From Sacrament
to Contract

for a cold
Fellow worker in
the vineyard.
With warm regards
John

SERIES EDITORS

DON S. BROWNING AND IAN S. EVISON

From
Sacrament to Contract

*Marriage, Religion, and Law
in the Western Tradition*

JOHN WITTE, JR.

Westminster John Knox Press
Louisville, Kentucky

Scripture quotations, unless otherwise noted, are from the Revised Standard Version of the Bible, copyright 1946, 1952, © 1971, 1973 by the Division of Christian Education of the National Council of the Churches of Christ in the U.S.A., and used by permission.

Book and cover design by Jennifer K. Cox

First edition

Published by Westminster John Knox Press
Louisville, Kentucky

This book is printed on acid-free paper that meets the American National Standards Institute Z39.48 standard. ∞

PRINTED IN THE UNITED STATES OF AMERICA

97 98 99 00 01 02 03 04 05 06 — 10 9 8 7 6 5 4 3 2 1

Library of Congress Cataloging-in-Publication Data

Witte, John, 1959–
      From sacrament to contract : marriage, religion, and law in the Western
   tradition / John Witte, Jr. — 1st ed.
            p.   cm. — (Family, religion, and culture)
      Includes bibliographical references.
      ISBN 0-664-25543-4 (acid-free paper)
      1. Marriage law—Religious aspects.   2. Marriage—Religious aspects—
   Christianity.   3. Marriage (Canon law)   I. Title.   II. Series.
   K675.W57   1997
   234'.165'09—dc21   97-23141

For my parents,
John and Gertie Witte

Contents

Series Foreword

There is an important debate going on today over the present health and future well-being of families in American society. Although some people on the political right and left use concern about the state of the family primarily to further their respective partisan causes, the debate is real, and it is over genuine issues. The discussion, however, is not well informed and is riddled with historical, theological, and social-scientific ignorance.

This is not unusual as political debates go. The American family debate, however, is especially uninformed and dogmatic. This is understandable, for all people have experienced a family in some way, feel themselves to be experts, and believe that they are entitled to their strong opinions.

The books in this series, The Family, Religion, and Culture, discuss these issues in ways that will place the American debate about the family on more solid ground. The series is the result of the Religion, Culture, and Family Project, which was funded by a generous grant from the Division of Religion of the Lilly Endowment, Inc., and took place in the Institute for Advanced Study in The University of Chicago Divinity School. Part of the project proceeded while Don Browning, the project director, was in residence at the Center of Theological Inquiry in Princeton, New Jersey.

The series advances no single point of view on the American family debate and gives no one solution to the problems concerning families today. The authors and editors contributing to the volumes represent both genders as well as a variety of religious and ethnic perspectives and denominational backgrounds—liberal and conservative; Protestant, Catholic, and Jewish; evangelical and mainline; and black, white, and Asian. A number of the authors and editors met annually for a seminar and discussed—often with considerable intensity—their outlines, papers, and chapters pertaining to the various books. The careful reader will notice that many of the seminar members did influence one another; but it is safe to say that each of them in the end took his or her own counsel and spoke out of his or her own convictions.

The series is comprehensive, with studies on the family in ancient Israel and early Christianity; economics and the family; law, feminism, and reproductive technology and the family; the family and American faith traditions; and congregations and families; as well as two summary books—one a handbook and one a critical overview of the American family debate.

This book, *From Sacrament to Contract,* shows how religion greatly influenced family law in Europe and America. Although this influence is all but forgotten, not only by contemporary churches but also by the present-day legal profession, it is essential in understanding the contemporary debate over the family. Few of us understand how medieval Catholic canon law shaped the marriage policies of the Protestant Reformation, how Luther and the Wittenberg reformers not only built on but also amended canon law to shape the legal marriage policies of Protestant Europe, how Calvin helped create the marriage laws of Geneva and Calvinist areas in Scotland, England, and America, and how these traditions have competed since the Enlightenment with an increasingly contractual and secular view of marriage and family.

From Sacrament to Contract is a path-breaking book that is based on original research, written with elegance and power, and full of stunning insights into our marriage and family traditions. One cannot read this book without feeling the loss of the full theology of covenant, the state, the public, and the secular that once informed our thinking about marriage and family. As Harold Berman, Witte's mentor and colleague, once said, "the secular has been secularized." This was not the case, however, at the time of Luther's Reformation when marriage and family were simultaneously seen as basically secular institutions and full of religious and sacred meaning.

This book will alter our mental picture of the family and encourage theology to contribute once again to the formation of our legal traditions on marriage and family.

Don S. Browning
Ian S. Evison

Acknowledgments

I would like to express my gratitude to a number of persons and institutions who have supported the preparation of this text.

It has been a privilege to be a part of The Religion, Culture, and Family Project at The University of Chicago Divinity School, which commissioned this text. I am especially grateful to Don S. Browning for his brilliant leadership of the Family Project as a whole and his sage mentorship of this text in particular. I have learned much from my interactions with him and with the dozens of scholars associated with this Project over the past four years, particularly those gathered in the annual fall seminars convened by the Project. I want to thank Carol Browning, Anne Carr, Bertram Cohler, Ian S. Evison, and John Wall for their leadership of this Project, and the Lilly Endowment, Inc., for its most generous financial support.

I was grateful to receive a Max Rheinstein Fellowship and Research Prize from the Alexander von Humboldt-Stiftung in Bonn, which allowed me to conduct research at several libraries in Brussels, Cologne, Dresden, Frankfurt am Main, Heidelberg, Tübingen, Leiden, and The Hague during the past two years. I was also grateful for the opportunity to serve as a visiting scholar at the Protestant Interdisciplinary Research Institute in Heidelberg in February and March 1995, and as the Jerald Brauer Seminar Scholar at the University of Chicago in April 1995, which provided splendid opportunities for research, writing, and lectures on various parts of this book.

Several friends and colleagues were kind enough to lend liberally of their advice and criticism. I would like especially to thank Harold J. Berman, R.H. Helmholz, Martin E. Marty, Max L. Stackhouse, and Steven E. Ozment, who each read large portions of the manuscript and made numerous edifying suggestions. Their comments have greatly improved my understanding of the subject, and I hope the quality of the book begins to approximate the quality of their advice. Several other friends have helped me with specific criticisms and suggestions, for which I am grateful. These include Frank Alexander, Tom Arthur, Wolfgang Bock, Michael Broyde, Rebecca Chopp, Nathaniel Gozansky,

Peter Hay, Timothy Jackson, Harriet King, Charles Reid, and Wolfgang Vögele.

Several joint degree candidates in the Law and Religion Program at Emory University have provided able and ample research assistance. I would like especially to thank Julia Belian, Scott Blevins, Heidi Hansan, M. Christian Green, and Joel Nichols for their invaluable help. I am also grateful for the stalwart support of my dean, Howard O. Hunter, and for the research support of the Emory Law Library staff, particularly Holliday Osborne and Will Haines.

It was a special pleasure to write a book about the virtues of marriage and family life, while enjoying the same in such abundance. My dear wife, Eliza, and our daughters, Alison and Hope, have given me constant love and support. Eliza has improved many of my ideas with her critical insights, and many of my passages with her keen editorial eye. Most important, she has improved all my life with her love, and for that I am most grateful of all.

This book is dedicated to my parents, John and Gertie Witte, who have provided me with a pristine model of marriage and parentage.

John Witte, Jr

Introduction

Oliver Wendell Holmes, Jr., once said that all the great questions of theology and philosophy must ultimately come to the law for their resolution. Holmes's claim, while overstated, has merit for this book. While theologians and philosophers have debated questions of the origin, nature, and purpose of marriage, jurists and judges have had to resolve them—in general statutes as well as in concrete cases. Such legal formulations have invariably reflected, and sometimes reified, prevailing theological ideas and ideals respecting marriage.

This book explores this interplay among law, theology, and marriage in the West. Its principal topical foci are Christian theological norms and Western legal principles of marriage and family life in the past half millennium. Its principal geographical focus is Western Europe, with some attention to its extension overseas to America. Its principal goal is to uncover some of the main theological beliefs that have helped to form Western marriage law in the past, and so to discover how such beliefs might help to inform Western marriage law in the future.

This book is, by design, more of a theological analysis than a sociological analysis of Western marriage law. It dwells principally on official lore and dips only intermittently into social practice. It draws more on marital statutes and summae than on testamentary documents and confessional practices. You will read more about the Marriage Acts of Lutheran Germany than about the acts of marriage by German gentlemen, more about papal pronouncements on lay sexual practices than about plaintiff petitions on clerical sexual abuse. For my principal interest is to come to terms with the cardinal religious sources and dimensions of the modern Western marriage law on the books.

To select this genre of writing is not to deprecate the great value of local and social histories of marriage and family life. Nor is it to ignore the dangers of writing a naked history of magisterial ideas. I do ground my analysis of marriage law and theology in concrete cases and other social data. I also acknowledge fully that not only theology, but also economics, politics, psychology, and numerous other factors have helped to shape Western ideas and institutions of marriage and family life. My principal goal, however, is to pull out of this thick fabric of family experience in the West the slender interwoven threads of Christian theology and marriage law and to examine some of their colors and patterns.

Models of Marriage

The Western Christian Church has, from its apostolic beginnings, offered four perspectives on marriage. A *religious perspective* regards marriage as a spiritual or sacramental association, subject to the creed, cult, and canons of the church community. A *social perspective* treats marriage as a social estate, subject to the expectations and exactions of the local community and to special state laws of contract, property, and inheritance. A *contractual perspective* describes marriage as a voluntary association, subject to the wills and preferences of the couple, their children, and their household. Hovering in the background is a *naturalist perspective* that treats marriage as a created institution, subject to the natural laws of reason, conscience, and the Bible. In Voltaire's quip: "Among Christians, the family is either a little church, a little state, or a little club" blessed by nature and nature's God.

These perspectives are, in an important sense, complementary, for they each emphasize one aspect of marriage—its religious sanction, communal legitimation, voluntary formation, and natural origin, respectively. These perspectives, however, have also come to stand in considerable tension, for they are linked to competing claims of ultimate authority over the form and function of marriage—claims by the church, by the state, by family members, and by God and nature. Some of the deepest fault lines in the historical formation and in the current transformations of Western marriage ultimately break out from this central tension of perspective. Which perspective of marriage dominates a culture, or at least prevails in an instance of dispute—the religious, the social, the contractual, or the natural? Which authority wields preeminent, or at least peremptory, power over marriage and family questions—the church, the state, the marital couple, or God and nature operating through one of these parties?

Historically, Catholics, Lutherans, Calvinists, Anglicans, and Enlightenment thinkers constructed systematic models of marriage to address these cardinal questions. Each group recognized multiple perspectives on marriage but gave priority to one perspective in order to achieve an integrated understanding. Their efforts have yielded five models of marriage for the modern West. These I have labeled: (1) the Catholic sacramental model; (2) the Lutheran social model; (3) the

Calvinist covenantal model; (4) the Anglican commonwealth model; and (5) the Enlightenment contractarian model.

These models of marriage are offered not as Weberian ideal types but as Niebuhrian conceptual constructs—ways of "stopping the endless Western dialogue" on marriage "at certain points," in Niebuhr's phrase, to test its theological meaning and to take its legal measure.[1] A full exposition of the details of any of these models could easily fill Elliott's proverbial five foot shelf of books. The sources are rich enough and the differences of perspective wide enough, even among close co-religionists, that one could easily subdivide these models into a battery of subtypes and hybrid types. Moreover, a full exposition of these models in action—portraying the day-to-day intimacies of the bedroom and the confessional, the patterns of paternity and inheritance, the indicia of wife and child abuse, the connivings of clerics and magistrates, the forms and forums of domestic stability and sexual discipline, and much more—could easily fill several more of Elliott's shelves. Selection, distillation, and truncation are necessary evils.

I have chosen as our "Niebuhrian stopping points" the mid-twelfth to mid-thirteenth centuries, the sixteenth and early seventeenth centuries, and the mid-nineteenth century and thereafter. These are watershed periods in the Western tradition of marriage—eras when powerful new theological models of marriage were forged that helped to transform the prevailing law of marriage. I have sought to sketch out just enough of the theology of each model to demonstrate its unique contribution to the Western legal tradition of marriage. And, in laying these models alongside each other, I have sought to give just enough of an account of the Western tradition of marriage to demonstrate its cardinal ideas and institutions. A brief profile of each model follows in an attempt to portray the overlapping colors and patterns. The subsequent five chapters fill in the picture of these models in more detail.

The *Catholic sacramental model* of the mid-twelfth century brought into a new concordance the discordant theological teachings of the apostles, fathers, and councils of the Western Church. The Catholic Church in this period and thereafter came to treat marriage and the family in a threefold manner—at once as a natural, contractual, and sacramental unit. First, marriage was a natural association, created by God to enable man and woman to "be fruitful and multiply" and to raise children in the service and love of God. Since the fall into sin, marriage had also become a remedy for lust, a channel to direct one's natural passion to the service of the community and the church. Second, marriage was a contractual unit, formed by the mutual consent of the parties. This contract prescribed for couples a lifelong relation of love, service, and devotion, to each other and proscribed unwarranted breach or relaxation of their connubial and parental duties. Third, marriage, when properly contracted and consummated among Christians, rose to the dignity of a sacrament. The temporal union of body, soul, and mind within the marital estate symbolized the eternal union between Christ and His Church, and brought sanctifying grace to the couple, the church, and the community. This sacramental perspective helped to integrate the natural and the contractual dimensions of marriage and to render marriage a central concern of the Church.

Though a sacrament and a sound way of Christian living, marriage, however, was not considered to be particularly spiritually edifying. Marriage was more of a remedy for sin than a recipe for righteousness. Marital life was considered less commendable than celibate life, propagation less virtuous than contemplation. Clerics, monastics, and other servants of the church were thus to forgo marriage as a condition for ecclesiastical service. Those who could not forgo marriage were not worthy of the church's holy orders and offices. Celibacy was something of a litmus test of spiritual discipline and social superiority.

From the twelfth century forward, the Catholic Church built upon this conceptual foundation a comprehensive canon law of marriage that was enforced by church courts throughout much of Western Christendom. By the early sixteenth century, the church's canon law was the predominant law governing marriage in the West.

Consistent with the naturalist perspective on marriage, the canon law punished contraception and abortion as violations of the created marital functions of propagation and childrearing. It proscribed unnatural relations, such as incest and polygamy, and unnatural acts such as bestiality and buggery. Consistent with the contractual perspective, the canon law ensured voluntary unions by dissolving marriages formed through mistake, duress, fraud, or coercion, and by granting husband and wife alike equal rights to enforce conjugal debts that had been voluntarily assumed. Consistent with the sacramental perspective, the church protected the sanctity and sanctifying purpose of marriage by declaring valid marital bonds to be indissoluble, and by dissolving invalid unions between Christians and non-Christians or between parties related by various legal, spiritual, blood, or familial ties. This canon law of marriage, grounded in a rich sacramental theology and ecclesiastical jurisprudence, was formalized and systematized by the Council of Trent in 1563 and greatly influenced Western marriage law for centuries thereafter.

The Lutheran, Calvinist, and Anglican traditions gave birth to three *Protestant models* of marriage. Like Catholics, Protestants retained the naturalist perspective of marriage as an association created for procreation and mutual protection. They also retained the contractual perspective of marriage as a voluntary association formed by the mutual consent of the couple. Unlike Catholics, however, Protestants rejected the subordination of marriage to celibacy and the celebration of marriage as a sacrament. According to common Protestant lore, the person was too tempted by sinful passion to forgo God's remedy of marriage. The celibate life had no superior virtue and was no prerequisite for ecclesiastical service. It led too easily to concubinage and homosexuality and impeded too often the access to and activities of the clerical office. Moreover, marriage was not a sacrament. It was instead an independent social institution ordained by God and equal in dignity and social responsibility with the church, state, and other estates of society. Participation in marriage required no prerequisite faith or purity and conferred no sanctifying grace, as did true sacraments.

From this common critique, the Lutheran, Calvinist, and Anglican traditions constructed their own models of marriage. Each Protestant tradition provided a different theological formula for integrating the inherited contractual, natural, and religious perspectives on marriage. Lutherans emphasized the social dimensions of marriage; Calvinists, the covenantal dimensions; and Anglicans, the commonwealth dimensions. Each Protestant tradition also assigned principal legal responsibility for marriage quite differently. Lutherans consigned legal authority mostly to the state; Calvinists, to both state and church; and Anglicans, mostly to the church. These differences in emphasis and authority among early Protestants were based, in part, on differences among their theological models of marriage

From 1517 onward, the *Lutheran tradition*, developed a *social model* of marriage, grounded in the evangelical doctrine of the heavenly and earthly kingdoms. Marriage, Luther and his colleagues taught, was a social estate of the earthly kingdom of creation, not a sacred estate of the heavenly kingdom of redemption. Though divinely ordained, marriage was directed primarily to human ends, to the fulfilling of "uses" in the lives of the individual and of society. Marriage revealed to persons their sin and their need for God's marital gift. It restricted prostitution, promiscuity, and other public sexual sins. It taught love, restraint, and other public virtues. All fit men and women were free to enter such unions, clerical and lay alike. Indeed, all persons were spiritually compelled to marry when they came of age, unless they had the rare gift of continence.

As part of the earthly kingdom, marriage was subject to the state, not the church. Civil law, not canon law, was to govern marriage. Marriage

was still subject to God's law, but this law was now to be administered
by magistrates who were God's vice-regents in the earthly kingdom.
Church officials were required to counsel magistrates about God's law
and to cooperate with them in publicizing and disciplining marriage. All
church members, as part of the priesthood of believers, were required
to counsel those who contemplated marriage and to admonish those
who sought annulment or divorce. But the church no longer had legal
authority over marriage.

This social model of marriage was reflected in the transformation of
marriage law in Lutheran Germany. Civil marriage courts replaced
church courts. Civil marriage statutes replaced canon law rules.
Lutheran jurists published treatises on marriage law, affirming and embellishing evangelical marriage theology. The new German marriage
law, like the new evangelical marriage doctrine, remained indebted to
the Catholic canon law tradition. Traditional marriage laws, like prohibitions against unnatural relations and against infringement of marital
functions, remained in effect. Impediments that protected free consent,
that implemented biblical prohibitions against marriage of relatives, and
that governed the couple's physical relations were largely retained. Such
laws were as consistent with the Catholic sacramental model as with the
Lutheran social model of marriage.

But changes in marriage doctrine also yielded changes in marriage
law. Because the Lutheran reformers rejected the subordination of marriage to celibacy, they rejected laws that forbade clerical and monastic
marriage, that denied remarriage to those who had married a cleric or
monastic, and that permitted vows of chastity to annul promises of marriage. Because they rejected the sacramental nature of marriage, the reformers rejected impediments of crime and heresy and prohibitions
against divorce in the modern sense. Marriage was for them the community of the couple in the present, not their sacramental union in the
life to come. Where that community was broken, for one of a number
of specific reasons (such as adultery or desertion), the couple could sue
for divorce. Because persons by their lustful nature were in need of
God's remedy of marriage, the reformers removed numerous impediments to marriage not countenanced by scripture. Because of their emphasis on the Godly responsibility of the prince, the pedagogical role of
the church and the family, and the priestly calling of all believers, the
reformers insisted that both marriage and divorce be public. The validity of marriage promises depended upon parental consent, witnesses,
church consecration and registration, and priestly instruction. Couples
who wanted to divorce had to announce their intentions in the church
and community and to petition a civil judge to dissolve the bond.

These changes in the laws of marital formation and dissolution introduced in Lutheran Germany—featuring parental consent, two witnesses, civil registration, church consecration, limited impediments, divorce for cause, remarriage for divorcees and widows—were widely advocated in all Protestant communities after the sixteenth century.

The *Calvinist tradition*, established in mid-sixteenth century Geneva, set out a *covenantal model* of marriage. This model confirmed many of the Lutheran theological and legal reforms, but cast them in a new ensemble. Marriage, Calvin and his followers taught, was not a sacramental institution of the church, but a covenantal association of the entire community. A variety of parties participated in the formation of this covenant. The marital parties themselves swore their betrothals and espousals before each other and God—rendering all marriages triparty agreements, with God as third-party witness, participant, and judge. The couple's parents, as God's lieutenants for children, gave their consent to the union. Two witnesses, as God's priests to their peers, served as witnesses to the marriage. The minister, holding God's spiritual power of the Word, blessed the couple and admonished them in their spiritual duties. The magistrate, holding God's temporal power of the sword, registered the couple and protected them in their person and property. Each of these parties was considered essential to the legitimacy of the marriage, for they each represented a different dimension of God's involvement in the covenant. To omit any such party was, in effect, to omit God from the marriage covenant.

The covenant of marriage was grounded in the order of creation and governed by the law of God. At creation, God ordained the structure of marriage to be a lifelong union between a fit man and a fit woman of the age of consent. God assigned to this marriage the interlocking purposes of mutual love and support of husband and wife, mutual procreation and nurture of children, and mutual protection of both parties from sexual sin. Thereafter, God set forth in reason, conscience, and the Bible a whole series of commandments and counsels for proper adherence to this ideal created structure and purpose of marriage.

God's moral law for the covenant of marriage set out two tracks of marital norms: civil norms, which are common to all persons; and spiritual norms, which are distinctly Christian. This moral law, in turn, gave rise to two tracks of marital morality: a simple morality of duty demanded of all persons regardless of their faith; and a higher morality of aspiration demanded of believers in order to reflect their faith. It was the church's responsibility to teach aspirational spiritual norms for marriage and family life. It was the state's responsibility to enforce mandatory civil norms. This division of responsibility was reflected in Geneva in the

procedural divisions between the church consistory and the city council. In marriage cases, the consistory was the court of first instance; it
would call parties to their higher spiritual duties, backing their recommendations with (threats of) spiritual discipline. If such spiritual counsel failed, the parties were referred to the city council to compel them,
using civil and criminal sanctions, to honor at least their basic civil duties for marriage.

This Calvinist covenantal model mediated both sacramental and contractual understandings of marriage. On the one hand, this covenantal
model confirmed the sacred and sanctifying qualities of marriage without ascribing to its sacramental functions. Marriage was regarded as a
holy and loving fellowship, a compelling image of the bond between
Yahweh and His elect, between Christ and His church. But marriage was
no sacrament, for it confirmed no divine promise. On the other hand,
this covenantal model confirmed the contractual and consensual qualities of marriage without subjecting it to the personal preferences of the
parties. Marriage depended for its validity and utility on the voluntary
consent of the parties. But marriage was more than a contract, for God
was a third party to every marriage covenant, and God set its basic terms
in the order and law of creation. Freedom of contract in marriage was
thus effectively limited to choosing maturely which party to marry—
with no real choice about the form, forum, or function of marriage once
a fit spouse was chosen.

Calvinists also modified the Lutheran social model of marriage. By su-
perimposing the doctrine of covenant on the two kingdoms framework,
Calvinists, in effect, added a spiritual dimension to marriage life in the
earthly kingdom, a marital obligation to spiritual life in the heavenly
kingdom, and complementary marital roles for both church and state in
the governance of both kingdoms. On the strength of this, Calvinist
communities added a variety of refinements to the Protestantized marriage law inherited from Lutheran Germany: The laws of marital formation, maintenance, and dissolution were tightened to ensure that only
fit parties entered this covenant, that only right conduct attended the
household, that only innocent spouses could dissolve the covenant.
Consistory, magistracy, and community alike were made responsible for
the proper functioning of the marital covenant and the proper enforcement of God's moral laws for marriage.

The *Anglican tradition*, particularly during the later Tudor and Stuart
periods from circa 1540 to 1640, brought forth a *commonwealth model*
of marriage. This model embraced the sacramental, social, and covenantal models but went beyond them. Marriage was at once a gracious symbol of the divine, a social unit of the earthly kingdom, and a solemn

covenant with one's spouse. But the essential cause, condition, and calling of the family was that it served and symbolized the common good of the couple, the children, the church, and the state all at once. Marriage was appointed by God as "a little commonwealth" to foster the mutual love, service, and security of husband and wife, parent and child. It was likewise appointed by God as a "seedbed and seminary" of the broader commonwealth to teach church, state, and society essential Christian and political norms and habits.

At first, this commonwealth model served to rationalize the traditional hierarchies of husband over wife, parent over child, church over household, state over church. After three decades of experimentation, England in the mid-sixteenth century had formally rejected most Protestant reforms of marriage. It returned to much of the medieval canon law of marriage administered by the church, but now under the supreme headship of the English Crown. To call the marital household "a little commonwealth" was to signal its subordinate place within the new hierarchy of social institutions that comprised "the great commonwealth" of England. It was also to call the household to an internal hierarchy of offices that matched the royal and episcopal offices of the great commonwealth. The commonwealth model was thus used to integrate a whole network of parallel domestic and political duties rooted in the Bible and English tradition. Moralists expounded at great length the reciprocal duties of husband and wife, parent and child, and master and servant that would produce a well-ordered little commonwealth. And, in keeping with the tradition of stability of the great commonwealth of England, they prohibited the dissolution of this little commonwealth of the family by divorce.

As the political concept of the English commonwealth was revolutionized and democratized in the seventeenth century, however, so was the English commonwealth model of marriage. The traditional hierarchies of husband over wife, parent over child, and church over family were challenged with a revolutionary new principle of equality. The biblical duties of husband and wife and of parent and child were recast as the natural rights of each household member against the other. The traditional idea of a created natural order of marriage, society, and state met with a new idea of marriage, society, and state formed voluntarily by contracts by individuals in the state of nature. Just as the English commonwealth could be rent asunder by force of arms when it abused the people's natural rights, so the family commonwealth could be put asunder by suits at law when it abused the couple's marital rights. Just as the King could be beheaded for abuses in the Commonwealth, so the paterfamilias could be removed from the head of the little commonwealth for abuses in the household. This revolutionary construction of the commonwealth model provided the rationale for the incremental liberalization of English marriage law in the course of the next two centuries. It also provided a stepping-stone for the development of the contractarian model of marriage during the Enlightenment era.

After the sixteenth century, these four models of marriage—each with multiple variants—lay at the heart of Western marriage law. The Catholic sacramental model flourished in southern Europe, Iberia, and France, and their colonies in Latin America, Quebec, Louisiana, and other outposts. The Lutheran social model dominated portions of Germany, Austria, Switzerland, and Scandinavia, together with their colonies. The Calvinist covenantal model came to strong expression in Calvinist Geneva and in dispersed Huguenot, Pietist, Presbyterian, and Puritan communities in Western Europe and North America. The Anglican commonwealth model prevailed in much of Great Britain and its many colonies across the Atlantic.

The *Enlightenment contractarian model* of marriage was adumbrated in the eighteenth century, elaborated theoretically in the nineteenth century, and implemented legally in the twentieth century. In various quarters of the Continent, England, and America, exponents of the Enlightenment gave increasing emphasis to the contractual perspective of marriage. The essence of marriage, Enlightenment thinkers argued, was not its sacramental symbolism, nor its covenantal associations, nor its social service to the community and commonwealth. The essence of marriage was the voluntary bargain struck between two parties who wanted to come together into an intimate association. The terms of their marital bargain were not preset by God or nature, church or state, tradition or community. The terms of the marital bargain were set by the parties themselves, in accordance with general rules of contract formation and general norms of a civil society. Such rules and norms demanded respect for the life, liberty, and property interests of other parties, and compliance with general standards of health, safety, and welfare in the community. But the terms of marriage were to be left to the parties themselves. Couples should now be able to make their own marital beds, and lie in them or leave them as they saw fit.

On the strength of these contractarian convictions, Enlightenment thinkers advocated the abolition of much that was considered sound and sacred in the Western legal tradition of marriage. They urged the abolition of the requirements of parental consent, church consecration, and formal witnesses for marriage. They questioned the exalted status of heterosexual monogamy. They called for the absolute equality of husband and wife to receive, hold, and alienate property, to enter into contracts and commerce, to participate on equal terms in the workplace. They castigated the state for leaving annulment practice to the church, and urged that the laws of annulment and divorce be both merged and expanded under exclusive state jurisdiction. They urged that paternal abuse of children be severely punished and that the state intervene where necessary to ensure the proper physical and moral nurture and education of children.

This contractarian gospel for the reformation of Western marriage law was too radical to transform much of the law of the nineteenth century, though it did induce greater protections for wives and children in their persons and properties. But this contractarian gospel anticipated much of the agenda for the transformation of marriage law in the twentieth century, particularly in America. In America, this transformation began slowly at the turn of this century, gained momentum with the New Deal, and broke into full stride during the 1960s and thereafter.

In the early part of the twentieth century, sweeping new laws were passed to govern marriage formalities, divorce, alimony, marital property, wife abuse, child custody, adoption, child support, child abuse, juvenile delinquency, education of minors, among other subjects. Such sweeping legal changes had several consequences. Marriages became easier to contract and easier to dissolve. Wives received greater independence in their relationships outside the family. Children received greater protection from the abuses and neglect of their parents, and greater access to benefit rights. And the state began to replace the church as the principal external authority governing marriage and family life. The Catholic sacramental concept of the family governed principally by the church and the Protestant concepts of the family governed by the church and broader Christian community began to give way to a new privatist concept of the family whereby the wills of the marital parties became primary. Neither the church, nor the local community, nor the paterfamilias could override the reasonable expressions of will of the marital parties themselves.

In the past three decades, the Enlightenment call for the privatization of marriage and the family has come to greater institutional expression. Prenuptial contracts, determining in advance the respective rights and duties of the parties during and after marriage, have gained prominence. No-fault divorce statutes are in place in virtually every state. Legal requirements of parental consent and witnesses to marriage have become largely dead letters. The functional distinction between the rights of the married and the unmarried has been narrowed by a growing constitutional law of sexual autonomy and privacy. Homosexual, bisexual, and other intimate associations have gained increasing acceptance at large, and at law.

Although *consensual* intimate relationships between adults have become increasingly impervious to state scrutiny, *nonconsensual* conduct has become increasingly subject to state sanction. Many state courts have opened their dockets to civil and criminal cases of physical abuse, rape, embezzlement, conversion, and fraud by one spouse or lover against the other. The ancient "marital exemption" in the law of rape, which often protected abusive husbands from criminal prosecution, is falling into desuetude. Fading too is the ancient spousal exemption in evidence law that discouraged spouses from testifying against each other. The arm of the state no longer knocks at the bedroom door with the same ease that it did in the past. But today, if a distressed party opens the bedroom door for it, the state will reach deeply into the intimacies of bed and board and punish severely those who have abused their autonomy.

From Sacrament to Contract

This is the grand movement of Western marriage law in the course of the past millennium. It is a movement "from sacrament to contract"— from a sacramental model that prioritizes canonical norms and ecclesiastical structures to a contractarian model that prioritizes private choice and contractual strictures. It is a movement fueled, in part, by the reciprocating shifts in the dominant theological models and legal structures of marriage.

This is a movement not so much of incremental secularization as of intermittent resacralization of Western marriage. The medieval Catholic model was every bit as secular in its theology and law of marriage as the Enlightenment contractarian model. The modern contractarian construction of marital equality was every bit as religious in inspiration as earlier Christian constructions of marital hierarchy. Each model has struck its own balances between church and state, clergy and laity, rights and duties, order and liberty, dogma and adiaphora in matters of marriage and sexuality. These balances were struck on the basis of deep religious convictions—whether Catholic, Protestant, Enlightenmentarian, or some combination of the same. To laicize, temporalize, or politicize marriage is not the same thing as to secularize marriage.

Historians will recognize that my title "from sacrament to contract" is a play on the words of Sir Henry Sumner Maine's thesis that legal history altogether moves "from status to contract." In a series of nineteenth-century classics, Maine had argued that all law must be viewed as part and product of the spirit of a people and their times—of a *Volksgeist und Zeitgeist,* as his German counterparts put it. As the spirit of a people changes, so inevitably does their law. Moreover, Maine had argued that, in earlier eras, a person's religious and familial status was a critical source of legal identity, rights, and duties, and that, by contrast, in his own day individually negotiated contracts were a more important source for the same.[2] These two general insights of Maine find a place in this book. The shifts in prevailing Western marriage law were, in part, products of shifts in the prevailing spirit and theology of a people, although they did not always follow the neat *post hoc propter hoc* development Maine sometimes suggested. Moreover, a person's marital status was historically defined much more fully by his or her standing in the sacramental, covenantal, or commonwealth communities than is the case today.

Maine, however, pressed his logic to all manner of fanciful conclusions that play no part in this book. For example, his descriptions of grand movements from religious primitivism to cultural custom to legal codes, and from fiction to equity to legislation, in my view depend on far too schematic and selective a treatment of the historical data. His preferences for legislation over natural law, individuals over communities, equality over hierarchy, rights over duties led him to a Whiggish historicism that seemed to render Victorian England the aspirational apex of every law and civilization. His repeated insistence that "the basic unit of an ancient society was the Family, and of a modern society the Individual" does justice neither to the place of the individual in ancient societies nor to the place of the family in modern societies.[3] It is going too far, in my view, to call Maine "a reactionary, a laissez-faire extremist in the Spencerian tradition, an ethnocentric imperialist, and a scholar whose British-based prejudices tainted his investigations of law and kinship with strong infusions of ideology."[4] But Maine must certainly be used with great caution.

Historians will also recognize that the beginning and end of this story of Western marriage law—represented by the terms "sacrament" and "contract" in my title—are well known. A long tradition of distinguished medievalists, represented in America today by James A. Brundage, R.H. Helmholz, and John T. Noonan, has brought the medieval sacramental theology and canon law of marriage to vivid light and life.[5] Their research has made clear that much of what we today call the "traditional family" and the "classic law" of the family was forged by canon lawyers and scholastic theologians in the early part of this millennium. The great medieval tradition of marriage—amply amended over the centuries, particularly by the Second Vatican Council in the early 1960s—lives on within the canon law of the Catholic Church today, and, in muted form, within the civil laws of many nations where Catholicism is strong. Given the rich literature on the subject, I have provided only a brief summary of the sacramental model in the opening chapter that follows, directing readers to the able and ample studies at hand.

Likewise, a long tradition of distinguished historians, represented in America by Mary Ann Glendon, Max Rheinstein, and Lawrence Stone, has described the rise of the modern contractarian model in Anglo-American law.[6] Their research has made clear what Professor Glendon saw already in 1977: that "beginning in the 1960s, there has been an unparalleled upheaval in the family law systems of Western industrial societies [that] equals and surpasses in magnitude that which occurred when family matters passed from ecclesiastical to secular authorities in the age that began with the Protestant Reformation."[7] The past generation of scholarship has produced innumerable books and articles describing, decrying, and defending these massive changes. Again, to avoid redundancy, I have given only a cursory summary of the rise of the contractarian model of marriage in the final chapter, directing the reader to the more substantial treatments readily at hand.

What is far less known are the chronological and conceptual movements between "sacrament" and "contract"—the "to" in my title "from sacrament to contract." I have thus devoted a good deal of this book to mining the theologies and laws of marriage in the Lutheran, Calvinist, and Anglican traditions of the early sixteenth-century forward, parsing many dusty old collections of canons, commentaries, and cases in the process. The stories of Luther burning the canon law books in 1520 and later condemning "jurists as bad Christians" (*Juristen böse Christen*) has, for many, obscured the reality that the Lutheran Reformation profoundly transformed Western public and private law, including the law of marriage. I have thus devoted chapter 2 to giving the reader something of a tour of the rich German Reformation archives on marriage.[8] The early Calvinist sources of a covenant theology and law of marriage have been almost entirely lost on modern historiography, and I have thus devoted chapter 3 to a close case study of Calvin's marital theology and the marriage law of sixteenth-century Geneva.[9] The remarkable evolution of early modern Anglican commonwealth understandings of marriage—from Thomas Becon to John Locke—is now known only in fragments to specialists, and I have thus devoted chapter 4 to a long discussion of this topic.[10] To choose this emphasis is not simply to play to my Protestant preferences, but to put forward new sets of ideas and institutions of marriage that have not played a sufficient part in the modern discussion of Western marriage.

To bring to light all these historical models of marriage is neither to wax nostalgic about a golden age of Western marriage, nor to offer a panacea to what Jean Bethke Elshtain calls "the sad and serious crisis of marriage in civil society."[11] We cannot delude ourselves with unduly romantic accounts of the Catholic, Protestant, or Enlightenment past. Nor can we seek uncritically to transpose its mores and morals into our day. To adduce these ancient sources is instead to point to a rich resource for the lore and law of modern marriage that is too little known and too little used today. Too much of contemporary society seems to have lost sight of the rich and diverse Western theological heritage of marriage and of the uncanny ability of the Western legal tradition to strike new balances between order and liberty, orthodoxy and innovation with respect to our enduring and evolving sexual and familial norms and habits. Too much of the contemporary Christian church seems to have lost sight of the ability of its forebearer to translate their enduring and evolving perspectives on marriage and family life into legal forms—both canonical and civil. There is a great deal more in those dusty old tomes and canons than idle antiquaria or dispensable memorabilia. These ancient sources ultimately hold the theological genetic code that has defined the contemporary family for what it is—and what it can be.

1

Marriage as Sacrament in the Roman Catholic Tradition

The law and theology of marriage was an important concern of the Christian church from the very beginning. Both Christ and St. Paul spoke at some length on the subject, and their teachings have been the cornerstone of the Western tradition of marriage for nearly two millennia.

Biblical and Patristic Teachings

New Testament Teachings

Christ taught that marriage was created by God as a union of a man and a woman who had been emancipated from their childhood homes. "Have you not read that he who made them from the beginning 'made them male and female,' and said, 'For this reason a man shall leave his father and mother and be joined to his wife, and the two shall become one flesh'? So they are no longer two, but one flesh" (Matt. 19:4–6). Christ opened his ministry by blessing the wedding feast at Cana with his first miracle of changing water into wine (John 2:1–11). He reserved one of his last words on the cross for bringing his mother Mary and his apostle John into a new family: "Woman, behold your son." Son, "[b]ehold your mother" (John 19:26–27).

Christ used the image of marriage and the family to teach the basics about the kingdom of God. "The kingdom of heaven may be compared to a king who gave a marriage feast for his son," Christ proclaimed. Only those who are invited may come to the feast. Only those who are ready for the feast when the bridegroom comes will gain entrance (Matt. 22:1–14; 25:1–13). The kingdom of God may also be viewed as an extended spiritual family, Christ intimated. "My mother and my brothers are those who hear the word of God and do it" (Luke 8:21). "Let the children come to me, and do not hinder them; for to such belongs the kingdom of God. Truly, I say to you whoever does not receive the kingdom of God like a child shall not enter it" (Luke 18:16–17). Even the most prodigal son and daughter, who come in childlike faith to seek forgiveness, can be part of this divine family (Luke 15:11–32). To be both a child of God and a brother or sister in Christ was the defining feature of the Christian.

Christians were not to elevate the demands of their own temporal families beyond the demands of the kingdom of God. Christ drove this lesson home in several jarring texts: "Do not think that I have come to bring peace to the earth; I have not come to bring peace, but a sword. For I have come to set a man against his father, and a daughter against her mother, and a daughter-in-law against her mother-in-law; a man's foes will be those of his own household. He who loves his father and mother more than me is not worthy of me; and he who loves son or daughter more than me is not worthy of me; and he who does not take up his cross and follow me is not worthy of me" (Matt. 10:34–38).[1] Christ commanded his twelve disciples to leave their families and vocations behind them and follow him. He commanded a man mourning the death of his father: "Follow me, and leave the dead to bury their own dead" (Matt. 8:21–22). "Truly, I say to you," he said to his disciples in a particularly pointed passage, "there is no man who has left house or wife or brothers or parents or children, for the sake of the kingdom of God, who will not receive manifold more in the age to come in eternal life" (Luke 18:29–30). Indeed, in "the age to come," Christ preached, persons "neither marry nor are given in marriage" (Matt. 22:30).

Christians were also not to subordinate the moral law of marriage taught by Moses to legal casuistry or to sinful calculus. In the Beatitudes, Christ set forth the letter and spirit of the new Christian law: "You have heard that it was said, 'You shall not commit adultery.' But I say to you that everyone who looks at a woman lustfully has already committed adultery with her in his heart" (Matt. 5:27–28). "It was also said, 'Whoever divorces his wife, let him give her a certificate of divorce.' But I say to you every one who divorces his wife, except on the ground of unchastity, makes her an adulteress; and whoever marries a divorced woman commits adultery" (Matt. 5:31–32). Christ returned to the subject of divorce in his famous colloquy with the Pharisees: "What God has joined together, let not man put asunder," he thundered. "For your hardness of heart, Moses allowed you to divorce your wives, but from the beginning it was not so. And I say to you, whoever divorces his wife, except for unchastity, and marries another, commits adultery" (Matt. 19:6, 8–9).[2]

Paul elaborated these sentiments in his letters to the new Christian churches. He used the image of marriage not only to describe the kingdom of God, as Christ had done, but also to define the nature of the budding Christian church. The church is the bride, Christ is the bride-groom, Paul said.[3] In this organic analogy lie the first principles of au-thority and submission, love and sacrifice that define both a Christian church and a Christian marriage. "[T]he husband is the head of the wife as Christ is the head of the church," Paul wrote to the Ephesians. "As the church is subject to Christ, so let wives be subject in everything to their husbands. Husbands, love your wives, as Christ loved the church and gave himself up for her. . . . [H]usbands should love their wives as their own bodies. He who loves his wife loves himself. For no man ever hates his own flesh, but nourishes and cherishes it, as Christ does the church, because we are members of his body. 'For this reason a man shall leave his father and mother and be joined to his wife, and the two shall be-come one flesh.' This mystery [*sacramentum*], is a profound one, and I am saying that it refers to Christ and the church" (Eph. 5:23–32).[4]

Paul translated Christ's teaching about the superiority of the kingdom of God to earthly families into a more general counsel about the superi-ority of celibacy to marriage. "It is well for a man not to touch a woman," Paul wrote to the church in Corinth. "I wish that all of you were [celi-bate] as I myself am" (1 Cor. 7:1, 7). Paul advised virgins to remain celi-bate and widows and widowers to avoid remarriage if they could, for marriage divided persons between spiritual and temporal loyalties and distracted them from divine service.[5] But Paul condoned marriage for those tempted by sin, saying it was "better to marry than to burn" (1 Cor. 7:9). And within marriage, he commended equal regard and rights for the sexual needs of both spouses. "[B]ecause of the temptation to im-morality, each man should have his own wife, and each woman her own husband. The husband should give to the wife her conjugal rights, and likewise the wife to her husband. For the wife does not rule over her own body, but the husband does; likewise the husband does not rule over his own body, but the wife does. Do not refuse one another except perhaps by agreement for a season, that you may devote yourselves to prayer, but then come together again, lest Satan tempt you with lack of self-control. I say this by way of concession, not of command" (1 Cor. 7:2–6).

Paul glossed Christ's words on sexual immorality with a number of specific prohibitions against adultery, fornication, lust, incest, homo-sexuality, sodomy, prostitution, polygamy, untoward primping, and other forms of sexual "immorality" and "perversion" (Rom. 1:24–27)[6]. He glossed Christ's words on divorce with an admonition that Chris-tians must remain in marriages even with an unbeliever, in the hope that they might convert him or her to the faith. But "if the unbelieving part-ner desires to separate, let it be so," Paul wrote; "in such a case the brother or sister is not bound. For God has called us to peace" (1 Cor. 7:15).

The Early Law and Theology of Marriage

These provocative biblical passages set out the first principles of Christian marriage. It was left to the church's theologians and jurists to translate these general principles into more specific precepts. Even before they had been incorporated into the biblical canon, these passages inspired the early church to develop a host of canon law rules for the governance of spiritual discipline. The earliest surviving church laws, such as the *Didache* (c. 120) and *The Teaching of the Apostles* (c. 250), repeated several of these passages and variations on the same. They also prohibited, with special emphasis, sodomy, adultery, pedophilia, fornication, and "eager gazing" on women, but commended chastity, celibacy, modesty of dress, and separation of the sexes during bathing and education.[7]

The seven ecumenical councils from 325 to 451, together with various local synods and church councils, promulgated increasingly detailed norms of a Christian ethic of marriage and sexuality. Bishops, clergy, monks, and other servants of the church were at first ordered to be chaste, heterosexual, and monogamous. By the late fourth century, the councils ordered them to be celibate and to avoid both marriage and concubinage on pain of losing their clerical offices. Lay Christians were enjoined to live in peaceful, monogamous, and heterosexual unions. They were prohibited from sexual sins of all sorts, with Paul's list now supplemented by specific commandments against bestiality, polygyny, and polyandry, and Paul's counsels to widows translated into a strong condemnation of "digamy" (remarriage after the death of a spouse). The laity were also forbidden from marrying heretics or heathens, from marrying parties with whom they had fornicated (save in the instance of pregnancy), from violating the Mosaic laws against marriage of blood and family relatives, and from marrying during Lent and other holy days.[8]

These same biblical teachings also inspired an ample stock of commentaries and sermons by the great Church Fathers: Ambrose, Athanasius, Augustine, Chrysostom, Clement, Gregory of Nyssa, Jerome, and Tertullian, among others.[9] The early Church Fathers, writing prior to the establishment of Christianity by Roman law in 380, set their doctrines of marriage and sexuality in sharp contrast to those of Roman society and law. They singled out for harsh criticism the Roman practice of temple harlotry, concubinage, transvestism, homosexuality, incest, polygamy, abortion, infanticide, and child abuse. They also occasionally spoke against the Roman practice of coercing young girls into marriage, of arranging marriages for reasons of property or diplomacy, and of restricting rights of divorce to husbands alone.[10] The late Church Fathers repeated and embellished these themes at great length—and helped to effectuate some modest reforms of the prevailing Roman law of marital formation, divorce, and sexual conduct.[11] The late Church Fathers also revealed an increasing preference for virginity, celibacy, and monastic chastity—sometimes pressing their preference to the point of outright opposition to intercourse and even to marriage itself. By the late fourth century, it was commonplace to treat marriage as the least virtuous Christian estate and to countenance sexual intercourse only for the purpose of procreation. As St. Ambrose of Milan put it: "[T]he virtue of chastity is threefold: one kind that of married life, a second that of widowhood, and a third that of virginity"—with the last on the list first in priority.[12]

No systematic theology of marriage emerges from what survives of these early Christian writings.[13] But various perspectives on marriage all find some place. For example, an array of natural, spiritual, contractual, and social perspectives on marriage are scattered throughout the writings of the leading Greek Church Father, St. John Chrysostom (345–407). Reflecting the *natural* perspective, Chrysostom wrote that marriage was created by God "to make us chaste, and to make us parents. Of these two, the reason of chastity takes precedence. When desire began, then marriage also began. It sets a limit to desire by teaching us to keep one wife."[14] "Marriage is not an evil thing," he wrote elsewhere. "Marriage is a natural remedy to eliminate fornication."[15] Reflecting the *spiritual* perspective, Chrysostom hinted at the sanctifying functions of marriage for Christians: "This, then, is what it means to marry in Christ: spiritual marriage is like spiritual birth, which is not of blood, nor of the will of the flesh . . . just as the soul is joined to God in an ineffable union which He alone knows. . . . How foolish are those who belittle marriage! If marriage were something to be condemned, Paul would never call Christ a bridegroom and the Church a bride."[16] Reflecting the *contractual* perspective, he urged that marriages be formed by special agreements that went beyond the material concerns of commercial contracts. "Who, when about to marry, inquires about the disposition and nurture of the damsel? No one; but straightaway about money, and possessions, and measures of property of various and different kinds: like as if he were about to buy something, or to settle some common contract." Such a crass contractualism is "to offer insult to the gifts of God," Chrysostom argued. Christians entering a marriage contract should look rather to the prospective spouse's "ways of life, and morals, and virtue of the soul."[17] For "marriage is not a business venture, but a fellowship for life."[18] Reflecting the *social* perspective, Chrysostom wrote: "The love of husband and wife is the force that welds society together. Because when harmony prevails, the children are raised well, the household is kept in order, and neighbors and relatives praise the result. Great benefits, both for families and states, are thus produced."[19] Such social goods can be achieved only if households are appropriately arranged under the authority of the paterfamilias, Chrysostom added with a nod to Paul: "The wife is a second authority. She should not demand equality, for she is subject to the head; neither should the husband belittle her subjection, for she is the body. If the head despises the body, it will itself die. Rather let the husband counterbalance her obedience with his love. . . . Where there is equal authority, there never is peace. A household cannot be a democracy, ruled by everyone; the authority must necessarily rest in one person."[20]

These same four perspectives on marriage can also be found scattered throughout the writings of the leading Latin Church Father, St. Augustine of Hippo (354–430).[21] Combining the *natural and spiritual* perspectives, Augustine called marriage a "true and loyal partnership" of faith, and referred to the procreation of children as "part of the glory of marriage and not of the punishment of sin."[22] Reflecting the *contractual* perspective, he insisted that marriage contracts be "read in the presence of all the attesting witnesses; and an express clause [be] there that they marry 'for the procreation of children.'"[23] Reflecting the *social* perspective, he called marriage the "seedbed of the city," and the household the "first step in the organization of men."[24] "[T]hat ordered agreement concerning command and obedience among those who dwell together in a household ministers to the ordered agreement concerning command and agreement among citizens."[25]

Augustine drew the natural, contractual, and spiritual perspectives of marriage somewhat closer together in his famous formulation of "the goods of marriage."[26] To be sure, following patristic convention, Augustine regarded marriage as less virtuous than virginity and chastity, and sexual intercourse as per se sinful. But marriage, as a creation of God, had its own inherited goods, which at least mitigated the sinfulness of sex. Marriage, Augustine wrote, "is the ordained means of procreation (*proles*), the guarantee of chastity (*fides*), and the bond of permanent union (*connubi sacramentum*)."[27] As a created and natural means of procreation, Christian marriage rendered sexual intercourse licit, and by nurturing and educating children helped to perpetuate the human species and to expand the church. As a contract of fidelity, marriage gave husband and wife an equal power over the other's body, an equal right to demand that the other spouse avoid adultery, and an equal claim to the "service, in a certain measure, of sustaining each other's weakness, for the avoidance of illicit intercourse."[28] As a "certain sacramental bond (*quoddam sacramentum*)" marriage was a source and symbol of permanent union between Christians.[29] "Once marriage is entered upon in the City of our God," Augustine wrote, "where also from the first union of the two human beings marriage bears a kind of sacred bond, it can be dissolved in no way except by the death of one of the parties. The bond of marriage remains, even if offspring, for which the marriage was entered upon, should not follow because of a clear case of sterility, so that it is not lawful for married people who know they will not have any children to separate and to unite with others even for the sake of having children."[30]

Augustine's theory of the marital goods of procreation, fidelity, and sacrament was the most integrated Christian theory of marriage offered by the Church Fathers. But this theory was only a foretaste of the robust sacramental model of the High Middle Ages. Augustine did not draw out many of the legal and theological implications of his theory, nor did he resolve all the tensions among even the three goods of marriage that he identified. Moreover, Augustine did not use the term "sacrament of marriage" in its later sense as an instrument or cause of grace instituted by Christ for the purpose of sanctification. For Augustine, the term *sacrament* meant only "symbolic stability."[31] Later Catholic theologians would call marriage permanent because it was a Christian sacrament. Augustine called marriage a Christian sacrament because it was permanent. His main goal was to distinguish Christian marriage from prevailing pagan marriages and from the attacks on the institution by Gnostic, Manichean, and other heresies. He sought to show that Christian marriage was a stable and permanent union. It allowed procreation with one's spouse even if continence was spiritually preferable. It demanded fidelity to one's spouse even if procreation was naturally impossible.

The Formation of the
Sacramental Model of Marriage

It was not until the revolutionary upheaval of the late eleventh through the thirteenth centuries that these early biblical and patristic sentiments were integrated into a systematic sacramental model of marriage. During the Papal Revolution of Pope Gregory VII (1073–1085) and his successors, the Catholic clergy threw off their royal and civil rulers and established the Roman Catholic Church as an autonomous legal and political corporation within Western Christendom. This event helped to trigger an enormous transformation of Western society. The West was renewed through the rediscovery and study of the ancient texts of Roman law, Greek philosophy, and patristic theology. The first modern Western universities were established in Bologna, Rome, and Paris with their core faculties of theology, law, and medicine. A number of towns were transformed into city-states. Trade and commerce boomed. A new dialogue was opened with the sophisticated cultures of Judaism and Islam. Great advances were made in the natural sciences, in mechanics, in literature, in art and architecture. The revolutionary era of the twelfth and thirteenth centuries, Harold Berman tells us, was the "first modern age" of the West.[32]

It was in this revolutionary context that the Roman Catholic Church developed a systematic theology and law of marriage. From the twelfth century forward, the church's doctrine of marriage was categorized, systematized, and refined, notably in Hugh of St. Victor's *On the Sacraments of the Christian Faith* (c. 1143),[33] Peter Lombard's *Book of Sentences* (1150),[34] and Thomas Aquinas's *Summa Theologica* (c. 1265–1273)[35] and the many later commentaries on these texts. From the twelfth century forward, the canon law of marriage was also systematized, first in Gratian's *Decretum* (c. 1140), then in a welter of later commentaries and new papal and conciliar laws.[36] These new theological and legal teachings on marriage were communicated not only through formal theological and legal tracts. They also found their way into sermons, catechisms, and confessional handbooks that eventually allowed these teachings to reach deeply into the lives of the laity.

Viewed collectively, these new theological and legal sources taught three broad perspectives on marriage. Marriage was conceived at once (1) as a created, natural association, subject to the laws of nature; (2) as a consensual contract, subject to the general laws of contract; and (3) as a sacrament of faith, subject to the spiritual laws of the church. These three perspectives were designed to be complementary, each emphasizing one aspect of marriage: its natural origin, its legal form, and its spiritual significance respectively. It was the sacramental quality of marriage, however, that provided the theological and legal integration of these three perspectives into a systematic model of marriage.

Natural Perspectives

First, marriage was regarded as a created natural association that served, in Augustine's phrase, both as "a duty for the sound and a remedy for the sick." Already in Paradise, God had commanded man and woman to "be fruitful and multiply." God had created them as social beings, naturally inclined to one another, and endowed them with the physical capacity to join together and beget children. God had commanded them to help and nurture each other and to inculcate within their children the highest virtue and love of the Divine. These qualities and duties continued after the fall into sin. But after the Fall, marriage also came to serve as a remedy for the individual sinner to allay lustful passion, to heal incontinence, and to substitute a bodily union with a spouse for the lost spiritual union with the Father in Paradise. Rather than allow sinful people to burn with lust, God provided the association of marriage wherein people could direct their natural drives and desires toward the service of the human community.[37]

Many writers, however—following Paul's teachings in 1 Corinthians 7 and that of the later Church Fathers—subordinated the duty of propagation to that of celibate contemplation, the natural drive for sexual union to the spiritual drive for beatitude.[38] For, as Peter Lombard put it:

> The first institution [of marriage in Paradise] was commanded, the second permitted . . . to the human race for the purpose of preventing fornication. But this permission, because it does not select better things, is a remedy not a reward; if anyone rejects it, he will deserve judgment of death. An act which is allowed by permission, however, is voluntary, not necessary. Now permission is received in various ways, as concession, as remission, as toleration. And there is toleration in the New Testament, for lesser good deeds and lesser evils; among the lesser good deeds is marriage, which does not deserve a palm, but is a remedy.[39]

After the fall into sin, marriage remained a duty, but only for those tempted by sexual sin. For those not so tempted, marriage was an inferior option. It was better and more virtuous to pursue the spiritual life of celibacy and contemplation than the temporal life of marriage and family, for marriage was regarded as an institution of the natural sphere, not the supernatural sphere. Though ordained by God and good, it served primarily for the protection of the human community, not for the perfection of the individual. Participation in it merely kept a person free from sin and vice. It did not contribute directly to his or her virtue. The celibate, contemplative life, by contrast, was a calling of the supernatural sphere. Participation in it increased a person's virtue and aided the pursuit of beatitude.[40] To this pursuit, Thomas Aquinas put it, "marriage is a very great obstacle," for it forces the person to dwell on the carnal and natural rather than the spiritual and supernatural aspects of life.[41]

As a created, natural institution, marriage was subject to the law of nature, communicated in reason and conscience, and often confirmed in the Bible. This natural law, medieval writers taught, communicated God's will that fit persons marry when they reach the age of puberty, that they conceive children and nurture and educate them, that they remain naturally bonded to their blood and kin, serving them in times of need, frailty, and old age. It prescribed heterosexual, lifelong unions between a couple, featuring mutual support and faithfulness. It required love for one's spouse and children.[42] It proscribed bigamy, incest, bestiality, buggery, polygamy, sodomy, and other unnatural relations. It prohibited contraception, abortion, infanticide, and other unnatural acts. The same lists of sexual sins set out by St. Paul and the Church Fathers reappeared with endless glosses and commentaries in the sources of the twelfth through the fifteenth centuries.[43]

Contractual Perspectives

Marriage was not simply a natural institution subject to the laws of nature. It was also a contractual relation subject to general rules of contract. Marriage depended on the mutual consent of the parties to be legitimate and binding. "What makes a marriage is not the consent to cohabitation nor the carnal copula," Peter Lombard wrote; "it is the consent to conjugal society that does."[44] The form and function of this conjugal society, and the requirements for entrance into it, were set by the laws of nature. But the choice of whether to enter this society lay with the parties. "Marriage, therefore," said Peter Lombard, "is the marital union between persons legitimate according to the [natural] law, who persevere in a single sharing of life."[45] John Duns Scotus glossed Lombard's definition with a reference to the conjugal debt that is inherent in the marital contract: "Marriage is an indissoluble bond between a man and his wife arising from the mutual exchange of authority over one another's bodies for the procreation and proper nurture of children. The contract of marriage is the mutual exchange by a man and wife of their bodies for perpetual use in the procreation and nurture of children."[46] Hugh of St. Victor stressed the requirement of conjugal fidelity: "What else is marriage but the legitimate association between a man and woman, an association in which each partner obligates (*debet*) himself to the other by virtue of mutual consent? This obligation can be considered in two ways, that one reserve oneself for the spouse, and that one not refuse oneself to the spouse. That is, he reserves himself in that after giving consent he does not go now to another union. He does not refuse himself in that he does not separate himself from that mutual association of one with the other."[47]

As a contract, marriage was subject to the general moral principles of contract that prevailed in medieval canon and civil law.[48] One such principle was freedom of contract, and this applied equally to marriage contracts.[49] "Marriages should be free." "No one is to be compelled to marry." "Matrimony should be freely contracted." These were commonplaces of medieval canon law, and medieval theologians endorsed them heartily.[50] Marriage contracts entered into by force, fear, or fraud, or through inducement of parents, masters, or feudal or manorial lords were thus not binding.[51] A second general principle of contract was that consensual agreements, entered into with or without formalities, were legally binding. Absent proof of mistake or frustration, or some condition that would render the contract unjust or unreasonable, either party could petition a court to enforce its terms. This general principle also applied to marriage contracts. Both husband and wife had an equal right to sue in court for enforcement even of a naked promise of marriage, for discharge of an essential and licit condition to marriage, or for vindication of their conjugal rights to the body of their spouse.[52]

Sacramental Perspectives

Marriage was not only a natural institution subject to natural law and a contractual institution governed by principles of contract. Marriage was also raised by Christ to the dignity of a *sacrament* and thus was subject to the church's spiritual jurisdiction.[53] As a sacrament, marriage was a visible sign of the invisible union of Christ with His church. Both the physical and the spiritual union of the married couple were symbolic. The harmony of their wills and minds reflected the concordance of the Church with the will and mind of Christ. Their physical and spiritual union in love symbolized the gracious union of spirit and flesh in the humanity of Christ. Like Christ's bond to His Church, the husband's bond to his wife was indissoluble and eternally binding.

Unlike the other six sacraments, marriage required no formalities and no clerical or lay instruction, witness, or participation. The two parties were themselves "ministers of the sacrament." Their consciences instructed them in the taking of the sacrament, and their own testimony was considered sufficient evidence to validate their marriages in a case of dispute. Although the Fourth Lateran Council of 1215 and later canon laws strongly encouraged the couple to seek the consent of their parents, to publish their banns for marriage in the church, to solemnize their union with the blessing of the priest, to invite witnesses to the wedding, and to comply with the marital customs of their domicile, none of these steps were absolute requirements. For as William Hay wrote, "it is not of the essence of marriage to contract it in the presence of the church and according to the custom of the country, but a matter of propriety. The fitness of the parties [and the consent between them] is of the essence of marriage."[54]

Like the other six sacraments, marriage was conceived to be an instrument of sanctification that, when contracted between Christians, caused and conferred grace upon those who put no obstacle in its way. Marriage sanctified the Christian couple by allowing them to comply with God's law for marriage, and by reminding them that Christ the bridegroom took the church as His bride and accorded it His highest love and devotion, even to death. It sanctified the Christian community by enlarging the church and by educating its children as people of God. The natural marital functions of propagation and education were thus given spiritual significance when performed by Christians within the extended Christian church.

When performed as a Christian sacrament, marriage transformed the relationship of a husband and wife, much as baptism transformed the character of the baptized. In baptism, the simple ritual act of sprinkling water on the forehead spiritually transformed the baptized party—canceling the original sin of Adam, promising the baptized party divine aid and protection in life, welcoming the baptized believer into the sanctuary of the church, into the spiritual care of the parents and godparents, into the community and communion of the congregation. Similarly in marriage, the simple ritual act of a Christian man and woman coming together in marriage spiritually transformed their relationship—removing the sin of sexual intercourse, promising divine help in fulfilling their marital and parental duties, welcoming them into the hierarchy of institutions that comprised the church universal.[55]

Twelfth- and thirteenth-century writers debated endlessly what step in the marital process rendered it sacramental. Several writers, building on Gratian's *Decretum*, insisted that sacramental grace was conferred only on consummation of the marriage through sexual intercourse—the final act of marriage. After all, the most startling feature of the sacrament was that it transformed sexual intercourse from an otherwise sinful act of lust into a spiritual act of great symbolic value. Moreover, it was well understood that a simple promise to marry in the future followed by intercourse rendered the couple married.[56] But the purely carnal act of intercourse, which was prone to great sinfulness even within marriage, seemed to be a most unlikely channel of grace. Moreover, some couples, such as Mary and Joseph, were truly married even though they did not have sexual intercourse. Such "spiritual marriages" seemed to be more worthy, rather than unworthy, of sacramental designation.[57]

Other writers, notably John Duns Scotus, insisted that it was the blessing of the priest during the church wedding that rendered marriage sacramental. This view was appealing because it hearkened to the role of the priest in other sacraments—the priest's sprinkling of water in baptism, his declaration of absolution from sin in penance, or his offering of bread and wine in the Eucharist.[58] But this view stood in tension with the social and legal reality that many marriages were contracted and consummated without church consecration. To declare such marriages "nonsacramental" was tantamount to removing them from the spiritual jurisdiction and sacramental care of the church.

By the late thirteenth century, it became widely accepted that it was the simple exchange of present promises between the parties that rendered it sacramental. This view became canonical. Neither consecration of the marriage through a church wedding nor consummation of the marriage through sexual intercourse was critical in the sacramental process. Even a secretly contracted, unconsummated marriage between a man and a woman capable of entering conjugal society in accordance with natural law could be an instrument of sacramental grace. It was the mutual exchange of wills, the genuine union of mind to be married, that triggered the conferral of sacramental grace. The fruits of that sacramental grace pervaded the institution from that time forward.[59]

Once this channel of sacramental grace was properly opened, it could no longer be closed. A marriage properly contracted between Christians, in accordance with the laws of nature, was thus an indissoluble union, a permanently open channel of grace. Thomas Aquinas captured this in a critical passage on the indissolubility of marriage:

> [S]ince the sacraments effect what they signify, it is to be believed that grace is conferred through this sacrament on the spouses, whereby they might belong to the union of Christ and the Church. And this is very necessary to them so that as they concern themselves with carnal and earthly matters, they do not become detached from Christ and the Church.
>
> Now since the union of husband and wife is an image of the union of Christ and the Church, the image must correspond with that which it imagines. Now the union of Christ and the church is a union of one person with one person, and it is to last in perpetuity. For there is only one Church, . . . and Christ will never be separated from His Church. As he himself says in the last chapter of Matthew, "Behold I am with you even unto the end of the world. . . ." It follows necessarily then that a marriage, in so far as it is a sacrament of the Church, must be a union that is indissoluble.[60]

Thomas bolstered this sacramental argument for the indissolubility of marriage with traditional patristic arguments from nature. "According to nature's intent marriage is oriented to the nurture of offspring. Thus it is according to the law of nature that parents save for their children and that children be heirs for their parents. Therefore, since offspring are the good of both husband and wife together, the latter's union must remain permanently, according to the dictate of the law of nature."[61] He also added a contractual argument that to preserve the marital bond was more advantageous to the couple and the broader community.[62] It was the argument from the sacramental quality of marriage, however, that gave his argument for indissolubility its cogency and canonical force.

The sacramental understanding of marriage both elevated and integrated the natural and the contractual dimensions of marriage. On the one hand, the sacramental quality of Christian marriage helped to elevate the natural acts of marriage to spiritual significance. At minimum, it helped to remove the stigma of sin in sexual intercourse and to elevate the procreation and nurture of children into an act useful for the church. More fully conceived, the sacramental quality effectively placed the natural institution of marriage into the hierarchy of church orders as something of an institution and instrument of grace, although one clearly subordinate to the celibate clerical and monastic orders.

On the other hand, the sacramental quality of Christian marriage helped to elevate the marriage contract into more than just a bargained-for exchange between two parties. At minimum, it rendered marriage an "adhesion contract" that was indissoluble: the terms of the marital bargain were already set by nature, and as a symbol of Christ's bond with his church, the marital bond was per force indissoluble. More fully conceived, the exchange of consent between the couple also signified an exchange of consent of the couple with God and the church. In essence, the parties consented to bind themselves to each other and to God and the church and thus to accept God's sacramental grace and the church's spiritual nurture for their marriage.

This understanding of the marriage sacrament, which was crystallized by theologians and canonists in the thirteenth century and thereafter, went beyond the formulations of St. Augustine and the other Church Fathers. Augustine called marriage a sacrament in order to demonstrate its symbolic stability. Thirteenth-century writers called marriage a sacrament to demonstrate its spiritual efficacy. Augustine said that marriage as a symbol of Christ's bond to the church *should* not be dissolved. Thirteenth-century writers said that marriage as a permanent channel of sacramental grace *could* not be dissolved.[63] Augustine simply scattered throughout his writings reflections on the natural, contractual, and spiritual dimensions of the marriage without fully integrating them. Thirteenth-century writers wove these three dimensions of marriage into an integrated sacramental framework.

Critics of the day, and in the centuries that followed, considered this new theology of marriage to be a self-serving attempt to bring marriage within the domain and power of the church.[64] There might be something to this allegation, given the revolutionary climate of the day and the great battles between popes and emperors, bishops and lords over questions of power and jurisdiction. Whatever the inspiration of twelfth- and thirteenth-century writers might have been, however, their theological construction of a sacramental model of marriage was a work of genius. It integrated nearly a millennium of inherited theological reflections on marriage and anticipated many of the hardest questions that would confront the church in subsequent centuries. The thirteenth-century sacramental model of marriage lies at the heart of Catholic theology still today—amply amended and emended over the centuries, but unchanged in its fundamental form.[65]

The Canon Law of Marriage

The Church's Jurisdiction

One reason that the Catholic sacramental model of marriage had such an enduring influence in the West was that it was both a theological and a legal model. The theological formulations of monks and professors were translated into the canon laws of popes and church councils. New canon laws of marriage were in turn given new theological apologiae. Since the late eleventh century, there was a constant cross-fertilization between the theology and law of marriage in the Roman Catholic Church.

It was the church's new legal and political prominence in the West that rendered this alliance of theology and law so powerful. In the Western world of 1200–1500, the church was not merely a voluntary association of like-minded believers gathered for worship. Its canon law was not simply an internal code of spiritual discipline to guide the faithful. The church was the one universal sovereign of the West that governed all of Christendom. The canon law was the one universal law of the West that was common to jurisdictions and peoples throughout Europe. The great nation-states of Western Europe were not yet born. The Holy Roman Empire was not yet real. In that interim, the Catholic Church with its canon law held preeminent authority.

The church claimed a vast jurisdiction—a power to proclaim and enforce law, literally "to speak the law" (*jus dicere*).[66] The church claimed personal jurisdiction over clerics, pilgrims, students, heretics, Jews, and Muslims. It claimed subject matter jurisdiction over doctrine, liturgy, ecclesiastical property, patronage, education, charity, inheritance, oral promises, oaths, moral crimes, and marriage. The church predicated these jurisdictional claims in part on Christ's famous delegation of the keys to Peter (Matthew 16:18)—a key of knowledge to discern God's word and will, and a key of power to implement and enforce that word and will by law. The church also predicated these new claims on its traditional authority over the form and function of the Christian sacraments. By the fifteenth century, the church had gathered whole systems of canon law around the seven sacraments of baptism, eucharist, penance, orders, extreme unction, confirmation, and marriage.

These jurisdictional claims rendered the church both legislator and judge of Christendom. The church issued a steady stream of papal decretals and bulls, conciliar decrees and edicts that were to prevail throughout Christendom. These legislative documents circulated singly and in heavily glossed editions of the six books that would later comprise the *Corpus iuris canonici*.[67] Formidable bodies of supplementary legislation promulgated by local prelates and synods also circulated, often glossed with commentary and the opinions of judges and jurists.

Church courts adjudicated cases (*causae*) in accordance with the substantive and procedural rules of the canon law. Most cases were generally heard first in the court of the archdeaconry, generally called the consistory court, presided over by the archdeacon or a provisory judge. Major disputes involving annulment of putative marriages or sexual felonies committed by or against clergy were generally heard by the consistory court of the bishop, presided over by the bishop himself or by his principal official. These courts operated with sophisticated rules of procedure, evidence, and equity, and had a battery of sharp spiritual weapons at hand to enforce their judgments and to put down their secular rivals.[68]

The church's canon law of marriage was the supreme law of marriage in much of the West. Temporal laws of marriage—whether of Roman, royal, customary, urban, feudal, or manorial stock—were considered subordinate to the canon law. In the event of conflict, civil courts and councils were to relinquish their jurisdiction over marriage to church courts and councils. The church could not always make good on its claim to exclusive jurisdiction and peremptory power over marriage. In polities governed by strong kings or dukes and weak ecclesiastics, civil authorities often enjoyed concurrent jurisdiction over marriage—

doubly so when the papacy was wracked with scandal in the fourteenth century. But, as a sacrament, marriage was at the heart of the church's jurisdiction, and its canon law was pervasive and powerful.

Marriage at Canon Law

The canon law distinguished three stages of consent in marriage: (1) the betrothal or promise to marry in the future ("I, Jack, promise to take you, Jill, to be my wife"); (2) the promise to be married in the present, which constitutes a true and valid union even without sexual intercourse ("I, Jill, now take you, Jack, as my husband"); and (3) the consummation of the marriage by voluntary sexual intercourse.[69]

None of these stages in the formation of marriage required much formality to be valid and enforceable. The first two steps required only the oral exchange of words, or (where parties were mute, deaf, or incapable of de facto exchange) some symbolic equivalent thereof. Parties could add much more to either stage—attaching legitimate conditions to the betrothal, swearing public oaths, or formalizing their wedding in a church followed by a public celebration, for example. But none of this was mandatory, even if preferred by the church. No formal writing or witnesses were required for the betrothal. No authorities (whether parental, feudal, political, or ecclesiastical) were required to approve or to preside at the marriage. The consummation of marriage through intercourse also required little beyond voluntary participation by both parties. Forced intercourse was sinful, even criminal in the extreme case.

The canon law recognized a variety of lawful impediments to the first stage of *betrothal*—that is, conditions under which either of the parties could break off the engagement without sin. A faithful party could spurn a fiancé(e) who had become a heretic or pagan; had abducted another (particularly a relative of the fiancé[e]); had been raped; had become impotent, severely deformed, or deranged after betrothal; had deserted him or her for more than two years; or had failed to make a present promise within the time of engagement agreed upon by the parties. In all these cases, the innocent party was advised to petition a church court to annul the betrothal. A religious vow to chastity or entry by either party into a religious order automatically nullified the agreement; the other party, in such instance, had no discretion to continue the relationship. A betrothal could also be dissolved by mutual consent of the parties.

A future promise to marry, followed by sexual intercourse, was viewed as a consummated marriage at canon law, and was considered valid, even if not licit. Intercourse after betrothal raised the presumption that the parties had implicitly consented to be truly married and to consummate their marriage. This presumption could be defeated if one of the parties proved that he or she had been forcibly abducted by the other. Even then the marriage was generally considered valid, though the abducting party was guilty of grave sin, which required penance.

The canon law also recognized several impediments to the second stage of marital consent, that of contracting of marriage in the present. These were of two types: (1) prohibitive impediments that rendered the contracting of marriage unlawful and sinful, but whose violation did not render the marriage invalid; and (2) diriment (or absolute) impediments that proscribed the contracting of marriage, and, if it was contracted, nullified and dissolved it completely, regardless of what the parties wished.

Prohibitive impediments dealt largely with cases of remarriage. A married person who had abducted a relative of his or her spouse or another married or betrothed person could not marry that person after his or her own spouse's death. For those who murdered their spouses, murdered a cleric, married a nun or monk, or had done public penance for a particularly egregious sin, marriage was proscribed altogether. To marry in the face of such impediments was a serious sin that required penance. But the marriage of such a party, particularly when the other spouse had no knowledge of this impediment prior to the marriage, could remain intact.

Diriment impediments nullified even fully consummated putative marriages, leaving parties free to remarry, but often saddled with serious charges of sin. The charges of sin were particularly grave if the parties secretly married in knowing violation of a diriment impediment. The charges of sin were still graver if the parties publicly married—with the participation of parents, peers, and priests—but kept secret their knowing violation of such a diriment impediment. Such an act was not only a sin against God; it was also a subterfuge against all others drawn into the ceremony.[70]

One set of diriment impediments sought to preserve the freedom of consent of both parties. Proof of extreme duress, fear, compulsion, or fraud (by parents, spouses, or third parties) impinged on consent and could invalidate a marriage contract, particularly if the action was brought soon after the union. A mistake about the identity of the other party, and in some cases of the virginity of the woman prior to marriage, was also a ground for nullification of a marriage.

A second set of diriment impediments defined which parties were free to give their consent. Parties who had, prior to the putative marriage, made religious vows of celibacy or chastity in one of the sacred orders of the church were eternally bound to God and thus could not bind themselves to another in marriage. Their marriage was thus automatically void. Christians could not contract marriage with infidels, Jews, or pagans, because the sacrament of baptism was a prerequisite for marriage; furthermore, such marriages could not symbolize the union of Christ with his faithful church. Marriages contracted with a non-Christian were thus automatically annulled on discovery. Moreover, if a party departed from the faith after consummation and remained incorrigible, a church court could declare the marriage void, particularly if the couple had children who would be forced to choose between their parents' faiths. Persons related up to the fourth degree either to a common ancestor or to a couple (whether or not married) who had engaged in sexual relations were prohibited from marrying. These were called the impediments of consanguinity and affinity set out in Leviticus. Parents could not marry their adopted children or grandchildren, nor the spouses of their adopted children. One who baptized or confirmed a party or who became a godparent could not marry him or her, for these persons were considered to be the "spiritual fathers or mothers" of the party who received the sacrament.

A third set of diriment impediments protected the ultimate sanctity and sanctifying function of the sacrament of marriage. Conditions attached to marriage promises that were illegal or repugnant to the sacrament or harmful to the offspring automatically rendered the marriage contract void. Thus a promise with the condition "that we abstain for a season" was valid. But a condition "that we engage in contraception," "that we abort our offspring," or "that we permit each other sexual liberty with others" nullified the marriage contract. Such conditions vitiated the spiritual purpose of marriage—to unite together in love and to raise children in the service of God. Likewise, permanent impotence, insanity, or bewitchment of either party were generally grounds for nullification, provided that such a condition was latent before marriage but unknown to the parties; if the parties knew of the condition before marriage or if it arose after consummation, they had no action for nullification.

Fourth, all bigamous and polygamous relations were annulled as contrary to the biblical command, even if the parties had children. Annulment for such an impediment required proof of one's spouse's prior marriage contract, which was not dissolved by the former spouse's death or by a formal annulment.

Today, the canon law doctrine of annulment is often described as the virtual equivalent of the common law doctrine of fault-based divorce. Any enterprising canon lawyer, it is said, can sift through the multiple impediments to marriage recognized at canon law and find one that applies sufficiently to allow an unhappy couple to dissolve their union. Historians have often assumed that the same was true in the canon law of the twelfth through the fifteenth centuries. They have been encouraged in this belief by sixteenth-century Protestant reformers who pummelled the canonists constantly with this charge, as we will see in succeeding chapters. "The conclusion has seemed logically to follow," writes R.H. Helmholz, "that energetic genealogical research coupled with legal ingenuity would almost always have produced sufficient grounds for the annulment of a marriage." But, says Helmholz on the strength of a career of close archival research, "the evidence of actual court practice . . . does not support this seemingly compelling conclusion. Court records from the Middle Ages produce many fewer cases in which such divorces occurred than expected." There are spectacular examples of ingeniously crafted arguments for annulment—not least that of Henry VIII in his attempts to escape his marriage to Catherine of Aragon. But one cannot write "history by anecdote," Helmholz warns, and the surviving records of more typical cases suggest that annulments were not so easily procured.[71]

The relationship of the parties once properly married was more closely regulated by the confessional norms of the inner forum than by the canon laws of the external forum.[72] The confessional books of the fourteenth and fifteenth centuries go on interminably in describing the appropriate household duties of husbands and wives, parents and children, masters and servants. Long sections of these confessional books were devoted to proper sexual etiquette within marriage: the proper "time, place, and manner" of sexual contact between husband and wife; the appropriate rules of dress, language, and decorum; the Christian response to impotence, sexual disease, and pregnancy. These same confessional books also glossed and illustrated at length the biblical lists of sexual sins—particularly Paul's injunctions against lust, fornication, concubinage, prostitution, sodomy, and "sexual perversion."[73] Many of the more mundane aspects of daily marital living were thus left to the private control of the sacrament of penance. Parties were to confess their sins secretly, including their sexual and marital sins, at least once annually. Once absolved, they were expected to do appropriate penitential works of purgation.

The canon law became more actively and openly involved when the conduct of the marital parties rose to the level of fault or crime. Neglect of a child's physical needs, spiritual nurture, or education might lead to intervention by a church court, particularly if pastoral reproof proved ineffective. Illegal transfers of property, through contract or testament, that violated obligations of minimal care for one's spouse or children could likewise trigger judicial intervention. Most important, violence against a wife or child, marital rape or incest, malicious desertion of one's spouse and family, and the commission of adultery, sodomy, or other grave sexual sins had dramatic legal effect. These actions, if proved, constituted canon law crimes that could be severely sanctioned—by both the church and any number of civil authorities. Moreover, proof of adultery, desertion, and cruelty could also support an action for divorce.

Divorce in the modern sense was not permitted at canon law. The sacramental bond, once consummated, remained indissoluble at least till the physical death of one of the parties—and ideally would be renewed in the life hereafter. Divorce at canon law therefore meant separation from bed and board (*a mensa et thoro*) alone. Both husband and wife were given standing to sue for divorce in church courts. During pendency of the divorce case, a church court could order a husband to pay his wife temporary alimony to sustain her, particularly if she had already moved out of the marital home out of fear or under pressure from her husband. If a church court found adequate grounds for divorce, it would order the estranged parties to live separately, and sometimes make further orders respecting custody and support of the children.[74]

A separated spouse, although freed from the physical bond of marriage, was not freed from the spiritual bond. "Separation can be of two kinds, corporeal and spiritual," reads a thirteenth-century canon law text, echoing Peter Lombard. "Spouses can be separated corporeally because of adultery, or by mutual consent in order to enter religious life, whether for a time or permanently. But they cannot be separated sacramentally as long as both live, provided they are married legitimately. For the marital bond remains between them even though, on separating, they should seek to marry other partners."[75] A subsequent marriage contracted before the death of one's estranged spouse was an act of bigamy—a mortal sin at canon law, and a serious crime at civil law.

The Tridentine Synthesis

The Roman Catholic tradition provided its own systematic distillation of these biblical, patristic, and medieval teachings on marriage in the work of the Council of Trent (1545–1563). This great council brought unity and reform to the Church on the scale of the great ecumenical councils of the past. And it set the basic theological and legal tone of the Catholic contribution to the Western tradition of marriage that lasted until the canon law revisions of 1917 and 1983 and the theological and structural transformations of the Second Vatican Council (1962–1965).

As Pope Paul III's 1542 Bull of Convocation made clear, the Council of Trent was prompted by "the many distresses [of] pastoral solicitude and vigilance" within the church and the many new "schisms, dissensions, and heresies" by which the "Christian commonwealth" was "wellnigh rent and torn asunder."[76] The Council was designed to respond forcefully to two centuries of humanistic attacks, two decades of Protestant dissent, and a host of political incursions into the church's jurisdiction. The First Decree of the Council proclaimed the Council's goals unequivocally: "for the advance and exaltation of the Christian faith and religion, for the extirpation of heresies, for the peace and unity of the Church, for the reform of the clergy and Christian people, for the suppression and destruction of heresies. . . ."[77]

Marriage was among the many subjects for which the Council issued comprehensive legislation. In the Decree Tametsi of 1563, the Council confirmed the medieval sacramental model of marriage—as a natural, contractual, and spiritual institution created by the Father and sanctified by the Son.

> The perpetual and indissoluble bond of matrimony was expressed by the first parent of the human race, when, under the influence of the divine Spirit, he said: *This now is bone of my bones and flesh of my flesh. Wherefore a man shall leave his father and mother and shall cleave to his wife, and they shall be two in one flesh.* But that by this bond two only are united and joined together, Christ the Lord taught more plainly when referring to those last words, as having been spoken by God, he said: *Therefore now they are not two, but one flesh,* and immediately ratified the firmness of the bond. . . .
>
> But the grace which was to perfect the natural love, and confirm that indissoluble union, and sanctify the persons married, Christ Himself, the instituter and perfecter of the venerable sacraments, merited for us by His passion, which Paul the Apostle intimates when he says: *Husbands love your wives, as Christ also loved the Church, and delivered himself up for it;* adding immediately: *This is a great sacrament, but I speak in Christ and in the Church.*
>
> Since therefore matrimony in the evangelical law surpasses in grace through Christ the ancient marriages, our holy Fathers, the councils, and the tradition of the universal Church, have with good reason always taught that it is to be numbered among the sacraments of the New Law. . . . [78]

On the strength of this decree, the Council issued a dozen canons that confirmed conventional medieval teaching and practice and condemned with "anathema" critics and customs to the contrary. Polygamy was forbidden. Mandatory clerical celibacy was confirmed. The spiritual superiority of celibacy and virginity to marriage was underscored. Medieval canon law impediments to betrothal and marriage and traditional prohibitions against marriage in certain seasons were confirmed. The church's power to grant dispensations from impediments was confirmed. Divorce meant only separation from bed and board, with no right of remarriage. Ecclesiastical judges were to enjoy exclusive marital jurisdiction.[79]

In the same Decree Tametsi, the Council of Trent also instituted several reforms to put down abuses which "experience teaches" had crept into the church. In an effort to curb the "evil" of clandestine marriages, the church sought to apply a "more efficacious remedy," based on earlier conciliar and patristic teachings. Minor children were to procure the consent of their parents to marry. Local parish priests were to announce the banns of marriage of a prospective couple on three successive festival days, forgoing such announcements only if "there should be a probable suspicion that a marriage might be maliciously hindered." Betrothed parties were to postpone cohabitation until after their wedding. Three days before consummation of their marriage, they were to make full and "careful" confession in the sacrament of penance and to "approach most devoutly the most holy sacrament of the Eucharist." Weddings were to be contracted in the church before a priest and "in the presence of two or three witnesses"—save during the seasons of Lent and Advent when marriage was forbidden. Failure to comply with these requirements was a great sin that "shall at the discretion of the ordinary [priest] be severely punished." And if the marriage contract was not consecrated by a priest it was deemed automatically "invalid and null," and the parties subject to spiritual and temporal sanctions. If the marriage was contracted properly, the priest was to record the names of the couple and their witnesses in the local parish register.[80]

To remedy some of the abuses of marital impediments and of dispensations from the same, the Council also instituted a number of changes. Baptized parties were to have only one godfather or godmother, with whom marriage was prohibited, and whose name was to be recorded in the local parish register. The impediment of public honesty (which could preclude marriage to and of a nonvirgin) was removed. The impediment of affinity (which precluded marriage to the relatives of a person with whom one had intercourse) was limited to relatives only in the second degree. Dispensations from impediments could be granted retroactively (allowing consummated marriages to stand) only if the parties had innocently violated these impediments. Persons who consummated their marriages in knowing violation of an impediment were subject to severe punishment and foreclosed from any dispensation.[81]

To protect against the "singularly execrable" abuses of the freedom of marital contract, the Council commanded "all, of whatever rank, dignity and profession they may be, under penalty of anathema to be incurred *ipso facto,* that they do not in any manner whatever, directly or indirectly, compel their subjects or any others whomsoever in any way that will hinder them from contracting marriage freely."[82] This provision was designed especially to end the practice of coerced and arranged marriages instituted by feudal or manorial lords, overbearing parents, or aristocratic or dynastic guardians eager to solemnize treaties and alliances with rivals through arranged or coerced marriages of their children or wards.

To deter the problems of abduction, rape, and kidnapping of young maidens, the Council imposed the ultimate sanction, declaring that any such party and his accomplices "shall be *ipso jure* excommunicated and forever infamous and disqualified for all dignities of any kind; and if they be clerics, they shall forfeit all rank." The woman who was abducted had no obligation to marry her abductor, although a despoiled virgin often had few choices besides marriage or entering a monastery. If she chose to marry her abductor, she could request an ecclesiastical judge to order him to pay her an endowment.[83]

To curb the common custom of concubinage, the Council also invoked the ultimate sanction of excommunication. Clergy were empowered to admonish concubinaries of their sin and demand them to separate. Those who persisted in their concubinage after three warnings "shall be punished with excommunication from which they shall not be absolved till they have in fact obeyed the admonition given them." Those who return to concubinage are to be punished "with a severity in keeping with the character of the crime."[84]

The marital reforms of the Council of Trent went beyond stark legal pronouncements that would guide the clergy and educated laity. The Council also authorized the preparation of a comprehensive new catechism aimed at children and uninstructed adults "who are in need of milk rather than solid food."[85] The Catechism, issued in 1566, included instructions on the "efficacy and use" of the seven sacraments, translated "into the language of the people and explained to the people by all parish priests."[86]

The Catechism provided a convenient distillation and integration of the contractual, natural, and sacramental dimensions of marriage.[87] Citing the "general opinion of the theologians," the Catechism defined marriage as "[t]he conjugal union of man and woman, contracted between two qualified persons, which obliges them to live together throughout life." A "perfect" marital contract requires "internal consent, external compact expressed by words, the obligation and tie which arise from the contract, and the marriage debt by which it is consummated." Consent alone is not enough for marriage. There must be a "mutual agreement," freely entered into and declared in words stated in the present tense one to the other—or where parties were deaf or mute, by some other token of genuine consent. "The marriage promise is not a mere promise, but a transfer of right, by which the man actually yields of the dominion of his body to the woman, the woman the dominion of her body to the man." Consummation of the marriage is not necessary to render it true and valid, although it is expected.

A marriage once contracted, the Catechism continued, must be understood both "as a natural union, since it was not invented by man but instituted by nature" and "as a Sacrament, the efficacy of which transcends the order of nature." As a natural union, created by God in Paradise, marriage has three reasons for its existence: (1) the "companionship of husband and wife," (2) "an antidote to avoid sins of lust," and (3) "the desire of family, not so much, however, with a view to leave after us heirs to inherit our property and fortune, as to bring up children in the true faith and service of God." This latter reason automatically renders contraception and abortion "a most heinous crime—nothing less than wicked conspiracy to commit murder."

As a sacramental union, marriage "is far superior . . . and aims at an incomparably higher end." "For as marriage, as a natural union, was instituted from the beginning to propagate the human race; so was the sacramental dignity subsequently conferred upon it in order that a people might be begotten and brought up for the service and worship of the true God and of Christ our Saviour." As a symbol of Christ's eternal bond to His Church, marriage introduces an indissoluble bond between husband and wife, a bond "of the greatest affection and love." The sacrament of marriage was anticipated already at creation, but it was not completed till the time of Christ. Christ perfected the institution and outlawed prior sinful practices of polygamy and divorce with his proclamation that "the two shall become one flesh" and "what God has joined together let no man put asunder."

Marriage brings three blessings, the Catechism states, echoing Augustine: offspring, if it is the Lord's will; fidelity, which is "a special, holy, and pure love"; and "sacrament," now in the Augustinian sense of stability and permanence. God confers those blessings where couples abide by His duties for marriage—set out in the natural law and elaborated in the Bible. "It is the duty of the husband to treat his wife generously and honorably," to be "constantly occupied in some honest pursuit with a view to provide necessaries for his family and to avoid idleness, the root of almost every vice." Wives, in turn, must "never forget that next to God they are to love their husbands, to esteem them above all others, yielding to them in all things not inconsistent with Christian piety, a willing and ready obedience."

This Tridentine synthesis of marriage theology and law became a rallying point for Catholic communities thereafter. Translated into multiple languages, and widely disseminated, the decree and catechism of Trent provided a common and familiar guide not only for the inner marital life of Catholic believers but also the public marriage law of Catholic countries. The rich sacramental model of marriage that was distilled in these simple documents came to be accepted throughout the early modern Catholic world—in Italy, France, Spain, and Portugal, and eventually in their colonies in Latin America, Mexico, Florida, California, Louisiana, Quebec, and beyond.[88]

2

Marriage as Social Estate in the Lutheran Reformation

Questions of marriage occupied Protestant theologians and jurists from the beginning of the Reformation. The founding fathers of the sixteenth-century Continental and English Reformations—Martin Luther and Philip Melanchthon; Martin Bucer and John Calvin; Thomas Cranmer and Thomas Becon—all prepared lengthy sermons and pamphlets on the subject. Scores of leading jurists and judges took up legal questions of marriage in their legal opinions and commentaries, often working under the direct inspiration of early Protestant theology and theologians.

The Protestants' early preoccupation with marriage was driven in part by their theology. Many of the core issues of the Protestant Reformation were implicated by the Roman Catholic theology and canon law of marriage that prevailed throughout much of the West on the eve of the Reformation. The Catholic Church's jurisdiction over marriage was, for the reformers, a particularly flagrant example of the Church's usurpation of the magistrate's authority. The Catholic sacramental concept of marriage, on which the Church predicated its jurisdiction, raised deep questions of sacramental theology and scriptural interpretation. The canon law impediments to marriage, its prohibitions against complete divorce, its close regulations of sexuality, parenting, and education stood in considerable tension with the reformers' interpretation of biblical teaching. That a child could enter marriage without parental permission or church consecration betrayed, in the reformers' views, basic responsibilities of the family, church, and state to children. Issues of marriage doctrine and law thus implicated and epitomized some of the cardinal theological issues of the Protestant Reformation.

The Protestants' early preoccupation with the theology and law of marriage was also driven by their politics. A number of early leaders of the Reformation faced aggressive prosecution by the Catholic Church and its political allies for violation of the canon law of marriage. Among the earliest Protestant leaders were ex-priests and ex-monastics who had forsaken their orders and vows, and often married shortly thereafter. One of the important symbolic acts of solidarity with the new Protestant cause thereafter was to marry, divorce, and remarry in open violation of canon law rules. King Henry VIII of England's famous flouting of the traditional canon law of annulment and Philip of Hesse's knowing violation of the canon laws of bigamy were only the most sensational cases.[1] Such acts of deliberate disobedience were quite common in the early years of the Reformation, among the highborn and lower classes alike. As Catholic Church courts began to prosecute these canon law offenses, Protestant theologians and jurists rose to the defense of their co-religionists—producing a welter of briefs, letters, sermons, and pamphlets that denounced traditional norms and pronounced a new gospel of marriage.

Political leaders rapidly translated this new Protestant gospel into civil law. Just as the act of marriage came to signal a person's conversion to Protestantism, so the Marriage Act came to symbolize a political community's acceptance of Protestantism. Political leaders—long envious of the church's lucrative jurisdiction over marriage and inspired by the new Protestant teachings—were quick to establish new civil marriage statutes. In Lutheran, Calvinist, and Anglican polities alike, a new civil law of marriage was promulgated within a generation after official acceptance of Protestantism. Protestant theologians and jurists played prominent roles both in formulating this new law and in defending it against detractors.

The following chapters take up the contributions of the Continental and English Reformations to the development of Western marriage law. This chapter analyzes the contribution of the Lutheran Reformation to the marriage law of sixteenth-century Germany, with passing attention to Swiss and Scandinavian developments. The following chapters take up, in turn, the contribution of the Calvinist and Anglican Reformations to Western marriage law.[2]

Despite their differences in theological orientation and legal emphasis, these three Protestant reformations of marriage had two broad features in common. First, they all replaced the traditional sacramental model of marriage with a new model that played up another dimension of marriage besides its spiritual qualities. Lutherans spoke of marriage as one of the three foundational social estates of the earthly kingdom, alongside the clergy and the magistracy. Calvinists called it a covenantal association of the civil and ecclesiastical order. Anglicans regarded it as a domestic commonwealth within the church and commonwealth of England. The common effect of these reconceptualizations was to reduce the role of the church and to increase the role of the state and the community in marriage formation, governance, and dissolution. Lutherans consigned much of the legal responsibility for marriage to the state and local community. Calvinists vested the law of marriage equally in the church and state. Anglicans ultimately returned much of the jurisdiction over marriage to the church courts, guided by ample Parliamentary legislation and occasional intervention from the royal and common law courts.

Second, despite the fiery anti-Catholic and anticanonical rhetoric of their early leaders—symbolized most poignantly in Martin Luther's 1520 burning of the canon law and confessional books before his faculty at the University of Wittenberg—each of these Protestant reformations accepted and appropriated a great deal of the traditional canon law of marriage. This could only be expected. Roman Catholic institutions had, after all, ruled effectively and efficiently in Europe for centuries. The canon law was a sophisticated system of law well known to the jurists and theologians who had joined the Reformation cause. Courses in canon law were regularly offered in both the law faculties and theology faculties of European universities, even after the Reformation. Indeed, canon law remained part of the common law (*jus commune*) of Protestant and Catholic Europe until the legal reforms and codification movements of the later eighteenth and nineteenth centuries. To be sure, in Protestant polities more than in Catholic polities, theologically offensive ecclesiastical structures and legal provisions, such as those directly rooted in notions of papal supremacy or spurned sacraments, were discarded. What remained, however, was readily used in service of the new Protestant theology and law of marriage.

The Case of Johann Apel

A 1523 case involving Johann Apel of Nürnberg provides an illuminating window on the budding reformation of marriage law in early sixteenth-century Germany.[3] Johann Apel was a canonist and a canon. He was trained first in his native Nürnberg, then at a Latin school in Wittenberg. In 1514, he enrolled at the University of Wittenberg, where he had passing acquaintance with a new professor of theology, Martin Luther. In 1516, he transferred to the University of Leipzig for legal studies. Like many law students in his day, Apel studied for a joint degree in canon law and civil law, and was awarded the *doctor utriusque juris* in 1519.[4] After a brief apprenticeship, Apel took holy orders and swore an oath of celibacy. Conrad, Bishop of Würzburg and Duke of

Francken, appointed him as a cathedral canon in Würzburg in 1523. He also licensed him as an advocate in all courts in his domain, both ecclesiastical and civil.

Shortly after his ecclesiastical appointment, Apel became enamored of a nun (whose name is not revealed in the records) at the local St. Marr cloister. The couple saw each other secretly for several weeks and carried on a brisk correspondence. The letters read into the court record hint that she became pregnant. Ultimately, she forsook the cloister and her vows and secretly married Apel. After a few weeks of further secrecy, the couple cohabited openly as a married couple. Upon hearing of these developments, Bishop Conrad privately annulled Apel's marriage and admonished him to confess his sin, return his putative wife to the cloister, and resume his duties. Apel refused, insisting that his marriage, though secretly contracted, was valid. Unconvinced, the Bishop indicted Apel and temporarily suspended him from office. Apel offered a spirited defense of his conduct in a frank letter to the Bishop.

Bishop Conrad, in response, had Apel indicted in the church court of audience, for breach of holy orders and the oath of celibacy, and for defiance of his episcopal dispensation and injunction. Apel adduced conscience and scripture in his defense, much as Luther had done two years before at the Diet of Worms. "I have sought only to follow the dictates of conscience . . . and the Gospel," Apel insisted, not to defy episcopal authority and canon law. Scripture and conscience condone marriage for fit adults as "a dispensation against lust and fornication." Apel and his wife had availed themselves of this dispensation and entered and consummated their marriage "in chasteness and love." Contrary to scripture, canon law commands celibacy for clerics and monastics, and thereby introduces all manner of impurity among them. "Who does not see the fornication and concubinage? Who does not see the defilement and the adultery?" Apel's alleged sin and crime of breaking "this little man-made rule of celibacy," he insisted, "is very slight when compared to these sins of fornication and breaking the law of the Lord." "The Word of the Lord is what will judge between you and me," Apel declared to the Bishop, and such Word commands acquittal.

The Bishop took the case under advisement. Apel took his cause to the evangelical community. He sought support for his claims among evangelical theologians and jurists in Nürnberg, Wittenberg, and elsewhere, who had already spoken against celibacy and monasticism. He published his remarks at trial under the title *Defense of Johannes Apel*, adorned with a robust preface by Martin Luther.[5]

Two weeks after publication of the tract, Bishop Conrad had Apel arrested and put in the tower, pending further proceedings. Apel's family pleaded in vain with the Bishop to release him. The local civil magistrate, Archduke Ferdinand, brother of the emperor, twice mandated that Apel be released, again to no avail. Jurists and councilmen wrote letters that denounced the Bishop's actions "as unduly savage and contrary to canon and imperial law," and that defended Apel's conduct as consistent with "the equitable commands of divine, natural, and human laws" and the "dictates and liberties of conscience." Emperor Charles V sent a brief letter urging the Bishop not to protract Apel's harsh imprisonment in violation of imperial law, but to try him and release him if found innocent. Apel himself wrote at least four supplications to the Bishop, arguing ever more sharply that lawful marriage is a "biblical commandment," whereas unlawful incarceration is a "diabolical connivance." Apel was finally tried three months later and was found guilty of several violations of the canon law and of heretically participating in "Luther's damned teachings." He was defrocked and excommunicated. Thereafter, Apel made his way to Wittenberg where, at the urging of Luther and a fellow reformer, Justus Jonas, he was appointed to the law faculty at the university.

For all of his bitter experience, however, Apel did not urge the abolition of the canon law of marriage. He collaborated with another fellow reformer, Lazarus Spengler, to publish a collection of early canon law texts for use at the University of Wittenberg faculty.[6] Despite Luther's heated protestations—which eventually prompted his famous remark that "jurists are bad Christians" (*Juristen böse Christen*)[7] —Apel also insisted that the Wittenberg law faculty continue to offer lectures and the doctoral program in canon law. Apel himself offered lectures on the canon law from his first year of appointment, and in 1528 developed a special course on the canon law of marriage, with Kaspar von Teutleben. His two famous books on legal science are peppered throughout with discussion of the canon law.[8]

Apel's case provides a miniature portrait of both the prevailing sacramental model and the budding social model of marriage in the sixteenth century. It illustrates the most pressing issues that divided proponents of these models—celibacy, concubinage, clerical marriage, secret marriage, easy annulments—issues that pressed with equal force in Calvin's Geneva, Zwingli's Zürich, and Henrician England. The Apel case also illustrates the organic connections that remained between these two models. Even while Luther was burning the canon law books, Apel, though badly burned by the canon law, insisted that this source remain at the core of the new Protestant theory and law of marriage.

The New Evangelical Theology of Marriage

Luther's Attack

Martin Luther attacked the traditional Roman Catholic theology and canon law of marriage with unbridled vehemence.[9] "[T]he estate of marriage has fallen into awful disrepute," he declared in a robust sermon of 1522.

> There are many pagan books which treat of nothing but the depravity of woman kind and the unhappiness of the estate of marriage. . . . Every day one encounters parents who forget their former misery because, like the mouse, they have now had their fill. They deter their children from marriage and entice them into priesthood and nunnery, citing the trials and troubles of married life. Thus do they bring their own children home to the devil, as we daily observe; they provide them with ease for the body and hell for the soul. [Furthermore,] the shameful confusion wrought by the accursed papal law has occasioned so much distress, and the lax authority of both the spiritual and the temporal swords has given rise to so many dreadful abuses and false situations that I would much prefer neither to look into the matter nor to hear of it. But timidity is no help in an emergency.[10]

According to Luther, evidence for the decrepit estate of marriage and marriage law was all around. Germany, he thundered, had suffered through decades of sexual indiscipline and immorality in the late fifteenth and early sixteenth centuries. Prostitution was rampant. High clerics and officials of government regularly kept concubines and visited the numerous brothels in German cities. The small fines incurred for such activity discouraged few. Drunken orgies were commonplace. Women were raped and ravaged, particularly by robber bands and soldiers. Lewd pamphlets and books exalting sexual liberty and license were published with virtual impunity. Writings by some Roman Catholics extolling celibacy and deprecating marriage and sex dissuaded many couples from marriage and persuaded many parents to send their children to monasteries and cloisters. The number of single men and women, of monasteries and cloisters, of monks and nuns had reached new heights.

Within the estate of marriage itself, Luther continued, instances of incest and bigamy appeared with alarming frequency. The canon laws governing the formation and dissolution of marriages were flouted or arbitrarily enforced in several parts of Germany. Laws prescribing care and education of children as well as laws proscribing abortion, abuse of family members, adultery, and desertion were regularly violated.[11]

Luther's forceful indictment of prevailing German marriage lore, law, and life, though somewhat hyperbolic, was neither without precedent nor without merit. Already in the previous century, a host of German Catholic writers had issued similar attacks and had already inspired a number of legal reforms within the cities.[12] Luther went beyond these Catholic critics, however, in attributing much of the decay of marriage not only to the negligence of authority and the moral laxness of society but also to the paradoxes in the traditional canon law and theology of marriage.

According to Luther, the canon law purported to govern in accordance with natural law and scripture. Yet it was filled with provisions not prefigured in natural law or scripture. The canon law discouraged and prevented mature persons from marrying by its celebration of celibacy, its proscription against breach of vows to celibacy and chastity, its permission to breach oaths of betrothal, and its numerous impediments that led to marital annulment. Yet it encouraged marriages between the immature by declaring valid secret unions consummated without parental permission as well as oaths of betrothal followed by sexual intercourse. The canon law highlighted the sanctity and solemnity of marriage by deeming it a sacrament. Yet it permitted a couple to enter this holy union without clerical or parental witness, instruction, or participation. Celibate and impeded persons were thus driven by their sinful passion to incontinence and all manner of sexual deviance. Married couples, not taught the scriptural norms for marriage, adopted numerous immoral practices.

Such paradoxes of the canon law of marriage, Luther and other evangelical reformers argued, were rooted in tensions within the Roman Catholic theology of marriage. Although Roman Catholic theologians emphasized the sanctity and sanctifying purpose of the marriage sacrament, they nevertheless subordinated it to celibacy and monasticism. Although they taught that marriage is a duty mandated for all persons by divine natural law, they excused many from this duty through the restrictions of canon law.

A true reformation of the law of marriage, therefore, required a new theological foundation. Accordingly, Luther, together with fellow reformers such as Philip Melanchthon, Martin Bucer, Johann Bugenhagen, Johannes Brenz, and several other leading theologians,[13] worked assiduously in the early years of the Reformation to lay this new theoretical foundation—often working in direct collaboration with like-minded jurists.[14]

The Social Model of Marriage

Like the Roman Catholics, the Lutheran reformers viewed marriage as a duty for the sound and a remedy for the sick, which were established by God. The duty of marriage stems from God's command that man and woman unite, help each other, beget children, and raise them as God's servants. The remedy of marriage is a gift that God provides to allay the sexual lust and incontinence born of the fall into sin. Unlike many Roman Catholics, however, the reformers taught that all persons should heed the duty and accept the gift of marriage—for the sake of both society and each person within it.

On the one hand, all persons should heed the duty of marriage for the sake of society. In the reformers' view, marriage was an important, independent institution of creation—in Luther's words, "a divine and holy estate of life," a "blessed holy calling," with its own created sphere of authority and responsibility, alongside that of the church and the state.[15] Indeed, marriage was the foundation of society, and of churches, states, schools, and other institutions that comprised it. "The earthly life has orders [Stände] and works [Werke] which serve to keep the human race, and are ordained by God, within certain limits and means," wrote Philip Melanchthon. "Matrimony is first, for God does not want human nature simply to run its course as animals do. Therefore, God has ordained marriage, Genesis 2 and Matthew 19 and 1 Corinthians 7, as an eternal inseparable fellowship of one husband and one wife. . . . [M]atrimony is a very lovely, beautiful fellowship and church of God if two people in true faith and obedience toward God live together, together invoke God, and rear children in the knowledge of God and virtue."[16] "All orders of human society," Justin Göbler concurred, "derive from the first estate, matrimony, which was instituted by God himself. On this origin and foundation, stand all other estates, communities, and associations of men. . . . From the administration of the household, which we call oeconomia, comes the administration of a government, a state being nothing more than the proliferation of households."[17]

The social estate of the family was to teach all persons, particularly children, Christian values, morals, and mores. It was to exemplify for a sinful society a community of love and cooperation, meditation and discussion, song and prayer. It was to hold out for the church and the state an example of firm but benign parental discipline, rule, and authority. It was to take in and care for wayfarers, widows, and destitute persons— a responsibility previously assumed largely by monasteries and cloisters. The social estate of marriage was thus as indispensable an agent in God's redemption plan as the church had been for the Roman Catholics. It no longer stood within the orders of the church but alongside it. Moreover, the social estate of marriage was as indispensable an agent of social order and communal cohesion as the state should be. It was not simply a creation of the civil law, but a godly creation designed to aid the state in discharging its divine mandate. Thus marriage should be viewed not as an inferior option but as a divine calling and a social status desirable for all people.[18] The early Church Fathers, such as Tertullian and Chrysostom, had recognized this, the reformers charged, but this lesson had been lost on more recent church leaders.[19]

Persons should accept marriage not only as a duty that served society, but also as a remedy against sexual sin.[20] Since the fall into sin, lust has pervaded the conscience of every person, the Lutheran reformers insisted. Marriage has become an absolute necessity of sinful humanity, for without it, the person's distorted sexuality becomes a force capable of overthrowing the most devout conscience. A person is enticed by his or her own nature to prostitution, masturbation, voyeurism, homosexuality, and sundry other sinful acts. The gift of marriage, Luther wrote, should be declined only by those who have received God's gift of continence. "Such persons are rare, not one in a thousand, for they are a special miracle of God." The Apostle Paul has identified this group as the permanently impotent and the eunuchs; few others can claim such a unique gift.[21]

This understanding of the created origin and purpose of marriage undergirded the reformers' bitter attack on celibacy and monasticism.[22] To require celibacy of clerics, monks, and nuns was beyond the authority of the church and ultimately a source of great sin. Celibacy was for God to give, not for the church to require. It was for each individual, not for the church, to decide whether he or she had received this gift.[23] By demanding monastic vows of chastity and clerical vows of celibacy, the church was seen to be intruding on Christian freedom and violating scripture, nature, and common sense.[24] By institutionalizing and encouraging celibacy the church was seen to prey on the immature and the uncertain. By holding out food, shelter, security, and opportunity, the monasteries enticed poor and needy parents to condemn their children to celibate monasticism. Mandatory celibacy, Luther taught, was hardly a prerequisite to true service of God. Instead, it led to "great whoredom and all manner of fleshly impurity and . . . hearts filled with thoughts of women day and night."[25] For the consciences of Christians and non-Christians alike are infused with lust, and a life of celibacy and monasticism only heightens the temptation.[26]

Furthermore, to impute to the celibate contemplative life superior spirituality and holier virtue was, for the reformers, contradicted by scripture. Scripture teaches that each person must perform his or her calling with the gifts that God provides. The gifts of continence and contemplation are but two among many and are by no means superior to the gifts of marriage and childrearing. Each calling plays an equally im-

portant, holy, and virtuous role in the drama of redemption, and its ful-
fillment is a service to God.[27] Luther concurred with the Apostle Paul
that the celibate person "may better be able to preach and care for God's
word." But, he immediately added: "It is God's word and the preaching
which makes celibacy—such as that of Christ and of Paul—better than
the estate of marriage. In itself, however, the celibate life is far inferior."[28] Luther's fellow reformer Johannes Brenz was more guarded:
"Matrimony, celibacy, and virginity . . . are equal in the eyes of God and
the words of the Gospel."[29]

The reformers' lengthy arguments *for* marriage as a natural and social
estate were also arguments *against* the Roman Catholic concept of marriage as a sacrament. For, in the context of the two kingdoms theory, to
place marriage and the family in the natural order of creation was to
deny it a place in the spiritual order of redemption. According to
Lutheran lore, God has ordained two kingdoms in which humanity is
destined to live: the earthly, or political, kingdom and the heavenly, or
spiritual, kingdom. The earthly kingdom is the realm of creation, of natural and civic life, where a person operates primarily by reason, law, and
passion. The heavenly kingdom is the realm of redemption, of spiritual
and eternal life, where a person operates primarily by faith, hope, and
charity. These two kingdoms embrace parallel temporal and spiritual
forms of justice and morality, truth and knowledge, order and law, but
they remain separate and distinct. The earthly kingdom is fallen and distorted by sin. The heavenly kingdom is saved and renewed by grace—
and foreshadows the perfect kingdom of Christ to come. A Christian is
a citizen of both kingdoms at once and invariably comes under the
structures and strictures of each.[30]

The Lutheran reformers regarded marriage as a social estate of the
earthly kingdom alone. Though divinely ordained to serve a holy purpose, it remains in Luther's words, "a secular and outward thing."[31] "No
one can deny that marriage is an external, worldly matter, like clothing
and food, house and property, subject to temporal authority, as the
many imperial laws enacted on the subject prove."[32] The sacraments, by
contrast, are part of the heavenly kingdom of faith and salvation. They
are spiritual instruments of salvation and sanctification.

By placing marriage within the earthly kingdom and sacraments
within the heavenly kingdom, the reformers sought to contrast the functions or uses of marriage and the sacraments. As part of the earthly kingdom, they argued, marriage is a gift of God for all persons, Christians
and non-Christians alike. Like law, marriage has distinctive uses or
functions within the life of the person and of society as a whole.[33] Marriage restrains people from yielding to sins of prostitution, incontinence,

and promiscuity, just as law restrains them from destructive cheating, feuding, and stealing; this is its civil use. Marriage reminds people of their lustful nature and their need for God's soothing remedy for lust, just as law reveals to them their sin and impels them to grace; this is its theological use. Marriage teaches people the virtues of love, patient co-operation, and altruism, just as law teaches them restraint, sharing, and respect for another's person and property; this is its pedagogical use. Marriage therefore not only has its own created tasks, but it also has distinctive social uses.

Marriage can, to be sure, symbolize for all people the union of Christ with His church, but that does not make it a sacrament. Sacraments are gifts and signs of grace ensuring Christians of the promise of redemption that is available only to those who have faith.[34] Marriage carries no such promise and demands no such faith. It remains an earthly institution. "[N]owhere in Scripture," writes Luther, "do we read that anyone would receive the grace of God by getting married; nor does the rite of matrimony contain any hint that that ceremony is of divine institution."[35] Scripture teaches that only baptism and the Eucharist confer this promise of grace. All other so-called sacraments are "mere human artifices" created by Roman Catholics through false interpretations of scripture for the purposes of augmenting the church's legal powers and filling its coffers with court fees and fines.[36]

Like the Roman Catholics, the Lutherans taught that a marriage contract could not be formed and dissolved spontaneously by anyone. Specific rules were needed to define which unions were proper and which could be dissolved. But, because marriage is a social estate of the earthly kingdom, not a sacrament of the heavenly kingdom, it is subject to civil law and civil authority, not canon law and the church. Marital questions are to be brought before civil courts, not church courts.

This does not mean that marriage is beyond the pale of God's authority and law, nor that it should be beyond the influence and concern of the church. "It is sheer folly," Luther opined, to treat marriage as "nothing more than a purely human and secular state, with which God has nothing to do."[37] The civil magistrate holds his authority from God. His will is to appropriate God's desire. His law is to reflect God's law. His rule is to respect God's creation ordinances and institutions and to implement God's purposes. His civil calling is no less spiritual than that of the cleric. Marriage is thus still completely subject to Godly law, but this law is now to be administered by a prince, not a prelate.[38]

Moreover, questions of the formation, maintenance, and dissolution of marriage remain important public concerns in which church officials and members must still play a nonlegal role. The church, the reformers argued, retained at least a fourfold responsibility for marriage. Through its preaching of the Word and the teaching of its theologians, the church had to communicate to the civil authorities and their subjects God's law and will for marriage and the family. Second, it was incumbent upon all church members, as members of the priesthood of all believers, to quiet, through instruction and prayer, the consciences of those troubled by marriage problems and to hold out a model of spiritual freedom, love, care, and equality in their own married lives. Third, to aid church members in their instruction and care, and to give notice to all members of society of a couple's marriage, the church was to develop a publicly available marriage registry that all married couples would be required to sign. Fourth, the pastor and consistory of the church were to instruct and discipline the marriages of its church members by blessing and instructing the couple at their public church wedding ceremony and by punishing sexual turpitude or egregious violations of marriage law with the ban or excommunication.[39]

The Transformation of
Marriage Law in Lutheran Germany

The reformers' new social model of marriage revolutionized the theology of marriage of sixteenth-century Germany. It also helped to transform prevailing German marriage law, for this social model of marriage was a self-executing program of action. It required civil authorities to divest the Roman Catholic Church of its jurisdiction over marriage and assured them that this shift in jurisdiction was a mandate of scripture, not a sin against the church. It called for new civil marriage laws that were consonant with God's Word but required that the church (and thus the reformers themselves) advise the civil authorities on what God's Word commands. Both the magistrates' seizure of jurisdiction over marriage and the reformers' active development of new marriage laws were thus seen as divine tasks.

The theology faculties and law faculties of the new Protestant German universities became the chief agents for the reform of marriage law in the early years of the Reformation. Lutheran theologians throughout evangelical Germany, several themselves trained in law, joined with university jurists to debate detailed questions of marriage also raised by scripture, Roman law, canon law, and local custom. At the University of Wittenberg, for example, Luther, Melanchthon, Bugenhagen, Jonas, and several other theologians gave courses and public lectures on marriage law along with such renowned jurists as Melchior Kling, Konrad Lagus, Johannes Apel, Hieronymous Schürpf, Basilius Monner, and several

others. By 1570, the Wittenberg theology and law professors together
published more than eighty tracts on marriage law questions, dissemi-
nating their ideas throughout Germany and beyond. Law professors and
theology professors at other German universities, particularly in such
evangelical centers as Marburg, Tübingen, Leipzig, Greifswald, Frankfurt an der Oder, and Köningsberg were active throughout the sixteenth
century in developing a learned civil law of marriage.[40]

This learned law did not remain confined to the academy or to books.
Three channels allowed it to penetrate directly into the law of the courts
and the councils of Lutheran cities and territories. First, civil courts regularly consulted both law and theology faculties of local universities
throughout the sixteenth century by use of what was called the "file-
sending" (Aktenversendung) procedure. Courts sent the written records
of marital cases raising difficult legal and moral issues to the law and theology faculties who would discuss the case and submit separate or joint
judgments. These judgments were frequently accepted by the courts
and issued as formal judgments. Studies of marriage law in Strasbourg,
Nürnberg, Goslar, and elsewhere have demonstrated the important influence of this Aktenversendung procedure on substantive marriage
law.[41]

Second, courts, councils, and litigating parties solicited opinions
(consilia) from prominent individual jurists,[42] as well as from the early
theological leaders.[43] Particularly the opinions of the new authorities on
marriage law were eagerly sought after, for they were frequently dispos-
itive of issues raised in court. For example, the Wittenberg jurist Hieronymous Schürpf—Luther's advocate at the Diet of Worms and the
best man at Luther's wedding to the former nun Katherine—was famous
throughout Germany and beyond for his learned consilia on difficult
marriage questions.[44] When not teaching at the University of Wittenberg, he traveled extensively throughout Germany, Scandinavia, and
Switzerland to dispense his opinions. His posthumously published collection of some 800 consilia remained a standard reference book for
more than two centuries thereafter.[45]

Third, from the early 1520s on, numerous new marriage ordinances
were promulgated—first as parts of the new church ordinances
(Kirchenordnungen) and public policy ordinances (Polizeiordnungen),[46]
and increasingly in the later sixteenth century as freestanding marriage
statutes (Eheordnungen).[47] University jurists and theologians (and their
students) were often directly involved in this legislative activity as ad-
visers, administrators, and draftsmen. Many of the early leaders of the
Reformation left their indelible imprints on this new matrimonial legislation.

New Marital Legislation

The first evangelical marriage laws appeared in 1523 in the towns of Zwickau and Leisnig, and in 1524 in Magdeburg, Annaberg, and Meissen. By 1530, at least eight other cities had promulgated such laws, including the influential centers of Nürnberg (1526), Braunschweig (1528), Hamburg (1529), Frankfurt am Main (1530), and Göttingen (1530). In subsequent decades, this urban legislation on marriage thickened, both in pages and in volumes, as existing laws were amended and other cities promulgated their first laws on the subject. By 1559, some sixty new city laws on marriage, drafted under evangelical inspiration, were on the books. Whereas many of the city councils could call on prototypes for this legislation reaching back to the mid-thirteenth century, the territorial and ducal councils began largely tabula rasa. Yet such legislation also began to appear rather quickly. Already in 1526, Landgrave Philip the Magnanimous of Hesse prepared, under Philip Melanchthon's instruction and inspiration, an ambitious plan for a secular system of marriage law in Hesse. Though Philip delayed official promulgation of this plan, it worked a considerable influence on practices in Hesse and surrounding territories, and ultimately was promulgated in truncated form in 1537 and in expanded form in 1566. Saxony issued Melanchthon's rudimentary rules in 1528, followed by more comprehensive legislation in 1533. Pomerania issued a territorial marriage law in 1535, followed by Brandenburg in 1540, Schleswig-Holstein in 1542, Braunschweig-Wolfenbüttel in 1543, and Württemberg in 1559.

The Lutheran reformers did not leave the promulgation of these new marriage laws to the vagaries of the political process. Many of the leading theological lights of the Reformation—Luther, Melanchthon, Brenz, Bugenhagen, and several others—participated actively both in drafting and defending these laws. The most fertile legislative pen was that of the Wittenberg theologian and town pastor Johannes Bugenhagen. Bugenhagen drafted the marriage provisions of the new laws of Braunschweig (1528 and 1543), Hamburg (1529), Lübeck (1531), Bremen (1534), Hannover (1536), and Hildesheim (1544). He also had a strong hand in drafting the marriage laws for the territories of Pomerania (1535), Schleswig-Holstein (1542), Brunswick-Wolfenbüttel (1543), and the kingdoms of Denmark and Norway (1537). Through correspondence and consultation, he also worked his ideas into the marriage laws of several other cities and territories in Germany and abroad, including Ostfriesland (1529), Mindener (1530), Göttingen (1530), Herforder (1532 and 1534), Soester (1533), Wittenberg (1533 and 1545), Ulm (1533–1534), Brandenburg-Nürnberg (1540), and Osnabrück (1543).[48]

The reformers made ample use of scissors and paste in crafting this legislation. They regularly duplicated their own formulations and those of their closest co-religionists in drafting new laws. They corresponded with each other about marriage laws and frequently circulated draft laws among their inner circle for comment and critique. They referred to and paraphrased liberally the theological writings of the leading reformers, particularly those of Luther, Melanchthon, Bucer, Bugenhagen, and Brenz. This close collaboration led to considerable uniformity among the marriage law provisions and considerable legal appropriation of the reformers' cardinal theological ideas on marriage and the family.

Despite the diversity of these new marriage laws over time and across the 350 odd polities that comprised Germany, three fundamental changes in the traditional German law of marriage can be discerned. The new civil law of marriage: (1) modified the traditional consent doctrine and required the participation of others in the process of marriage formation; (2) sharply curtailed the number of impediments to betrothal and to putative marriages; and (3) introduced divorce, in the modern sense, on proof of cause with a right to remarriage. Such changes, taken together, simplified the laws of marriage formation and dissolution, provided for broader public participation in this marriage process, and protected the social functions of marriage and the family.

The Law of
Consent to Marriage

As in canon law, so in the new civil law, the marriage bond was to be formed by a free consensual union between two parties. Many of the reformers, however, accepted the traditional consent doctrine only after: (1) modifying the canonists' threefold distinction between the betrothal or future promise to marry, the present promise to marry, and the consent to consummate the marriage through sexual intercourse; (2) requiring that parents and witnesses participate in the marriage process; and (3) enlarging the task of the church in the process of marital formation.

Luther was the most ardent advocate for these reforms. For Luther, the three forms of consent accepted at canon law were scripturally unwarranted, semantically confusing, and a source of public mischief. The Bible, said Luther, makes no distinction between the present and future promise of marriage. Any promise to marry, freely given in good faith, creates a valid, indissoluble marriage before God and the world; this marriage is consummated through sexual intercourse. Even before consummation, however, scripture makes clear that breach of this promise through sexual relations with, or a subsequent marriage promise to, another is adultery.

Furthermore, the distinction between present and future promises of marriage depends upon "a scoundrelly game" (*ein lauter Narrenspiel*) in Latin words that have no equivalent in German and thus confuse the average person. The Catholic Church courts usually interpreted the promise "*Ich will Dich zum Weibe haben*" or "*Ich will Dich nehmen; Ich will Dich haben; Du sollst mein sein*," as a future promise, though in common German parlance these were usually intended to be present promises.[49] A present promise, traditional church courts insisted, must use the terms "*Accipio te in uxorem*" or "*Ich nehme Dich zu meinen Weibe*," though neither phrase was popular in lay or popular circles. Such a post hoc interpretation of promises, Luther charged, preyed on the ignorance of the common people, disregarded the intent of the couple, and betrayed the presumption of the church courts against marriage. By interpreting many promises to be betrothals, church courts had availed themselves of the much more liberal rules for dissolving betrothals and thus had been able to dissolve numerous marriages. Through their combined doctrines of construing marriage promises as betrothals and of permitting the religious vow to dissolve betrothal, the canon lawyers had thus covertly subsidized celibacy and monasticism.

To allay the confusion and reverse the presumption against marriage, Luther proposed that all promises to marry be viewed as true binding marriage vows in the present (*sponsalia de praesentia*) unless either party had expressly stipulated some future condition or event. A promise in any language with a verb in the future tense was not enough to defeat the presumption. An expressly stated condition was required.

Luther and his followers did not attach such solemnity and finality to the marriage promise without safeguards. First, they insisted that, before any such promise, the couple seek the consent of their parents or, if they were dead or missing, of their next of kin or guardian. Such consent, they argued, had always been mandated by scripture (in the Decalogue Commandment to honor one's parents) as well as by natural law, Roman law, early canon law, reason, and equity. The parents played an essential role in the process of marriage formation. They judged the maturity of the couple and the harmony and legality of their prospective relationship. More important, their will was to reflect the will of God for the couple. Like the priest and like the prince, the parent had been given authority as God's agent to perform a specific calling in the institution of marriage. Parents, Luther wrote, are "apostles, bishops, and priests to their children." By giving their consent to the couple, parents were giving God's consent. Where parents withheld their consent unreasonably, ordered their child to lead a celibate life, or used their authority to coerce a child to enter marriage unwillingly, they no longer performed a Godly task. In such cases Luther urged the child to petition the civil magistrate for his approval; the magistrate would thus surrogately represent God's will. If the magistrate, too, was unreasonable or coercive, Luther urged the child to seek refuge in another place. Marriages contracted without such parental or surrogate parental consent were, in Luther's view, void altogether. Other theologians deemed these unions voidable, but subject to validation if the parents gave their consent post hoc.[50]

Second, Luther insisted that the promise to marry be made publicly, in the presence of at least "two good and honorable witnesses." These witnesses could, if necessary, attest to the event of the marriage or to the intent of the parties and could also help instruct the couple of the solemnity and responsibility of their relationship—a function tied to Luther's doctrine of the priesthood of all believers.[51]

Third, Luther and his followers insisted that, before consummating their marriage, the couple repeat their vows publicly in the church, seek the blessing and instruction of the pastor, and register in the public marriage directory kept in the church. Luther saw the further publicizing of marriage as an invitation for others to aid and support the couple, a warning for them to avoid sexual relations with either party, and a safeguard against false or insincere marriage promises made for the purpose of seducing the other party. Just as the parental consent was to reflect God's will that the couple be married, so the priest's blessing and instruction was to reflect God's will for the marriage—that it remain an indissoluble bond of love and mutual service.[52]

With these requirements of parental consent, witnesses, and church registration and solemnization, Luther deliberately discouraged the secret marriages that the canon law had recognized (though not encouraged). He made marriage "a public institution," advocating the involvement of specific third parties throughout the process of marriage formation. Luther did, however, insist that private vows followed by sexual intercourse should constitute a valid marriage if the woman was impregnated or if the intercourse became publicly known. This was to be a case-by-case exception to the usual rule that a private promise was not an adequate basis for a valid marriage. Luther made the exception to protect the legitimacy and life of the child and to prevent the woman from falling victim to "the strong prejudice [against] marrying a despoiled woman."[53]

It was left to the jurists to work out the legal implications of these reforms of the law of marital consent. Luther's conflation of future and present marriage promises found support only among later jurists who had joined the evangelical cause. Earlier jurists, such as Kling, Schürpf, and Lagus—despite Luther's arguments with them—retained the traditional canon law distinction between present and future promises to marry and insisted on a separate group of impediments for each promise. Although they urged courts to interpret promises in accordance with the common German language, they silently rejected Luther's other recommendations.[54] Only in the second half of the sixteenth century were Luther's teachings made, in Rudolf Sohm's words, "the general Protestant doctrine and praxis which lasted into the eighteenth century."[55] Beust, Schneidewin, Goden, Monner, Mauser, and other later evangelical jurists rejected or severely diminished the distinction between the present promise to marry and the public unconditional betrothal. Like Luther, they inveighed against the secret marriage, and many affirmed, for the same reason as Luther, the exception for private marriages whose consummation became publicly known or resulted in pregnancy.[56]

Luther's reforms of the law of marital consent also came to expression in the new civil law. Many statutes used the terms "betrothal" (Verlöbnis) and "marriage" (Ehe) interchangeably and deemed the public betrothal to be a completed (geschlossen) marriage.[57] Several other statutes, while retaining the traditional distinction between promises of betrothal and marriage, attached far greater importance and finality to public unconditioned betrothals, providing (1) that these promises take precedence over all secret betrothals (even those made subsequently); (2) that promiscuity by either betrothed party is punishable as adultery; and (3) that these promises can be dissolved only on grounds also permitted for divorce.[58] The functional distinction between future and present promises was thus considerably narrowed at German civil law.[59]

The requirement of parental consent to marriages, particularly for children who had not yet reached the age of majority, won virtually unanimous acceptance in sixteenth-century Germany among jurists and legislators alike. Parental consent was a particularly prominent topic of discussion among the jurists. They adduced evidence in support of this change from Roman, early canon, and Germanic law. For several of the early jurists, like Kling and Schürpf, who advocated general allegiance to canon law, parental consent was highly commendable but not absolutely necessary. Couples who married without parental consent should be fined by the state and disciplined by the church, but neither the parents nor one of the parties should be able to annul the marriage because of this omission. Several later jurists, such as Monner, Mauser, and Schneidewin, argued that such clandestine marriages should be annulled unless the parties had consummated their private vows; post hoc consent by the parties should have no effect. Virtually all the jurists urged that the couple seek the approval of both fathers and mothers. Where the parents were dead or missing, they assiduously listed in the order of priority the next of kin, tutors, curators, and others whose consent should be sought. Finally, the jurists discussed in detail the conditions that parents could attach to their consent. Reasonable conditions of time ("You may marry my daughter but only after a year"), of place (". . . only in the church of Wittenberg"), or of support (". . . only when you secure a job") were generally accepted by the jurists. But they carefully denied parents the opportunity to use the consent doctrine to place coercive demands or unreasonable restrictions on the couple. Monner and Mauser, in fact, argued that parents or guardians who abused their consensual authority be fined, even imprisoned, in cases of serious abuse.[60]

Given the prominent attention to parental consent by theologians and jurists, it is not surprising that most of the new civil statutes required such consent. Very few statutes, however, ordered that all marriages contracted without parental consent be nullified.[61] The presence of witnesses or the public declaration of betrothal in a church was usually accepted as an adequate substitute, though several statutes ordered stern civil and ecclesiastical penalties for parties who failed to gain parental consent.[62] The ambit of the parents' authority in the marriage process was also carefully circumscribed in the new statutes. Courts were instructed to prohibit parents from entering their unwilling children in cloisters or monasteries or from obstructing children who wanted to leave their sacred orders. Children saddled with severe conditions or restrictions on their prospective marriages were granted rights of appeal to the local court; where the court found for the child, the parents (or guardians) were subject to fines and other penalties.[63] In most jurisdictions, parental consent was no longer required once the child reached the age of majority.[64]

The requirement of at least two good and honorable witnesses to the marriage promise was accepted by virtually all jurists and legislative draftsmen. A few early statutes denied outright the validity of an unwitnessed marriage promise, but, in most jurisdictions, the validity of these promises was left to the discretion of the court.[65] At first, unwitnessed marriages were rarely dissolved. But as the scandal of premarital sex and pregnancy grew and courts were faced with time-consuming evidentiary inquiries into the relationship of litigating couples, these private promises were increasingly struck down. Parties who consummated their private promises were fined, imprisoned, and, in some jurisdictions, banished. In the later sixteenth century, a number of territories also began to require either that the couple invite a government official as one witness to their promises or that they announce their promises before the city hall or other specified civic building.[66]

In many jurisdictions, the church was assigned an indispensable role in the process of marriage formation. Couples were required, on pain of stiff penalty, to register their marriage with local church officials.[67] The public church celebration of the marriage and the pastor's instruction and blessing were made mandatory even for couples who had earlier announced their betrothal and received parental consent.[68] Several ordinances explicitly ordered punishment for betrothed couples who consummated their marriages before participating in the church ceremony.[69] By the 1550s, this "anticipatory sex" was grounds for imprisonment or banishment from the community as well as excommunication from the church.[70]

These four interrelated reforms introduced into the German civil law of marriage—the equation of unconditioned future and present promises to marry, along with the requirements of parental consent, of witnesses, and of church registration and celebration for marriage—remained standard provisions in the next three centuries, not only in Germany but also in many other Western nations. These reforms were based, in part, on the new theology of the Lutheran social model of marriage. But they were also based on earlier Roman law and canon law provisions, which had fallen into desuetude by the eve of the Reformation.

As we saw in chapter 1, the Council of Trent made comparable changes to the canon law of marital formation—appealing to the same canon law and Roman law precedents, but grounding these reforms in the distinctive sacramental theology of the Catholic tradition. In the Decree Tametsi in 1563, the Council decreed that (1) to contract a valid marriage, parties had to exchange present promises in the company of a priest and witnesses; (2) all betrothals had to be announced publicly three times before celebration of the marriage; and (3) each parish was required to keep an updated public registry of marriage. The Council further encouraged (but did not require) parents to counsel their children in choosing compatible spouses.[71]

The Law of Impediments to Marriage

Lutheran theologians and jurists strove with equal vigor to reform the canon law of impediments. For the reformers, a number of these grounds for annulment of betrothals and marriage were biblically groundless. Several others, though grounded in the Bible, had become a source of corruption and confusion.

According to the Bible, as the reformers understood it, marriage is a duty prescribed by the law of creation and a right of persons protected by the law of Christ. No human law could impinge on this divine duty or infringe on this God-given right without the warrant of divine law. No human authority could obstruct or annul a marriage without divine authorization.[72] "It is contrary to faith as well as to love," wrote Andreas Osiander, "when man puts asunder, without God's command, what God has brought together."[73] Impediments, therefore, that were not commands of God could not be countenanced. Thus the impediments protecting the sanctity of the marriage sacrament were untenable, for the Bible (as the reformers understood it) does not teach that marriage is a sacrament. Impediments protecting religious vows of celibacy or chastity were unnecessary, for scripture subordinates such vows to the vows of marriage.

Even the biblically based impediments of the canon law had, in the reformers' view, become sources of corruption and confusion. It had long been the official practice of the Roman Catholic Church to relax certain impediments (such as consanguinity and affinity) where they worked injustice to the parties or to their children. Parties could receive a dispensation from these impediments and be excused from the legal strictures. This "equitable" practice met with little criticism. The reformers' concern was with the abuse of this practice in certain bishoprics in Germany. Certain corrupt clerics, in their judgment, had turned their "equitable" authority to their own financial gain by relaxing any number of impediments if the dispensation payment was high enough. This clerical bribery and trafficking in dispensations from impediments evoked caustic attacks from the reformers. "[T]here is no impediment to marriage nowadays," Luther charged, "which they cannot legitimize for money. These manmade regulations seem to have come into existence for no other reason than raking in money and netting in souls."[74] Such abuses not only desecrated the priestly office, but resulted in a liberal law of impediments for the rich and a constrictive law for the poor. Furthermore, the reformers averred, the impediments had become so intricate that they were confusing to the common person. The confession manuals were filled with ornate legalistic discussions of the impediments, incomprehensible to the uninitiated and frequently not in the language of the common people.[75]

Acting on these general criticisms, the reformers developed a simplified and, in their view, more biblical law of impediments. They (1) adopted most of the physical impediments; (2) accepted, with some qualification, the impediments protecting the parties' consent; (3) adopted a severely truncated law of personal impediments; and (4) discarded the spiritual impediments protecting the sanctity of the sacrament.

Given the importance attached by the reformers to the physical union, they were understandably receptive to the canonists' *physical impediments*. Thus the impediment of permanent impotence and prohibitions against polygamy and bigamy were unanimously accepted, on the strength of the same favorite passages in Moses, the Gospels, and the Pauline epistles that the canonists had adduced.[76]

By accepting the consensual theory of marriage, the reformers also accepted the traditional impediments that guaranteed *free consent*. Thus a man and a woman who had been joined under duress, coercion, or fear were seen as "unmarried before God" and thus free to dissolve their union. Both Lutheran theologians and jurists, however, required that the pressure exerted on the couple be particularly pervasive and malicious—a requirement that they based on patristic authority. The reformers, like the canonists, accepted errors of person as grounds for annulment. Luther, Bucer, and Brenz, however, urged Christian couples to accept such unions as a challenge placed before them by God—a recommendation that is repeated in some of the statutes. A number of reformers also permitted annulment of marriage based on errors of quality, the mistaken assumption that one's spouse was a virgin. For, as the Mosaic and Pauline law made clear, one's prior commitment to marriage, whether through a promise or through sexual intercourse, prevented him or her from entering any true marriage thereafter. Thus the second putative marriage was void from the start.[77]

In developing the civil law of *personal impediments*, the reformers were far less faithful to the canon law tradition. They rejected several of these impediments and liberalized others in an attempt to remove as many obstacles to marriage and as many obfuscations of scripture as possible.

First, the reformers rejected impediments designed to protect the celibate and the chaste. The canon laws prohibiting marriage to clerics, monks, and nuns were unanimously rejected as unscriptural.[78] Several statutes explicitly condoned clerical marriage and enjoined subjects to accept their offspring as legitimate children and heirs.[79] Canon laws forbidding remarriage to those who had initially married a cleric, monk, or nun had no parallel in the new civil law. The traditional assumption that vows to chastity and celibacy automatically dissolved betrothals and unconsummated marriages found acceptance only among the early conservative jurists, such as Kling, Schürpf, and Apel. For Luther and many others, these were "accursed man-made regulations which seem only to have entered the church to multiply the dangers, the sins, and the Devils there!"[80]

Second, the reformers rejected or simplified the intricate restrictions on those related by blood, family, spiritual, and legal ties. Only early Lutheran jurists and legislators accepted the canon law formulation of the impediment of consanguinity that permitted annulment of marriages between parties related by blood to the fourth degree.[81] Several reformers permitted restrictions on parties related by blood only to the third or to the second degree, and both positions found statutory expression.[82] Luther's repeated arguments for adopting only the slender group of impediments of consanguinity set forth in Leviticus were routinely rejected.[83] Similarly, the canon law impediments of affinity and public decorum—which annulled marriage between a person and the blood relative of his or her deceased spouse or fiancé(e) to the fourth degree—were accepted in qualified form only by early Lutheran jurists and legislators.[84] The arguments by theologians to reduce these restrictions to "in-laws" in the third, second, or even first degrees all came to legislative expression.[85]

Third, the spiritual impediments, prohibiting marriages between godparents and their children, were rejected by virtually all the reformers and legislators.[86]

Fourth, legal impediments, proscribing marriages between a variety of parties related by adoption, were liberalized, and in some jurisdictions abandoned altogether.[87]

Fifth, a number of jurisdictions that had accepted Luther's conflation of future and present marriage promises rejected the canon law impediment of multiple relationships. The canonists had maintained that any betrothal was dissolved if one of the parties made a subsequent marriage promise to, or had sexual relations with, another. This rule was adopted by the reformers only for conditioned betrothal promises. They regarded unconditioned public promises of betrothal as indissoluble and thus superior to any subsequent physical or verbal commitments to marriage.[88]

The reformers rejected the *spiritual impediments* of unbelief and crime that had been designed to protect the sanctity of the marriage sacrament. The canon law had prohibited marriage between Christians and non-Christians and permitted annulment when one party had permanently left the church. Only those couples who had been sanctified by baptism and who remained true to the faith could symbolize the union of Christ and His church. To the reformers, marriage had no such symbolic Christian function and thus no prerequisites of baptism or unanimity of faith.[89] The canonists had also prohibited marriage to the person who had done public penance (for mortal sin) or who was guilty of certain sexual crimes, for his or her marital union would be constantly perverted by this grave former sin. Thus neither the mortal sinner nor the spouse could receive the sanctifying grace of the sacrament. To the reformers, marriage imparted no such sanctifying grace and thus required no such prerequisite purity. To be sure, Luther writes, "sins and crimes should be punished, but with other penalties, not by forbidding marriage. David committed adultery with Bathsheba, Uriah's wife, and had her husband killed besides. He was guilty of both crimes, still he [could take] her to be his wife."[90] A number of jurists and legislators concurred.

The Law of
Divorce and Remarriage

The reformers' attack on the canon law of impediments was closely allied with their attack on the canon law of divorce. Just as they discarded many impediments as infringements on the right to enter marriage, they rejected the canon law of divorce as an abridgement of the right to end one marriage and to enter another.

The Roman Catholic Church had, for centuries, taught that (1) divorce meant only separation of the couple from bed and board; (2) such separation had to be ordered by a church court on proof of adultery, desertion, or cruelty; divorce could not be undertaken voluntarily; and (3) despite the divorce, the sacramental bond between the parties remained intact, and thus neither party was free to remarry. Once properly established, the marriage bond could never be severed, even if the parties became bitter enemies.

In practice, the canon law of divorce was partly mitigated by the law of impediments, which allowed parties to dissolve putative marriages and enter others. But the declaration of annulment simply meant that the marriage never existed because it had been contracted improperly, and it required proof in a church court of an absolute (diriment) impediment. A declaration of annulment often also meant that the parties had sinned gravely in joining together and were subject to penitential discipline and, at times, also legal punishment. Such annulments were not nearly so easy to come by as some sixteenth-century writers seemed to imagine. They were particularly difficult to procure if the parties had consummated their marriages and had children.[91]

The Lutheran reformers rejected this traditional doctrine with arguments from scripture, history, and utility. Scripture teaches, the reformers insisted, that marriage is a natural institution of the earthly kingdom, not a sacramental institution of the heavenly kingdom. The essence of marriage is the cleavage and the community of husband and wife in this life, not their sacramental union in the life to come.[92] For a couple to establish "a true marriage" in this earthly life, wrote Martin Bucer, "God requires them to live together and be united in body and mind. . . . The proper end of marriage is . . . the communicating of all duties, both divine and human, each to the other with the utmost benevolence and affection."[93] Irreconcilable separation of the parties was tantamount to dissolution of the marriage, for the requisite benevolent communion of marriage could no longer be carried out. The Roman Catholic teaching that permanently separated couples were still bound in marriage rested on the unbiblical assumption that marriage is an eternally binding sacrament.

Furthermore, the reformers charged, for the Catholic Church to equate divorce with judicial separation and to prohibit divorcees from remarrying had no basis in scripture. The term "divorce" (*divortium*) as used in scripture means dissolution of marriage, not simply separation. No philological evidence from biblical or early patristic times suggests otherwise. The Roman Catholics had improperly introduced their interpretation of the term in order to support their sacramental concept of marriage.[94] Where scripture permits divorce, the reformers believed, it also permits remarriage. "In the case of adultery," for example, Luther wrote, "Christ permits divorce of husband and wife so that the innocent person may remarry."[95] Other reformers considered the sentence of divorce and the right of remarriage to be "one and the same."[96] For the divorcee, like any single person, had to heed God's duty to form families and to accept God's remedy against incontinence and other sexual sins. To deprive the divorcee of the spiritual and physical benefits of marriage, as the Roman Catholic Church had done, could not be countenanced. It was unbiblical and led to all manner of sexual sin.

The reformers bolstered these scriptural arguments for divorce and remarriage with arguments from history. They adduced support for their biblical exegesis from the commentaries of the Church Fathers. They found a wealth of precedent for laws of divorce and remarriage in the Mosaic law based on Deuteronomy 24:1, the canon law of the early church, and the decrees of the Christian Roman emperors, particularly the *Theodosian Code* (438) and Justinian's *Code* (534) and *Novellae* (565).

These historical laws of divorce, however, were hardly commensurate with the teachings of the gospel. Christ had permitted divorce only on grounds of adultery and only as a special exception to the general command "what God has joined together, let not man put asunder" (Mark 10:2–12; Luke 16:18; Matt. 5:31–32, 19:3–19). The laws of Moses, of the early church, and of the Roman Empire, however, had put marriages asunder for many other reasons besides adultery. The Mosaic law had permitted divorce for indecency and incompatibility of all kinds. In Roman law, a person could divorce a spouse who was guilty of treason or iconoclasm, who had committed one of many felonies or fraudulent acts against third parties, or who had abused, deserted, threatened, or, in other ways, maltreated members of their family. Divorce was also permitted if a husband wrongly accused his wife of adultery or if a wife was guilty of shameful or immoral acts (such as abortion, bigamy, or exhibitionism), became delinquent, insolent, or impotent, or persistently refused to have sexual relations. In the later Roman Empire, divorce was even permitted by mutual consent of the parties. The innocent party was, in most instances, permitted to remarry another.[97] The early church not only acquiesced in this liberal law of divorce but was the first to advocate the adoption of some of its provisions.[98] Such liberal laws remained in constant tension with Christ's command that all but the unchaste must remain indissolubly bound.

The reformers resolved this tension by distinguishing between moral laws designed for chaste Christians in the heavenly kingdom and civil laws designed for sinful citizens of the earthly kingdom. Christ's command, the reformers taught, is an absolute moral standard for Christians. It demands of them love, patience, forgiveness, and a conciliatory spirit. It sets out what is absolutely right, what the true law would be if the earthly kingdom were free from sin and populated only by perfect Christians. The earthly kingdom, however, is fallen, and many of its sinful citizens disregard the moral law. Thus it becomes necessary for civil authorities to promulgate laws that both facilitate and protect marriage and its social functions as well as maintain peace and order in sinful society. The positive laws of the German princes, like those of Moses and the Roman emperors, therefore, must inevitably compromise moral ideals for marriage. They must allow for divorce and remarriage.[99] "It might be advisable nowadays," Luther wrote, "that certain queer, stubborn, and obstinate people, who have no capacity for toleration and are not suited for married life at all, should be permitted to get a divorce. Since people are as evil as they are, any other way of governing is impossible. Frequently something must be tolerated even though it is not a good thing to do, to prevent something even worse from happening."[100] "The reality is that some households become broken beyond repair," Bugenhagen continued. This is "an eye sore both to the church and the state" and is better removed lest "it cause further evil."[101] The law of divorce and remarriage, like other positive laws, must thus be inspired by the moral norms of scripture as well as by pragmatic concerns of utility and good governance.

By conjoining these arguments from scripture, utility, and history, the reformers concluded that (1) divorce in the modern sense had been instituted by Moses and Christ; (2) the expansion of divorce was a result of sin and a remedy against greater sin; and (3) God had revealed the expanded grounds for divorce in history. On this basis, the reformers successfully advocated a new civil law of divorce and remarriage. They specified the proper grounds for divorce and the procedures that estranged couples had to follow.

The Protestant reformers and legislators of Germany unanimously accepted adultery as a ground for divorce on the stated authority of scripture and frequently also of Roman law and early canon law.[102] Theologians such as Luther and Bugenhagen, however, advocated that the couple first be given time to resolve the matter privately. They instructed adulterers to seek forgiveness and innocent spouses to be forgiving. They further urged pastors and friends to sponsor the mending of this torn marriage in any way they could. These recommendations found statutory support. A number of marriage ordinances repeated the reformers' prescriptions.[103] Criminal statutes provided that punishment of the adulterer could not commence until the innocent party sued for divorce. Absent such suits, a judge could begin criminal proceedings against an adulterer only if his or her violation was "open, undoubted, and scandalous."[104] Even in such cases, authorities preferred less severe penalties (not banishment or imprisonment) that would still allow the couple to rejoin. Where efforts of private reconciliation failed, and continued cohabitation of the parties yielded only misery and threats to the safety of the parties and their children, the innocent spouse could sue for divorce. Husbands and wives had equal rights to sue for divorce. Thereafter, the innocent party was permitted to remarry, after a time of healing—usually a few months or a year.[105] The adulterer faced stern criminal sanctions scaled to the egregiousness of the offense. These ranged from fines or short imprisonment to exile or execution in the case of repeat adulterers. The call by many reformers to execute all divorced adulterers found little acceptance among the authorities, though many jurisdictions, in response, stiffened their penalties for adultery.[106] Only the egregious repeat offender was subject to execution.[107]

Although a few theologians and early legislators accepted adultery as the only ground for divorce,[108] many others defended a far more expansive divorce law. Desertion or abandonment was a widely accepted ground for divorce among the reformers. A party who deserted his or her spouse and family destroyed the bond of communal love, service, and support needed for the marriage to survive and for children to be properly nourished and reared. Not every absence of a spouse, however, could be considered a form of desertion. Theologians such as Bugen-hagen and jurists such as Schneidewin insisted that the abandonment be notoriously willful and malicious, a requirement that was repeated in several statutes.[109] No divorce was thus permitted if the absent partner was serving the prince's army, engaged in study or business abroad, or was visiting a foreign place. Divorce for desertion was permitted only where the partner's absence was completely inexcusable and in-equitable, left the spouse and family in grave danger, or was so unrea-sonably prolonged that the party had presumably died or fallen into delinquency or adultery. The deserted spouse was in such cases free to remarry. If the long-lost deserter returned, he or she was presumed guilty of adultery until proven innocent.[110] If the deserter never re-turned, the spouse could, after a designated period of time, petition for an *ex parte* divorce and for the right to marry another.

Quasi-desertion, the unjustifiable abstention from sexual intercourse, found limited acceptance as a ground for divorce. Luther, Brenz, Bucer, and the jurist Clammer argued that voluntary abandonment of such an essential aspect of marriage was tantamount to abandonment of the marriage itself. Furthermore, it violated Paul's injunction in 1 Corinthi-ans 7 that spouses abstain from sex only by mutual consent. Luther counseled the deprived spouse to warn the other spouse of his or her discontent, and to invite the pastor or friends to speak with the spouse. If the spouse remained abstinent, Luther permitted the deprived spouse to sue for divorce and remarry.[111] Only a few statutes adopted this teaching.[112]

At the urging of several more liberal reformers, most notably Martin Bucer, numerous other grounds for divorce sporadically gained accep-tance in Lutheran territories. Already in the 1520s, Zürich and Basel un-der Huldrych Zwingli's inspiration recognized, alongside adultery and desertion, impotence, grave incompatibility, sexually incapacitating ill-nesses, felonies, deception, and one spouse's serious threats against the life of the other spouse as grounds for divorce.[113] By the 1550s, confes-sional differences between the couple, defamation of a spouse's moral character, abuse and maltreatment, conspiracies or plots against a spouse, acts of incest and bigamy, delinquent frequenting of "public games" or places of ill repute, and acts of treason or sacrilege all came to legislative expression as grounds for divorce.[114] Although no single mar-riage statute in this period explicitly adopted all these grounds for di-vorce, a few statutes did permit divorce "on any grounds recognized by Scripture and the Roman law of Justinian."[115]

The reformers insisted that divorce, like marriage, be a public act. Just as a couple could not form the marriage bond in secret, so they could not sever it in secret. They had to inform the community and church of their intentions and petition a civil judge to order the divorce.[116] This requirement of publicity was a formidable obstacle to divorce. Couples who publicized their intent to divorce invited not only the counsel and comfort of friends and pastors but frequently also the derision of the community and the discipline of the church. Furthermore, judges had great discretion to deny or delay petitions for divorce and to grant interim remedies short of this irreversible remedy. Particularly in conservative courts, the petitioner had a heavy burden of proof to show that the divorce was mandated by statute, that all efforts at reconciliation had proved fruitless, and that no alternative remedy was available.[117]

Continuity and Discontinuity

The Lutheran Reformation introduced a new social model of marriage into the Western tradition, alongside the Catholic sacramental model. Like the Catholics, Lutherans taught that marriage was a natural, created institution subject to godly law. But, unlike the Catholics, Lutherans rejected the subordination of marriage to celibacy. The person was too tempted by sinful passion to forgo marriage. The family was too vital a social institution in God's redemption plan to be hindered. The celibate life had no superior virtue and no inherent attractiveness vis-à-vis marriage and was no prerequisite for ecclesiastical service.

The Lutheran reformers replaced the sacramental model of marriage with a new social model. Marriage, they taught, was part of the earthly kingdom, not the heavenly kingdom. Though a holy institution of God, marriage required no prerequisite faith or purity and conferred no sanctifying grace, as did true sacraments. Rather, it had distinctive uses in the life of the individual and of society. It restricted prostitution, promiscuity, and other public sexual sins. It revealed to humanity its sinfulness and its need for God's marital gift. It taught love, restraint, and other public virtues and morals. All fit men and women were free to enter such unions, provided they complied with the laws of marriage formation.

As an estate of the earthly kingdom, marriage was subject to the prince, not the pope. Civil law, not canon law, was to govern marriage. Marital disputes were to be brought before civil courts, not church courts. Marriage was still subject to God's law, but this law was now to be administered by the civil authorities who had been called as God's vice-regents to govern the earthly kingdom. Church officials were required to counsel the magistrate about God's law and to cooperate with him in publicizing and disciplining marriage. All church members, as priests, were required to counsel those who contemplated marriage and to admonish those who sought annulment or divorce. But the church no longer had legal authority over marriage.

The reforms of German marriage law introduced during the Lutheran Reformation reflected this reconceptualization of marriage. Civil marriage courts replaced church courts in numerous Lutheran territories, frequently at the instigation of the reformers. New civil marriage statutes were promulgated, many replete with Lutheran marriage doctrine and scriptural marriage laws. Lutheran jurists throughout Germany published treatises on marriage law, affirming and embellishing the basic marriage doctrine set forth by the theologians.

This new civil law of marriage had a number of important innovations that can be directly traced to the theology and advocacy of Luther, Bucer, Brenz, Bugenhagen, Melanchthon, and their evangelical colleagues. Because the reformers rejected the subordination of marriage to celibacy, they rejected laws that forbade clerical and monastic marriage, that denied remarriage to those who had married a cleric or monastic, and that permitted vows of chastity to annul vows of marriage. Because they rejected the sacramental nature of marriage, the reformers rejected impediments of crime and heresy and prohibitions against divorce in the modern sense. Marriage was for them the community of the couple in the present, not their sacramental union in the life to come. Where that community was broken, for one of a number of specific reasons (such as adultery or desertion), the couple could sue for divorce. Because persons by their lustful natures were in need of God's remedy of marriage, the reformers removed numerous legal, spiritual, and consanguineous impediments to marriage not countenanced by scripture. Because of their emphasis on the Godly responsibility of the prince, the pedagogical role of the church and the family, and the priestly calling of all believers, the reformers insisted that both marriage and divorce be public. The validity of marriage promises depended upon parental consent, witnesses, church consecration and registration, and priestly instruction. Couples who wanted to divorce had to announce their intentions in the church and community and petition a civil judge to dissolve the bond. In the process of marriage formation and dissolution, therefore, the couple was subject to God's law, as appropriated in the civil law, and to God's will, as revealed in the admonitions of parents, peers, and pastors.

It must be stressed, however, that the Lutheran reformers appropriated a great deal of the canon law in their formation of the civil law of marriage. Canon law doctrines that grounded marriage in the mutual consent of the parties continued with only minor changes. Canon law prohibitions against unnatural relations and against infringement of

natural marital functions remained in effect. Canon law impediments
that protected free consent, that implemented scriptural prohibitions
against marriage of relatives, and that governed the couple's physical relations were largely retained. Such canon laws were as consistent with
Roman Catholic as with Lutheran concepts of marriage, and they continued largely uninterrupted.

Moreover, Lutheran jurists and judges turned readily to canon law
texts and authorities in formulating their doctrines of marriage law. Pro-
fessorial and court opinions of the late sixteenth century on cases of disputed betrothals, wife abuse, incest, child custody, desertion, adultery,
divorce, annulment, and the like are chock-full of citations to the *Decretum,* Decretals, and various canonists.[118] Legal dictionary and handbook entries on marriage, prepared by Lutheran jurists, cite Catholic
theological and canon law sources with great frequency and authority.[119] Learned tracts on marriage law, prepared by Lutheran jurists, often made greater use of canon law and Roman law authorities than the
new Protestant texts.

The 1543 *Tract on Matrimonial Cases* by Melchior Kling, Luther's
friend and colleague at Wittenberg, illustrates and explains this appetite
for traditional canon law forms. Kling stated several times, in this tract,
that he accepted the "new [evangelical] theology of marriage." But he
said: "I have generally followed the canon law in this writing, which at
the time of the [Roman] Empire was used to frame opinions in matrimonial cases. For even though other laws may have been extant, which
might seem more worthy and outstanding—customs and examples both
predating and following the time of Moses, the law of Moses itself, the
New Testament, and Roman law—these are not completely sufficient or
comprehensive for our time."[120] The canon law, Kling believed, had appropriated the most valuable parts of the Old and New Testaments, Roman law, and local custom, and had refined its doctrine for centuries.
"Surely, we could not go back to the simple Mosaic rules of marital impediments" or "return to the pre-Mosaic customs of concubinage and
polygamy," he reasoned. "Nor could we easily follow both the Mosaic
[and] . . . New Testament laws of divorce," let alone try to "observe the
multiple causes for divorce [recognized at Christian] imperial law." The
canonists had worked through all these conflicts of law and had systematized a "Christian and equitable" source of law, which evangelicals
should not, and could not, simply cast aside. To begin on a biblical *tabula rasa* was "foolish," Kling concluded. "We should begin with tradition" and amend and emend it as the Bible and new theological
doctrines compel.[121] Kling practiced what he preached. Though he cited
most frequently to the Bible, the Digest, the "doctors," and the "theolo-

gians" (presumably of Wittenberg), his tract is peppered throughout with references to the *Decretum,* the Decretals, Panormitanus, Hostiensis, Johannes Andreae, and several other canonists.[122]

These caveats of Luther's own day warn us that the reformation of marriage law in Lutheran Germany was not so radical as the early reformers had envisioned, and as some historians have assumed. The Lutheran reformers worked within the Western tradition of marriage. Their new theology of marriage, though filled with bold revisions, preserved a good deal of the teaching of the Roman Catholic tradition. Their new civil law of marriage was heavily indebted to the canon law that it replaced. What the Lutheran reformers offered was a new social model for marriage, which stood alongside the traditional sacramental model and within the Western tradition.

3

Marriage as Covenant
in the Calvinist Tradition

The theology and law of marriage developed by evangelical Lutherans provided a paradigm for Protestants. The Lutheran reformers
defined the principal theological differences with the prevailing Catholic
tradition and drafted many of the enduring principles of Protestant marriage law. Lutheran theological and legal tracts on marriage and family
life enjoyed such wide circulation and authority in sixteenth-century
Europe that one exuberant authority wrote: "All that the Reformation offered to the Western tradition of the family was born in Wittenberg."[1]

If Wittenberg was the Bethlehem of Protestant marriage law, Geneva
was the Nazareth. This small independent city, newly converted to the
Protestant cause in 1536, provided an ideal environment for the slow
maturation of a distinctive law and theology of marriage that would
come to dominate a good deal of the Protestant world in subsequent
centuries.

The leader of the Genevan reformation was John Calvin, an exiled
French jurist and theologian, who joined the Protestant cause in 1532.
During his Geneva tenure from 1536 to 1538, and again from 1541 till
his death in 1564, Calvin led a sweeping reformation of Genevan marriage and family life, alongside many other religious, political, and legal
institutions. So profound and enduring was his influence on the Western legal tradition that, two centuries later, even a religious skeptic like
Jean-Jacques Rousseau had only praise for his compatriot: "Those who
consider Calvin only as a theologian fail to recognize the breadth of his
genius. The editing of our wise laws, in which he had a large share, does
him as much credit as his *Institutes [of the Christian Religion].* . . . [S]o
long as the love of country and liberty is not extinct among us, the mem-
ory of this great man will be held in reverence."[2]

Calvin's reformation of marriage law and theology fell into two distinct phases. In the first half of his career, Calvin the *jurist* was primarily at work. Content to repeat theological commonplaces on marriage,

he directed most of his energy to the establishment of a new marriage law for Geneva. Comprehensive Marriage Ordinances of 1545 and 1547 brought old canon law rules and new civil law reforms into an impressive new synthesis. Ecclesiastical Ordinances of 1541 and 1547 brought the city council and the church consistory into an imposing new alliance for the enforcement of these laws. When these legal reforms met with widespread resistance in Geneva in the 1550s, Calvin the *theologian* went to work. In a series of letters, sermons, and biblical commentaries prepared in the last twelve years of his life, Calvin laid out a comprehensive covenant theology of marriage and family life that served to integrate and rationalize much of the new legal structure. This theological apologia, together with the stepped-up activities of the Genevan consistory, helped to render the new marriage law on the books a new law of action—in Geneva and, eventually, in the dispersed reformed communities of France, England, Scotland, the Netherlands, and their colonies.

The Case of the
French Noblewoman

A 1552 case before the Geneva consistory provides a good opening view of this new law and theology of marriage, and the tensions that lingered between them in Calvin's mind. A "certain noblewoman from Paris," as she anonymously identified herself, sent a long letter to the consistory on June 24, 1552.[3] The noblewoman's choice of anonymity was deliberate, for she wrote to complain bitterly of her husband's "idolatry and persecution of Christians" and to inquire whether "the law of marriage compels her to live with her husband, or whether the Gospel permits her to leave him and to seek liberty [in Geneva]." The prevailing *civil* law of Geneva gave husband and wife alike an equal right to sue for divorce on proof of adequate cause—a procedural equality for which Geneva had already become quite famous. Thus, if she moved to Geneva, this noblewoman could easily press an *ex parte* case against her husband for divorce. The prevailing popular stigma against divorce, however, rendered such suits very dangerous for a woman, particularly this one. By leaving her husband and homeland, she would at minimum put her liberty and property at risk. By filing a divorce suit against her husband, she would likely imperil her own life and limb as well.

Ten years before, this noblewoman had converted from Catholicism to the evangelical cause—contrary to her husband's confession and command. At first, he had indulged her somewhat, she writes, "though he held her all the time to the papal idolatry, forcing her to go to Mass and to undertake journeys and pilgrimages and make vows to the saints." Six years later, however, he and his relatives began a ruthless campaign against her and her Protestant co-religionists. "Some he throws into prison; others he charge[s] before the judge and nobility." "He forbids [his wife] to speak to any of them." He censors her letters, shadows her movements, threatens her servants with "the fire" not to conspire in her heresy. He forbids her to perform charity or to "sing Psalms or hymns or anything else in the praise of the Lord." He forces her continued compliance with "papal idolatry." If she disobeys him, he "threatens to throw her into the water or some other secret death"—suggesting that he might "amuse himself by having her burned or killing her slowly in a permanent dungeon." Till now, she has suffered "in becoming Christian silence," she writes, indicating that she fears relating any more in her letter lest her husband find her out. She assures Calvin and his colleagues, however, that she has endured "grievous and severe assaults [and] . . . every kind of affliction of both spirit and body." She urges the Geneva consistory "to meet together to formulate a reply to her sad request so that she may have a resolution of her case, for she has no desire to live any longer in such idolatry."

Calvin's opinion, on behalf of the "unanimous" Geneva consistory, vacillates between pastoral gentleness and biblical legalism.[4] Calvin, the pastor, opens with a few lines of "pity and compassion" for the noblewoman's "most severe and cruel servitude" suffered on account of "her true and pure religion." "[W]e bear in mind the perplexity and anguish in which she must be, . . . praying God that it would please Him to give her relief."

Calvin, the jurist, however, had little relief to give her. "Since she has asked for our counsel, regarding what is permissible," he writes, "our duty is to respond, purely and simply, on the basis of what God reveals to us in his Word, closing our eyes to all else." The new Genevan law followed the strict biblical view that divorce is permitted only on grounds of adultery (and, in rare cases, malicious desertion). Cruelty and abuse were insufficient grounds for divorce, and "voluntary divorce" by either or both parties was out of the question. A marital couple's differences in religion were also an insufficient ground for divorce. To the contrary, said Calvin, citing 1 Corinthians 7:13 and 1 Peter 3:1, "a believing party cannot, of his or her own free will, divorce the unbeliever . . . but should endure bravely and persevere with constancy . . . and make every effort to lead her partner into salvation." It would be an irony, said Calvin, "to abrogate the order of nature" in marriage for the sake of one form of Christianity over another. The parties must continue to live together, "and no matter how great his obstinacy might be, she must not let herself be diverted from the faith, but must affirm it with constancy and steadfastness, whatever the danger."

A little later in his opinion, Calvin the pastor softened this interpretation, and seemed to be charting a road to relief. "If the party should be persecuted to the extent that she is in danger of denying her faith" or imperiling her life, he writes, "then she is justified in fleeing." A spouse need not put soul and body in mortal jeopardy for the sake of the marriage, but may leave when faced with such a dire threat. "This does not constitute a voluntary divorce," said Calvin. The apostasy and cruelty together are tantamount to dissolution of the marriage itself, and an innocent party need not endure them. Given what the noblewoman had described in her letter—"grievous and severe assaults and every kind of affliction of both spirit and body"—this seemed to provide a rationale for finding in her favor.

Calvin the jurist had the final word in the case, and he found against her. His judgment rested on a rather technical legal point of notice, which he read into the same passages of 1 Corinthians 7:13 and 1 Peter 3:1 already cited. Contrary to what scripture requires, Calvin concluded, the noblewoman had not given adequate notice to her husband of her religious dissatisfaction. "What she says in her letter is that she is only silent and dissimulates. When pressed to defile herself with idolatry, she yields and complies. This being so, she has no excuse for leaving her husband, without having made a more adequate declaration of her faith"—although, as Calvin recognized, she would doubtless have to endure "greater compulsion" as a consequence of such declaration. "If thereafter," Calvin concluded, "she finds herself in grave peril, with her husband persecuting her to death, she may avail herself of the liberty which our Savior grants to His followers for escaping the fury of wolves."

This was a quite typical petition, and a quite typical response.[5] With the deaths of Huldrych Zwingli, Martin Luther, and Martin Bucer by the early 1550s, Calvin had emerged alongside Philip Melanchthon as the leading Protestant authority on the Continent. Private litigants and political magistrates from throughout Europe sought his counsel on sundry questions of marriage theology and law.[6] A number of parties, particularly women, moved to Geneva to avail themselves of its more egalitarian marriage procedures and the possibilities of finding relief from oppressive homes and laws. Many of these parties, while not always so desperate in their plight as this French noblewoman, often raised the same kind of basic issue—how to balance biblical and civil laws on marriage and divorce, formal and equitable interpretations of the law, church and state responsibilities in the formation, maintenance, and dissolution of marriage.

Calvin's own vacillations in this case—between theological principles and civil precepts, pastoral equity and legal formality—capture in miniature the central tension of his broader reformation of marriage in Geneva. In 1552, Calvin was in the interim between the first phase of his reformation of marriage, which was focused almost exclusively on law, and the second phase of his reformation, which blended law more fully with theology. As he moved from his first to his second phase, Calvin often tempered his earlier legalism, even while confirming most of his laws. On questions of spousal oppression and apostasy, Calvin remained firm in his judgment not to grant a divorce unless the soul and body of the innocent spouse were truly imperiled. This was consistent with (perhaps even caused by) his judgment not to countenance revolt against oppressive and apostate magistrates unless the soul and body of the citizen were truly imperiled.[7] On many other marital questions, Calvin's early legal views underwent considerable theological tailoring and tempering as he moved into the second phase of his career. It is to those two phases of his career in marital reformation that we now turn.

The Early Reformation
of Marriage Law

As a young Protestant neophyte in his early twenties, Calvin naturally came under the influence of the first generation of Reformation leaders. In the years immediately following his conversion in 1532, Calvin read several writings of the leading Protestant lights: Martin Luther, Philip Melanchthon, Martin Bucer, Heinrich Bullinger, and Huldrych Zwingli. In his early travels, he also came upon the new church ordinances of Basel, Berne, Brunswick, Strasbourg, and Zürich, which already enjoyed wide circulation and authority in the rapidly expanding Protestant world.[8]

Calvin's first formulations on marriage—from his 1536 *Institutes* to his 1545 Marriage Ordinance and its amendments—drew liberally from these disparate Protestant sources. His theology of marriage remained rather rudimentary in these early writings, constituting little more than a distillation of prevailing Protestant principles. His legal formulations on marriage were more learned, ultimately yielding an impressive integration and elaboration of the Reformation's most daring legal reforms.

Calvin's emphasis on the law of marriage, rather than its theology, could be expected during the first phase of his career in Geneva. Calvin was still young in his theology, and the ready acceptance of Protestant marriage teachings in Geneva allowed him to direct his initial theological forays to more central and controversial doctrines. Calvin was more learned in law, having studied canon law and civil law with the great jurists Pierre l'Estoile, Guillaume Budé, and Andreas Alciat, and having learned the basics of Protestant marriage law from Bucer, Melanchthon, and his Geneva colleague, Guillaume Farel.[9] Since Geneva still lacked a comprehensive new marriage law when he arrived, Calvin focused most of his initial efforts there.

Calvin's Early Theology of Marriage

Calvin repeated, with only modest embellishment, the familiar Protestant attack on the prevailing Catholic theology of marriage. Like the Lutheran reformers, he grounded his attack in the theory of the two kingdoms.[10] "[T]here is a twofold government in man," he wrote. "One aspect is spiritual, whereby the conscience is instructed in piety and in reverencing God; the second is political, whereby man is educated for the duties of humanity and civil life that must be maintained among men. These are usually called the 'spiritual' and the 'temporal' kingdoms (not improper terms) by which is meant that the former sort of regime pertains to the life of the soul, while the latter has to do with the concerns of the present life—not only with food and clothing but with laying down laws whereby a man may live his life among other men honorably and temperately. For the former resides in the mind within, while the latter regulates only outward behavior."[11]

Marriage, family, and sexuality are matters of the earthly kingdom alone, Calvin believed. Marriage is "a good and holy ordinance of God," designed to procreate children, to remedy incontinence, to promote "love between husband and wife."[12] Its morals and mores are subject to the laws of God that are written on the "tablet" of conscience, rewritten in the pages of scripture, and distilled in the Ten Commandments. Marriage, however, is not a sacrament of the heavenly kingdom. Though it symbolizes the bond between Christ and His Church, marriage confirms no divine promise and confers no sanctifying grace, as do true sacraments. Though it is a righteous mode of Christian living in the earthly kingdom, it has no bearing on one's salvation or eternal standing.[13]

Moreover, celibacy is not an obligation of the earthly kingdom. The celibate life is a "special gift of God," commended only to those "rare persons" who are continent by nature. "[I]t is the hypocrisy of demons to command celibacy," and "giddy levity" to exult the celibate state over the marital estate, Calvin charged. For the Church to command celibacy is to "contend against God" and to spurn God's gracious "remedy" for lust. For the Church to subordinate marriage to celibacy is to commit the spiritual "arrogance" of supplanting God's ordinance with a human tradition.[14] Two decades before, such teachings would have been revolutionary. By the late 1530s, they had become familiar refrains in the Protestant litany.

Critique of Canon Law

Calvin took up, with more originality, the Protestant attack on the Catholic canon law of marriage, which had governed Genevan life continuously until just before his first arrival there in 1536.[15] He issued a lengthy and bitter broadside against the arguments from scripture, tradition, and the sacraments that the Catholic Church had adduced to support its ecclesiastical jurisdiction. "[T]he power to frame laws was both unknown to the apostles, and many times denied the ministers of the church by God's Word," he insisted. "[I]t is not a church which, passing the bounds of God's Word, wantons and disports itself to frame new laws and dream up new things" for spiritual life.[16] The Bible alone is a sufficient guide for a person's Christian walk and a church's corporate life. For the Church to impose new laws upon its own members is to obstruct the simple law and liberty of the gospel. For the Church to impose its own laws upon civil society is to obscure its essential pastoral, prophetic, and pedagogical callings. To be sure, said Calvin quoting Paul, "all things [must] be done decently and in order." Certain rules and structures "are necessary for internal discipline [and] the maintenance of peace, honesty, and good order in the assembly of Christians." But the church has no authority to impose laws "upon consciences in those matters in which they have been freed by Christ"—in the so-called adiaphora, the external and discretionary things of life that do not conduce to salvation.[17] Marriage and family life are among these adiaphora. Laws governing such matters lie within the province of the state, not the church.

Particularly the Catholic Church's sacramental theology of marriage, Calvin argued, has led all Christendom down a "long legal trail of errors, lies, frauds, and misdeeds."[18] Calvin singled out for special critique the familiar targets of earlier Protestant attacks—the Church's "usurpation" of marital jurisdiction from secular judges, its condonation of secret marriages of minors without parental consent, its restrictions on the seasons for betrothal, its long roll of marital impediments beyond "the law of nations and of Moses," its easy dispensations from marital rules for the propertied and the powerful, its prohibitions against divorce and remarriage. "[P]apal tyranny" and "iniquitous laws," he wrote, have "so confused matrimonial cases . . . that it is necessary to review the controversies that often ensue therefrom in light of the Word of God" and "to make certain new ordinances by which [marriage] may be governed."[19]

Ecclesiastical Ordinances

The city council of Geneva soon made "certain new ordinances" for the governance of marriage—inspired and instructed, in part, by Calvin and his ministerial colleagues. The 1541 Ecclesiastical Ordinances of Geneva, drafted by Calvin and revised by the city councils, set out the church's new role in the family life and law of the community.[20] The church's "four offices" of pastors, teachers, elders, and deacons were to propound a purely biblical ethic of marriage and family life among its members—freed from the distortions of the canon law and free from the directions of a central episcopacy. Pastors were to expound relevant biblical passages from the pulpit; teachers were to explain them more simply to students and catechumens. Elders were to discipline sexual license and marital discord among church members; deacons were to aid orphans, widows, and the sexually abused. All church leaders were to set an example of sexual modesty, chastity, and integrity in their lives. Any pastor, the Ordinance ordered, caught in fornication, "dissolute dancing," or sexual "scandal" was to be summarily dismissed.

The 1541 Ecclesiastical Ordinance established a central consistory for Geneva to work "hand-in-hand" with the Small Council in the governance of marital matters.[21] The Small Council, which was the chief magisterial body of the city, operated with several standing specialty committees—for finance, public works, charity, and the like. The consistory was established as a new standing committee to aid the Small Council in its governance of the moral, religious, sexual, and familial life of the city. The presiding officer of the consistory was one of the four leading syndics of the Small Council. The members of the consistory included both laity and clergy divided into two companies: (1) a Company of Elders (10–12 citizens elected from the three other representative city councils); and (2) a Company of Pastors (comprised of up to 12 pastors drawn from local churches). The "Moderator" of the Company of Pastors was John Calvin, who by his office and by his learning exerted a formidable influence on the consistory's deliberations.

The Genevan consistory came to serve as something of a hearings court of first instance and a mediator of last resort in cases of sex, marriage, and family life (among many other subjects).[22] The consistory met once per week for several hours. Parties could petition the consistory voluntarily or be subpoenaed to appear—often on the recommendation of a local pastor or magistrate. Pleadings were oral. Proceedings were recorded by a notary. Testimony was given under oath.[23] Parties and witnesses could be questioned by any consistory member. Documentary or physical evidence could also be demanded and examined. The consistory process was designed to be less formal and more flexible than that of a courtroom, although it was doubtless equally unnerving to parties and witnesses, who generally appeared without legal counsel and without any guarantee of procedural rights. Over time, the Geneva consistory became rather famous, as we saw in the case of the French noblewoman, and parties throughout the Protestant world would look to it or write to it for directions and judgments on questions of marriage and family life.

The Ecclesiastical Ordinance explicitly barred the consistory from exercising any jurisdiction over marriage—any power to make and enforce civil or criminal laws. The consistory could administer only spiritual sanctions of admonition, catechization, or public confession to conduct its affairs—a spiritual arsenal supplemented, after a long fight, with the power of excommunication. Cases or issues that required legal action or orders were referred to the Council for disposition. In such instances, the consistory's findings of fact and recommendations of action were probative but not binding on the Council.

Critics of the day saw little distinction between this new Protestant consistory and the old Catholic church courts that had enjoyed plenary jurisdiction over marital matters in Geneva until five years before. The Ecclesiastical Ordinance, however, sought to safeguard against such a "reversion" by appointing to the consistory both lay and ministerial officers led by a powerful lay syndic, and by expressly curtailing the consistory's legal power: "[M]inisters have no civil jurisdiction and wield only the spiritual sword of the Word of God, as St. Paul commands them," the Ordinance reads. "Disputes in marital cases are not spiritual matters but are mixed up with politics, and must remain a matter for the magistracy." "There must be no derogation by the consistory from the authority of the civil council or magistracy; the civil power must proceed unhindered."[24]

The civil power must not proceed unguided, however. Clear and comprehensive rules are "the sinews of the commonwealth [and] the souls of the civil power," Calvin believed. Such rules were especially critical for governing the tender subjects of sex, marriage, and family life.[25] The Genevan city council had already, since the 1480s, supplemented a good deal of the canon law of crimes with its own criminal prohibitions against sexual sins punishable by secular authorities: prostitution, adultery, fornication, rape, incest, bigamy, sodomy, bestiality, and the like.[26] These criminal laws were tightened and amended, in part at Calvin's urging, in the early 1540s.[27] But Geneva still lacked a civil law of marriage to replace the canon law system.

The 1545 Marriage Ordinance

In 1545, Calvin and four members of the Council thus drafted a comprehensive Marriage Ordinance for Geneva and surrounding rural polities—cleverly culling its provisions from an array of biblical, canonical, and civil law sources. The Ordinance was not a legal code, though Calvin called it that. The Ordinance neither moved from general principles to specific rules, nor covered all relevant subjects equally or systematically. It was instead a large, learned, and (sometimes) loose collection of rules for the governance of marital formation, maintenance, and dissolution. Though the Ordinance was debated and amended several times before its formal adoption in 1561, its basic provisions served from the start as an authoritative statement of the new common law of marriage for Geneva.[28]

Betrothals and Weddings

The Ordinance dwelt at length with betrothals—seeking to safeguard against secret marriages and to secure the consent of the couple, their parents, and the broader community to this vital first step of intimate union. The consent of the couple was the essence of betrothal, and the drafters took pains to secure it. Betrothal promises had to be made "simply," "unconditionally," and "honorably in the fear of God." Ideally, such betrothals were to be initiated by "a sober proposal" from the man, accepted by the woman, and witnessed by at least two persons of "good reputation," although deviations from this procedure were tolerated. Betrothals made in secret, qualified with conditions, or procured by coercion were automatically null, and the couple themselves, and any accomplices in their wrongdoing, faced punishment. Betrothals procured through trickery or "surprise," or made "frivolously, as when merely touching glasses when drinking together," could be annulled on petition by either party. Betrothals involving a newcomer to the city were not valid until the parties produced proof of the newcomer's integrity of character and eligibility for marriage. Absent such proof, the couple had to wait a year before they could marry.[29]

The consent of the couple's parents was also vital to the validity of the betrothal. The consent of fathers was the more critical; maternal consent was required only when fathers were absent, and would be respected only if (male) relatives would concur in her views. In the absence of both parents, guardians would give their consent, again with priority for the male voice. Minor children—men under 20, women under 18—who entered marriage without such parental consent could have their betrothals unilaterally annulled by either set of parents or guardians.[30] Adult or emancipated children could proceed without their parents' consent, though "it is more fitting that they should always let themselves be governed by the advice of their fathers." The Ordinance makes clear that parental consent was only a supplement to, not a substitute for, the consent of the couple themselves. Parents were prohibited, on pain of imprisonment, from coercing their children into unwanted engagements or withholding their consent or payment of dowry until the child chose a partner whom they favored. Parents were further prevented from forcing youngsters into marriage before they were mature enough to consent to and participate safely in the institution. Minor children "observing a modest and reverent spirit" could refuse to follow their parents' insistence on an unwanted fiancé(e) or a premature engagement. Other children, confronting a "negligent or excessively strict" father, could "have him compelled to give a dowry" in support of their marriage.

The consent of the broader state and church community also played a part in the betrothals. Betrothed couples were to register with a local civil magistrate, who would post notices of their pending nuptials and furnish the couple with a signed marriage certificate. Couples were to file this registration of marriage thereafter with a local church, whose pastor was to announce their banns from the pulpit on three successive Sundays.[31] Such widespread notice was an open invitation for fellow parishioners and citizens alike to approve of the match or to voice their objections. Any number of objections could be raised at this stage—for example, that one of the parties was "incompetent" by reason of youth, imbecility, contagion, or a "wild spirit," or that the parties were "incompatible" because of differences in age, religion, social rank, or economic status. These objections were not necessarily fatal to the betrothal, and officials were given wide discretion regarding their disposition. No such discretion was allowed if it was proved that the parties fell within one of the biblical degrees of consanguinity or affinity, that one of the parties had an "incurable contagious disease," or that the prospective bride "taken to be virgin is not so." All objections to betrothal, the Ordinance insisted, had to be voiced privately to the consistory and only by citizens or by persons of good reputation. Such precautions helped to avoid the prospect of "defamation or injustice," particularly "to an honorable girl." Those who objected to the betrothal in an untimely or improper manner could be sued for defamation by the couple or their parents.

A couple, once properly betrothed, had little time to waste and little room to celebrate. Neither their publicly announced betrothal nor the civil registration of their marriage was sufficient to constitute a marriage. A formal church wedding had to follow—within three to six weeks of betrothal. If the couple procrastinated in their wedding plans, they would be reprimanded by the consistory; if they persisted, they would be "sent before the Council so that they may be compelled to celebrate it." If the prospective groom disappeared without cause, the woman was bound to her betrothal for a year. If the prospective bride disappeared, the man could break off the engagement immediately, unless there was evidence that she had been kidnapped or involuntarily detained.[32] Cohabitation and consummation prior to the wedding were strictly forbidden to the parties, on pain of imprisonment. Pregnant brides-to-be, though spared prison, were required to do public confession for fornication prior to the wedding and on the day of the wedding had to wear a veil signaling their sin of fornication.[33] Weddings were to be "modest affairs," "maintaining the decorum and gravity befitting Christians" and featuring a mutual swearing of oaths by the couple, as well as by their witnesses, followed by the blessing and sermon of the pastor.[34]

Marriage, Annulment, and Divorce

A marriage, once properly contracted, consecrated, and celebrated, was presumed permanent. The married couple was expected to maintain a common home. Both parties could be called to account for privately separating from bed or board, particularly if there was suspicion of adultery, harlotry, concubinage, or sodomy. Couples who "wrangled and disputed with each other" were to be admonished by the consistory to "live in peace and unity," with severe cases of discord reported to the congregation for popular reproof or to the Council for criminal punishment. Husbands were forbidden to "ill treat," "beat," or "torment" their wives, and were subject to severe criminal sanctions if they persisted. The Ordinance made no provision, even in extreme cases, for the traditional canon law remedy of separation from bed and board (without divorce). An ethic of perpetual reconciliation of husband and wife coursed through the Ordinance, with ministers, magistrates, and members of the broader community all called to foster this end.

The presumption of permanent marriage was not irrebuttable, however. In instances of serious marital impediments or individual fault, a party could sue for annulment or divorce. The Ordinance rendered the process of marital dissolution as open and communal as it had rendered the process of marital formation—requiring open hearings in the consistory, and if necessary, the city council.

A judgment of *annulment* required proof that a putative marriage was void from the start by reason of some defect (called an impediment) present at the time of the wedding but unknown to either of the marital parties. Either party could sue for annulment on discovery of a blood or familial relationship between them that violated biblical commands.[35] Upon annulment both were left to remarry. A husband could sue if he discovered that his wife lacked presumed virginity, was incurably diseased, or refused to correct a "defect of her body" that prevented intercourse—again, leaving both parties free to remarry. A wife could sue on grounds of the impotence or incurable disease of her husband—leaving her free to remarry, but him "forbidden to misuse any woman again." In all such cases, the parties were expected to prepare a register of their individual and collective properties and, with appropriate judicial supervision, reach an "amicable" parting of property and person.[36]

A judgment of *divorce* required proof in open court that a marriage, though properly contracted, was now broken by reason of the adultery or desertion of one of the parties. In cases of adultery, husband and wife were accorded an equal right to sue—a deliberate innovation to "ancient practice" in Geneva, which the Ordinance grounded in Paul's teaching that husband and wife have a "mutual and reciprocal obligation" in "matters of intercourse of the bed." Only an entirely innocent plaintiff could bring such a suit; any evidence of mutual fault, fraud, or collusion in the adultery was fatal to the case. Failure to bring suit in a timely manner was taken as a sign of forgiveness, and cut off the suit for divorce. After bringing suit, the plaintiff was urged to reconcile with the wayward spouse—and was doubtless told that such reconciliation would likely exonerate the latter from criminal punishment. But the plaintiff could insist on the divorce, and in such instance, the case would be referred to the Council for adjudication. The innocent party was free to remarry thereafter. The adulterer faced criminal punishment—imprisonment in the usual case, banishment or execution by drowning in an egregious case.[37]

Parties could also sue for divorce on grounds of desertion. These divorce cases were procedurally more complicated and substantively less egalitarian in their treatment of husband and wife. In cases where the husband left home for a legitimate reason (such as for business or military service), but inexplicably did not return and could not be found, the wife had to wait ten years before he could be presumed dead and she would be permitted to remarry. In cases where the husband left "through debauchery or some other evil disposition," the wife was to find him and to request his return. If she could not find him, she would have to wait one year before proceeding further. If she did find him and he refused to return—or the year of waiting had expired—she was to request three biweekly announcements of his desertion, both by the minister in the church and by the lieutenant of the city council. If he still failed to respond, she was to summon two or three of his relatives or close friends to try to find him and urge his return. If that proved futile, she could appear before the consistory to state her case and, with their approval, petition the magistrate for an order of divorce. The return of the husband anytime before issuance of such an order would end the proceedings. The husband would be admonished for his desertion. The wife would be compelled to welcome him back to bed and board. If the husband repeated his desertion, he faced prison. If he deserted habitually, the wife could sue for divorce *ex parte,* with no further notification requirements.

A husband who brought suit for his wife's desertion followed the same procedures, but with three simplifications. First, cases of intentional desertion and legitimate departure by the wife were treated alike. Second, husbands had no obligation to wait for one year (let alone ten) if he could not locate his wife; the public announcements of her departure and petition for divorce could commence immediately. Third, even if a wife returned, her husband could reject her if he had "suspicion that she has misconducted herself." The consistory would urge their reconciliation, but if he insisted, they would investigate her conduct while away. If they found no evidence of misconduct, he would be compelled to accept her. If they reached "a very emphatic presumption that she committed adultery or kept bad and suspect company and did not conduct herself honorably as a good woman," the Ordinance reads, "the husband's petition shall be heard, and he shall be granted what reason dictates."

Marriage Litigation

The 1545 Marriage Ordinance provided generous guidance for the governance of marriage and family life in Geneva. It was left to the consistory and the Small Council to put these rules into action: "All matrimonial causes concerning personal relationships and not goods shall receive attention in the first instance in the consistory where an amicable solution, if one can be found, shall be effected in the name of God," the Ordinance concludes. "If it is necessary to pronounce some judicial sentence, the parties shall be sent to the Council with a statement of the decision of the consistory so that the definitive sentence may be given."

A vivid picture of the Marriage Ordinance in action can be seen in the case law of 1546, the year after the first draft was issued.[38] A dozen cases on questions of marriage and sexuality are reported in the consistory register for that year, touching many aspects of the marriage process and implicating many rules of the new draft ordinance. All but one of the cases ended in the consistory, with guilty parties simply admonished and open questions left for later resolution or for action by one of the consistory members. This picture of the Marriage Ordinance in action is rendered all the more colorful in that John Calvin participated in all these cases, as Moderator of the Company of Pastors, the clerical "bench" of the consistory.

Four cases reported in 1546 dealt with challenges to betrothal. A man, who testified that his fiancée was "corrupt" and wanted to be "separated" from him, was released from his betrothal provided that his fiancée would come to the consistory to corroborate his story.[39] A young couple who became engaged while the woman was tippling was ordered to reappear before the consistory with their parents "in order for the parents to declare that the promise of marriage was frivolous, and to be admonished to take better care of their children."[40] Another young couple, who had married without the consent of the woman's parents, was deemed "not properly contracted" and was ordered to return to the consistory for further counsel.[41] A Genevan woman, whose engagement with a man from Gex was challenged by a woman in the city of Berne, was given an extension on her engagement and permission to join with her fiancé in order to answer the objection.[42]

Three cases dealt with spousal desertion, discord, and neglect. A maid, deserted by her husband for twelve years, came to inquire about a rumor that her husband was involved in a case in the town of Guyon. The consistory court's decision was that "Calvin should write to the consistory of Guyon" and ask for information about the case.[43] A widower was hauled into court apparently on suspicion that he had grossly neglected his wife before she died. Though the record is cryptic, the notary reports: "The decision is that it will be a scandal to open the door to many to kill their wives, when it appears that this woman was complaining futilely [of her ailment] and died in sadness."[44] A disaffected married couple was summoned to the consistory for investigation. The husband complained of his perennial unhappiness and of his wife's "horrible" conduct. The wife complained of his apostasy and disaffection, despite her best efforts to indulge and cajole him. She threatened to leave for another city if she was forced to endure him. He refused to describe her "horrible conduct," which would allow the consistory to determine the appropriate remedy. Exasperated, the consistory referred the case to Calvin to give pastoral guidance and reproof.[45] The couple did not appear before the consistory again.

Four cases of improper sexual behavior fell to the consistory to resolve. A young man was admonished for frequenting a dance hall, for, as Calvin warned him on behalf of the consistory, "dancing leads to debauchery."[46] Another man, suspected of fornication, was admonished for "hugging his maid lustfully in an open street" and not accepting his own pastor's reproof for such conduct.[47] A woman was reprimanded for becoming pregnant and for failing to disclose her condition in time for the consistory to intervene. Her testimony that she had extracted a marriage promise from her lover did not seem to impress the consistory, given its new charge to outlaw secret betrothals.[48] A young man was admonished for fathering an illegitimate child in a nearby town. When he denied the charge "with many words," he learned that the woman's own local consistory had reported the case to the central Geneva consistory, that Calvin had been dispatched to investigate, and that his findings were that the woman "wears makeup and is reputed to be sexually promiscuous." This evidence was sufficient, despite the young man's denials, to yield the consistory's decision to "procure a written certificate" from the woman's hometown—presumably a certificate for a "shotgun wedding" between the fornicating parties.[49]

The consistory court dealt more fully and firmly with the marital conflicts and infidelities of an elderly Genevan aristocrat, Sir François Favre.[50] On February 18, 1546, the consistory haled Favre before it and demanded that he account for "scandalous rumors" that "there is conflict between him and his wife" and that "she has departed for an unknown reason"—perhaps because "a maid was pregnant before she left the house." According to the notary, "Favre responded that he is old, and would just like to have someone to take care of his house. Sir Calvin admonished him that this response was nonsense. The father of a household should account for his maid," Calvin insisted, pressing Favre for a better answer. Favre tried again, saying "he knows nothing [about the maid's pregnancy] and that his wife simply left with her property, under pressure by someone who wants to use that property." There was no marital conflict, Favre argued. "He did not beat her." His wife, he said, would corroborate his testimony on her return. Favre was "admonished, indeed well admonished," the notary reports, noting in the margin of the register that this was Favre's third wife. The consistory decided to refer the matter to the city prosecutor to collect further information about Favre from the pregnant maid. They later decided to send a letter to the nearby consistory of Gex, asking them to summon Casper Favre, apparently François' son, to Geneva to testify.

The case was reopened two years later when François Favre appeared voluntarily before the consistory court, now pleading for permission to divorce his wife *ex parte*. The notary reports as follows:

Favre demanded to be divorced from his wife because she had numerous lawsuits [against her], and her properties were situated in Morges where he was unable to attend to them. He had not taken her on this condition. Moreover, he confessed to having committed adultery, an action which his wife also condemned, in agreeing to the action for divorce. After this [plea], Sir Calvin began to give his opinion. He affirmed that adultery is a sufficient cause for a woman to seek a divorce. For though the husband has preeminence over the wife, yet in this there is equality—[see] St. Paul, 1 Cor[inthians] 7: "the husband has not power over his body," etc. However, here it is necessary [for the consistory] to consider when this fornication or adultery has taken place, whether it was before the marriage was contracted, and if it was during the marriage, whether the wife's consent to continue living with her husband after the adulterous act would cancel the fault. The members of the consistory were urged in addition to beware, lest there be collusion between the parties, which would open the door to the dissolution of many marriages. Finally, it was pointed out that the wife, who was an interested party in the case, had not brought an action, although she had [per his testimony] accused him of disgraceful conduct.[51]

Favre's divorce case was thus dismissed. Shortly thereafter, Favre was again accused of fornicating with his maid servants, as well as perjuring himself before the consistory and resisting its spiritual discipline. On the recommendation of the consistory, the Geneva authorities imprisoned him and forced him into a lengthy public apology. Favre eventually left Geneva to spare himself further scrutiny and embarrassment.[52]

These marital cases in 1546 were quite typical of the cases heard by the consistory in the 1540s and early 1550s. The consistory would hear some ten to forty cases per year dealing with marriage, family, and sexuality. Virtually all these cases were of modest proportion: disputes over secret, conditional, or coerced betrothals; petitions for protection from parental or spousal coercion or neglect; inquiries into fornication or debauchery; reprimands for discord or abuse; charges of spousal desertion or delinquency. Almost all these cases met with either stern spiritual admonition or with simple avuncular advice and action, and ended there.[53] Few cases during Calvin's tenure, let alone in the 1540s, rose to the level of social intrigue and legal complexity evident in the Favre case.[54]

The New Marriage Law
in Comparative Perspective

The Marriage Ordinance of Geneva—on the books and in action— was a watershed in the evolution of Protestant marriage and family law.

The Ordinance collected and combined the most enduring provisions of the old Catholic canon law and the most daring reforms of the new Protestant civil law. The Ordinance retained the canonists' distinctions of betrothal, marriage, and consummation. But it imported various Protestant rules to simplify, abbreviate, and police the process. The Ordinance repeated the canonists' requirement that the couple mutually consent to marriage. But it incorporated Protestant demands for the further consent of parents, parishioners, and citizens in the process. The Ordinance accepted the canonists' biblically based impediments of consanguinity, affinity, and infirmity. But it rejected, in typical Protestant fashion, the impediments rooted in Catholic sacramental theology. The Ordinance repeated the canonists' injunction that marriage is an indissoluble estate. Yet it followed Protestant (and Roman law) views that adultery and desertion are themselves acts of marital dissolution, triggering rights for divorce and remarriage at least for the innocent party. The Ordinance adopted the canon law pattern of involving clergy in the governance of marriage. But it left to the Protestant magistrate both civil and criminal jurisdiction over sex, marriage, and family life.[55]

This Marriage Ordinance was more than a synthesis of earlier laws, however. Through this enactment, Calvin and his colleagues also introduced several innovations, or novel emphases, in prevailing Protestant marriage law that came to have a formidable influence on the Western legal tradition.[56] A dozen such contributions deserve mention: (1) the strict prohibitions against frivolity, drunkenness, and conditionality in contracting betrothals; (2) the substantial protections of children from parental coercion into engagements; (3) the elevation of paternal over maternal consent in the process of betrothal; (4) the abbreviation and careful communal policing of the interim between betrothal and marriage; (5) the absolute impediments of impotence and contagion to betrothal and marriage; (6) the mandatory publication of banns by both magistrates and ministers; (7) the dual requirements of state registration and church consecration to constitute marriage; (8) the deprecation of the right of separation from bed and board, and the strong emphasis on reconciliation between husband and wife; (9) the equal standing for women to sue for annulment on grounds of impotence and for divorce on grounds of adultery; (10) the disparate treatment of husbands and wives in suits for desertion, (11) the stern prohibition against wife abuse; and (12) the establishment of a mixed clerical and lay consistory to serve as a hearings court of first resort and a mediator of last resort in marital cases.

Taken together, these innovations of Genevan marriage law helped to render both mental consent and sexual ability indispensable features of marriage. They helped to render betrothal, marriage, and dissolution central concerns of church, state, and society alike. And they helped to promote what André Biéler once called a "differential equality"—such progressive gender equality on some issues that Geneva was named a "women's paradise," such regressive patriarchy on other issues that Geneva was described at the same time as "a woman's abyss."[57]

The most surprising feature of the new marriage law of Geneva is its intensely legalistic quality. Unlike other Protestant laws on marriage, both the Marriage Ordinance of 1545 and the marriage cases of 1546 are almost silent on any sources of law beyond the command of the sovereign. A typical Protestant ordinance of the day would begin at least with a bit of homiletic throat clearing, if not a fuller recitation of its sources in the Bible, reason, conscience, tradition, and custom. An elaborate law, such as this one, would usually also provide a crisp distillation of the polity's favorite theological doctrines supporting its basic provisions—a common feature of polities that established religion by civil law.[58] In a dozen reported cases on a heated religious topic like marriage, one could expect to find a liberal peppering of citations to everyone from Moses to Martin Luther, particularly with someone of Calvin's erudition in the room. But the new Geneva marriage law leaves its religious sources and its theological rationale almost completely hidden. First Corinthians 7 is mentioned twice in passing, but both times to make the claim (contrary to earlier Geneva civil law) that, in cases of adultery, women and men should have equal rights to sue for divorce. For the rest, the rules are stated categorically and the decisions announced confidently, with very little by way of citation to religious authority and even less by way of theological explication.

The Marriage Ordinance mirrors Calvin's method in this first phase of marital reformation in Geneva. Law came first in his early reform efforts, theology a distant second. "The purity of our families depends on the purity of our laws," Calvin declared to the Geneva Small Council in urging their adoption of his Marriage Ordinance.[59] The purification of marriage law was thus his first ambition.

Calvin's Later Reformation of Marriage Theology

Popular Contempt

"Rules without canons will either harden or wither over time," Lord Acton once said. "Whether hardened or withered, they come to little effect." Calvin learned this lesson the hard way in his reformation of

Genevan marriage law. However refined his early legal formulations on marriage may have been, they did not admit of easy political adoption or popular acceptance. Genevan political officials dithered for nearly two decades before finally yielding to most of his legal reforms. Genevan parishioners and subjects resisted, with increasing contempt, the authority of Calvin and the consistory to deal with marital matters.

Two cases of popular contempt appear already in the consistory register of 1546, when the Marriage Ordinance was first circulating. In one case, a man charged Calvin with posturing as "the new pope" of marriage.[60] In another case, a man flatly asserted that the consistory "lacked the authority" to dissolve his sister's betrothal, punctuating his remarks with a few insulting jabs at Calvin.[61] Such jurisdictional challenges become more pointed and frequent in subsequent years, as anticlericalism escalated in Geneva.[62] Why should the church consistory enjoy such authority over a civil estate like marriage? Why should the city magistrates be swayed by the pastors' teachings on sexuality and domesticity? Why should ministers have such powers to probe the intimacies of bed and board? Why should rights to participate in the sacrament of Eucharist turn on wrongs pertaining to the adiaphora of marriage? How was the magistrate or minister to parse and police the line between the pastoral functions of the consistory and the judicial functions of the Council? Had not Calvin simply created a new church court under his authority, wielding much of the same power and prerogative as the former episcopal and inquisitorial courts of Catholicism, but now lacking any final appeal to Rome? Dozens of litigants and pamphleteers voiced such criticisms in the later 1540s and 1550s.[63] Calvin had no ready answers.

Not only the jurisdiction but also the substance of the new marriage law came under increasing challenge. Calvin may well have ingeniously cut and pasted what he considered to be the best of Catholic and Protestant laws on marriage, suitably amended with his own favorite norms. But why should these laws be binding on Geneva? Why could Geneva not adopt some of the more liberal rules of a Zürich or a Strasbourg, or the more conservative laws of a Rome or a Paris? What was to prevent piecemeal or wholesale reform or rejection of these new rules? What was to check the growing marital and sexual license in Geneva about which Calvin and other pastors complained bitterly: the sharp increases in adultery, desertion, and discord within the home; the escalation of fornication, harlotry, and sumptuousness outside the home; the rapid exploitation of the new rights to divorce and remarriage by the Genevan elite; the sharp increases in "ribaldry" of music and literature and "lewdness" of manner and speech among the youth—pathos, which Calvin denounced with all the passion and prescience of any modern-day Jeremiah.[64]

Such challenges sent Calvin scurrying to his library, pulpit, and letter desk to develop and defend a more elaborate theology of marriage and family life than he had earlier offered. In a long series of biblical commentaries, sermons, and letters prepared in the last twelve years of his life, he provided a rich theological apologia both for his marriage law system as a whole and for many of the individual rules that he had prescribed.[65] Calvin's late-life ailments and early death in 1564 kept him from fully elaborating, let alone systematizing, these new theological sentiments. But even in its somewhat scattered form, Calvin's new theology of marriage made an impressive and enduring contribution to the Western canon. Later reformed theologians and jurists, in Europe and America, elaborated many of the basic theological insights that he had adumbrated.

Such challenges also steeled Calvin and his consistory colleagues to enforce the new marriage laws of Geneva with greater rigor and vigor. Convinced of the biblical warrant for the new marriage law, the consistory of the 1550s and thereafter set out with new resolve to break the political and popular resistance to the new marriage law regime. Using a blend of pastoral cajolery and spiritual coercion, they worked hard to translate the new marital law on the books into a new law of social action. The following two sections take up these theological and legal developments in turn.

Covenant Theology of Marriage

Calvin's early theology of marriage had been grounded in the Lutheran doctrine of the two kingdoms. Marriage, he had argued, was an institution of the earthly kingdom alone—"a good and holy ordinance of God, just like farming, building, cobbling, and barbering."[66] Christians should participate in the institution—not to be justified or sanctified, but to keep themselves free from the sins of lust and incontinence. Church leaders should cooperate in the governance of marriage—not as spiritual lords of the Christian conscience, but as pastoral aides to the Christian magistrate. This early theology may have allowed Calvin to counter Catholic claims that marriage is a sacrament subject to the church's jurisdiction. But it did not allow him to counter either the political laxness in marriage law or the popular license in marriage life that prevailed in mid-sixteenth-century Geneva.

Calvin's mature theology of marriage was grounded in the biblical doctrine of covenant. The idea of a divine covenant or agreement between God and humanity had long been taught in the Western Church. Theologians, at least since the time of Irenaeus in the second century,[67] had discussed the interlocking biblical covenants: (1) the covenant of works whereby the chosen people of Israel, through obedience to God's law, are promised eternal salvation and blessing; and (2) the covenant of grace whereby the elect, through faith in Christ's incarnation and atonement, are promised eternal salvation and beatitude. The covenant of works was created in Abraham, confirmed in Moses, and consummated with the promulgation and acceptance of the Torah. The covenant of grace was created in Christ, confirmed in the Gospel, and consummated with the confession and conversion of the Christian.[68] These traditional teachings on the covenant were well known to the early Reformers, and Calvin had already used them to fortify his doctrines of sin and salvation, law and gospel, man and God.[69]

In his later years, Calvin used the doctrine of covenant to describe not only the vertical relationships between God and man, but also the horizontal relationships between husband and wife. Just as God draws the elect believer into a covenant relationship with him, Calvin argued, so God draws husband and wife into a covenant relationship with each other. Just as God expects constant faith and good works in our relationship with Him, so God expects connubial faithfulness and sacrificial works in our relationship with our spouses.[70] "God is the founder of marriage," Calvin wrote. "When a marriage takes place between a man and a woman, God presides and requires a mutual pledge from both. Hence Solomon in Proverbs 2:17 calls marriage the covenant of God, for it is superior to all human contracts. So also Malachi [2:14] declares that God is as it were the stipulator [of marriage] who by his authority joins the man to the woman, and sanctions the alliance."[71]

God participates in the formation of the covenant of marriage through his chosen agents on earth, Calvin believed. The couple's parents, as God's "lieutenants" for children, instruct the young couple in the mores and morals of Christian marriage and give their consent to the union.[72] Two witnesses, as "God's priests to their peers," testify to the sincerity and solemnity of the couple's promises and attest to the marriage event.[73] The minister, holding "God's spiritual power of the Word," blesses the union and admonishes the couple and the community of their respective biblical duties and rights.[74] The magistrate, holding "God's temporal power of the sword," registers the parties, ensures the legality of their union, and protects them in their conjoined persons and properties.[75] This involvement of parents, peers, ministers, and magistrates in the formation of marriage was not an idle or dispensable ceremony. These four parties represented different dimensions of God's involvement in the marriage covenant, and they were thus essential to the legitimacy of the marriage itself. To omit any such party in the formation of the marriage was, in effect, to omit God from the marriage covenant.

The Law of the Marriage Covenant

God participates in the maintenance of the covenant of marriage not only through the one-time actions of his human agents, but also through the continuous revelation of his moral law. Calvin repeated his earlier definition of the moral law: as God's commandments, engraved on the conscience, elaborated in scripture, and distilled in the Decalogue.[76] He now used sundry terms to describe this moral law: "the voice of nature," "the law of nature," "the natural order," "the inner mind," "the rule of equity," "the natural sense," "the sense of divine judgment," "the testimony of the heart," "the inner voice"—terms and concepts that he did not adequately sift or synthesize.[77] For our purposes, these are all synonyms to describe the basic norms created by God, and confirmed in the covenant, for the right ordering of our marital and sexual lives.

The covenant of marriage is grounded "in the creation and commandments of God," and "in the order and law of nature," Calvin believed.[78] At creation, God ordained the structure of marriage to be a lifelong union between a fit man and a fit woman of the age of mature consent. God assigned to this marriage three interlocking purposes: (1) the mutual love and support of husband and wife, (2) the mutual procreation and nurture of children, and (3) the mutual protection of both parties from sexual sin.[79] In nature, man and woman enjoy a "common dignity before God" and a common function of "completing" the life and love of the other.[80] In marriage, husband and wife are "joined together in one body and one soul," but then assigned "distinct duties" and "different authorities."[81] God has appointed the husband as the head of the wife. God has appointed the wife, "who is derived from and comes after the man," as his associate and companion—literally his "help meet."[82] "The divine mandate [in Paradise] was that the husband would look up in reverence to God, the woman would be a faithful assistant to him, and both with one consent would cultivate a holy, friendly, and peaceful intercourse."[83]

This created subordination of the wife to the husband was exacerbated by the fall into sin, Calvin believed. "The woman had previously been subject to her husband, but that was a liberal and gentle subjection. Now she is cast into servitude to man"—consigned perennially to a life of child bearing and domestic service, while the husband presides over her material and spiritual welfare and that of their children.[84]

Calvin reminded women of their God-given domestic roles many times—sometimes with a level of insult and misogyny that warrants criticism, even when judged by sixteenth-century standards.[85] But Calvin also made clear that husbands were not to abuse their superior offices within the marital estate, on pain of spiritual and civil sanctions.[86] He called marital couples repeatedly to the mutual love and nurture that God had prescribed for marriage.[87] He insisted, more than once, that the domestic vocation is equal in status to all other vocations. He further insisted that, despite the headship of the man within the home, the woman must enjoy both connubial and parental equality.[88] "While in other things, husband and wife differ both as to duty and as to authority," Calvin wrote, "with respect to their mutual obligations in bed . . . they are bound to mutual benevolence."[89] And again: "[A]uthority is distributed as much to one parent as to the other. . . . God does not wish the father alone to rule the child; the mother must also have a share in the honor and the preeminence."[90]

Calvin used this understanding of the created structure and purposes of marriage to integrate a variety of biblical morals and mores for life within the covenant of marriage. In Calvin's view, these biblical norms had different implications (1) for the believer versus the nonbeliever, and (2) for the married couple versus the unmarried party. Calvin spelled out these distinctions in some detail, for to him they were critical to resolving some of the tensions that might appear between and within biblical and natural norms for marriage.

Calvin explained the first distinction (the differential impact of biblical marital norms on believers and nonbelievers) in the context of his broader theory of the "uses" of the moral law.[91] Like other Protestant reformers, Calvin believed that the moral law provides no pathway to salvation. Prior to the fall into sin, the law was a recipe for righteousness. But since the Fall, no person has been capable of perfectly abiding by the law and thereby earning salvation by good works alone. Salvation now comes through faith and grace, not by works and the law, said Calvin. Nonetheless, from God's point of view, the moral law continues to be useful in this earthly life—to have "uses." God uses both its basic norms known to all persons and its more refined norms known only to believers through the Bible to govern and guide humanity.[92]

On the one hand, said Calvin, the moral law has a "civil use" of defining for all persons what is absolutely necessary to maintain a modicum of civil and domestic order. In this sense, God uses "the moral law as a halter to check the raging and otherwise limitlessly ranging lusts of the flesh. . . . Hindered by fright or shame, sinners dare neither execute what they have conceived in their minds, nor openly breathe forth the rage of their lust."[93] The moral law thus imposes upon them a "constrained and coerced righteousness," a "civil morality."[94] "[E]ven the pagans," therefore, have always recognized the natural duties of sexual restraint, heterosexual monogamy, marital fidelity, procreation of children, bondage to kin, and the like, which are essential to the survival of marriage.[95]

On the other hand, the moral law has a "spiritual use" of defining for believers what is aspirationally needed to attain a measure of holiness or sanctification. Even the most devout saints, Calvin wrote, still need the moral law "to learn more thoroughly . . . the Lord's will [and] to be aroused to obedience."[96] In this sense, the moral law teaches them not only the "civil righteousness" that is common to nonbelievers, but also the "spiritual righteousness" that is becoming of believers. The moral law not only coerces them against violence and violation, but also cultivates in them charity and love. It not only punishes harmful acts of adultery and fornication, but also prohibits evil thoughts of passion and lust.[97]

God's moral law for the covenant of marriage thus gives rise to two tracks of marital norms: civil norms, which are common to all persons; and spiritual norms, which are distinctly Christian. This moral law, in turn, gives rise to two tracks of marital morality: a simple "morality of duty" demanded of all persons regardless of their faith, and a higher "morality of aspiration" demanded of believers in order to reflect their faith.[98] In Calvin's mind, commandments and counsels, musts and shouldsts, absolutes and adiaphoras for marriage can thereby be distinguished.

This two-track system of marital morality, Calvin believed, corresponds roughly to the division of marital responsibility between church and state in this earthly life. It was the church's responsibility to teach aspirational spiritual norms for marriage and family life. It was the state's responsibility to enforce mandatory civil norms. This division of responsibility fit rather neatly into the procedural divisions between the consistory and the council in Calvin's Geneva. In marriage cases, the consistory would first call parties to their higher spiritual duties, backing their recommendations with (threats of) spiritual discipline. If such spiritual counsel failed, the parties were referred to the city council to compel them, using civil and criminal sanctions, to honor at least their basic civil duties for marriage.[99]

With this first distinction in mind, Calvin spelled out various biblical norms for married and unmarried parties, grounding and integrating many of these norms in the created structure and created purposes of marriage.

The Structure
of the Marriage Covenant

Calvin grounded various biblical rules against illicit sexual unions in the created *structure* of marriage—a lifelong monogamous union of a fit man and a fit woman. Citing Moses and Paul, he condemned as "monstrous vices" sodomy, buggery, bestiality, homosexuality, and other "unnatural" acts and alliances—arguing cryptically that to "lust for our own kind" or "for brutes" was "repugnant to the modesty of nature itself."[100] He condemned as "incestuous" marriages contracted between the blood and family relatives identified in Leviticus, arguing that God had prohibited such unions to avoid discord, abuse, rivalry, and exploitation among these relatives.[101] This Levitical law against incest, said Calvin, "was not simply a civil law of Israel . . . nor one of those laws which can be repealed in accordance with the circumstances of time and place. It flows from the very font of nature, and is grounded in the general source of all laws, which is permanent and inviolate."[102] Thus, "unfit relatives" who were innocently married and later discovered their Levitical impediment must have their marriages immediately annulled.[103] Those who knowingly married in violation of these Levitical prohibitions must face not only annulment, but also civil and spiritual sanctions.[104]

Calvin condemned, at greater length, the traditional Hebrew practice of polygamy, which had again become fashionable in a few quarters of sixteenth-century Europe.[105] To allow polygamy, Calvin argued, is to ignore the creation story of "the one man and the one woman" whom God had created and joined together in Paradise.[106] "God could have created two wives for Adam if he wanted to," Calvin preached. "But God was content with one."[107] "Since this mutual union was consecrated by the Lord, the mixture of three or four persons is false and wicked" and "contrary to the order and law of nature."[108] To hold up as normative the polygamous practice of Solomon, David, and other Old Testament figures, Calvin continued, is to elevate the customs of the Jews above the laws of Christ.[109] God had tolerated the practice of polygamy among the Jews to accommodate their waywardness and disbelief, but even then, the prophets had condemned the institution unequivocally.[110] "Today, this liberty accorded to the Jews [of entering into polygamy] is not permitted to us. For Jesus Christ has revealed himself in this world, and declared the will of God to us more fully."[111] Christ and His apostles teach that the "two shall become one flesh."[112] For Calvin, that was the end of the matter, and he left it to his Genevan colleague Theodore Beza to work out further details of his argument.[113] When Calvin encountered the institution again in a later biblical commentary, he dismissed the issue facetiously: "He that takes two wives is worthy to be cut down the middle, he that takes three to be cut in three pieces."[114]

The Special Case of Adultery

Calvin saved his greatest thunder for the sin of adultery outlawed in the Decalogue. He read the commandment "Thou shalt not commit adultery" expansively to outlaw various illicit alliances and actions, within and without the marital estate.

Within marriage, the obvious case of adultery, of course, is sexual intercourse or "any other form of lewd sexual act" with a party not one's spouse.[115] Calvin regarded this form of adultery as "the worst abomination," for in one act the adulterer violates his covenant bonds with spouse, God, and the broader community.[116] "It is not without cause that marriage is called a covenant with God," Calvin thundered from his Geneva pulpit. "[W]henever a husband breaks his promise which he has made to his wife, he has not only perjured himself with respect to her, but also with respect to God. The same is true of the wife. She not only wrongs her husband, but the living God."[117] "She sets herself against His majesty."[118] Other parties are also vicariously injured. When a woman commits adultery, for example, "she injures her husband, exposes him to shame, despoils also the name of her family, despoils her unborn children, despoils those already born to her in lawful marriage."[119]

Given its disparate and devastating impact, adultery had to be counted among the worst offenses—"even graver" than idolatry, heresy, or impiety. For "one can be idolatrous, heretical, or impious, and still hold to matrimonial obligation. But to be both adulterer, and spouse, to be these two things at once, is impossible."[120] In Calvin's view, the moral law therefore "denounces capital punishment for adultery," and he decried the modern-day habit of treating the offense more lightly. "The punishment of death was always awarded to adultery. Thus it is all the more base and shameful that Christians do not emulate Gentiles at least in this. Adultery is punished no less severely by the Julian [i.e., Roman] law than by the law of God. Yet those who boastfully call themselves Christian are so tender and remiss that they punish this execrable offense only with a very light reproof."[121]

Though Calvin lamented this laxness of punishment, he addressed directly the consequences of adultery for the innocent spouse. Automatic execution of the adulterer would have left the innocent party with the stark but simple choice of remaining single or remarrying. Sparing the adulterer from execution complicated matters. The fate of the marriage rests in the hands of the innocent spouse, Calvin believed.[122] The innocent spouse has power either to forgive the fault and restore the marriage or to condemn the fault and confirm its dissolution.

The innocent spouse's confirmation of the dissolution of the marriage was expressed by filing for divorce on grounds of adultery. "Christ has allowed" the innocent spouse to seek divorce and even remarry thereafter if so inclined, said Calvin.[123] But a true believer should reconcile with the wayward spouse, following the example of Joseph's indulgence of the Virgin Mary when he first learned of her pregnancy.[124] God has instituted divorce as "a concession" to our sinfulness, "permitting it only within the common civil order, which serves to bridle men here below," and not within the higher spiritual order "where the children of God ought to be reformed by the Holy Spirit. Though God does not punish those who divorce on reasonable and lawful grounds, He meant that marriage should always remain inviolable."[125]

Calvin refused to expand the grounds for divorce beyond adultery, but was generous about entertaining divorce suits brought for adultery. Christ teaches that a proven case of adultery is the only "reasonable and lawful ground" for divorce, Calvin argued. To expand the grounds for divorce beyond adultery is both bad theology and bad policy. "Those who search for other grounds ought justly to be set at nought, for they choose to be wise above the heavenly teacher."[126] They also invite endless amendment to the moral law: "Some say that leprosy is a proper ground for divorce, because the contagion of the disease affects not only the husband but also the children. . . . Another man develops such a dislike of his wife that he cannot endure to keep company with her. Will [divorce or] polygamy cure this evil? Another man's wife falls into palsy or apoplexy, or becomes afflicted with an incurable disease. May the husband reject her under the pretense of incontinence?"[127] Obviously not, said Calvin, as he drew the line firmly at adultery alone as a legitimate ground for divorce.[128]

When properly pled on grounds of adultery, Calvin believed, divorce actions had to be made equally available to husband and wife. "[T]he right to divorce belongs equally and mutually to both sides for both have a mutual and equal obligation to fidelity. Though in other matters the husband is superior [to the wife], in matters of the marriage bed, the wife has an equal right. For he is not the lord of his own body; and therefore, when, by committing adultery, he has dissolved the marriage, his wife is set at liberty."[129] The same is true in reverse for the husband. Once at liberty, the innocent spouse is free to remarry, said Calvin, following conventional Protestant teaching.

Calvin went beyond Protestant convention, however, in his surprising solicitude for the parties after divorce. Both parties, he wrote, would be severely tempted to sexual sin, and both should be granted relief to avoid still greater sin. For the innocent party, Calvin countenanced remarriage—even, if necessary, before issuance of the magistrate's final divorce decree: "[I]f adultery is proven, *even if no sentence is passed,* a Christian church may proceed to marry those who can produce such hearings."[130] Likewise, the wayward party should eventually be allowed to remarry. "Adultery has not been punished as severely as it should have been, and the lives of those who violate the marriage bond have been spared," Calvin wrote glumly in a late-life letter. But then he turned quite pragmatic: "But it would be harsh to prohibit a man from marrying during his whole lifetime if his wife has divorced him for adultery, or to prohibit a woman who has been repudiated by her husband, especially if they have difficulty with being sexually continent; one indulgence necessarily brings the other along with it." Calvin would not allow the guilty party "to fly off immediately to another marriage. The freedom to remarry should be put off for a time, whether for a definite period of time or until the innocent party has remarried."[131]

Calvin considered various other acts within the marital estate—besides sexual intercourse with a third party—to be tantamount to adultery. On one extreme, he regarded sexual perversity with one's own spouse as a violation of the spirit of the Seventh Commandment. "We know to what end marriage was ordained—that persons should live honestly together, and that there should be no beastly looseness and or coupling themselves together like dogs and bitches, or bulls and cows." Married couples "should show that they do not bear God's image in vain."[132] And again: "If married couples recognize that their association is blessed by the Lord, they are thereby admonished not to pollute it with uncontrolled and dissolute lust. . . . For it is fitting that a marriage, once covenanted in the Lord, be called to moderation and modesty."[133] Calvin saw this more as a spiritual law of sexual prudence than a civil law against marital prurience. But he did occasionally press the Genevan Council to reprimand couples who proved too sexually raucous, and issued several stern admonitions on sexual modesty to parishioners and correspondents alike.

On the other extreme, Calvin regarded one spouse's desertion of the other, or both spouses' voluntary separation from each other, as virtual forms of adultery. Husband and wife, he said flatly, "must live together and stay together till death."[134] Any undue separation from bed or board, beyond what was necessary for a spouse to carry out normal civic and vocational obligations, "is close to the appearance of adultery," particularly "if it is prompted by capriciousness or sexual desire."[135] Any abandonment of one's spouse is doubly suspect, especially if done angrily or maliciously.[136] Calvin pressed this logic not only for the simple reason that virile spouses, left on their own, might be tempted to adultery—in mind, if not in fact. He was also concerned that such separations violated God's literal command that husband and wife be joined together permanently in soul, mind, and body. "[I]t is the law of marriage that when a man joins himself to a wife, he takes her to be a companion to live with her and die with her. If the nature of marriage is such, . . . a married man is only half a person, and he can no more separate himself from his wife than cut himself into two pieces."[137]

Calvin thus stood opposed to the traditional canon law and civil law remedy of separation from bed and board. He stood even more firmly opposed to the new social fashion of couples separating simply because "their manners were not congenial, or their appearance did not please, or some other [trivial] offense."[138] Calvin advocated perpetual union of bed and board between husband and wife—by force of law and arms, if necessary.[139] He ordered separated couples to reconcile with each other, deserting spouses to return to their homes, abandoned spouses to forgive the desertion. Where reconciliation proved impossible, Calvin preferred to treat the marriage as dissolved by reason of the presumed adultery of one party, rather than perpetuated without the cohabitation of both parties.[140] This was consistent with his strict biblical reading that adultery is the sole ground for divorce granted by the moral law.

Calvin was not always consistent in his treatment of separation, however. As we saw in the opening story of the French noblewoman, where one party deviates from the faith and abuses the other, Calvin generally allowed only for separation by the innocent spouse, with no right of remarriage.[141] In cases of malicious desertion, he sometimes insisted that the innocent spouse bring proof of actual adultery before a divorce action could lie.[142] Calvin was aware that he thereby left the innocent party subject to sexual temptation. He offered only a vague homily in reply: "Would it not be inhuman to refuse [the innocent party] the remedy of [re]marriage when constantly burning with desire? My answer is that when we are prompted by the infirmity of our flesh, we must have recourse to the remedy; after which it is the Lord's part to bridle and restrain our affections by his Spirit, though matters should not succeed according to our desires."[143]

On this point, Calvin's associate Theodore Beza was more insistent and consistent than Calvin in treating "desertion as adultery" and allowing divorce and remarriage to the innocent party. A party deserted "in soul," through a difference of religion, or "in body," through malicious abandonment, is like the innocent spouse in a case of adultery, said Beza. The innocent party has power either to forgive the fault and restore the marriage or to condemn the fault and confirm its dissolution. The innocent party should seek reconciliation with the wayward spouse "only so long as conscience allows." Thereafter, he or she can abandon the dissolved marriage by filing for divorce, and contract a new marriage if so desired.[144]

For Calvin, the commandment against adultery was equally binding on the unmarried, and equally applicable to both illicit sexual activities per se and various acts leading to the same. Calvin condemned with particular vehemence the sin of fornication—sexual intercourse or other illicit acts of sexual touching by a nonmarried party.[145] He decried at length the widespread practice of casual sex, prostitution, concubinage, premarital sex, nonmarital cohabitation, and other forms of bed hopping that he encountered in modern-day Geneva, as well as in ancient Bible stories. "Today it is not only the common man who flatters himself into thinking that fornication is not such a great and mortal sin. We even see high born persons making light of God by calling fornication a natural sin and a matter of little consequence. There are actually such shameless swine that talk that way."[146] All these actions, Calvin believed, openly defied God's commandment against adultery, and God's commendation of chaste and holy marriage.[147] Calvin had simple biblical counsel to offer against the "scourge of fornication": preach against it constantly, punish it severely by spiritual and criminal sanctions,[148] and portray everything from an individual case of syphilis to a community's encounter with pestilence as God's retribution for the offense.[149] He followed this counsel to the letter.

Calvin stretched the reach of the Seventh Commandment far beyond the sin of actual fornication. For believers abiding by the spiritual law, such an extension was natural, for as Christ taught in the Beatitudes: "Continence involved not only keeping the body free from fornication, but also keeping a chaste mind."[150] But Calvin urged a comparable extension of the civil law of adultery. In his more exuberant moments, he tended to treat all manner of mildly sexual activities—lewdness, dancing, bawdy gaming, sexual innuendo, coarse humor, provocative primping, suggestive plays and literature, and much more—as forms of adultery, punishable by the state.[151] Calvin would not tie the sexy dresser and the swarthy whoremonger to the same stake for flogging or execution. He viewed these more attenuated forms of adultery as violations of milder criminal laws against sumptuousness, punishable by admonition and fines.[152] But he was insistent that even such attenuated

sexual conduct was a form of adultery that deserved both spiritual reproof and criminal sanctions.

The Purpose of
the Marriage Covenant

Starting with the created *structure* of the marriage covenant, Calvin
was able to integrate various biblical and natural norms against bestiality, homosexuality, polygamy, adultery, desertion, and fornication, and
to smuggle in a tepid endorsement of divorce and firmer prohibition
against separation. Turning to the created *purposes* of marriage—mutual
love of husband and wife, mutual procreation of children, and mutual
protection from lust—Calvin was able to integrate several other such
norms.

Sexual dysfunction, Calvin insisted, was an absolute barrier to marriage, for it vitiated all three purposes of marriage. Thus, putative marriages of prepubescent children were null, even if the parties have
reached sufficient maturity to consent to marry, for "the terms of the
marriage cannot be carried out."[153] Marriages of "the frigid and eu-
nuches" were likewise null, for such unions "completely obviate the nature and purpose of marriage. For what is marriage except the joining
of a male and female, and why was it instituted except to produce children and to remedy sexual incontinence?"[154] Calvin called for automatic
annulment of any marriage of a permanently dysfunctional party, and
called for penalties if the condition had been kept secret prior to the
wedding.[155]

Calvin grounded a number of prudential norms for the *unmarried believer* in the created purposes of marriage. Citing both Moses and Paul,
he counseled Christians against marrying unbelievers, for such unions
would invariably jeopardize all three created functions of marriage. The
unbeliever could not know the true meaning of love reflected in Christ,
would not know how to raise children in the love of God, and might not
resist the temptations to lust that marriage was supposed to remedy.[156]
Calvin did not regard differences in religion as an absolute bar to the
contracting of marriage, let alone a ground for annulment or divorce, as
we have seen.[157] Instead, he wrote simply: "When a man is to marry, he
should (so far as possible) choose a wife who will help him in the worship of God . . . who knows God and his word, and who is ready to give
up all idolatry." To do otherwise, said Calvin, was "spiritually unlawful,"
though civilly permissible.[158]

Citing Moses' account of the evil world on the eve of the Flood—"the sons of men saw that the daughters of men were fair and took to wife such as them as they chose"—Calvin counseled against entering marriage with undue levity or lust.[159] "Marriage is a thing too sacred to allow that men should be induced to it by the lust of their eyes," he wrote.[160] "Elegance of form" may certainly have a place in the calculus of marriage.[161] But we "profane the covenant of marriage" when "our appetite becomes brutal, when we are so ravished with the charms of beauty, that those things which are chief are not taken into account."[162]

Calvin laid out "those things which are chief" in his account of what he sought in his own wife: "I am none of those insane lovers who embrace also the vices of those they are in love with, where they are smitten at first sight with a fine figure. This only is the beauty which allures me, if she is chaste, if not too nice and fastidious, if economical, if patient, if there is hope that she will be interested about my health," and if she could produce children.[163] Calvin could not have been surprised that this account did not bring an overwhelming response from eligible women. He did eventually find and marry Idelette de Bure, a pious widow of evangelical stock with two grown children. During their seven years of marriage, they had a son, who died in infancy—"a severe wound," as Calvin put it.[164] His pain was doubled by Idelette's premature death and his stepdaughter Judith's "lustful rush" into marriage and divorce a few years later on account of her adultery.[165]

Calvin chose thereafter to remain a widower and seemed to use this experience in advising other widows and widowers. Citing Paul, he urged widows and widowers to refrain from remarriage if they were beyond childbearing years and "altogether beyond the danger of incontinence."[166] For, in such instances, the marital purposes of procreation and perhaps even mutual love would be compromised, and "the inconveniences of mixed married life" might well not be worth it.[167] "Women are no less at liberty than men to marry a second time upon becoming widows," Calvin insisted, reiterating both his concern for gender equality in questions of sexuality and his condemnation of mandatory celibacy. But neither elderly widows nor elderly widowers should rush to marry too easily.[168] Building on this same moral, Calvin discouraged marriages between young men and elderly women, arguing that such unions "were contrary to the order of nature," for they would not yield children, and "contrary to the law of conscience," for they would tempt the young husband to adultery.[169] He sometimes pressed this counsel in the obverse case as well, even to the point of condemning the late-life espousal of his dear friend and fellow reformer Guillaume Farel to a young maiden.[170]

Calvin also grounded several biblical norms for *married parties* in the created purposes of marriage. Most important, he urged that married couples retain a healthy sex life, even after their childbearing years. "Satan dazzles us . . . to imagine that we are polluted by intercourse," said Calvin.[171] But "when the marital bed is dedicated to the name of the Lord, that is, when parties are joined together in his name, and live honorably, it is something of a holy estate."[172] For "the mantle of marriage exists to sanctify what is defiled and profane; it serves to cleanse what used to be soiled and dirty in itself."[173] Husband and wife should not, therefore, "withhold sex from the other." Nor should they "neglect or reject" one another after intimacy or intercourse.[174] Couples may forgo their sexual obligations for a season, said Calvin, echoing the traditional position on the "Pauline privilege." But such abstinence should occur only by mutual consent and only for a finite period, lest one party be tempted to adultery by too long a wait.[175] The traditional option of maintaining a sexless "spiritual marriage" was anathema to Calvin.[176]

If a couple proved barren, Calvin urged them to accept this as God's providential design. "We are fruitful or barren as God imparts his power," he wrote. Those who are barren should sponsor or adopt orphans or find other ways of serving the next generation.[177] Calvin would hear nothing of concubinage or surrogate motherhood as a viable alternative to sterility, despite the example of Abraham and other Old Testament figures. In taking Hagar as his concubine, "Abraham took a liberty" that God had not countenanced, Calvin believed, and his reward was the perpetual strife between Sarah and Hagar, Isaac and Ishmael, and their many descendents. This, for Calvin, was proof enough that concubinage was no viable option for the modern day.[178] Calvin would also hear nothing of divorce on grounds of sterility. Procreation was only one created purpose of marriage, he counseled. Where it could not be achieved, a couple had to double their efforts to achieve the other purposes of mutual love and mutual protection from lust, "treating each other with chaste tenderness" even where God would not bless them with children.[179]

If, after a time, one marital party became incapable of sexual performance because of frailty, impotence, or sickness, Calvin urged understanding and patience on the part of the other spouse. Here, too, he would hear nothing of concubinage, separation, or divorce as a remedy or a result of this later sexual incapacitation.[180] There was a rather blurry line between automatic annulment of a new marriage where one party proved permanently impotent or frigid, and automatic perpetuation of a long-standing marriage where a spouse once capable of intercourse later became incapacitated. Calvin did little to clarify the line. Theodore Beza and his colleagues on the Geneva consistory did, favoring perpetuation of any such marriage and opting for annulment only if the sexually active party sought it within a few months of the wedding and (obviously) only if the couple lacked children.[181]

If one party contracted leprosy or some other form of contagious disease, Calvin again urged "Christian patience" by the healthy party, and sexual restraint by the afflicted party. He again flatly prohibited concubinage, separation, or divorce as options.[182] In one extreme case, Calvin did allow for separation from bed and board, where a husband had been afflicted with "elephantitis," a disease that dramatically increased his sexual appetite but was highly contagious and dangerous to his wife.[183] It would be "cruel," said Calvin, "to obligate the woman to share a home and marriage bed with a husband who is forgetful of all the laws of nature. We feel that she must be allowed to live as a widow, after a legal investigation by judges has intervened. Meanwhile, she should continue to attend her husband and perform any duties she can, provided that he does not require of her anything virtually unnatural."[184]

The Covenant Model of Marriage in Comparative Perspective

Calvin's covenant theology of marriage was neither very systematic nor entirely consistent. The foregoing account is no simple report from a chapter or two of Calvin's *Institutes* or other systematic works. It is a patchwork quilt, stitched together from many thin strands of argument strewn all over Calvin's late-life commentaries, sermons, letters, consilia, and legal fragments. And, even granting all of Calvin's close distinctions—between believers and nonbelievers, couples and singles, spiritual and civil laws, Old Testament customs and New Testament canons—this patchwork account is not free from anomaly. For example, Calvin harvested a thick sheaf of modern-day prescriptions for marriage from the creation story of Adam and Eve, often reading the Genesis passages inventively and with anticipation of New Testament teachings and customs. But he would take no modern lessons from the Bible's descriptions of Abel's incest, Abraham's concubinage, or Solomon's polygamy, condemning all such "unnatural" actions unequivocally. Calvin read into a few pastoral asides from Paul a very progressive understanding of equality of women in rights to marital sex, parentage, and divorce. But he squeezed out of the creation story a general principle of subordination of women in all other matters, even to the point of denying women a right to propose marriage to a prospective husband.[185] Calvin insisted that any marital impediments of blood and family be grounded in a strict reading of the Bible or be discarded. But he imported, rather casually, various impediments of crime, religion, and quality that had only the shallowest grounding in the Bible. Calvin read the term *adultery* in the Seventh Commandment to include a fantastic range of illicit conduct—from a husband's torrid affairs with a third-party relative to a bit of suggestive sexual innuendo with one's own spouse. But when discussing Christ's permission to divorce on grounds of the same term *adultery,* he read the term narrowly as proven illicit intercourse by one's spouse and a third party. Calvin was remarkably solicitous for the sexual needs and temptations of divorcées, even suggesting that they could remarry before the state issued a divorce decree. But he offered only bland injunctions to "Christian patience" to allay the sexual burning of both single and married persons for whom no natural and licit sexual outlet was available. Even a sympathetic parsing of Calvin's opening distinctions and a generous appreciation for his sixteenth-century rhetorical style cannot explain away these and other anomalies in his presentation.

Such anomalies were inevitable and not fatal. Given the loose literary forums and forms in which Calvin worked, it was inevitable that loose ends and loose logic would remain, undetected. This was doubly inevitable given the conditions during which Calvin wrote in his later life: rapidly deteriorating health, escalating demands for his pastoral and political counsel, bitter controversies over the execution of Michael Servetus, and a proliferation of other demands associated with subjects of reform that had nothing to do with marriage and family life.[186] In that context, it was remarkable that Calvin was able to rise to the level of refinement and comprehension that he did.

The profundity of Calvin's insights for marriage was not lost on his contemporaries or his followers. Even in prototypical form, Calvin's covenant theology of marriage proved to be a powerful Protestant model for marriage that exercised an enormous and enduring influence on the Western tradition.

Calvin's covenantal model mediated both the sacramental and the contractual models of marriage that pressed for recognition in his day. On the one hand, this covenantal model confirmed the sacred and sanctifying qualities of marriage, without ascribing to it sacramental functions. Calvin now held a far more exulted spiritual view of marriage than he had earlier espoused. He described marriage in sweeping spiritual terms as "a sacred bond," "a holy fellowship," "a divine partnership," "a loving association," "a heavenly calling," "the fountainhead of life," "the holiest kind of company in all the world," "the principal and most sacred . . . of all the offices pertaining to human society."[187] Conjugal love is "holy" when "husband and wife are joined in one body and one soul."[188] "God reigns in a little household, even one in dire poverty, when the husband and the wife dedicate themselves to their duties to each other. Here there is a holiness greater and nearer the kingdom of God than there is even in a cloister."[189] Calvin had come a long way from his earlier glum description of marriage as "a good ordinance, just like farming, building, cobbling, and barbering."

With this more exulted spiritual view of marriage, Calvin also described more fully the biblical uses of marriage to symbolize the relationship of God and humanity. He analyzed at length the Old Testament image of Yahweh's covenant of marriage with Israel, and Israel's proclivity for "playing the harlot"—worshiping false gods and allying with Gentile neighbors, much as delinquent spouses abandon faith in God and faithfulness to each other.[190] He returned repeatedly to the New Testament image of Christ's marriage to the church, holding up Christ's faith and sacrificial love toward us as a model to which spouses and parents should aspire.[191] He went so far as to say that "marriage is the holiest bond that God has set among us," for it is "a figure of the Son of God and all the faithful," "a symbol of our divine covenant with our Father."[192] But then, almost in self-chiding, Calvin reiterated his earlier position that marriage, though symbolic of God's relationship with persons, is not a sacrament, for it does not confirm a divine promise. "Anyone who would classify such similitudes with the sacraments ought to be sent to a mental hospital."[193]

On the other hand, Calvin's covenantal model confirmed the contractual and consensual qualities of marriage, without subjecting it to the personal preferences of the parties. "It is the mutual consent of the man and the woman that . . . constitutes marriage," Calvin insisted, echoing traditional views.[194] Lack of true consent—by reason of immaturity, drunkenness, insincerity, conditionality, mistake, fraud, coercion, or similar impairment—perforce breaks the marriage contract, just as it breaks any other contract.[195]

But marriage is more than a contract and turns on more than the voluntary consent of the parties. God is a third party to every marriage, Calvin believed, and God has set its basic terms in the order and law of creation. "Other contracts depend on the mere inclination of men, and can be entered into and dissolved by that same inclination."[196] Not so the covenant of marriage. Our "freedom of contract" in marriage is effectively limited to choosing which party to marry from among the mature, unrelated, virile members of the opposite sex available to us. We have no freedom to forgo marriage—unless we have the rare gift of natural continence—for else we "spurn God's remedy for lust" and "tempt our nature" to sexual perversity.[197] We also have no freedom to abandon marriage, "for otherwise the whole order of nature would be overthrown."[198] "Consider what will be left of safety in the world—of order, of loyalty, of honesty, of assurance—if marriage, which is the most sacred union, and ought to be most faithfully guarded, can thus be violated," Calvin thundered.[199] "In truth, all contracts and all promises that we make ought to be faithfully upheld. But if we should make a comparison, it is not without cause that marriage is called a covenant with God," for it cannot be broken.[200]

Calvin's covenantal model of marriage not only mediated the sacramental and contractual models of marriage that he encountered in Geneva. It also modified the social model of marriage that he inherited from Wittenberg. Using the two kingdoms theory, Luther and his colleagues had treated marriage as a social estate of the earthly kingdom alone—an institution fundamentally earthly in nature, social in function, civil in governance. Calvin echoed and endorsed these evangelical teachings on marriage.[201] But he also superimposed on this two kingdoms framework a doctrine of marriage as covenant. The effect of this was to add a spiritual dimension to marriage life in the earthly kingdom, a marital obligation to spiritual life in the heavenly kingdom, and complementary marital roles for both church and state in the governance of both kingdoms.

Marriage was an earthly order and obligation for all persons, said Calvin, echoing Luther. But it also had vital spiritual sources and sanctions for Christians. Marriage required the coercive power of the state to preserve its integrity. But it also required the spiritual counsel of the church to demonstrate its necessity. Marriage was grounded in the will and consent of the parties. But it was also founded in the creation and commandments of God. Marriage deterred sinful persons from the lust and incontinence of this earthly life. But it also symbolized for them the love and sacrifice of the heavenly life. Marriage served the social purpose of procreation and protection from sin. But it also served the divine purpose of sanctification and edification by grace. None of these sentiments was altogether original with Calvin, nor were they entirely unknown to Luther. But, using the doctrine of covenant, Calvin was able to cast these traditional teachings into a new ensemble, with new theological emphases and new legal implications.

Calvin's covenantal model of marriage also helped to refine and rationalize many of the rules set out in the Geneva Marriage Ordinance of 1545 and its amendments. For example, the doctrine of covenant provided Calvin with a sturdy new rationale for the familiar Protestant requirement that the formation of marriages be intensely public affairs. Earlier Protestant reformers (as well as later Catholic theologians at the

Council of Trent) had grounded the involvement of various parties in the formation of marriage in discrete biblical passages, with no general theory to integrate them. Parental consent was based on the Fourth Commandment of the Decalogue and Paul's admonitions to parents and children. Mandatory witnesses to betrothals and espousals was rooted in Peter's disquisitions on the priesthood of believers. Church consecration and celebration of the marriage was grounded in Christ's delegation of the power of the keys to Peter and the apostles. Civil registration and publication of marriage banns was based on Paul's general descriptions of state power in Romans 13. Calvin repeated, and also embellished, these familiar biblical rationales for the involvement of each party in the process of marriage formation.[202] But he also integrated these separate biblical rationales by treating all four of these parties as allied agents of God in the formation of the marital covenant. He thereby rebuffed the agitation in his day for the truncation of the public formalities and functionaries of marriage formation. He also helped to confirm the place of parents, peers, ministers, and magistrates in the marriage process for centuries to come. Subsequent generations of reformed theologians and jurists—building on Calvin's work as well as that of his contemporary, Heinrich Bullinger, who espoused similar sentiments,[203] and contemporaneous Anabaptist writers[204]—elaborated at length this covenantal conception of a public marriage process.

Similarly, the doctrine of covenant allowed Calvin to tighten the rules and standards for entering and exiting marriages. The 1545 Marriage Ordinance distinguished clearly between betrothal and marriage, annulment and divorce. But at the same time, it conflated terms like rescission, dissolution, nullity, voidness, and the like, leaving unclear the precise legal effect of a given defect, impediment, or illicit action.[205] Calvin's exposition on the moral law for the covenant of marriage made this somewhat clearer. Betrothals and marriages were automatically annulled if the parties breached Levitical impediments or involved a sexually dysfunctional party. Betrothals could be broken by either party, or at the instigation of a third party, for any number of reasons of Christian prudence—differences in religion or quality, concerns for compatibility, maturity, security, and the like. Marriages once entered were virtually permanent. The rules of Christian prudence that could annul betrothals could not annul marriages. Separation from bed or board was not an option, save in the most dire case of danger to an innocent spouse's body and soul. Divorce could be granted on strict biblical grounds of adultery or a fully proven case of malicious desertion that was tantamount to adultery.

Geneva's New Law
of Marriage in Action

This new covenantal understanding of marriage and family life did not remain confined to sermons, commentaries, and letters. In the course of the 1550s and thereafter, it also came to vivid legal application in the work of the Geneva consistory—led by Calvin, still serving as the Moderator of the Company of Pastors. Newly convinced of the biblical value and validity of Geneva's statutory reforms of marriage, Calvin and his consistory colleagues set out to render this new law on the books a new law in action.

The Geneva Consistory

The consistory's stepped-up activities in the enforcement of Genevan marriage law was driven not only by new theological conviction but also by new political power. For more than a decade after his return to Geneva in 1541, Calvin and other new emigrés to the city had been caught up in an escalating battle of political wills with the local landed aristocracy. One gravamen of their dispute concerned the refugees' access to citizenship, suffrage, and attendant political and professional positions (Calvin, despite his political prominence, did not gain Genevan citizenship in Geneva until December 1559, less than five years before his death.) The other issue was the degree of legal and religious control that could be exercised by the consistory and clergy of the new reformed churches, an issue exacerbated by the controversial execution for heresy of Michael Servetus on October 27, 1553. Open riot over both these issues broke out in Geneva in early 1555, and episodes of insurrectionary violence erupted several times thereafter. The party in favor of Calvin and his colleagues ultimately prevailed, leading to the removal of their more hardened opponents from prominent political positions—and indeed the withdrawal of several of them from Geneva altogether.[206]

A crucial new weapon won in this political battle was the consistory's unequivocal power to enforce its spiritual discipline by using the ban (preclusion from the Eucharist) and excommunication (exclusion from the church altogether). The consistory announced and defended this prize proudly in front of the entire assembly of Genevan officials. The notary reports: "John Calvin, in the name of the consistory, together with the ministers of the city who are present with him, most adequately refuted the arguments which had been advanced for the diminution, indeed the demolition, of the Consistory's authority. He showed, on the basis of passages in the Holy Bible and from the consistent practice of the pure [apostolic] church, what the true practice of excommunication was, and to whom was given the power to excommunicate or admit to communion. Despite every effort of Satan to overthrow so Godly and useful an order [as excommunication and the ban] . . . God has been victorious."[207]

This "Godly victory" helped to restore to the Geneva consistory a good deal of the power of the traditional Catholic Church courts over questions of marital morality, but now on a new theological grounding. The Catholic Church had based its power to ban and excommunicate on the sacrament of penance. All baptized believers, the Church had taught, were required to confess their sins and to reconcile themselves to God, on pain of eternal punishment. The Church had claimed the authority to define the vices that required confession, to hear the sinner's confession, to absolve him from eternal punishment, and to prescribe virtuous works of purgation. Failure to adhere to the Church's moral regimen, for marriage and many other moral matters, could lead to the ban or, in extreme cases, excommunication—a great peril to eternal life.[208]

The Reformed Church of Geneva based its jurisdiction over morality on the sacrament of the Eucharist (which they called Holy Communion or the Lord's Supper). Baptized believers, who sought to partake of communion, the Geneva Church taught, were required "to examine their hearts and confess their sins," lest they "profane and pollute" the sacrament and "eat and drink judgment upon themselves" and upon the whole congregation.[209] To be banned from communion or excommunicated altogether was not necessarily threatening to eternal life. But in the small community of Geneva, it was a threat to civil life. Banned or excommunicated parties often faced various civil deprivations—the denial or cancellation of professional licenses, the loss of business clients, the suspension of voting rights, the denial of standing to press civil suits, the abridgment of criminal procedural protections—as well as many unofficial forms of social shunning.[210] Thus the addition of the ban and excommunication to its arsenal of spiritual weapons considerably enhanced the consistory's power over questions of sexuality, marriage, and family life in Geneva.

A picture of the Geneva consistory's enhanced involvement in marriage questions can be seen in the cases that came before it in the first nine months of 1557—the time before the harvest, when marital litigation was at its briskest. This was the first full season of hearings after the political tumult of Geneva had died down, when Calvin and his colleagues could set about their consistory work in earnest. In this nine-month period, the consistory heard some eighty cases on questions of marriage, family, and sexual conduct—up to seven cases per week. As in its cases of a decade before, the consistory still adhered closely to the rules of the Marriage Ordinance of 1545 and various complementary civil and criminal norms. But now the consistory often offered more by way of legal and theological rationale for its decisions. It made considerable use of the ban—though not excommunication—to enforce its discipline, particularly in cases of sexual misconduct or abuse. And it collaborated more closely and fully with the Council on cases involving difficult issues, recalcitrant parties, or disputed testimony. This was not only theologically commended, but strategically wise. The Geneva Council held far broader powers of arrest and subpoena and had license to extract evidence from obstinate witnesses by force, by torture if necessary.[211]

Disputed Betrothals and Marriages

Cases of disputed betrothals occupied a good deal of space on the consistory's docket in 1557. A few of these cases were simple disputes between the betrothed parties. A woman was relieved of her engagement to a young man who had since their engagement contracted syphilis. In the consistory's view, the disease not only betrayed his unfaithfulness to her, but to proceed to marriage would also endanger her health and that of her children. The woman was freed from her engagement. The man was sent to the Council for punishment for his presumed fornication.[212] Another woman "requested the consistory for the right not to marry [her fiancé] even though they were engaged." The notary reports no stated reason for her disaffection, though the record hints at his "lack of employment." Her fiancé testified that "it was by his own will and deliberation to have her as his wife." The consistory concluded that it "finds nothing to stop the marriage from having effect" and ordered the couple to marry after he had found employment.[213] A man requested the consistory to permit him to marry on the strength of a prenuptial contract that he and his fiancée had executed some time earlier. The consistory ordered the man to prove that he had made appropriate arrangements with the woman's family and that the contract was legitimate.[214] The man was back before the consistory the following week, accompanied by a lawyer, to corroborate the legitimacy of the contract and the arrangement. The consistory was convinced and ordered the marriage to proceed with all due speed "according to God."[215]

Most of the disputed betrothal cases heard in 1557 concerned the consent of parents or guardians to the pending nuptials. A young woman and her father were reprimanded for entering a prenuptial contract for marriage without procuring the consent of the future groom's father.[216] Another father was ordered to procure a letter of consent from the father of the minor groom, even though he lived in a distant foreign city, and procurement of the letter could well delay the wedding unduly.[217] A guardian was questioned closely about his delayed consent to his ward's betrothal; only when he had assured the consistory that he consented fully to the union, and was legitimately delayed in giving his consent, did the consistory allow the marriage to proceed.[218] A bickering pair of parents was sent to the Council to sort out conflicting testimony over whether the father had in fact consented to the marriage of his minor daughter.[219] A young orphaned woman, who promised marriage to two gentlemen seriatim, was sent with her guardian and two prospective husbands to the Council for investigation and reproof.[220] The Council decided to dissolve the first secret betrothal, which both the young woman and the guardian "did not like," and to confirm the second betrothal, because this was the match that the guardian had suggested and approved.[221]

The consistory did reserve the right to second-guess parents suspected of acting in bad faith. It nullified the engagement of a handicapped fourteen-year-old girl, despite the father's insistence on her marriage and production of a fully executed prenuptial contract. The consistory considered the woman too young to be married, and judged that her disabling "hump" would likely obstruct childbearing, perhaps even intercourse.[222] It confirmed the engagement and marriage of another couple, despite the loud post hoc protests of the girl's father. The father had consented to his daughter's engagement. Thereafter, the couple had been properly married in a church, but apparently without his knowledge. The father shortly thereafter withdrew his consent to the engagement and marriage, and forcibly took his daughter back into his own custody. When questioned by the consistory, the father charged that his son-in-law had not tendered to him the full dower payment he had promised, causing the father to lose some properties he had intended to buy with the promised funds. The consistory tried to force the young man to make the payment, but the father said he would refuse it, if tendered, because he now believed the young man to be dishonest. The consistory decided to send the matter to the Council for final disposition, recommending that "such marriage should not be broken and may not be dissolved, for this would open the door to many others."[223] The Council, on investigation, concurred and, through the consistory, ordered the father to return his daughter to her husband, and for the marriage to continue, even without his consent.[224]

The consistory also periodically dissolved engagements that violated other rules of Christian prudence. The consistory applied rather literally Calvin's recommendations against marriages between parties with sharp differences in age. It annulled the engagement of a twenty-five-year-old man to a woman "at least as old as his mother," arguing that "women should not be married with men who are not close to them in age, and those who are no longer able to bear children should not marry younger men." Calvin and two colleagues were commissioned to report the matter to the Small Council so "as to avoid the consequences that even the pagans do not suffer" and "so that the order of nature would not be broken."[225] The consistory ruled similarly in a case of a betrothal between a twenty-two-year-old man and a widow of forty, who reportedly already had more than twenty children. The consistory not only annulled the betrothal, but because the parties had already consummated their engagement, the consistory also banned both parties from the Lord's Supper and referred them to the Council for punishment of their fornication.[226]

The consistory pressed this same logic to order the annulment of "a marriage already contracted" between a widow, over seventy years old, and a servant of hers, aged twenty-seven or twenty-eight. The sole stated ground for the annulment was "too great an inequality of age" between the couple. There was no reported evidence of fraud or stratagem by the young man, though marriage between servants and their masters was much frowned upon in that day. The Council agreed with the consistory, holding that such marriages were "against the order of nature" and placed the young man in "sore temptation to adultery."[227] The consistory apparently rethought its position shortly thereafter—or, more likely, just applied it differently in the case of a widower—for it confirmed, despite Calvin's sharp protestations, the engagement of the 68-year-old Geneva reformer Guillaume Farel and a young woman some four decades his junior.[228]

A few of these betrothal cases were considerably more involved and required protracted evidentiary hearings and considerable legal discernment from the consistory. In these cases, Calvin's legal talents shone through. In one case, the consistory was asked to determine whether an engaged man and woman were bound by a long-standing, but now stale, betrothal. Three years before, the man had procured the consent of the woman's father for permission to marry and had given an engagement ring to the woman. The woman had accepted his proposal for marriage, but on condition that both of her parents consent to their union and that the man make an additional dowry gift, of considerable value, to her family. The man apparently never made the additional gift, nor did he procure her mother's consent. The betrothed parties, who had grown disenchanted with each other over the years, asked whether the marriage needed to go forward. Calvin undertook the consistory's investigation, the notary reports, questioning at length the woman's mother (without oath) as well as the parties and their siblings. An obvious ground for annulment of the betrothal was that the parties had strayed well beyond the statutory six-week window between betrothal and wedding. Without stating his grounds, Calvin eventually found that there was no real marriage, and the parties could "with a clear conscience be set free from any obligation" to marry.[229]

Another case of protracted betrothal raised more sinister facts. A father petitioned the consistory to determine the legitimacy of a betrothal between his minor daughter and a man of the age of consent. The father had approved the match more than two years before. The man had then deserted his fiancée inexplicably. The young man testified that he had been imprisoned in France for his adherence to the evangelical cause. He further testified that he and his fiancée had reconciled since his return and that he had made appropriate arrangements with her family. The consistory took the case under advisement and ordered him to reappear with corroborating witnesses.[230] Two weeks later, the same father was back before the consistory, now with witnesses who testified that the young man was fraudulently exploiting the one-year period that deserted maidens had to wait before being freed from their betrothals. The young man, they said, "did not want to take her for his wife, but he would return here every year to prevent the girl from getting married, and he would oppose any man who would like to marry her." Calvin cross-examined the man at length and discovered that he, in fact, had married someone else in France and had children. Moreover, rather than being imprisoned for his evangelical sentiments, he had, it seemed, voluntarily partaken of the Catholic mass and Eucharist. Calvin, on behalf of the consistory, reprimanded the young man severely, ordered him to bring his wife and children to Geneva, banned him from the Lord's Supper, and, later, ordered him to appear before the Council for criminal sanctions.[231]

The consistory was asked to determine the legitimacy of a betrothal between a young man and a young woman, both under the age of majority. The young man had apparently used ample gifts of liquor to induce her family to consent to the union and had, since receiving the same, fraternized rather freely with the woman, much to her family's chagrin. On hearing these developments, the consistory ordered the young woman to remain in her parents' home while the case was pending. It then ordered that the marriage could proceed only if both sets of parents would state their consent to the union.[232] The young man's parents appeared the following week to protest the marriage—loudly. Given the amount of putative sexual contact between the couple to date, the consistory removed the case to the Small Council, recommending dissolution of the betrothal and a permanent prohibition against the parties' seeing each other again. The Council agreed.[233]

The consistory judged the legitimacy not only of these budding new unions but also of the existing marriages of couples newly arrived in Geneva. New emigrés were generally required to register with the city clerk and provide proof, inter alia, of their marital status. A sealed marriage certificate together with a letter of introduction from the syndic of the foreign city was generally adequate, and such cases were rubber-stamped if and when they came to the consistory for approval.[234]

Absent such proof of the foreigners' marriage, however, the consistory would review the evidence more closely. Three such cases in 1557 involved the secret marriages of former Catholic priests newly converted to the Protestant cause. In one case, the consistory investigated a couple who had moved to Geneva in order to experience "a true Reformation of the Gospel." The couple and several witnesses testified that they had been secretly married in the Catholic Church but, given the man's clerical status at the time, "without the promises required." They had lived faithfully in marriage ever since, and adduced several credible character witnesses. After considerable deliberation, the consistory decided simply to "confirm the marriage."[235] In another case, the consistory investigated the marriage of a former Catholic priest and his former maid. The man testified that he had secretly married the woman when he was a priest and that they had a daughter, now fully grown. Though they had no character witnesses, and though he had been delayed for some time before joining his wife in Geneva, the consistory seemed convinced of their sincerity. The decision was that "the marriage should be done again in this city, and the judge should be asked to sign their banns" of marriage, which would then be announced from the pulpit.[236] The consistory reached the same conclusion in the case of a former priest who said that "his marriage was not done according to God, and wants it to be confirmed and approved in the congregation of believers." He was referred to the Council for appropriate action.[237]

Sexual Offenses

The consistory's briskest business came in the enforcement of Geneva's expansive laws against fornication and adultery. The consistory dealt summarily with minor sexual offenses. A young man was reprimanded for kissing a young woman without the permission of her father or guardian, and ordered not to see her again.[238] Another single man was admonished for regularly frequenting the house of a married woman while her husband was away, and forbidden from returning to her home on pain of spiritual punishment.[239] A man was banned from the Lord's Supper, and recommended to the Council for dismissal from the position of city guard for allowing his betrothed daughter and fiancé secretly to celebrate and consummate their marriage in his own house.[240] Another man was likewise banned for secretly and "with bad intentions" "putting his hand under a widow's apron and saying that they should have a drink." The woman was banned as well, for good measure, since "she should change her behavior."[241] A group of raucous partygoers was reprimanded and banned from the Lord's Supper for "singing bad songs"—presumably sexually ribald or blasphemous songs, given the severity of the punishment.[242]

Cases of fornication and premarital sex were quite common, and generally met first with stern spiritual sanctions aimed at extracting confessions from the parties. A young man was banned from the Lord's Supper for fornicating with a maid and not confessing his sin.[243] Another young man, who had excused himself from the Lord's Supper because of his fornication with a maid, successfully petitioned the consistory to forgive him and allow him to communion.[244] A fornicating couple was reprimanded and, when they failed to confess their sin, were sent to the Council for punishment.[245] A secretly betrothed couple, now expecting a child, was banned from the Lord's Supper for their secret engagement, their fornication, and their earlier participation in the Lord's Supper while having their secret sins unconfessed.[246] An unmarried man, who had already confessed to fathering an illegitimate child, was questioned whether he was now having sex with his maid. He pled innocence and offered to dismiss the maid if the consistory recommended it. The consistory at first declined his offer and banned him from the Lord's Supper instead. But, on further deliberation, they reversed themselves, accepted his offer to dismiss the maid, and dismissed him with admonition.[247]

The consistory generally insisted on "shotgun weddings" for parties whose sexual experimentation led to pregnancy. The consistory recommended to the Council to order such a wedding between a woman, newly with child, and her lover, who lived in the city of Berne.[248] In another case, it ordered a local man to appear for spiritual reproof and marital instructions after he had, with promises of marriage, wooed and impregnated a maid. Both parties were banned from the Lord's Supper for fornication; the ban was lifted after they agreed to marry.[249] In another case, the consistory subpoenaed an unmarried and pregnant maid to testify whether a suspect fellow servant was the father of her child. She admitted that the servant had fondled her, but that she did not have sex with him. The father of the child, she said, was a Frenchman who had sojourned briefly at the house but was now beyond reach. The maid was spiritually admonished for her fornication. When it was discovered she had already secretly borne an illegitimate child, she was sent to the Council for punishment "so that the city may be purged."[250]

The consistory generally collaborated with the Small Council on cases involving more serious sexual misconduct or more recalcitrant parties. In one case, the consistory haled before it a whole battery of witnesses who testified to the purported adulterous affair of two married parties. The consistory heard enough hearsay testimony and circumstantial evidence of adultery to cause anyone to blush, but the sole eyewitness was a young girl whose testimony was not considered sufficient. When the consistory ordered the accused parties to confess their adultery, they both steadfastly maintained their innocence, despite threats of the ban. The consistory decided to refer the matter to the Council for further inquiry, sending along a thick file of collected testimony.[251] In another case, after several witnesses testified, a man confessed to seducing a married woman. He then made light of his action, however, saying that "though he was a great sinner, . . . the Lord was an even greater forgiver." Perhaps so, but the consistory was not so forgiving. They banned him from the Lord's Supper and sent him to the Council "in order to purge the city of such rabbles."[252]

A man and a widow, newly engaged, were reprimanded for visiting and talking to each other "as husband and wife," and enjoined from further such contact until their wedding day.[253] When the Council later reported that the couple continued to see each other, the consistory came down hard on the couple: "They must be punished for being sexually immoral and disobedient." Moreover, the consistory decided to investigate their actions while the widow had still been married, and if there was any hint of adultery, "their marriage should be forbidden and broken."[254] The consistory was equally hard on a man alleged to have raped at least one of his maids and impregnated one or two others. A flock of witnesses testified against him. He denied the charges flatly. He was threatened with the ban and removal of the case to the Council for severe corporal punishment. He persisted in his denial. The consistory followed through on their threat, "leaving him to deal with his conscience."[255]

The consistory investigated at some length the adulterous pursuits of Jean Fabri, a Geneva minister, with a married woman parishioner.

According to the woman's testimony, Fabri had visited her home with some regularity, "coming into her garden and into her house." He enticed her "many times, saying that her husband was too skinny, and that she should not have children with him." Fabri also "enticed her into her bedroom and sought to kiss her and touch her." The woman had reported these attempted seductions to her husband, who apparently had banished her from their home. When confronted by the consistory, Fabri confessed that "Satan has seduced him, and he has enticed her, having conceived bad thoughts . . . but he never wanted to kiss her or touch her." Speaking for the consistory, Calvin denounced the entire affair as "a great scandal." Fabri was eventually stripped of his office and subjected to imprisonment and a severe flogging. The woman was referred to the Small Council for protection from her husband during her banishment.[256]

Only one other case of wife abuse is reported in the consistory record of 1557. A husband was reprimanded and temporarily banned from the Lord's Supper for beating his wife. He testified that "he would quit entirely and go to the Catholic Church if he could not beat his wife if she did displeasing things." Calvin, on behalf of the consistory, reprimanded him. After the man apologized for his actions and testimony, the ban was lifted, and he "was accepted to the Lord's Supper, so long as he set a good example for others."[257]

Annulment and Divorce

Disputed betrothals and marriages and sexual misconduct by the married and unmarried comprised the vast bulk of the consistory's business in 1557. Only a small handful of cases of marital dissolution came before it, although some such cases were also heard directly by the Small Council. Two consistory cases touched on questions of desertion. In one case, a woman requested a divorce on grounds of her husband's desertion. She introduced into evidence several letters from him attesting to his desertion. The consistory found the letters—which were apparently submitted only in translation and unsigned by the husband—"not sufficient enough to grant her a divorce at present," and ordered her to wait the prescribed one-year period.[258] The woman's case does not appear in the record again. In a second case, the consistory investigated the propriety of an Italian man's rather aggressive courtship of a deserted wife in Geneva. The woman testified that she had been deserted for more than a year. Her suitor had brought her the news of her husband's death. She had consulted Calvin about the propriety of courting this new gentleman, and he had approved. The woman's sisters-in-law, however, testified that her husband (their brother) was still alive, and that her suitor was acting in bad faith. The consistory, on investigation, found that the gentleman suitor had indeed acted "fraudulently" in reporting her husband's death. They enjoined him from further courtship of the woman and "advised the Italian prosecutor to be aware."[259] A year later, the woman successfully brought an *ex parte* divorce action for desertion.

One case dealt with involuntary annulment of an "incestuous marriage," presumably a marriage between persons related by a prohibited degree of consanguinity. Apparently, the parties had married with knowledge of their impediment, for, on discovery, the wife was whipped and banished from the city "to avoid scandal." The husband was granted temporary domicile in the city to collect their property. Ironically, he was also told "if he wants to have her, he may go live with her," provided they stay out of the city. If he returned to the city, the marriage would be deemed dissolved, and the parties would be punished for their incest.[260]

The clear cause célèbre of 1557 was the divorce of John Calvin's brother, Antoine, from his socially prominent wife, Anne Le Fert, a case recently brought to life by Robert Kingdon.[261] Antoine and Anne lived with John, in the parsonage, throughout their married lives. The relationships between Antoine and Anne, and John and Anne were perennially testy, occasionally tempestuous. Already in 1548, John Calvin had, on his own initiative, called on the consistory to investigate his sister-in-law on "suspicion of adultery" with Jean Chantemps, the son of a local noble. Jean had been frequenting Calvin's house regularly, particularly when the Calvin brothers were away. He had brought Anne a gift of a ring and had eaten meals there several times. What had "greatly afflicted his heart," Calvin reported to the consistory, was that Jean had visited Anne under very suspicious circumstances one Sunday when John and Antoine were at church services. The following week, he had broken into her bedroom in the middle of the night. Jean admitted to "hugging" Anne lustfully and behaving "indecently," but said she had spurned him.

The consistory (having recused Calvin) conducted its investigation and pressed the parties to confess their adultery. They refused and were referred to the Small Council for imprisonment and further investigation. No charges were ultimately brought. The case was returned to the consistory, and Anne, Antoine, and John were called to "a ceremony of reconciliation," in Kingdon's apt phrase, featuring Anne's public kneeling before Antoine and John and begging their forgiveness for her untoward behavior.[262]

Forgiveness for one presumed sexual offense did not inoculate Anne against condemnation for another. John and Antoine Calvin were back before the consistory in early 1557, now asking that Antoine be "given the right to divorce his wife" on account of her second alleged act of adultery.[263] Anne was now charged with fraternizing with one of her disabled servants—the "hunchback" Pierre, as he was called in the record. Both the consistory and the Council investigated the case at great length, summoning several rounds of witnesses, commissioning three expert opinions, and cross-examining Anne and "the hunchback" repeatedly, sometimes together, sometimes separately. John Calvin, though again recused from the consistory's deliberations, served actively as legal counsel to his brother and seems to have had a considerable hand in crafting his brother's petition and in influencing the Council's activities. Anne and Pierre were imprisoned throughout the proceedings, and in later interrogations before the Council, Anne was twice tortured in an effort to extract a confession of adultery. Neither party confessed. The testimony of sundry witnesses and the circumstantial evidence of repeated meetings and suspicious conduct by the two were enough to convince the Council to grant the divorce on grounds of Anne's adultery. She was permanently banished from Geneva—on twenty-four hours notice—and ultimately remarried a few years later. Antoine was released from his marriage and remarried a few years later in Geneva.[264]

Patterns of Litigation

The pathbreaking work in the Genevan archives by Robert Kingdon, Cornelia Seeger, and Walter Köhler, among others, suggests that this case law of 1557 was quite typical of the Genevan law in action in the 1550s and thereafter.[265] The consistory had seized upon its new marital jurisdiction with alacrity in the aftermath of the 1555 riots in Geneva. They maintained a comparably full docket of cases for the next two decades, addressing many of the same issues as the consistory of 1557, with similar results.[266]

The consistory and Council heard numerous cases of disputed betrothals. They automatically annulled betrothals on the discovery of a Levitical impediment of a blood or family relationship between the parties, potential bigamy by one party, or obvious impotence or other sexual dysfunction of one party. Parties who sought to conceal these conditions before marriage were subject to rather severe spiritual and criminal sanctions. The consistory and Council generally annulled betrothals of minors who were immature, prepubescent, lacked parental consent, or were coerced or tricked into the betrothal—again, often sanctioning guilty parties in the process. They also generally annulled betrothals if one party contracted a contagious disease or was convicted for a crime, or if the parties were separated by too great a difference of age, religion, quality, and, in a few instances, even social status. They rarely annulled betrothals if parties failed to have their banns published, delayed their wedding unduly, cohabited or experimented sexually, were delinquent in dower payments, or disputed among themselves over jobs, property, or living arrangements. In most such instances, the consistory preferred to subject the parties to spiritual or civil sanctions, but compel them to get married. Malicious desertion of a fiancé(e) generally broke the engagement and exposed the deserter to spiritual and civil sanctions. But a mere change of heart by either party was often not a sufficient ground for annulment of a betrothal, particularly if prenuptial contracts were executed and dower payments had been tendered.[267]

While betrothals were relatively easy to annul, consummated marriages were not. The consistory and Council did annul marriages on the stated statutory grounds of consanguinity, affinity, bigamy, or impotence. They generally dissolved marriages where, shortly after their wedding, the husband discovered the woman taken to be a virgin was not so. They also lent a sympathetic ear to parties who, shortly after the wedding, complained that the spouse had become fiercely antagonistic and abusive, contracted a contagious disease, or was charged with a serious crime committed before the wedding. Most other pleas for annulment, even those brought by disheartened parents who learned of their minor children's marriage after the fact, were not successful, although the children could face serious spiritual and criminal sanctions for their disobedience and had little recourse if their parents chose to retaliate by disinheriting them.[268]

The consistory and Council were even more reserved about granting divorces of consummated marriages. The only stated statutory grounds for divorce were proven adultery and malicious desertion, and the reported cases did nothing to create new grounds. The burden of proof on the innocent party was quite high—"absurdly high" for women petitioners, according to Cornelia Seeger.[269] Petitioners had to walk a tightrope between the consistory's spiritual counsel to be reconciled and the Council's evidentiary demands to prove their spouse's wrongdoing and their own innocence at the same time. The vast majority of parties could not meet this burden of proof. Fewer than forty divorces were granted during Calvin's Geneva tenure from 1541–1564, almost all with male petitioners, and most on grounds of adultery.[270] This was a very low rate of divorce, which persisted for the next two centuries. Divorce rates in Geneva at the *opening* of the twentieth century were one-hundred times higher.[271]

A cause and consequence of such low divorce rates in sixteenth-century Geneva was that the Geneva Council and consistory reinstituted the traditional canon law remedy of separation from bed and board, despite Calvin's strong protestations against it. In cases of severe wife or child abuse, perennial fighting between couples, habitual desertion, contagious disease, habitual frigidity, and the like, the consistory and Council would simply separate the parties if all efforts at reconciliation failed.

Preservation and Colonization

The reformation of marriage introduced in sixteenth-century Geneva did not die with John Calvin in 1564. Calvin and his followers had worked hard to preserve the new theology and law of marriage in a variety of media. The Geneva Bible included suggestive notes on marriage in the margin of the relevant texts of the Gospels and the Pauline epistles. The Geneva Catechism and student handbooks of the Geneva Academy included ample discussions of marriage, divorce, and sexual conduct. A growing number of published letters, sermons, opinions, and biblical commentaries by Calvin and Beza placed before the reader a large cache of learned theological discussions of marriage. The Geneva Ecclesiastical Ordinance of 1561 incorporated Calvin's Marriage Ordinance of 1545, amply amended and emended with further norms suggested by the intervening years of litigation. "Change nothing!" was Calvin's famous deathbed instruction to his followers who had gathered to hear his final advice. On marriage matters, at least, his immediate followers obliged him.

This rich literary preservation of Calvin's reformation work not only ensured its survival in Geneva and surrounding rural communities in subsequent generations. It also helped in the colonization of Calvinist communities in various parts of Europe and eventually overseas to America. A host of new communities, inspired by the writings of Calvin, Beza, and their Genevan colleagues, sprang up in the later sixteenth century and thereafter: French Huguenots, Dutch Pietists, Scottish Presbyterians, English and New England Puritans, and various smaller communities in the German Palatinate, Poland, Czechoslovakia, Hungary, and eventually South Africa.[272] Many of the first leaders of these communities were educated in the Geneva Academy. Many later leaders were weaned on the rich corpus of Calvin's writings that came available to them, often in local translations.

These farflung Calvinist communities were not replicas of Geneva.

Their leaders did not repeat in every particular the theological formulations of John Calvin and his colleagues. Indeed, while Lutheran communities in Germany and Scandinavia tended to settle into common routinized patterns in the seventeenth century, contemporaneous Calvinist communities tended to pluralize into a number of national and regional variations on Genevan themes. The nature of these variations turned in part on the temperament of their leaders, in part on the historical and theological contexts in which the local reformations occurred.

Among the hallmarks of these later Calvinist communities was their preservation and their pluralization of Calvin's theology and law of marriage. Covenantal theologies of marriage sprung forth in ever greater varieties in these early modern Calvinist communities. Genevan civil laws governing marriage formation, maintenance, and dissolution gave rise to a variety of local legal progeny.

A great deal has been written on the covenantal theology and the state law of marriage among these later Calvinist groups. William Haller, Edmund Leites, and James Turner Johnson, for example, have demonstrated the influence of Calvinist ideas on Anglican marital theology and ecclesiastical law reforms in later Tudor and Stuart England.[273] George Howard, Edmund Morgan, and John Demos have described in exquisite detail the Calvinist theological and legal contours of the Puritan family in various New England colonies.[274] The patterns of marital reformation in French, Scottish, and German Calvinist communities have likewise attracted ample study.

The Dutch Example

The Calvinist Reformation of marriage in the Netherlands has not been part of the conventional literature. It deserves a few words both by way of introduction to English-speaking readers and by way of distillation of the main themes of the Calvinist reformation of marriage.

The Protestant Reformation came comparatively late to the Netherlands. The region had been under Spanish imperial rule until the mid-sixteenth century and was subject to the canon law of marriage administered by the Bishop of Utrecht. After the violent upheaval against their Spanish rulers from 1566 to 1581, however, the seven northern provinces of the Netherlands turned abruptly to the reformed cause.[275] Civil authorities assumed jurisdiction over a variety of subjects previously governed by church courts, including marriage, promulgating a welter of new statutes and codes.[276] Civil jurists produced systematic syntheses of the new civil laws and offered learned opinions in explication and elaboration of these new laws.[277] The new legislation and learned law on marriage drew upon a variety of Catholic canon law and Genevan civil law prototypes.[278]

The new Dutch civil law of marriage retained the traditional Catholic canon law definition of the formal betrothal or engagement (*verloving, trouwbelofte*) as the first step to marriage. It also accepted the Catholic canon law and Protestant civil law impediments to betrothal that allowed either party to break the engagement without issue—if one party became a heretic or lunatic, became engaged to or was abducted by a third party, became physically or emotionally abusive of the other, or became impotent or deformed.

Following Genevan prototypes, however, the Dutch civil law rejected the canon law rule that prior or subsequent religious vows to celibacy automatically annulled the betrothal. It also insisted on far more stringent formal requirements for the betrothal, each enforced by stiff fines. Couples under the age of majority were required to receive consent from both sets of parents (or, guardians, tutors, or curators). They were required to announce their betrothals before at least two good and honorable witnesses. They were required to register their betrothal with the consistory of the local reformed church, to receive spiritual instruction on marriage from the minister or an elder, and to request the minister to announce their betrothal banns from the pulpit for at least three successive Sundays. They were required to petition the local magistrate in their domicile for a certificate showing that they were single, in good standing, and free from communicable disease and criminal delinquency. All these changes in the traditional law of betrothals reflected Calvin's axiom that marriage was an inherently public institution in which parents, peers, and pastors all played a vital role.

The new Dutch civil law also accepted the basic canon law definition of the marriage itself (*huwelijkssluiting*) as a free consensual union between a fit man and a fit woman. It likewise accepted the common Catholic and Protestant impediments that protected the free consent of both parties and annulled marriages based on fear, duress, fraud, and errors of person and quality. It accepted the physical impediments recognized at canon law that annulled marriages where one party was rendered impotent or physically impaired. It accepted the canon law impediments of consanguinity and affinity, but only to the third degree, or in some provinces to the second degree.

Following Geneva prototypes, however, the Dutch civil law rejected the canon law impediments that annulled marriages where one party had departed from the faith or committed a mortal sin. It also rejected canon law impediments that prohibited remarriage to anyone who had previously married a cleric, monk, or nun.

The Dutch civil law departed from both pre-Tridentine canon law as well as Genevan civil law in requiring that parties solemnly repeat their vows before, and procure a marriage certificate from, either a reformed minister or a magistrate. Calvin had insisted that marriage certificates be issued by the magistrates but that the wedding itself be celebrated in a church. Dutch Calvinists accorded equal authority to both church and state to certify and solemnize the marriage, leaving the choice of forum to the parties. This innovation became popular among seventeenth-century Calvinists in England and America.[279]

A similar blend of Catholic and Calvinist sources is evident in the Dutch civil law of divorce. Unlike Calvin, Dutch Calvinist authorities retained the traditional canon law remedy of separation of bed and board. Indeed, from the seventeenth-century case law it seems that they far preferred this remedy to that of outright divorce. Unlike the canonists, they ordered separation from bed and board for any number of causes: adultery, violence, contagion, wife and child abuse, confessional differences, defamation of a spouse's moral character, acts of incest or lewdness, habitual drunkenness and gaming, among other causes. Like Calvin, they allowed for outright divorce in the modern sense, with a right of remarriage to both parties. But while Calvin sought to restrict divorce to proven cases of adultery, the Dutch civil authorities recognized divorce on proof of desertion—not only physical desertion, but spiritual, sexual, emotional, and other forms of desertion as well. The expansive interpretation of the concept of desertion provided "the peg on which was later hung the doctrine of divorce by mutual consent in the Enlightenment era."[280]

4

Marriage as Commonwealth in the Anglican Tradition

The Lutheran and Calvinist reformations of marriage followed inverse patterns. The Lutheran reformation began with a new theology of marriage, which eventually assumed new legal forms. The Calvinist reformation began with a new law of marriage, which eventually attracted new theological norms. The Lutheran reformation of marriage was pluralistic at the start, led by a score of strong theologians and jurists who inspired their own brands of marital reformation. Over time, these reformation ordinances settled into a common legal pattern for Germany and Scandinavia. The Calvinist Reformation was more uniform at the start, centered in the work of Calvin and the Geneva consistory. Over time, this Genevan reformation was colonized and pluralized in various Huguenot, Pietist, Presbyterian, Puritan, and Reformed communities of Europe and North America.

The Anglican reformation of marriage introduced a new, cyclical pattern of reform. Radical theological and legal reforms of marriage crashed onto the scene in one generation only to be put down by the restoration of traditional forms in a subsequent generation. But, in each of these cycles of reform and restoration, small changes were made in the prevailing theology and law of marriage that gradually transformed the English marital tradition. This transformation of English marriage law was much slower than its Continental counterparts. What the Continental reformers enacted over three decades, the English reformers protracted over three centuries. But what the Continental reformers provided for small integrated towns and territories, the English reformers provided for a vast and diverse commonwealth, eventually on both sides of the Atlantic.

The first grand cycle of reform and restoration came in the Tudor era. Catalyzed by the sensational annulment case of Henry VIII and Catherine of Aragon in 1527–1533, reformers such as Thomas Cranmer and Thomas Becon set out to supplant the inherited canon law tradition of marriage with new Protestant forms. They replaced the traditional sacramental model of marriage with various covenantal and social models drawn from the Continent, notably those of Heinrich Bullinger and Martin Bucer. They also imported familiar Protestant principles governing marriage, divorce, and remarriage. A good deal of ingenuity and energy was directed to legal reform. From 1533 on, Parliament introduced a series of laws, culminating in the 1552 *Reformation of Ecclesiastical Law*. These legal reforms promised to bring sweeping liturgical, doctrinal, and canonical changes to the institution of marriage. This first effort at legal reform largely failed. Queen Mary's midcentury legal repeals broke the momentum of the reform. Queen Elizabeth's settlement after 1559 restored only a few piecemeal changes to the law of marriage. England in the later sixteenth century circled back to much of the marriage law of the medieval Catholic tradition. It largely spurned both the bold common law reforms proffered by the Protestants and the milder canon law refinements promulgated by the Council of Trent.

A second grand cycle of reform came in the turbulent seventeenth-century reign of the Stuarts, a dynasty interrupted by the Puritan Revolution of 1640–1660 and terminated by the Glorious Revolution of 1689. The most dramatic changes affecting marriage in this second cycle of reform were theological. In an attempt to defend and extend the settled English law of marriage, English theologians developed a new commonwealth model of marriage. "[M]arriage was made and appointed by God himself to be the foundation and seminary of all sorts and kinds of life in the commonwealth and the church."[1] The marital household is "a little commonwealth, by the good government whereof, Gods glorie may bee aduaunced, the common-wealthe whiche standeth of several families, benefited, and all that live in that familie, may receiue much comfort and commoditie."[2] Such sentiments, typical in seventeenth-century English theology, embraced earlier sacramental, social, and covenantal models of marriage, but went beyond them. Marriage was at once a gracious symbol of the divine, a solemn covenant with one's spouse, and a social unit alongside church and state. But the essential cause, condition, and calling of marriage was that it simultaneously served and symbolized the commonwealth—that is, the common good—of the couple, the children, the church, and the state.

This commonwealth model of marriage initially provided a refined rationale for prevailing English laws and structures of marriage. It helped to substantiate the traditional hierarchies of husband over wife, parent over child, church over household, state over church, and to integrate the sundry biblical duties that attached to each of these offices. The family was assigned a subordinate place in the natural hierarchy of social institutions crowned by the King. Persons within the family were assigned their subordinate places in the natural hierarchy of family offices headed by the paterfamilias.

But as the political concept of the English commonwealth was revolutionized and democratized during the seventeenth century, so was the theological concept of the family commonwealth. The traditional hierarchies of husband over wife, parent over child, and church over family were challenged with a revolutionary new principle of personal and institutional equality. The biblical duties of husband and wife and of parent and child were recast as the natural and contractual rights of each household member vis-à-vis the other. The traditional idea of a hierarchical natural order of marriage, society, and state was challenged with a new idea of marriages, societies, and states that were voluntarily contracted by free individuals in the state of nature. Just as the English commonwealth could be rent asunder by force of arms when it abused the natural rights of the people, so the family commonwealth could be put asunder by suits at law when it abused the marital rights of either spouse. Just as the King could be relieved of his head for abuses in the English Commonwealth, so the paterfamilias could be removed from his headship for abuses in the domestic commonwealth.

This revolutionary construction of the commonwealth model, captured poignantly in the writings of John Milton and John Locke, provided a new rationale for the transformation of English marriage law. Inspired by this reconstructed commonwealth model, Parliament in 1653 introduced a series of reforms of marriage law and government that reflected the new principles of liberty and equality within the household, and that shifted marital jurisdiction from church courts to local magistrates. This experiment, too, largely failed. The 1653 law was repealed during the Restoration of 1660. Yet a few of its provisions on marital formation and divorce were retained, and more of them slowly soaked into English law and life in the next century. This reconstructed commonwealth model of marriage, together with this growing body of legal reforms, provided a key stepping-stone for the development of the Enlightenment contractarian model of marriage, discussed in the next chapter.

It is commonly argued that Anglican theology struck a *via media*, a middle way, between the teachings of Rome and Wittenberg, Paris and Geneva. This was a broad middle way that allowed the Church of England to embrace a wide range of theological opinions that nudged against Catholic and Protestant poles on each side. As the great seventeenth-century Anglican poet John Donne put it: "From extreme to extreme, from east to west, the angels themselves cannot come, but by passing the middle way between; from that extreme impurity in which Antichrist had dampened the church of God, to that intemperate purity in which Christ had constituted his church, the most angelical reformers cannot come but by touching, yea, and stepping upon some things in the way. . . . God reaches out his hand to the receiving of those who come towards him; and nearer to him, and to the institutions of his Christ, can no church, no not of the Reformation, be said to have come than ours does."[3]

While this *via media* image does not adequately describe many aspects of Anglican theology, it does help to describe the Anglican theology of marriage. The Anglican tradition, from the start, contemplated a fantastic range of opinions on marriage, from the Anglo-Catholic to the Anglo-Puritan, from the sacramental to the contractarian. These differences in English theologies of marriage were sometimes quite profound. It is misleading simply to equate the teachings of the Church *of* England with those of the churches *in* England, particularly after the Toleration Act of 1689 gave license for English Protestant dissenters to maintain doctrines and practices that, by definition, lay beyond the boundaries of the Anglican way.[1] But, on questions of marriage, it has been the special genius of the Anglican tradition over the centuries to find a way to accommodate widely diverse and even discordant teachings and yet retain a distinct denominational identity and standard.

Today, it is *The Book of Common Prayer,* with its timeless language, liturgy, and lectionary, that seems to hold worldwide Anglicanism together. Historically, English law played a critical role as well. The law set the outer boundaries and defined the middle line of this theological *via media.* This was one virtue of establishing Anglicanism by law. Establishment laws defined the core theological doctrines of marriage, from which no dissent was tolerated. But these establishment laws also left the penumbral doctrines and practices of marriage, family, and sexuality open to wide speculation, experimentation, and variation. Invariably, what had been penumbral, even heretical, doctrines in an earlier generation were established as core doctrines in a later generation. It was this inherent fluidity and flexibility of the Anglican theology and law of marriage—grounded as it was in an emerging English epistemology of probability and reasonableness—that eventually gave the Anglican tradition a uniquely eclectic and dynamic quality.[5]

While the sacramental, social, and covenantal models of marriage eventually hardened with growing canonization, the commonwealth model inevitably softened with growing liberalization. Thus we see the great irony of the Anglican contribution to the Western tradition of marriage: What began in the sixteenth century as the most conservative

Christian tradition of marriage in all of Christendom ultimately gave birth to the most liberal Christian tradition of marriage three centuries later. It is to this ironic tale that we now turn, analyzing a wider chronological swath of material than in previous chapters in order to see the irony at last begin to unfold.

The Cases of
Henry VIII and Catherine of Aragon

It is worth recounting King Henry VIII's mighty struggle to seek dissolution of his marriage with Catherine of Aragon. This dispute was the catalyst of the English Reformation in general and of the English reformation of marriage in particular. Given its sensational soap opera qualities, the case had a way of focusing the English mind on the arcane details of canon law rules of marriage formation and dissolution—and the intense casuistry that could attend their application.[6]

The familiar facts of the case require a bit of historical background to appreciate. Henry VIII's father, Henry VII, had come to the English throne in 1485, a victor in the bloody War of the Roses over the question of royal succession. Henry VII's first son, Prince Arthur, was his heir apparent. Arthur's siring of a son was critical to ensuring a male successor to the English throne for at least two more generations. Prince Arthur was thus betrothed as an infant to Catherine of Aragon, the daughter of Ferdinand and Isabella of Spain—a betrothal that helped to seal favorable diplomatic relations between England and Spain. Arthur and Catherine were married in 1501. Prince Arthur died in 1502—childless.

Henry VII's second son, Henry (VIII), now became heir to the throne. In a continued effort to secure peace between England and Spain, the twelve-year-old Prince Henry was betrothed to his brother's widow, Catherine, in 1503. This betrothal of a widow to her former brother-in-law raised a difficult legal question, however. The Mosaic law spoke thrice to the issue and not altogether clearly. Leviticus 18:16 stated: "You shall not uncover the nakedness of your brother's wife; she is your brother's nakedness." Leviticus 20:21 underscored this prohibition with a threat of infertility: "If a man takes his brother's wife, it is impurity; he has uncovered his brother's nakedness; they shall be childless." But Deuteronomy 25:5 provided: "If brothers dwell together, and one of them dies and has no son, the wife of the dead shall not be married outside the family to a stranger; her husband's brother shall go in to her, and take her as wife, and perform the duty of a husband's brother to her." These Mosaic laws can be reconciled by reading the first two Leviticus passages to govern relations when both brothers are alive, and the

Deuteronomy passage to govern only after one brother has died. But neither the rabbinical nor the canonical authorities over the centuries had
accepted this reading unequivocally.

The prevailing Catholic canon law on the subject treated the relationship of a man and the widow of his brother as one of affinity. This
relationship was an impediment to marriage and would lead to the involuntary annulment of a putative marriage contracted in ignorance or
in knowing violation of it. Already in the late thirteenth century, however, canonists had maintained that the pope, as final interpreter of the
canon law, could grant a dispensation from this and other Levitical impediments in a specific case. Such dispensations were viewed as equitable exceptions to the usual rules. In this case of affinity, a dispensation
could be especially compelling, given the injunction of care for a
brother's widow in Deuteronomy 25:5. In the late fourteenth century,
popes began to exercise this right of dispensation, waiving impediments
of affinity in a number of cases of budding royal and aristocratic marriages. Indeed, Catherine's sister Isabella was granted precisely such a
dispensation from an impediment of affinity in 1500, under pressure on
the papacy by her father, Ferdinand.

On petition to Pope Julius II in 1504, therefore, Catherine was given
a dispensation to marry her late husband's brother, Prince Henry. They
were married in 1509, just after Henry VIII had succeeded to the English throne. Catherine gave birth to six children, including two princes,
but they were all stillborn or died in infancy except Mary, born in 1516.
Popular sentiment of the day described this ill fate as the scourge of
childlessness promised by Leviticus 20:21. The lack of a male successor
carried more than the usual disappointment to the hopeful couple and
nation. Against the backdrop of the War of the Roses, it posed a real
threat of renewed civil war. In desperation—or infatuation—Henry VIII
had taken a mistress named Mary and sired an illegitimate son, Henry
Fitzroy. But the claim of this bastard child to succeed to the throne was
dubious at best.

Henry VIII grew disenchanted with Catherine. Already in 1524, word
circulated of his desire to end his marriage with Catherine and to sire a
legitimate son with another wife. By 1527, Henry had come upon the
legal formula to achieve this end. He announced to his advisors that he
had become convinced that his marriage to Catherine was against the
law of God set forth in Leviticus 18. This law had been improperly
waived by Pope Julius II's dispensation in 1504. It would violate his
"scruple of conscience," Henry said, to continue his marriage in open violation of God's law.

Early in 1527, at Henry VIII's urging, the Archbishop of York,

Cardinal Thomas Wolsey, convened a secret *ex officio* inquisitorial trial, which canon law empowered him to do. At trial, Henry was accused of violating the divine law of Leviticus 18 that prohibited his marriage to his brother's widow. Henry's defense was that the papal dispensation of Julius II granted him permission to marry. The promoter for the inquisitorial court then predictably attacked, at length, the procedural propriety and substantive legitimacy of the dispensation. Henry evidently thought that this legal maneuvering would end the matter. Pope Julius's 1504 dispensation from the impediment of affinity would prove illegitimate and be reversed. Henry's marriage to Catherine would thus be illegitimate and automatically annulled. He would perform a requisite penance for his sin of violating Leviticus 18. He would then be free to marry again. And a new woman to marry was at hand. Everyone thought that the intended new wife was to be Mary, Henry's former mistress. A marriage of Henry VIII and Mary would render their bastard son Henry Fitzroy's claim to the throne considerably stronger. Henry, however, secretly desired to marry not Mary, but Mary's sister, Anne Boleyn.

Cardinal Wolsey suspended proceedings of the inquisitorial court and took the case under advisement. He soon learned that the case was not nearly so easy as Henry may have imagined. First, he discovered that the canon law authorities were divided on whether an inquisitorial court could reverse a papal dispensation. The preponderance of authority was against him. Even if the inquisitorial court reversed the 1504 dispensation, therefore, it was unlikely that it would stand up on appeal to a papal court.

Moreover, Catherine, who had since learned of the secret proceeding, stood up to fight for continuation of her marriage. She introduced a vital new fact that changed the legal question dramatically. Catherine claimed that her marriage to Arthur had never been consummated through sexual intercourse. She was thus a virgin at the time of her marriage to Henry, she argued, and Henry in fact knew this. According to canonists who regarded consummation as critical to the formation of marriage, this meant she was technically not the wife or widow of Arthur, and no impediment of affinity precluded her marriage to Henry. According to other canonists who regarded a contract as critical to the formation of marriage, this meant that the only impediment that stood in the way of her marriage to Henry was the impediment of public honesty. Dispensations from such a man-made impediment were routinely issued and could be covered by Julius's 1504 dispensation, or easily procured after the fact and applied retroactively. In either case, Catherine intimated, the validity of Pope Julius II's dispensation was not critical, and Henry's scruple of conscience was not pressing. Then to make the case even more difficult, Catherine demanded, as canon law allowed, that she be made a party to the case and given legal counsel, not only from England but also from abroad. What was supposed to have been a bit of secret legal maneuvering had suddenly escalated well beyond what Henry could have imagined.

The case was rendered even more complicated by Henry's secret desire to marry Anne Boleyn. The same impediment of affinity under dispute in Henry's relationship with Catherine also stood in the way of Henry's intended marriage to Anne Boleyn. By having already consummated his relationship with Anne's sister Mary, Henry had, in effect, married her. His "marriage" to Mary created an impediment of affinity to marrying Mary's sister Anne Boleyn. For Leviticus 18 had likewise precluded a man from marrying his (deceased) wife's sister. Henry thus found himself in a most untenable position. In the case of his current wife, Catherine, he had just argued that the impediment of affinity could not be dispensed with, and an annulment must be granted. In the case of his intended new wife, Anne, he would have to argue that the impediment of affinity must be dispensed with, and permission to marry must be granted. The contradiction was too plain to ignore.

Henry sought to escape this dilemma by appealing to the new Pope, Clement VII, for a dispensation to marry Anne Boleyn. His counselors related Henry's intentions, together with several draft dispensations. Clement was trapped—both by precedent and by politics. According to prevailing canon law authorities, the granting of a dispensation in this case was premature, given Henry's current marriage to Catherine. And to dispense with the impediment of affinity in this case was tacitly to confirm the propriety of Julius II's dispensation from the impediment of affinity in 1504. Moreover, Clement had just surrendered to Catherine's nephew, Charles V, the Holy Roman Emperor, who had sacked Rome. Clement was in no position to alienate his captor by ill treatment of his captor's aunt, Catherine. Neither sovereign could be entirely disappointed, and Clement sought to assuage both. To assuage Henry, Clement granted him on April 13, 1528, a dispensation to marry Anne, pending resolution of his case with Catherine. To assuage Charles, Clement on the same day commissioned his own legatine inquisitorial court to rehear the case for annulment, taking the matter out of Cardinal Wolsey's discretion and placing it beyond Henry's immediate control.

The legatine court commenced a public inquisition in England on May 31, 1529. Both before and during trial, counsel for Henry and Catherine debated at length the propriety of Julius II's 1504 dispensation that enabled the royal couple to be married. The former arguments continued—whether Catherine was a virgin at the time of her marriage to Henry, and whether Pope Julius's dispensation was for the impediment of affinity or the impediment of public honesty. Counsel for Henry now added a third argument that brought long rejoinder—that in 1504, the twelve-year-old Henry was too young to understand or consent to the dispensation and that the basis for the betrothal (continued peace with Spain) was fictional, since a peace treaty between the two countries was already contracted. Counsel for Henry also ventured a fourth argument—that the impediment of public honesty was not just a trivial man-made construction, but a serious natural law impediment that Pope Julius had no power to dispense.

The legatine court ordered both Henry and Catherine to appear for testimony. Henry appeared. Catherine demurred. On June 16, 1528, Catherine appealed formally by mandate to Pope Clement VII to have the case moved from England to Rome—an appeal that Henry's functionaries in Rome delayed delivering to Clement for several weeks. On June 18 and 21, Catherine appeared before the legatine court and both formally protested the court's jurisdiction over her and the case and pronounced in open court her virginity at the time of her marriage with Henry. She then withdrew and refused to appear again, despite charges of contumacy and the cajolery and threats of several royal and legatine visitors.

On July 16, 1529, Pope Clement VII responded to Catherine's appeal by suspending the legatine court sitting in England and ordering the entire case removed to Rome. This move was in accordance with the canon law procedure of advocation. On October 7, 1529, Clement responded to Catherine's claims of virginity by sending a private letter to Henry, inquiring into his view of the matter. Henry made no answer. On March 7, 1530, Clement amended his earlier dispensation and ordered Henry to suspend his planned marriage to Anne pending the papal court's final resolution of his case against Catherine. When Clement learned of Henry's open consorting with Anne, he issued a stern letter to Henry on January 25, 1532, threatening to excommunicate him if he did not leave Anne and return to Catherine.

These events set afoot the famous sequence of events that ultimately led to the break between England and Rome. Already in late 1529, both Henry and Clement began marshaling canon law authorities from throughout England and the Continent to speak to the propriety of both Julius's 1504 dispensation and Clement's 1529 advocation. A number of English, French, and Italian faculties and professors of law and theology supported Henry's cause. The German faculties and isolated professors from the rest of Europe sided primarily with the papacy. Despite intense negotiations—ultimately involving ambassadors from throughout the Continent—relations between Clement and Henry and between Catherine and Henry eroded. Henry refused to participate in the case in Rome. He refused to reconcile himself to Catherine.

On July 11, 1533, the papal court in Rome began hearings in the annulment case. After long argument, and adjournment, the papal court solemnly pronounced on March 23, 1534, that the marriage of Henry and Catherine "was and is valid and canonical."[7]

By this time, however, Henry had taken matters into his own hands. In the autumn of 1532, he had impregnated Anne—with the later Queen Elizabeth—and on January 25, 1533 had secretly married her. In early March 1533, he pushed through Parliament the Act in Restraint of Appeals to Rome, which provided that all "causes of matrimony and divorces . . . shall from henceforth be heard and definitively adjudged and determined within the king's jurisdiction and authority."[8] The objections of Sir Thomas More and Bishop Fisher, among other clergy, led to their summary and savage execution.

On March 30, 1533, the King's favorite, Thomas Cranmer, was appointed Archbishop of Canterbury. Within a month, Cranmer convened yet another *ex officio* inquisitorial trial on the propriety of Henry's marriage to Catherine. Cranmer summoned Henry and Catherine to appear to answer the charges against them of violating the Levitical law of impediments. Catherine refused to appear and was cited for contumacy. The same tired arguments on both sides, now swollen with supporting opinions collected from throughout Europe, were again presented. On May 28, 1533, Cranmer declared the marriage of Henry and Catherine annulled, accepting the arguments that Catherine had consummated her marriage with Arthur and that an impediment of affinity rendered void her marriage to Henry. Shortly thereafter, Cranmer ratified the secret marriage of Henry and Anne, saying nothing about the impediment of affinity between them.

On April 4, 1534, Parliament confirmed Archbishop Cranmer's sentences in the Act of Succession. The Act declared that Prince Arthur had "carnally known" Catherine, that the marriage between Henry and Catherine was thus "against the Laws of Almighty God" and "utterly void and annulled," and that the marriage of Henry and Anne "shall be established and taken for undoubtful, true, sincere, and perfect ever after."[9] This Act guaranteed the legitimacy of their daughter Elizabeth's claim to the throne. If any doubt of the pope's control lingered, Henry pushed through Parliament the Supremacy Act of 1534, declaring himself to be "the only supreme head in earth of the Church of England."[10]

Catherine died in 1536, under suspicious circumstances. When Anne Boleyn proved incapable of producing a male heir, she was condemned and executed for adultery in 1536. Henry then married Jane Seymour, who produced Edward VI in 1537, but died in childbirth. Edward VI would succeed Henry to the throne in 1547. Mary, daughter of Henry and Catherine, would succeed him in 1553. Elizabeth, daughter of Henry and Anne, would succeed her in 1559.

Few matrimonial cases, before or since, have reached this level of complexity, intrigue, and machination. Thomas Cranmer later called it "the case of the century," and for centuries thereafter historians and playwrights have sifted through its sordid and scintillating details to produce endless interpretations. For the average English soul in the 1520s and 1530s, the case was surely bewildering. Arcane arguments about canon law impediments; papal dispensations granted, modified, suspended, and reversed; sordid discussions over whether Arthur and Catherine had sexual intercourse; ecclesiastical tribunals convened, suspended, and removed; learned canonists taking diametrically opposite positions on simple legal questions; great churchmen rewarded or beheaded for their views of the moment; the King's contumacy celebrated but the Queen's contumacy castigated; the King's concubinage rewarded but his concubines executed—all this and much more could not have inspired much confidence in the prevailing system of theology or law.

After the dizzying events surrounding the birth of the English Reformation, theologians and jurists began to take stock of prevailing doctrines and to press for reforms that would both immunize England from such machinations in the future and routinize the salutary changes that had already taken place. The disputed doctrines of impediments, annulment, and divorce would loom large in these calculations.

The Tudor Reformation
of Marriage Theology

Henry's celebrated marriage case triggered an explosion of new Protestant literature in England both on marriage and its dissolution and on the canon law of marriage and its reformation.[11] Some of this literature was indigenous, building on a two-century tradition of English antipapalism and anticanonicalism inaugurated by John Wycliff, William of Ockham, and others.[12] Some of this literature was Continental. The writings on marriage by Luther, Melanchthon, Bullinger, Bucer, Calvin, Beza, and many others enjoyed wide circulation in Tudor England—sometimes fully translated and reproduced with attribution, often excerpted in sermons and pamphlets or published under pseudonyms.[13]

Thomas Becon

The writings of Thomas Becon—student of Anglican divines Hugh Latimer and George Stafford and chaplain to Archbishop Cranmer—provide a good illustration of both types of literature on marriage. Becon peppered many of his seventy-odd devotional and catechical tracts with a variety of spicy Protestant sentiments on marriage, which he drew together in a circa 1560 title *The Booke of Matrimonie*.[14] Several of Becon's tracts were best-sellers in Tudor and Stuart England, and remain among the classics of Anglican theology. Becon also helped to produce English editions of the influential marriage tracts of Continental reformers Heinrich Bullinger and Martin Bucer; the Bullinger tract, in fact, was printed under Becon's pen name. In this range of writings, both the covenantal model and the social model of marriage developed on the Continent can be seen, together with the rudiments of a budding commonwealth model of marriage, which would come to full flower in England at the turn of the seventeenth century.

Becon's own prolific writings—like those of other Anglican divines in the early sixteenth century—propounded no fully systematic theology of marriage and family life. But they did provide a substantial cache of popular Protestant marriage principles.

Like his Continental brethren, Becon inveighed bitterly against the decay of marriage in his day and laid much of the blame on the canon law. In Becon's view, the canon law had "most filthely corrupted, mangled, and defiled all the misteries of God, of his holy worde, and blessed Sacramentes" and had "moste vilely and most wickedly embased, caste downe, and made almost of no reputation . . . the moste holy state of godly Matrimony."[15] "[T]he glory of this christen matrimony is now greatly obscured, yea almost utterly extin[ct] and quenched throwe the abominable whoredom, stinckinge adultery, wicked fornication, and all kinde of uncleannes, which is used now a dayes among us."[16]

On the one hand, Becon charged, the canon law requirement of clerical celibacy had unleashed all manner of sexual pathos upon England. "The synagogue[s] of Satan are such and so great enemies to matrimony, that they had rather have their subdeacons, deacons, and priests, their monks and their friars, their canons and nuns . . . to be most filthy fornicators, abominable adulterers, stinking sodomites, and to be defiled with all kind of beastly and unnatural uncleanness, than once to suffer them to embrace holy wedlock." England's "plage" of prostitution, bastardy, homosexuality, syphilis, and much else was, in Becon's view, "ayded and abeted" by the "evyl commaund" of clerical celibacy.[17]

On the other hand, Becon charged, the canon law had confused lay marital life through its imposition of unwieldy and unbiblical impediments to marriage, its recognition of secret marriages without church consecration, and its prohibitions against divorce for adultery and against the remarriage of widows and widowers.[18] Becon condemned, with particular vitriol, the "evyl canons" that allowed immature "child" marriages based on lust. When the inaptly married party comes to "see [an]other whome they coulde finde in theyr harte to fansie and love better, than many of them beginne to hate one another." This, in turn, Becon charged, ushered in an insidious pattern of easy annulments for the rich who can pay for a dispensation, and of permanently unhappy households for the poor who have no payment to dispense. Such households feature "frowning, ouerwharting, scolding, and chiding," and such prevalent abuse of wives and children "that the whole house is filled full of these tragedies eue vnto the toppe" and "shortly after the whole towne is in a rore." "What a wicked and hellyke life."[19]

Becon offered familiar Protestant reforms to end this perceived wickedness. He summarized his suggestions in a series of pithy paragraphs contrasting "The Acts of Christ and of Antichrist [the Pope]" on questions of marital formation and dissolution:

> Christ saith: "Honor thy father and thy mother": in which comandment is required of children that they give not themselves to marriage without the consent of their godly parents. . . . Antichrist in the bestowing of children in marriage, requireth not the consent and good-will of the parents. . . .
>
> Christ, by being present at a marriage with his mother and with his disciples, teacheth evidently that matrimony ought to be solemnly and openly proclaimed and celebrated, and that it ought not to be done in corners. Antichrist, for money, granteth dispensations for all men for to marry where they will, when they will, and with whom they will. All things are decent and lawful, if money come. All things obey money.
>
> Christ in his doctrine did never forbid marriage to be contracted between any persons, except those degrees only which his heavenly Father had tofore forbidden by his servant Moses. Antichrist in his law prohibiteth many and divers degrees to marry together whom God hath set at liberty . . . except they purchase a license of him for money: for money maketh all things lawful in the court; neither are his laws any other thing than nets for money.
>
> [Christ] suffereth those that be god-fathers and god-mothers (as they term them) to be one child at baptism, to marry together, if they be loose and at liberty, and not forbidden by the law Levitical. [Antichrist] plainly forbiddeth this thing, and maketh the matter a spiritual consanguinity and a ghostly kindred, of much

more force and strength than any carnal strength or fleshly consanguinity is.

Christ freely permitteth marriage to all degrees, none excepted,
if they have not the gift of continency: neither doth he appoint any
time where it shall not be lawful to solemnize matrimony, but
giveth liberty to all men at all times freely to marry. Antichrist . . .
denieth marriage to all his clattering clergy, rather suffering them
to burn and run awhoring. . . . [H]e forbids at certain times of the
year to celebrate matrimony; insomuch that whosoever presumeth
in those forbidden times to marry is not only accursed, but his marriage also is not lawful.

[Christ gives] liberty to the guiltless and innocent man, having
an harlot to his wife . . . not only to be divorced from that harlot,
sometime his wife, but also to marry again. . . . Antichrist in his law
saith, If a man have an whore to his wife, it shall be lawful for him
to be divorced from her, both from bed and board; but he may by
no means marry again, live as he may. . . .

[Christ gives] liberty to the faithful man or woman [to divorce
an idolater and remarry]. Antichrist will by no means suffer any divorcement so to be made so that marriage shall follow, although
the guiltless person burn so greatly.[20]

Each of these Protestant reforms of the canon law—parental consent to
marriage,[21] church proclamation and consecration of marriage,[22] limitations of impediments to biblical forms,[23] permission for clergy to
marry,[24] propriety of divorce for cause with rights of remarriage,[25] and
propriety of remarriage by widows and widowers[26]—while not unequivocally accepted, found substantial endorsement in the writings of
the Anglican divines. William Tyndale, Thomas Cranmer, John Hooper,
John Jewel, Hugh Latimer, and Edmund Grindal in particular adduced
an ample arsenal of ancient Christian and classical sources in support of
many of these reforms. Several others took the further familiar step, on
which Becon dithered,[27] of denying the sacramental character of marriage altogether, thereby also questioning the propriety of the church's
jurisdiction over marriage.[28]

Becon sketched out what he considered to be a more proper understanding of marriage. Marriage was not a condition to be despised or
subordinated in dignity to the single, contemplative life. To the contrary, marriage is the "best estate," a "thynge of great excellency and in-
comparable dignitie," created by God to "mayntayn," "preserue," and
"prottytte the common weale and also set forth the glorye of God, of nature, and of man."[29] Marriage is a "great vocation and destinye," which
clergy and laity alike should embrace and enjoy. Marriage is, as Becon
put it in his summary definition that was often repeated in later sermons

and pamphlets: "an hie, holye and blessed order of life, ordayned not of man, but of God . . . wherein one man and one woman are coupled and knit together in one fleshe and body in the feare and loue of God, by the free, louing, harty, and good consente of them both, to the extent that they may dwel together, as one fleshe and body of one wyl and mynd in all honesty, vertue and godliness, and spend theyr lyues in equal partaking of all such thinges as god shal send them with thankes geuynge."[30] "Matrimony is, instituted of God, celebrated in paradise, sanctified by the holy Ghost, and beautified with the first fruits of Christes wonderful miracles."[31]

God ordained marriage for three causes, Becon wrote—love, procreation, and deterrence from sin, in that order of priority.[32] I underscore this point, for conventional scholarship has treated marital love and amicability as an invention of seventeenth-century Puritanism or eighteenth-century affective individualism. Becon's mid-sixteenth century writings, as well as those of Bullinger and Bucer, belie this assumption. "The first cause" of marriage, Becon wrote, "is, that for asmuch as the solitary life is a sorowfull and uncomfortable life, and man in nature is desirous of compeny, and gladly liveth not alone: God . . . appointed this most holye order of life, and commaunded one man and one woman to live in the same, and that one of them might be a comfort, joye and help to another in all honest and godly things. . . . to have his familie and name extended, is greate gladnesse and felicitye, and the swete consolation of travaile."[33] Becon stressed these virtues of marital love several times, treating love as the sine qua non of marriage and the sacramental symbol and seal of Christ's love for his church.[34] The second cause of marriage, said Becon, is procreation, which must continue not only to perpetuate one's family name, but also that "the nomber of th'elect and chosen people of God be fulfilled."[35] The third cause of marriage is to avoid "fornication, adultry, incest, Sodomitry, and all other kinde of uncleannesse."[36]

Becon left it mostly to others to define the legal steps for forming and maintaining this ideal state of matrimony. His own advice—like that of many of his fellow divines—was mostly homiletic. To wit: "Art thou a father or mother, master or mistress? Bring then up thy family in the nurture of the Lord, and so art thou truly faithful. Art thou a married man? Look how thou cleave unto thy wife: love her as thy own flesh, and as Christ loved the congregation. So shall thy faith appear to be unfeigned. Art thou a married woman? Be obedient to thine own husband, and seek above all things to please him, and so shalt thou shew thyself to be truly faithful."[37] In his famous catechism, he further urged husbands to love, support, and defend their wives and children in an exercise of true godliness, and wives, in turn, to obey their husbands, to educate their children, and "to be chast, pure and honest in dede, in word, in gesture, in apparrell and in all her behaviour."[38]

Becon offered more substantial advice in his several glosses on the Commandment "Thou shalt not commit adultery." Like his Catholic and Protestant contemporaries, he viewed this Commandment as a source and summary of a biblical ethic on sexuality and marriage.[39] The Commandment helped to systematize sundry biblical and natural commandments and counsels for married persons. Becon summarized its lessons in sweeping terms:

> And forasmuch as matrimony is a holy state of life, God in the aforesaid precept requireth of all married persons, that they lead a pure, clean, and blameless life, that they be faithful and loving one to the other, that they break not the marriage vow, that they know not the company of any strange flesh, that they defile not themselves in mind with evil lusts and in the body with uncleanness; but that they be pure both in body and spirit, utterly estranged from all adultery, incest, whoredom, and whatsoever is unclean in the sight of God, living together in all godliness and honesty. And that the married folk may the better this do, God requireth also of them in this precept, that they suffer no fleshly thoughts to rise and rule in their hearts, but that they suppress them straightaways through earnest and hearty prayer, and through the diligent consideration of God's holy will, and through the fervent meditation of the sacred scripture; again, that they frequent the company of no lewd or ill-disposed persons, whereby they may be the rather provoked unto the breach of this commandment and unto dissolution of life: Item, that they avoid all wanton pasttimes, all filthy communications, all uncomely gestures, all nice and lascivious apparel, all reading of wanton books, all beholding of unpure images or pictures, all banqueting and excess of eating and drinking, and besides, whatsoever may entice or move unto the filthy pleasure of the flesh; and finally, that in all their words and deeds there appear nothing in them but gravity, modesty, and honest behaviour, unto the good ensample of such as be their youngers and inferiors, . . . that God may bless them and their marriage, and make them joyful parents of many children, which in this world may be good members of the Christian commonweal, and in the world to come blessed citizens of that glorious and heavenly Jerusalem.[40]

The Commandment similarly enjoined unmarried persons against the "mortal folly" of fornication, incest, "and such other corporal uncleanness" as well as "filthy talk, wanton countenances, singing of bawdy ballads, reading of amorous books, idle jesting, vain pasttimes, and whatsoever maketh unto the provocation of fleshly appetite."[41]

In other glosses on this same Commandment, Becon thundered prophetically against "the louse and lascyvyous lyvyng" of his country-men, particularly their habits of glibly contracting and dissolving mar-riages to "the great dishonour of God's institution." He even courted treason charges by intimating that the life of Henry VIII was both an il-lustration and instigation of undue sexual license. He called for a return to the "ancient byblycal remedyes" of severe punishment for sexual sin-ners, execution for convicted adulterers and fornicators.[42] In cases of proven adultery, he followed the Gospel literally, allowing the innocent spouse to divorce and remarry, after all attempts at reconciliation had failed.[43]

Besides offering his own writings, Becon helped to introduce two sys-tematic Protestant tracts from the Continent that came to work a con-siderable influence on the later Anglican theology of marriage: (1) *The Golde Boke of Christen Matrimonye* by Zürich reformer Heinrich Bull-inger, an eighty-page exposition of a covenantal model of marriage;[44] and (2) *De Regno Christi (On the Kingdom of Christ),* by Strasbourg re-former Martin Bucer, nearly half of which was devoted to elaborating a social model of marriage.[45]

Heinrich Bullinger

Heinrich Bullinger's *Golde Boke of Matrimonye* set out, in accessible terms, a covenantal model of marriage. Bullinger had propounded his model of marriage on the foundation of Huldrych Zwingli's work and had effectively used this model to advocate several legal reforms in Zürich in the 1540s and 1550s. "Wedlocke," he wrote, "is a couvenante, a couplinge or yokynge together" of one man and one woman "by the good cosente of the bothe."[46] "Holy wedlocke was ordyned of God him-selfe in Paradise. . . . God was the fyrst causer of wedlocke, and [spliced] and knyt them together, & blessed them."[47] It is thus an "honorable and holy" estate, enjoyed by the "holiest, & most vertuous, the wysest & most noble menne" in the Bible, and commended to all persons today—clerical and lay, young and old, single and widowed, rich and poor.[48]

God had created marriage so that a man and woman "may lyve to-gether honestlye and frendlye the one with the other, that they maye avoyde uncleannesse, that they maye brynge up children in the feare of God, that the one maye helpe and comforte the tother."[49] Bullinger fol-lowed conventional arguments regarding the marital purposes of protection from lust and procreation of children, arguing that marriage is God's "remedy & medicyne unto our feble and weake flesh" and that children are "the greatest treasure" of a marriage.[50] But, like Becon, he placed special emphasis on marital love and friendship, returning to the theme several times in this and other writings.[51] At creation, he insisted, God planted in Adam and Eve "the loue, the harte, the inclinacion & naturall affecion that it besemethe the one to have towarde the other." The "mouthe of God thereby declareth the dewty knot and couenant of maried folkes, namely that the hyghest loue, bonde, and unite among them should be this, that no man seperate them asunder, but only death. . . . The loue therefore in mariage ought to be (next unto God) above all loues," with couples rendering to each other "the moost excellennt and unpayneful seruyce, diligence and earnest labour, . . . one doying for an-other, one louyinge, dependyng, helpyng & forbearyng another, suffer-yng, also lyke joye and lyke payne one with another."[52]

Such an ideal state of matrimony, Bullinger insisted, could be achieved only if the covenant of marriage were "framed ryght accordyng to the word and wyll of God."[53] Bullinger recognized the conventional steps of betrothal, wedding, and consummation, and glossed each step with ample avuncular advice based on biblical sources. Parties should enter marriage only by a "mature and mutual consente" that is free from coercion, fraud, or the inducements of "carnall lust, mony, good, [or] flattery."[54] They should marry only fellow believers, for "mariage also concerne the soule and inwarde man," and be insistent that their spouse show true "feare of God" and a whole host of Godly virtues.[55] They should avoid marriages with blood or family relatives listed in Leviticus, ending unions immediately if such a relationship is discovered.[56] They should procure their parents' consent, which ought to be given fairly, soberly, and with due admonition of the solemnity of the union.[57] They should be married in a public church wedding officiated by "Gods min-ister" and "receave the blessying & commytte themselues to the com-mon prayers of the congregation, and entone the same."[58] By so doing, it is "openly declared in the sight of all the world, that it is God which knytteth the knot of mariage" and that "euery one is warned, faythfully to kepe his promyse, made and given to his spouse." After a suitable and "sober" celebration, they must enter their "first dwellyng together."[59]

Bullinger did not leave the newly married couple untutored. The first few months of cohabitation are a "moost daungerous" time, he believed, and he thus devoted a third of his tract to describing the interlocking "dutyes of domestycyty" required by the marital covenant between hus-band, wife, and God.[60] Bullinger went on for several pages advising cou-ples about sex, food, dress, and other details of domestic economy,

warning against excess in any of these. He then set out the couple's respective duties of "ordinate obedyence and coniugall love mutuall," following New Testament leads, and holding up the relationship of Christ
and His Church "for an ensample or myrrour to the state of wedlocke
and conjugal covenantal love."[61] The wife owes her husband the duties
of obedience, service, respect, devotion, modesty, courtesy, support,
faithfulness, and honesty.[62] The husband is the head of the wife, "her
defender, teacher, and comforte," called to exhibit the selfless sacrificial
love of Christ himself and the virtues of clemency, wisdom, integrity,
and faithfulness.[63] The wife must give proper care to the home, exhibiting cleanliness, industry, thrift, and judiciousness in her treatment
of servants and neighbors. The husband must "labour for the common
weal" of his family, exhibiting industry, honesty, integrity, and charity.[64]
Couples with children could turn to a dozen pages of Bullinger's instructions on the parental duties of breast-feeding, nurture, discipline,
education, and dress of children, and, later, their courtship and contracting of marriage with a suitable partner.

This genre of writing about the interlocking covenantal duties of husband and wife, and of parent and children within the household—a
blending of catechism, confessional book, and instructional manual into
a sort of spiritual "Dr. Spock"—became a trademark of the Anglican tradition. The "dutyes of domestycyty" that Heinrich Bullinger pressed into
thirty pages of terse text in 1540 became the subject of some six hundred pages of prolix prose by William Gouge eighty years later.[65]
Dozens of such books appeared in the later sixteenth and seventeenth
centuries, written by divines of both Anglo-Catholic and Anglo-Puritan
inclination.[66]

Even properly contracted marriages and dutifully maintained households can be rent asunder, Bullinger continued. The "shamefull, vycious
and abhominable" sins of adultery, harlotry, and lust can affect even the
noblest couple and drive them to defy their "sacred covenantal dutyes"
to God, spouse, and children.[67] In the event of one party's adultery or
malicious desertion (which is tantamount to adultery), Bullinger wrote,
"[d]ivorce is permitted of God." Christ allowed divorce "for the helth &
medicyne of man, and for amendment in wedlok," even though this was
a "perilous & pitefull" regimen.[68] This "medicyne" of divorce could not
be administered by the couple themselves, but by a disinterested judge,
who had to hear their petitions and find adequate cause for the dissolution of their marriage. Adulterous parties must be severely punished—
executed in egregious cases. Innocent parties must be free to remarry,
for to prohibit remarriage is "violently to cast a snare about poore peoples neckes and to drave them unto vyce and synne."[69]

The first English edition of Bullinger's tract was printed anonymously in 1541. It was censored immediately, doubtless because of its open advocacy of clerical marriage and of divorce and remarriage—teachings (let alone practices) that remained illegal in England until 1547.[70] The book was republished the following year under a new title, *The Golde Boke of Christen Matrimonye,* and (at the instance of "the hungry printer") under Thomas Becon's famous pen name.[71] The suspect chapters on clerical marriage and divorce were quietly dropped from the new edition, together with two other controversial chapters on impediments to marriage. This Becon edition of Bullinger's tract was regularly reprinted, and various abridgments and summaries of it became standard texts for Anglican clerics for the next two centuries.[72]

Becon added a long preface to this 1542 edition of Bullinger's *Golde Boke,* which extolled marriage not only for the spiritual good of the couple and their children, but also for the civil good of the commonwealth and church. By marriage, Becon wrote with ample bombast, "many noble treasures chaunce unto us, vertue is mayntayned, vice is exchewed, houses are replenished, cities are inhabited, the ground is tylled, sciences are practised, kingdomes floryshe, amitie is preserued, the publique weale is defended, naturall succession remaynethe, good artes are taught, honest order is kepte, Christedome is enlarged, Goddes word promoted, and the glory of God hyghly auaunced and sette further."[73] On the stability of "this householde common weale" hangs the security of the whole commonwealth of England.[74]

Martin Bucer

Becon's emphasis on the social utility of the "householde common weale" is central to Martin Bucer's 1550 manifesto *On the Kingdom of Christ (De Regno Christi).* Bucer was one of the great Continental Protestants, an intimate associate of Luther and Melanchthon, an influential mentor of the young Calvin, and a leading reformer of the theology and law of Strasbourg. Through Becon's influence in part, Bucer had been appointed to a chair at Cambridge University in 1549. Bucer produced his *De Regno Christi* shortly after his arrival, summarizing his lifelong reflections on the reformation of the earthly kingdom, particularly the reformation of family lore and law. The work was formally dedicated to the young English King Edward VI, but was functionally more significant in helping to shape an emerging theology of marriage in England.[75]

Like Bullinger, Bucer taught that marriage is a "first and most sacred union of man and woman." Marriage was to be "established in a holy way" in accordance with the laws of God. Persons should enter into it "gravely, deliberately, religiously, as befits those who have professed piety."[76] Bucer proffered many of the same prescriptions for the proper contracting of marriage that Bullinger had outlined, periodically echoing Bullinger's description of marriage as a "compact" and "covenant" that symbolized the loving union of Christ with His Church.[77] He likewise endorsed Bullinger's rendition of the interlocking purposes of marriage—for mutual love and friendship, procreation of children, and protection from lust—with a similar emphasis on marital love, friendship, and sacrifice. Married couples, he wrote in summary, must be "united not only in body but in mind also, with such an affection as none may be dearer and more ardent among all the relations of mankind, nor of more efficacy to the mutual offices of love, and of loyalty. They must communicate and consent in all things both divine and human, which have any moment to well and happy living. The wife must honour and obey her husband, as the Church honours and obeys Christ her head. The husband must love and cherish his wife, as Christ his Church. Thus they must be true to each other, if they will be true man and wife in the sight of God, whom certainly churches must follow in their judgement. Now the proper and ultimate end of marriage is not copulation, or children, for then there was no true matrimony between Joseph and Mary the mother of Christ, nor between many holy persons more, but the full and proper and main end of marriage is the communicating of all duties, both divine and humane, each to the other, with utmost benevolence and affection."[78]

Unlike Bullinger, however, Bucer placed special emphasis upon the social quality and utility of this divinely ordained institution. Following the conventions of the Lutheran two kingdoms theory, he insisted that "marriage is a *res politica*," "a civil thing." It is an institution of the "earthly kingdom, not the heavenly kingdom." It is subject to Godly norms, but directed to human ends. It is an institution created for the "common good," which Bucer defined as both the "internal good" of members of the household and the "external good" of subjects of the commonwealth. "[H]oly wedlock [is] the fountain of and seminary of good subjects," designed for the "decency and well-being of the commonwealth," for the "springing up of good men, and a right constitution of the commonwealth." "[W]ho knows not that chastity and pureness of life can never be restored or continued in the commonwealth, unless it first be established in private houses, from whence the whole breed of men is to come forth."[79]

This emphasis on the social utility of marriage was hardly startling. Many fellow divines, including Becon, said things similar, and one could trace these sentiments back to Chrysostom, Augustine, and other Church

Fathers. But Bucer pressed this logic to conclusions radical for his own day and prescient of reforms urged a century later by John Milton. Marriage must be maintained if it caters to the common good, Bucer said. But it must be dissolved if it detracts from the common good. Serving the common good became, for Bucer, not an aspirational goal of marriage, but an essential condition for its continuance. There are "four necessary properties" to any "proper and useful" marriage, he wrote: "(1) That the [couple] should live together. . . . (2) That they should love one another in the height of dearness. . . . (3) That the husband bear himself as the head and preserver of the wife, instructing her to all godliness and integrity of life; that the wife also be to her husband a help, according to her place, especially furthering him in the true worship of God, and next in all the occasions of civil life. And (4) That they not defraud each other of conjugal benevolence." Marriages that exhibit these four properties must be maintained and encouraged. But "where only one [property] be wanting in both or either party . . . it cannot then be said that the covenant of matrimony holds good between such." Improper separation, loss of love, or defiance of religious devotion, marital duty, or conjugal debts each breaks the marriage bond. For each of these lapses betrays an essential condition of marriage and thus denies its reason for being.[80]

To perpetuate the formal structure of marriage after a "necessary property" is lost is a destructive custom, Bucer believed. It is also an unbiblical practice. "[T]he Lord did not only permit, but also expressly and earnestly commanded his people, by whom he would that all holiness and faith of the marriage covenant be observed, that he could not induce his mind to love his wife with a true conjugal love, might dismiss her that she might marry to another" who is more meet and good.[81]

On this foundation, Bucer advocated the replacement of the canon law of divorce with the more liberal divorce provisions of the earlier Christianized Roman law. He dismissed the canon law remedy of separation from bed and board, with no right of remarriage, as just the kind of destructive custom that should be avoided. He likewise replaced the small list of causes for divorce recognized at Catholic canon law with the more ample roll of causes recognized at Christianized Roman law. Bucer intimated strongly that divorce should be granted on grounds of "mutual consent alone," as earlier Roman law had (for a time) allowed.[82] Though he later seemed to retreat from this position, he confirmed a wide range of causes for divorce recognized at Roman law that were considered deleterious to the common good of family, state, or church:

> If the husband can prove the wife to be an adulteress, a witch, a murderess, to have bought or sold to slavery any one free born, to

have violated sepulchers, committed sacrilege, favored thieves and robbers, desirous of feasting with strangers, the husband not willing, if she lodge forth without a just and probable cause, or frequent theaters and sights, he forbidding, if she be privy with those that plot against the State, or if she deals falsely, or offers blows [he may divorce her]. And if the wife can prove her husband guilty of any of those forenamed crimes, and frequent the company of lewd women in her sight, or he beat her, she had the like liberty to quit herself, with this difference, that the man after divorce might forthwith marry again, the woman not till a year after, lest she might chance to have conceived.[83]

All such pernicious conduct by a husband or a wife had to end the marriage, in Bucer's view, for to perpetuate the union thereafter served neither the internal good of the household nor the external good of the community.

Bucer's emphasis on the social dimensions of marriage also led him to advocate exclusive state jurisdiction over marriage. Bucer was in favor of local parishes and clerics maintaining internal codes of spiritual discipline to guide their members on questions of marriage and sexuality. But he stood firmly against any exercise of legal or political authority by the clergy over questions of marital formation, maintenance, and dissolution.[84] It was up to the Christian king, he wrote, "to take up the just care of marriages," following the tradition of the ancient Hebrew monarchs and Christian Roman emperors.[85] "[P]ious princes and commonwealths both may and ought [to] establish" a civil law of marriage.[86] To Bucer, this was self-evident, given that marriage was a "civil thing" of the earthly kingdom. "[N]o wise man can doubt," he wrote confidently, "that it is necessary for princes and magistrates first with severity to punish whoredom and adultery; next to see that marriages be lawfully contracted, and in the Lord, then that they be faithfully kept; and lastly, when that unhappiness urges, that they be lawfully dissolved, and another marriage contracted, according as the law of God, and of nature, and the constitutions of pious princes have decreed."[87]

Becon, Bullinger, and Bucer set out many of the main themes of the emerging Anglican theology of marriage. From different perspectives, each of these influential writers insisted on chipping away various canon law accretions from biblical and apostolic norms of marriage. Each criticized the sacramental construction of marriage, the subordination of marriage to celibacy, the inflation of impediments to betrothal and marriage, the restriction of divorce to separation from bed and board, among other canon law institutions. Each insisted on the familiar

Protestant requirements of mutual, parental, and communal consent to marriage, church consecration and registration of new unions, marriage for clergy and laity alike, divorce for cause, rights of remarriage for innocent divorcées and for widows and widowers. Each treated marriage as a natural, contractual, social, and spiritual union that was held together by the mutual love and duties of husband and wife, and by the mutual nurture of church and state. Each insisted that marriage was a covenant involving God, husband and wife, and the broader community, which was created to serve the ends of mutual love, mutual protection from sin, and mutual procreation and nurture of children.

Bullinger and Bucer added their own variations on these common themes. Bullinger stressed the internal covenantal duties of domestic love, devotion, and support between husband and wife, parent and child. Bucer stressed the external common goods of the household for the church, state, and broader commonwealth. Bullinger stressed the church's role in the communication and enforcement of biblical duties of the domestic covenant. Bucer vested the state with principal governance of the formation and dissolution of marriage. Bullinger adduced primarily biblical sources for his construction of marriage. Bucer added a variety of norms from natural law, the law of nations, and Christianized Roman law. Bullinger focused on marital formation and adumbrated various biblical norms governing betrothals, weddings, and initial cohabitation. Bucer focused as well on marital dissolution and adduced various historical norms justifying separation, divorce, and remarriage.

In the mid-sixteenth century, the Church of England had not yet developed an integrated model of marriage to mediate among these variations on Protestant marriage doctrines. But the writings of Becon, Bullinger, Bucer, and other divines provided a fertile seedbed out of which would grow a rich theology of marriage in subsequent centuries. The companionate view of marriage, which is usually traced to seventeenth-century Puritan communitarianism and eighteenth-century "affective individualism," was already in place among Anglican theologians of the mid-sixteenth century.[88] The covenantal conception of the household, which is often treated as a unique contribution of seventeenth-century English Puritanism, was in fact already an integral part of Anglican thought by the mid-sixteenth century.[89] The commonwealth model of marriage as the prototype and progenitor of the English commonwealth, which would become the paradigm of seventeenth-century marriage theology, had its roots in the writings of Becon and Bucer, and can be traced to even earlier Protestant and Catholic prototypes.

Legal Reformation
and Legal Reversal

It was left largely to Parliament to establish the preferred norms and habits for the Church and Commonwealth of England. The legislation passed in the heat of Henry's marital disputes with the papacy laid the constitutional groundwork for a robust legal reformation of marriage and many other topics. The 1533 Act in Restraint of Appeals barred the papacy's appellate jurisdiction over the English "empire" and declared that "all causes of matrimony and divorces" now lie exclusively "within the King's jurisdiction and authority."[90] The 1534 Supremacy Act declared the King to be "the only supreme head in earth of the Church of England" with "full power and authority . . . to reform" all doctrines, liturgies, and laws, including those affecting marriage.[91] Acts of 1533 and 1535 called for a Reform Commission of spiritual and temporal leaders of the commonwealth to recommend systematic reform of prevailing canon law, including the law of marriage.[92]

Preliminary Legal Changes

Even before the Reform Commission began its work, Parliament made several piecemeal changes to the prevailing canon law of marriage, family, and sexuality that were consistent with the agitations of the Protestant reformers. Impediments of consanguinity and affinity were restricted to those set out in Leviticus.[93] Judges and clerics were forbidden "to dispense with God's Lawes" on the subject, either by expanding these impediments beyond the Levitical degrees or by offering dispensations to parties to marry in violation of them.[94] The canon law impediment of precontract, which had earlier allowed fully consummated marriages to be broken on discovery of a prior contract to marriage, could now be enforced only if the subsequently married couple had no children.[95] Parishes were ordered to keep a marriage registry, putting the public on notice of existing marriages.[96] Priests were granted freedom to marry, without prejudice to their person, property, or profession, and guaranteed the same punishment as the laity if convicted for adultery or fornication.[97] Children of properly solemnized and consecrated marriages were to be treated as presumptively legitimate; all others were to be treated as bastards who were subject to severe civil restrictions and deprivations.[98] Various sexual crimes, particularly buggery, bestiality, and sodomy, were newly and repeatedly condemned as capital offenses.[99] These piecemeal legislative changes were viewed by many as steps along the way to a more systematic reformation of the liturgy, doctrine, and discipline of marriage.

Liturgical Reform

Systematic liturgical reform came in *The Book of Common Prayer*. The Parliaments of 1549 and 1552 mandated versions of the Prayer Book, which were repealed by Queen Mary.[100] Elizabeth's First Parliament promulgated a comprehensive new Prayer Book, which ultimately became a centerpiece of Anglican unity and identity.[101] This 1559 *Book of Common Prayer* provides a timeless distillation of prevailing sentiments on marriage, and a wedding ritual that is still widely practiced today:

> [H]oly matrimony . . . is an honorable estate, instituted of God in paradise in the time of man's innocency, signifying unto us the mystical union, that is betwixt Christ and his Church: which holy estate Christ adorned and beautified with his presence and first miracle that he wrought in Cana of Galilee, and is commended of St. Paul to be honorable among all men, and therefore is not to be enterprised nor taken in hand unadvisedly, lightly, or wantonly, to satisfy men's carnal lusts and appetites, like brute beasts that have no understanding, but reverently, discreetly, advisedly, soberly, and in the fear of God, duly considering the causes of which matrimony was ordained. One was, the procreation of children to be brought up in the fear of the Lord, and praise of God. Secondly, it was ordained for a remedy against sin, and to avoid fornication, that such persons as have not the gift of continency might marry, and keep themselves undefiled members of Christ's body. Thirdly, for the mutual society, help, and comfort, that the one ought to have of the other, both in prosperity and adversity.[102]

The Prayer Book repeats the traditional requirement of publication of banns of marriage on three successive Sundays or holy days prior to the wedding, during which occasion the couple, their parents, and other parties could voice objections to the budding union.[103] The wedding itself was to be celebrated as a public event, in a parish church, with a set liturgy. During the service, the officiating priest invited guests for the final time to state "any just cause why they may not be lawfully joined together." He admonished the couple that "if either of you do know any impediment why ye may not be lawfully joined together in matrimony, that ye confess it. For be ye well assured, that so many as be coupled together on [other grounds] than God's Word doth allow, are not joined together by God, neither is their matrimony lawful."[104] Thereafter, the couple exchanged ritualized oaths of marriage. The husband delivered the wedding ring to the woman. (The 1662 Prayer Book revision mandated exchange of rings.) The priest declared them married, adding Christ's familiar warning: "Those whom God hath joined together, let no man put asunder." There followed a series of ritualized blessings, prescribed Bible readings, set prayers, a homily, and public celebration of the Eucharist.

The 1559 *Book of Common Prayer* was passed by statute and mandated for use in all churches in England. All other prayer books and liturgies were declared to be "utterly void and of none effect."[105] Royal and local visitors were commissioned to ensure its uniform and universal adoption throughout England. Dissenters from the Prayer Book were subject to prosecution in church courts—sometimes vicious persecution, especially in the wake of anti-Catholic and antisectarian legislation in the 1570s and periodically thereafter.[106] The language and liturgy of the Prayer Book's section on the Solemnization of Matrimony has remained virtually unchanged until the twentieth century despite the comprehensive Prayer Book revisions of 1604 and 1661/62, and the 1789 adoption of a new *Book of Common Prayer* for the Protestant Episcopal Church in America.

Doctrinal Reform

Systematic doctrinal reform came in the Thirty-Nine Articles of Religion (1571). The Articles, however, both in their final form as well as in the provisional drafts of 1553 and 1562, had relatively little to say about marriage and family life. Echoing the new theological and legal sentiments of the day, the Articles did permit clerical marriage as a matter of church dogma: "Byshops, Priestes, and Deacons, are not commaunded by Gods lawe eyther to vowe the estate of single lyfe, or to abstayne from marriage. Therefore it is lawful *also* for them, as for all Christian men, to mary at ther owne discretion, as they shall judge the same to serue better to godlynesse."[107] The Articles explicitly denied the sacramental quality of marriage as a matter of church dogma: Only Baptism and Eucharist are the "two Sacramentes ordayned of Christe our Lorde in the Gospell," the Articles read. The sacrament of marriage is a state of "lyfe alowed in the Scriptures: but . . . not any visible signe, or ceremonie, ordayned of God."[108] The Thirty-Nine Articles had little else to say about marriage, save giving a nod to the homilies on marriage in the Prayer Book.[109]

Failed Reforms
of Ecclesiastical Law

These relatively modest changes in the established liturgy and doctrine of marriage left it to the Reform Commission to make the most radical changes in the inherited canon law tradition. A body of thirty-two leading theologians, bishops, civilians, and common lawyers, led by

Archbishop Thomas Cranmer, seemed equal to the task.[110] In 1552, they presented to Parliament a comprehensive *Reformation of Ecclesiastical Law*.[111]

This *Reformatio legum* includes a crisp primer on Protestant marriage theology and law. Softening the quasi-sacramental language of the Prayer Book, the *Reformatio* holds up equality of partners, mutuality of obligations, and temporality of purposes as the main marks of marriage: "Marriage is a legal contract, inducing and effecting a mutual and perpetual union of a man with a woman, by the order of God, in which each surrenders to the other power over his body, for the purpose of begetting offspring or of avoiding harlotry, or of controlling life by means of reciprocal obligations."[112]

"Since marriage is a lawful and devout custom, and prevents the disgrace of many shameful things," the *Reformatio* continues, "we do not want to keep any persons of any condition, rank, or age whatsoever from marriage," including the clergy.[113] All parties are free to enter this union, provided they are fit for such unions and follow the conventional steps of betrothal and espousal. Parties may enter betrothals once they have reached the age of consent—twelve for girls, fourteen for boys. Parents or guardians of both parties must give their consent to the pending union. Parish ministers must publicly announce the banns for marriage on three successive Sundays or holy days. Weddings must be public religious ceremonies in the parish church of either party, following the prescribed liturgy and ritualized exchange of oaths set out in the Prayer Book.[114] Betrothed parties must postpone their cohabitation or consummation until after the ceremony. Violation of any of these rules automatically nullifies the marriage.

The *Reformatio* adopted a truncated list of impediments to betrothal and marriage. Discovery of a prior, undissolved marriage by either party or discovery of a blood or family relation between the parties proscribed in Leviticus led to automatic annulment and potential punishment of the parties for bigamy or incest. Postmarital discovery of an error respecting the person or quality of one spouse or the impotence or another defect that precluded intercourse allowed either party to bring an action for annulment. Proof of coercion or threats into marriage could also break betrothal or marriage. Insanity, contagion, and heresy were sufficient grounds to break betrothals, but not consummated marriages. "Spiritual associations" by either party "ought not to impede at all the course of marriage"—a reversal of traditional canon law rules respecting the superiority of vows of chastity and holy orders.[115]

The *Reformatio* granted both husband and wife an equal right to sue for complete divorce and the right to remarry, on proof of cause. Such causes included adultery, desertion, deadly hostility, and prolonged ill-treatment, with a hint that even perennial "disagreements or grounds of offense" might ripen into a sufficient cause for divorce. In all such cases, couples were urged to reconcile and continue their marriage. Absent reconciliation, innocent parties could file a petition before an ecclesiastical judge. Innocent parties were warned against any conspiring in, or falsely charging, their spouses' marital fault, on pain of severe penalty. Husbands were required to continue to pay their wives "a seemly and fit allowance" while the divorce proceeding was pending, regardless of who was plaintiff.[116] A successful suit for divorce brought criminal sanctions of banishment or imprisonment on the guilty party. Separation from bed and board was not a recognized remedy, nor was voluntary withdrawal from one's spouse a legitimate act. A couple was either to remain married and cohabiting or seek divorce following proper ecclesiastical procedures, thereby sundering the union permanently and leaving the former spouses free to remarry.

The *Reformatio* included traditional prohibitions against sexual offenses: adultery, fornication, bigamy, polygamy, incest, premarital sex, and conspiracy in the same. The church courts were to punish these with public penance, the ban, or excommunication. More serious sexual crimes of rape, sexual battery, kidnapping, and the like were left to the magistrate to punish, with corresponding spiritual sanctions where appropriate.[117] The law urged "shotgun" weddings for betrothed parties whose premarital sex had led to pregnancy, on pain of a man's forfeiture of ample property and a woman's banishment or imprisonment. It demanded fathers to support illegitimate children that they had sired. It urged mothers, even of illegitimate children, to nurse their own children rather than send them to wet nurses.

Virtually every provision on marriage and divorce in the *Reformatio* had antecedents in the marriage ordinances of Wittenberg, Zurich, Strasbourg, and Geneva, and the attendant writings of Luther, Bullinger, Bucer, and Calvin. Luther's and Calvin's emphases on formal betrothals and the policing of the conduct of betrothed parties prior to the wedding are evident. Bullinger's emphasis on a highly ritualized consecration of marriage in church comes through clearly. Bucer's liberal doctrine of divorce, on grounds beyond adultery, and rights of remarriage are likewise manifest. The Continental Reformers' common emphases on the civil qualities of marriage, clerical marriage, restricted impediments, and divorce rather than separation all find a place in the law. These Protestant prototypes were well known to Cranmer and many of his colleagues, and they had skillfully appropriated them in the *Reformatio*. The only provisions not common in Continental Protestant marriage laws were the requirements of mothers to nurse their own children, husbands to support their wives during divorce suits, and fathers to support their illegitimate children—and these provisions were known at English canon law prior to the Reformation.

Though theologically commonplace, these provisions proved politically unpersuasive. The 1553 Parliament, which had already passed prototypes of the Thirty-Nine Articles and *The Book of Common Prayer,* refused to promulgate this *Reformation of Ecclesiastical Law.* The 1571 Parliament likewise demurred. In each instance, it was a single, strong layperson who led the opposition on largely political grounds—the Duke of Northumberland in the House of Lords in 1553, Queen Elizabeth herself in 1571. There is no evidence that the Reformatio's articles on marriage and divorce themselves met with any serious criticism. But, as part of a more comprehensive reformation of the canon law and ecclesiastical structures of England, they did not pass muster.[118]

Legal Settlement

The rejection of the *Reformatio* was an affirmation of much of the medieval canon law of marriage. To be sure, earlier legislation allowing clerical marriage and restricting impediments of blood, affinity, and prior contracts remained in effect.[119] With the legal establishment of the Prayer Book and Thirty-Nine Articles, Parliament also indirectly sanctioned clerical marriage, publication of banns, and church consecration of marriages. But the early sixteenth-century Catholic canon law of marriage, as amended by statute, remained the law governing marriage. Neither the more radical Protestant reforms of the 1552/71 *Reformatio legum,* nor even the more modest Catholic reforms of the 1563 *Decree Tamesti* of the Council of Trent were accepted. Such reforms would not be fully implemented for at least three more centuries.[120] The *Reformatio* came to stand, in the English tradition, as something of a futuristic liberal ideal to which subsequent legal reforms moved ever so slowly.

The English ecclesiastical law of marriage in the late sixteenth century thus looked very much like the Catholic canon law of marriage of a century or two before.[121] The law distinguished between betrothal, marriage, and consummation. Parties could contract betrothals after the age of seven, marriages after the age of twelve for girls, fourteen for boys—although in reality, the common practice of feudal wardships tended to extend the marriage age to sixteen and twenty-one respectively, and social custom discouraged marriages before parties had reached their mid twenties.[122] Legitimate betrothals required a mutual promise to marriage in the future ("I shall take you for my husband/

wife"). Public betrothals, especially those backed by oaths, were preferred, though private betrothals were legitimate and enforceable. Consummation by the couple after betrothal led automatically to marriage.
Absent consummation, the affianced parties could break off their betrothals for any number of reasons: on grounds of mutual consent; by
reason of one party's desertion, fornication, abuse, cruelty, or crime; on
discovery of coercion, fraud, infancy, contagion in either party; or by
breach of a condition (such as failure to deliver promised property). Parents and third parties could also press the parties to forgo their union
because of differences of status, person, or religion, and many other
causes. Church courts could, on their own initiative, dissolve a betrothal
on discovery of a relationship of consanguinity, affinity, or precontract.
All that was missing from the traditional canon law of betrothal was the
prohibitive impediment of a prior or subsequent vow of celibacy or
chastity by either party. But, absent proof of an impediment of consanguinity, affinity, or precontract, the betrothed couple had the final word
and act respecting their marriage. Legitimate marriages required only a
mutual promise of marriage in the present ("I take you for my hus-
band/wife"). No parental consent, testimony of witnesses, publication of
banns, ceremony in church, or sexual consummation were necessary,
although, again, it was customary to attend to each of these formalities.[123]

Marriages, once contracted, could be dissolved either by annulment
or divorce. An order of *annulment* required proof of one of the impediments to marriage that survived Tudor statutory reform—a blood or
family relationship between the parties prohibited by Leviticus, a precontract to an earlier marriage by one of the parties, or the impuberty,
frigidity, or impotence of either or both parties.[124] A declaration of annulment was a judgment that the putative marriage had been void from
the start and that parties were free to marry another. Annulments had
hidden costs, however, beyond the costs of litigation. The annulment
dissolved a woman's right to collect dower interests in her former husband's estate.[125] It reduced any children born of the union to the status
of bastards, with severely truncated rights of inheritance from their parents along with other civil and political deprivations.[126] And, if granted
on grounds of precontract, the annulment could also expose the previously contracted party to prosecution for bigamy, now a capital offense.[127]

A decree of *divorce* required proof of adultery, desertion (for more
than seven years), or protracted ill treatment—beyond the normal physical beatings that English law allowed a husband to visit upon a recalcitrant or belligerent wife.[128] A judgment of divorce was an order for

separation from bed and board alone, with no right of remarriage for either party while the other spouse was still alive.

1604 Canons

The 1604 Canons and Constitutions Ecclesiastical—the only major English legislation on marriage before passage of Lord Hardwicke's Act in 1753—both softened and hardened this inherited canon law tradition.[129] On matters of marital *formation,* the 1604 Canons softened the medieval canon law slightly. Seven years before, Convocation had thundered its support for the traditional canon law rules of private consent, despite the problem of clandestine marriages: "consent in marriage is specially to be regarded, and credit of kindred, honour, wealth, contentment, and pleasure of friends be rather matters of conveniency than necessity in marriage."[130] The 1604 Canons encouraged more publicity in marriage formation by confirming the Prayer Book's requirement of public banns and church consecration for marriage, and by introducing the requirement that children under twenty-one years must procure the consent of their parents or guardians before contracting and consummating their marriage.[131]

The 1604 Canons, however, also confirmed the traditional licensing exception, which eventually undercut the effectiveness of these reforms as deterrents to secret marriages. Parties could be exempted from the publication and public consecration requirements by procuring a marriage license from an authorized ecclesiastical official.[132] "Licensed marriages" were initially conceived as narrow exceptions to the usual rules, reserved for instances where necessity, such as imminent travel or military service, demanded an abbreviated engagement. At first, only the Archbishop of Canterbury and a few of his delegates were formally authorized to issue marital licenses, and they were expected to demand the presence of two good and honorable witnesses, strict proof of no prior impediment or pending marital litigation affecting the couple, and formal proof of parental consent from both sets of parents.[133] In the course of the seventeenth century, however, this license exception came to be treated as an attractive alternative method of marrying without the involvement of church, family, or community. Licensing officials proliferated, licensing requirements eroded, and false licenses abounded. Couples who sought to marry secretly could easily steal away to a remote parish to be married, or make their way to one of the many licensing booths that sprang up around the Fleet Prison and near the ports. This "underground marital industry," as Lord Hardwicke would later call it, thrived in the seventeenth and eighteenth centuries, despite the increasingly stern prohibitions of Parliament and Convocation against it.[134]

The problem of secret and premature marriages—which had earlier taxed the Catholic Church and led to the firm publicity requirements of the Council of Trent—thus continued to plague the Anglican Commonwealth. It was now spurious lax licensors and licenses, however, that provided parties with the convenient means for circumventing the laws requiring public marriage formation.[135] Parliament's opposition to such secret marriages had several motivations, not all entirely unselfish: the dangers of exploitation and abuse of youngsters; the social costs of inaptly formed marriages that would be impossible to dissolve; the parents' loss of control over their children and their properties; and the commonwealth's loss of revenue from license taxes and wedding fees, among other factors. The famous 1753 Parliamentary Act for the Better Preventing of Clandestine Marriage (Lord Hardwicke's Act) sought to put a forceful end to this practice by returning the licensing exception to its traditional limits, and by requiring formal banns, church consecration, parental consent, and two witnesses as a condition for legitimate marriage.[136]

On matters of marital *dissolution,* the 1604 Canons held fast to the substance of medieval canon law and introduced reforms to ensure its faithful execution. Seven years before, Convocation had complained bitterly about an "epidemic" of "disorderly marriages" and annulments and divorces "slightly passed."[137] The 1604 Canons took steps to end the disorder and to narrow the passage. All annulment and divorce proceedings were to be held in open church court, staffed by a duly authorized ecclesiastical judge, with no secret dispensations or equitable tinkering with dissolution requirements allowed. Parties were required to offer testimonial, documentary, or physical evidence in support of their dissolution petitions. The uncorroborated testimony of the parties themselves, even if uncontested, was no longer deemed sufficient evidence to dissolve a marriage.[138]

In cases of divorce, the 1604 Canons were doubly insistent on the traditional remedy of separation alone, with no right of remarriage to the innocent party. Ecclesiastical judges were required to enjoin divorced parties to "live chastely and continently; neither shall they during each other's life, contract matrimony for any other person. And, for the better observation of this last clause, the said sentence of divorce shall not be pronounced, until the party or parties requiring the same have given good and sufficient caution and security into the court, and they will not any way break or transgress the said restraint or prohibition."[139] Judges were threatened with a one-year suspension of office for failure to extract this pledge.[140] Divorced parties who did remarry prior to the death of their ex-spouse (or presumed death in cases of desertion) faced prosecution for bigamy, a capital offense.[141] These firm measures were designed to put an end to the protracted disputes among jurists and theologians about the meaning of divorce, and to cut off any further experimentation with granting divorced parties a right to remarriage.[142]

These restrictions on marital dissolution, confirmed by the 1604 Canons, worked a particular hardship on women caught in abusive marriages. Once emancipated from their childhood homes, most women were dependent upon their husbands for security and support. Under the doctrine of coverture, their person and property effectively merged with that of their husbands. Absent special arrangements made through prenuptial contracts or the procurement of a special legal status of a "feme sole" or "feme covert," married women were restricted severely in their contractual, testamentary, commercial, and other legal capacities.[143] A major mitigating factor, however, was that women were granted rights of dower. This was a legal claim to at least a third of the marital estate, which even the most conniving husband found hard to overcome.

The restrictions on marital dissolution put the right to dower in direct competition with the right to remarry. An annulment gave a woman the right to remarry, but no right to collect her dower. A divorce preserved her right to dower, but gave her no right to remarry.[144] Neither circumstance was attractive to a woman without independent wealth and "must have deterred many a woman from pursuing her legal rights against an abusive or adulterous husband."[145]

It was this intolerable circumstance that led to one important reform of the prevailing ecclesiastical law—the introduction at the turn of the seventeenth century of the modern practice of awarding *alimony*. Historically, husbands could be required to make payments of daily maintenance to their wives while their divorce case was pending, a provision that found its way even into the 1552 *Reformation of Ecclesiastical Law*. But now the obligation to pay alimony could be extended, temporarily or permanently, after issuance of the divorce decree. Innocent wives who had divorced adulterous or abusive husbands could petition a court for payments of reasonable costs of their maintenance and support for a set time or for life.[146] Courts insisted on proof of the wife's innocence and the husband's prior guilt before honoring any such petition and would hear nothing of a husband suing for alimony from his wife. Any evidence of collusion or fraud by the wife would automatically cut off her rights. Once convinced of the wife's right to alimony, however, courts would calculate the award much in the same manner as they do today—weighing the length of the marriage, the size of the wife's pre-marital estate, the relative wealth and needs of the parties at the time of the divorce, the ages and needs of any children, the severity of the husband's fault during the marriage, among other factors.[147]

At first, only the Court of High Commission could hear petitions for alimony, and such awards were relatively rare. But, in the course of the seventeenth century and thereafter, orders for alimony became a staple practice of lower ecclesiastical courts, despite the repeated attacks from common law judges and jurists that church courts had no business ordering transfers of property among the laity. The practice persisted in the church courts till the nineteenth century, when it was taken over by the common law courts in the Matrimonial Causes Act of 1857.[148]

Given these modest changes in the prevailing law on the books, "marriage litigation in sixteenth and seventeenth-century England continued to look much as it had during the Middle Ages."[149] As the pathbreaking archival work of R.H. Helmholz, Ralph Houlbrooke, Martin Ingram, Eric Carlson, and others has shown, English church courts throughout this period continued to enjoy plenary jurisdiction over questions of marriage, family, and sexuality—interrupted only briefly during the Commonwealth period of 1640–1660. They adjudicated disputes over betrothals and marriages, with the vast preponderance of cases involving contractual and property disputes between parties who had made clandestine or oral contracts of marriage and now sought specific performance or injunctive relief from the other. They heard petitions for annulment and divorce, although the new procedural and property restrictions rendered such actions considerably less common than they had been prior to the Reformation. They presided over cases of wife and child abuse, desertion, deprivation, and the like—often sharing such jurisdiction with various royal and common law courts in serious cases involving crime. They meted out discipline for fornication, adultery, incest, premarital pregnancy, and the like, using the ecclesiastical censures of penance, admonition, ban, and excommunication—sometimes supplemented by heavy fines as well as corresponding criminal sanctions administered by the appropriate civil court.

The church courts' jurisdiction over marriage in the Tudor and Stuart eras was considerably more effective than the typical caricature would allow. It was typical of seventeenth-century Puritan writers, and twentieth-century historians who accepted their judgments, to dismiss the church courts as corrupt, dilatory, expensive, and ineffective. According to Professors Helmholz, Houlbrooke, and Ingram, this judgment is simply not borne out by the case law evidence of the period. The church courts were far from perfect in exercising their marital jurisdiction; no judicial system is perfect, including notoriously our own. Although imperfect, the church courts were effective—streamlining marital formation, curbing marital abuses, reducing illegitimacy, protecting wives and children, curtailing separation and desertion, and in general "reinforcing the ideals of personal chastity, communal responsibility for sexual behaviour and stable matrimony."[150]

Marriage as Commonwealth in Seventeenth-Century England

Traditional Formulations

The legal settlement of marriage questions also brought considerable theological settlement. Seventeenth-century English theologians—from the Anglo-Puritan to the Anglo-Catholic—generally agreed that marriage was not a sacrament, although it was a divinely ordained institution. Celibacy was not a prerequisite for clerical service, although it was a commendable state for the naturally continent.[151] Marriage was to serve the goals of love, procreation, and continence, although these goals were variously described and prioritized.[152] Mutual consent of a fit man and a fit woman was the essence of marriage, although arranged marriages, bordering on compulsion, were still commonly defended. The consent of parents or guardians was an essential step for the contracting of marriage, although marriages contracted without such consent were still tolerated. Contracts of betrothal and marriage were still distinguished, although the length of time and the conduct of the parties in the interval were variously described.[153] Church consecration of marriage was an essential step to the formation of marriage, although the exchange of rings and the celebration of the Eucharist remained controversial ceremonies in some circles.[154] Impediments of consanguinity, precontracts, impotence or frigidity were the principal grounds for annulment of marriages, although impediments of crime and heresy were sometimes defended as well. The legal establishment of these core doctrines of marriage ended the heated theological debates about them. Those who could not accept these basic established doctrines had to keep silent or to leave—on pain of punishment.

Rancorous debate continued about the doctrine of divorce, however, despite the firmness of the law established by the 1604 Canons. Deuteronomy 24, Matthew 19, and 1 Corinthians 7 all taught that "divorcement" was a proper remedy in certain cases—of "uncleanness," "fornication," or "departure of the disbeliever," respectively. The 1604 Canons had confirmed the traditional Catholic interpretation of these biblical passages. The term *divorce* meant only separation from bed and board, not absolute divorce with a right to remarriage. This traditional doctrine of divorce was forcefully defended by a variety of leading Anglican divines throughout the seventeenth century, and a few Puritans as well.[155]

The 1604 Canons had not accepted, however, the sacramental theology of marriage upon which this medieval interpretation had been founded, and therein lay the controversy. Historically, the Catholic Church had prohibited complete divorce on the theory that marriage was an eternal sacramental bond between husband and wife. Marriage began in this life and continued more perfectly in the life to come. This sacramental bond of marriage symbolized the eternal bond of grace between Christ and his church. To allow absolute divorce and remarriage to an estranged couple was both to legitimate serial polygamy and to symbolize divine infidelity. Neither course could be countenanced. It was better for estranged couples to be separated from bed and board, yet remain married in this life. Their marital bond could be restored and redeemed in the life hereafter, if not before. And, even if the couple remained estranged for the rest of their temporal lives, their bond could still bring some measure of sanctifying grace to their children and the church, if not to themselves. God could use even a broken marriage to communicate his sacramental grace.[156]

By officially denying the sacramental character of marriage in the Thirty-Nine Articles, the Anglican Church and English Parliament had undercut this traditional rationale for prohibiting absolute divorce. No systematic substitute rationale was yet at hand. This inevitably led to strident theological attack against the established doctrine—not only from many Puritans, but also from some Anglicans.[157] Some early seventeenth-century Anglican theologians, such as Vicar Edmund Bunny, simply returned to traditional sacramental rationales for this doctrine of limited divorce—in defiance of official Anglican dogma.[158] Others, such as Bishop Lancelot Andrewes argued that the 1611 King James Version of the Bible had simply not captured the nuance of Christ's words in Matthew 19:9. This Authorized Version reads: "Whosoever shall put away his wife, except it be for fornication, and shall marry another, committeth adultery." But, properly understood, Andrewes argued, the verse should read: "He that putteth away his wife (which but for adultery is not lawful) and marrieth another, comitteth adultery himself." This reading, together with the injunction, "What God hath joined together, let not man put asunder," said Andrewes, makes clear that the Bible grants only the right of separation, not remarriage.[159] But such counterdogmatic and countertextual logic could not be convincing in the long term. A new rationale was needed.

The *commonwealth model of marriage* provided the new rationale. This model served at once to rationalize and routinize the many marital doctrines that had been settled, and to seek settlement over the disputed doctrine of divorce. The commonwealth model was not universally endorsed in seventeenth-century England. But it was a popular construction of the nature and purpose of marriage that appealed broadly to English theologians—from the Anglo-Catholic to the Anglo-Puritan.[160]

Seventeenth-century theologians began where Thomas Becon and Martin Bucer had ended in the mid-sixteenth century—with the belief that "marriage is a little common weale" created "for the common good."[161] In 1590, William Perkins put it thus: "[M]arriage was made and appointed by God himself to be the foundation and seminary of all sorts and kinds of life in the commonwealth and the church. . . . [T]hose families wherein the service of God is performed are, as it were, little churches; yea, even a kind of paradise on earth."[162] Robert Cleaver opened his famous 1598 tract *A Godly Form of Householde Gouernment* with an oft-repeated maxim: "A household is as it were a little commonwealth, by the good government whereof, Gods glorie may bee aduaunced, the common-wealthe whiche standeth of several families, benefited, and all that live in that familie, may receiue much comfort and commoditie."[163] William Gouge premised his massive 1622 tome *Of Domestical Duties: Eight Treatises* on the same belief that "the family is a seminary of the Church and the Common-wealth," and indeed in its own right, "a little church, and a little commonwealth, whereby a tryal may be made of such as are fit for any place of authority, or subjection in Church or commonwealth."[164] Daniel Rogers, a sharp critic of Gouge on many points, nonetheless embraced the commonwealth model of marriage: "Marriage is the Preservative of Chastity, the Seminary of the Common-wealth, seed-plot of the Church, pillar (under God) of the world."[165] Such sentiments "represent the consensus" of those writing on marriage in the late sixteenth and early seventeenth centuries.[166]

Theologians predicated this commonwealth model on both natural and biblical arguments. Systematic theologians regarded the interlocking commonwealths of state, church, and family as something of an earthly form of heavenly government. Dudley Fenner, for example, suggested that "the divine polity of Father, Son, and Holy Spirit" was reflected in "the covenanted polities of state, church, and family." State authorities are the Father's vice-regents called to rule in accordance with the natural laws of creation. Church authorities are the Son's representatives called to preach

Christ's word and to administer His sacraments. Family authorities are the Spirit's agents, called to provide daily Godly instruction, protection, and edification to its members. Just as the divine polity and persons of God are mutually dependent and edifying, so are these human polities.[167]

Biblical theologians grounded this commonwealth construction in the Fifth Commandment of the Decalogue: "Honour thy father and thy mother." This Commandment, Robert Pricke maintained, was "the Foundamentall Ground . . . of all Christian subjection and of like Christian gouernment, as well in Church and Common-wealth, as in every Schoole and Private Familie."[168] This Commmandment, John Dod added, was also the "fundamental ground" of the Second Table of the Decalogue. It played much the same role that the First Commandment played for the First Table of the Decalogue. Only those who obey the First Commandment, "Thou shalt have no other gods before me," can fully obey the subsequent Commandments on graven images, swearing, and the Sabbath. Likewise, only those who obey the Fifth Commandment of honoring parents can fully obey the later Commandments against killing, stealing, adultery, perjuring, and coveting.[169]

The domestic commonwealth was created as a hierarchical structure, English theologians believed. God had created Eve as "a help meet" for Adam. God had called Adam and Eve to mutual society among themselves and mutual procreation of children (Gen. 1:28, 2:18). After the Fall, God had commanded that Adam "shall rule over" Eve (Gen. 3:16). As heir of Adam, the modern husband was thus the head of his wife. As heir of Eve, the modern wife was his subject, his "help meet." Together husband and wife were the heads of their children and the rest of the household. Each of these offices in the family hierarchy was bound by a series of duties, rooted in the Bible and natural law.

The dozens of household manuals and catechisms published in the early seventeenth century copiously described this hierarchy of duties and offices within the domestic commonwealth. Robert Cleaver's four hundred-page manual on *A Godly Form of Householde Gouernment* offered a typical description. "All gouernment of a familie," Cleaver wrote, must be directed to two ends: "First Christian holinesse, and secondly the things of this life." "Religion must be stirring in Christian families, and that good gouernment looketh to bring godly behauior into families, as well as thrift and good husbandrie."[170]

The paterfamilias must play the leading role in achieving this domestic ideal, Cleaver believed. As a husband, he must "liue with his Wife discreetely." He must "cherish and nourish" her as Christ loves and supports His Church. He must "use her in all due benevolence, honestlie, soberly, and chastly." And he must "gouern her in all duties, that properly concern the state of marriage, in knowledge, in wisedome, judgement, and justice." A husband must not be "bitter, fearce, and cruell" to his wife and must "never beate her" even if he, as her head, must reproach and admonish her. Instead, "as a man of knowledge," he must "edify her, both by a good example, and also, by good instructions."[171] As a father, the married man must lead his household in private devotions, daily prayer, catechization, and Bible reading. He must ensure that children and servants are faithful in public worship and Sabbath observance. He must be vigilant in offering his children instruction and admonition with wisdom, punishment and rebuke with patience.[172]

The duty of the married woman is to be "faithful and loving" to her husband, "wise and prudent" to her family. She must "reverence her husband" and "submit herself unto him," as scripture enjoins. She must not "wear gorgeous apparell beyond her degree & place." She must avoid sloth and the keeping of idle and untoward company. She must be thrifty, just, charitable, and prudent in her choice of friends. She must keep order and help maintain "the exercise of religion within the household." She must tend especially to the care of her daughters and maidens, teaching them and exemplifying for them the norms and habits of Christian womanhood.[173]

Husband and wife also have a variety of mutual duties to each other and to their children. Husband and wife "must love one another with a pure heart fervently." They must be "faithful" to each other, constantly "bending their wits, and al their endeavours, to the helpe each of other, and to the common good of the family." They must pray together, "admonish one another," and serve as "mutuall helpes, each to other, in matters concerning their owne salvation, and the service of God." Together, they must "instruct and bring up their children even from their cradle, in the feare and nourture of the Lord, . . . in shamefastnesse, hatred of vice, and love of all vertue." When the children mature, they must "bring them up in some profitable & lawfull calling, by which they may live honestly, & Christianly, & not be fruitless burdens of the earth . . . or commonwealth." They must also "provide for the disposing of them in marriage," counseling them in their courtship and consenting to their marriage when they come of age and have chosen wisely among available spouses.[174] In response to this, "the duties of the naturall child" are very simple: "Reverence, Obedience, and Thankfulnesse"—exemplified notably in seeking their parents' consent to their own marriage, and in caring for their parents when they become elderly or disabled.[175]

Faithful maintenance of this hierarchy of offices and duties, Cleaver believed, was the best guarantee of order within the domestic commonwealth. "For as in a Citie, there is nothing more unequal, then that

every man should be like equall: so it is not convenient, that in one
house every man should be like and equal another. There is no equalli-
tie in that citie, where the private man is equall with the Magistrate, the
people with the Senate, or the servants with the master, but rather a confusion of all offices and authoritie. The husbands and wives are Lords of
the house. . . . The husband without any exception is maister over all
the house, and hath as touching his familie more authority than a King
in his own kingdome. The wife is ruler of all other things, but yet under
her husband."[176]

Faithful maintenance of these domestic duties and offices was also the
best guarantee of order within the broader commonwealths of church
and state, Cleaver insisted. Indeed, properly functioning marriages and
households were indispensable to civic flourishing. "[I]f maisters of families do not practise at home catechising, and discipline in their houses
& joyne their helping hands to Magistrates, and Ministers," social order
and stability will soon give way to chaos and anarchy.[177] "[I]t is impossible for a man to vunderstand to gouerne the common-wealth, that
doth not knowe to rule his owne house, or order his owne person, so
that hee that knoweth not to gouern, deserueth not to raigne."[178]

This was common lore among Cleaver's fellow divines. "A con-
scionable performance of household duties . . . may be accounted a pub-
like work," William Gouge wrote. For "good members of a family are
likely to make good members of church and commonwealth."[179]
"[M]ost of the mischiefs that now infest or seize upon mankind throughout the earth, consist in, or are caused by the disorders and ill-
governedness of families."[180] "There was never any disorder and
outrage, in any family, Church, or Commonwealth" when domestic offices were respected and domestic duties discharged, Robert Pricke insisted. For domestic duty and discipline allow persons "to rise up to the
knowledge of the Souveraigne Lord, and to give unto him the reverence
and honour due to his divine Majestie." It also teaches them not only the
personal virtues but also the civic habits that "upholdeth, and continueth
all these estates, degrees, and orders" of the broader commonwealth.[181]
Daniel Rogers wrote more generally that a stable marriage and household
served as "the right hand of providence, supporter of lawes, states, orders, offices, gifts, and services, the glory of peace, . . . the foundation of
Countries, Cities, Universities, . . . Crownes and Kingdomes."[182] In the
mid-sixteenth century, Thomas Becon had described himself as "a very-
tyble voice cryinge in the wildernesse" of English divinity against the conventional deprecation and distortion of marriage. Half a century later, his
prophetic voice was part of a loud ecumenical chorus extolling the

domestic commonwealth for its indispensable personal, social, and moral goods.

Some writers pressed the commonwealth model to even further service and came to treat the domestic commonwealth not only as a valuable resource for political stability but as the very source of political authority. Sir Robert Filmer (John Locke's famous antagonist) posed this thesis forcefully in his defense of monarchical government. In his *Patriarcha* of c. 1638 and later essays, Filmer sought to prove that the domestic and political commonwealths are essentially the same, and that both are subject to the absolute authority of the male head.[183] Adam and Eve, Filmer believed, were the founders not only of the first marriage and family, but also of the first state and society. Adam was the first husband and father, but also the first patriarch and ruler. Eve was the first wife and mother, but also the first helper and subject. Together with their children, they comprised at once a domestic and a political commonwealth.[184]

Over time, Filmer argued, this first domestic and political commonwealth of Paradise was duplicated and differentiated. New marriages, new families, new societies, new states proliferated. But, for all their diversity, these institutions retained the same basic patriarchal structure created by God for the first commonwealth. The highest authority within these institutions was vested in the eldest entitled male, the patriarch descended from Adam. Duties of obedience and subjection fell on all others, as they had fallen on Eve and in turn on her children. This pattern of authority and subjection was not a matter of a social contract or a voluntary choice by the ruler or the ruled, Filmer insisted. It was the nature of things, the design of God's creation. "Every man that is born is . . . by his very birth . . . a subject to him that begets him: under which subjection he is always to live, unless by immediate appointment from God, or by the grant or death of his Father, he becomes possessed of that power to which he was subject."[185]

On these premises, Filmer defended a monarchical form of government modeled on the domestic hierarchy. The hierarchy of the family under the paterfamilias is replicated in the political hierarchy of the state under the King, he believed. "Kings now are the fathers of their people."[186] "If we compare the natural duties of a Father with those of a King, we find them to be all one, without any difference at all but only in the latitude or extent of them. As the Father over one family, so the King, as Father over many families, extends his care to preserve, feed, clothe, instruct, and defend the whole commonwealth."[187] The King enjoys "a natural right of a supreme Father over every multitude" and is deserving of the reverence, obedience, and subjection that natural children owe to their fathers. Thus the Fifth Commandment, "which enjoins obedience to Kings is delivered in the terms of 'Honor thy Father' as if all power were originally in the Father. If obedience to parents be immediately due by a natural law, and subjection to princes, but by the mediation of a human ordinance, what reason is there that the law of nature should give place to the laws of men, as we see the power of the Father over his child gives place and is subordinate to the power of the magistrate."[188]

Filmer recognized the inherent limitations of this extended interpretation of the commonwealth. Though analogous in hierarchy and duty, the modern commonwealths of state, church, and family were not identical. Each of these "commonwealths" had its own calling, constitution, and character that could not be conflated. The state had a unique power of the sword and the law. The church had a unique power of the Word and the sacrament. The marital household had a unique power of love and duty. Though he noted them, Filmer did not elaborate these differences among the political, ecclesiastical, and domestic commonwealths. Particularly in his later years, he tended increasingly toward a patriarchal monism.

Filmer's theological contemporaries did elaborate these differences, and in so doing emphasized the unique "companionate" qualities of the domestic commonwealth. "There is no Societie more neere, more entire, more needfull, more kindly, more delightfull, more comfortable, more constant, more continuall, than the Societie of Man and Wife," wrote Thomas Gataker.[189] "Conjugal love," Daniel Rogers insisted, is the "mayne and joint duty of the married." Marital love is the highest love, for it is simultaneously spiritual and sensual, Christian and carnal—a sweete compounde of both religion and nature."[190] "[M]arriage is the Queen of friendships," Jeremy Taylor insisted, "in which there is a communication of all that can be communicated by friendships"[191] Even William Gouge, who rivaled Filmer in patriarchal sternness, could bring himself to say that "with true matrimonial love and affection" a man and a woman reached "the nearest of equality that may be," becoming "after a sort even fellows and partners."[192] Dozens of paeans to romance, sensuality, intimacy, tenderness, friendship, companionship, sharing, equality, and other soft affections between husband and wife flowed from the pens of seventeenth-century English writers. Seventeenth-century writers were fully aware that marriage could also be, what William Whately called "a little hell," featuring poverty, rape, violence, abuse, and other forms of pathos.[193] But marital love was an ideal to be held up.

Marital love thus stood alongside marital duty in defining the domestic commonwealth. English Puritans certainly emphasized this, as William Haller, James T. Johnson, and Edmund Leites have all ably and amply shown.[194] But Anglican divines embraced the theme of marital love as well. To be sure, there was little romance in the austere Anglican tomes of a Richard Hooker—even less perhaps than appears in the cold Puritan calculus of a William Gouge. But just as Gouge does not represent average Puritan feeling, so Hooker does not capture the range of Anglican teaching on marital love. Already *The King's Book* of 1543 had listed "mutual aid and comfort" as the first purpose of marriage, before procreation and deterrence, and had urged that "man and wife ought to live together in perfect unity and concord, and to love each other as their own bodies, and to use the same in all cleanness, unity, and honour, even as Christ himself loved his espouse the church."[195] At the same time, Becon, Bullinger, Bucer, Sandys, Whitgift, and other divines had treated marital love and affection as a "necessary," even "indispensable," property of marriage. Without true marital love, the institution could not, and in Bucer's view should not, continue. These sentiments echoed in subsequent Anglican summae and sermons, and even more loudly in plays and poems of the day—just think of Shakespeare, Herbert, and Donne.[196] Even the rather reserved *Book of Common Prayer* of 1559 and 1662 commanded newly married couples to have "one accord of heart and mind" and to embrace "pleasant and sweet love." This passage, together with the more expansive biblical passages on love that the Prayer Book appointed for the marriage service, inspired many grand homiletic descriptions and prescriptions of marital love, affection, and companionship.[197] These themes were well known and repeated by such Anglican churchmen as Lancelot Andrewes, John Cosin, Jeremy Taylor, and others in the seventeenth century and beyond.

The concept of marital love and companionship was no invention or monopoly of seventeenth-century English Puritanism. It was a common feature of the English commonwealth model of marriage, alongside concepts of marital duty, hierarchy, and order. And all these concepts had Protestant theological roots reaching early into the sixteenth century, and Catholic theological roots reaching back several centuries more.[198] What was new about these marital concepts in the seventeenth century was not their formulation, but their integration in the commonwealth model.

The commonwealth model of marriage provided a sturdy new framework to rationalize the established law of marriage in England. English theologians, of course, repeated and glossed endlessly the biblical and traditional arguments for each of the rules of marital formation, maintenance, and dissolution, drawing on both medieval Catholic and various

Protestant sources in so doing. But it was the commonwealth understanding of marriage—as the first society created by God, the foundation of the Church and Commonwealth of England, the progenitor of civil society and morality—that gave these traditional interpretations a new sense of unity and gravity.

The steps for marital formation had to be carefully negotiated, for much was at stake in this union, both theological and political. The couple was not merely joining in covenant with each other and with God, as Continental Protestants taught. They were not merely symbolically representing the mysterious union of Christ and His Church, as Catholics taught. The couple was also, in effect, joining in covenant with the Church and Commonwealth of England—past, present, and future. They were promising, in William Heale's words, "to stake not onlie the temporal and eternal happynesse of themselves and theyr childr'n, but the verie vertue, stabilitie, order, and securitie of all England" on their marital promise.[199] A successful marriage would earn them and all others great reward; a failed marriage would bring great hardship.

Fraught as it was with personal, social, and eternal consequences, the step into matrimony thus required all the maturity, deliberation, and participation that the laws of marital formation demanded. Marriage required formal betrothals with a delay before nuptials so that all parties could calculate their companionability and compatibility.[200] It required the consent and counsel of parents and guardians, for they represented the wisdom of past generations of the commonwealth. It required the consecration of priests and approbation of magistrates, for they represented the current rulership of the commonwealth. It required the desire to procreate and the capacity to educate, for children would become the future generation of the commonwealth, to the benefit of family, church, and state alike.[201]

"They that enter into the state of marriage," Jeremy Taylor wrote, "cast a dye of the greatest contingency, and yet of the greatest interest in th'world, next to the last throw for eternity."[202] "Most gravely doth our Communion Booke admonish such as come to be married that they ought enter into this estate, not rashly, lightly, unadvisedly . . . but discreetly, advisedly, soberly, and in the feare of God," William Whately wrote. For persons who marry without full awareness of the gravity of their office do so "with much hazzard to their soules, and much unquietnesse to themselves, families, and neighbors . . . [and] indeede the very Common weal."[203] "Marriage of al humane actions is the one & only weightiest," William Heale continued. "It is the present disposall of the whole life of man: it is a Gordian knot that may not bee loosed but by the sworde of death: it is the ring of union whose poesie is Pure and endlesse. In a word it is that state which either imparadizeth a man in the Eden of felicitie, or els exposeth him vnto a world of miserie. Hence it is that so mature deliberation is required, before such an eternal bond be united. The mutual affection of each partie, the consent of parents, the approbation of friends, the trial of acquaintance: besides the e'pecial observance of disposition, of kindred, of education, of behaviour. Now then if a man solemnize marriage upon these due respects, he can hardly make his choice amissse, because hee is guided by vertue, which never faileth her followers."[204]

A similar argument was used to rationalize the restricted rules of marital dissolution and divorce. English theologians repeated and glossed with endless enthusiasm biblical passages on the maintenance of a "godly household." They grounded the patriarchal structure of the household on the Fifth Commandment and the texts of Paul. They grounded the impediments of precontract, consanguinity, and frigidity on Old Testament commandments on bigamy, incest, and procreation. They grounded the limited doctrine of divorce on New Testament counsels to be faithful to one's spouse even in the face of poverty, oppression, heresy, sickness, and other adversity.

It was the commonwealth understanding of marriage, however, that gave these traditional biblical rules their urgency and integrity for many seventeenth-century writers. The domestic commonwealth was the foundation of the English commonwealth. Its hierarchy of offices and duties was the model, even the source, of political authority and civic obligation. Its patriarchal construction was the foundation on which the monarchy and episcopacy of England was built. Its definition and discharge of duties was essential for civic order, liberty, and rule of law. Such a progenitive union could not be broken unless it defied God's explicit laws for marital formation. To break marriage for any other cause was, in Bishop Lancelot Andrewes' words, to act "against nature," "against the church," "against the commonwealth," indeed, "against the whole state of mankind."[205]

This was a new rationale for the English law of limited divorce and dissolution. In Catholic sacrament theology, marriage was presumed permanent because God had chosen this instrument to dispense his grace on the Church. In Anglican commonwealth theology, marriage was presumed permanent because God had chosen this institution to convey his law for the Commonwealth. In Catholic theology, even a broken marriage had to be maintained lest a channel of God's grace be prematurely closed to the Church. In Anglican theology, even a broken marriage had to be retained, lest a source of God's law and order be permanently lost on the Commonwealth. Catholic divorce doctrine tended to be more sacramental and otherworldly in inspiration; Anglican divorce doctrine tended to be more social and utilitarian.

To be sure, Anglicans in the seventeenth century and thereafter continued to speak of the sacramental qualities of marriage. But this was more a revival of an Augustinian concept of *sacramentum* than the survival of a Catholic theology of sacramentalism. In Catholicism, marriage was presumed to be permanent because it was a sacrament. In Anglicanism, marriage was presumed to be sacramental because it was permanent.

Liberal Revisions

Until the mid-seventeenth century, this commonwealth model had considerable intuitive appeal. The English commonwealths of family, church, and state, as conventionally understood and organized, had parallel hierarchical structures under a single head. The King, subject to God, stood at the head of the political commonwealth. The Archbishop, subject to God and King, stood at the head of the episcopal commonwealth. The paterfamilias, subject to God, King, and Bishop, stood at the head of the domestic commonwealth. With such a neat and orderly construction, it was easy for some to believe the speculation of a Dudley Fenner that these three commonwealth hierarchies were somehow models of God's creation order, perhaps even of the Triune Godhead itself.[206]

Such speculations were harder to follow when the English world—in Christopher Hill's apt phrase—"was turned upside down" by the English Revolutions of 1640 to 1689.[207] The 1640 Revolution was, in part, a rebellion against the excesses of the political commonwealth, headed by King Charles. The landed aristocracy and merchants chafed under oppressive royal taxation raised to support unpopular wars. Clergy and laity suffered under harsh new establishment laws that drove religious nonconformists first out of their families and churches, then out of England altogether. Much of the country resented the increasingly belligerent enforcement of royal measures by the prerogative courts—Star Chamber, Admiralty, High Commission, and Requests. When Parliament was finally called into session in 1640, after an eleven-year hiatus, its leaders seized power by force of arms. Civil war erupted between the supporters of Parliament and the supporters of the monarch. The Parliamentary party prevailed and passed an Act "declaring and constituting the People of England to be a commonwealth and free state." Parliament abolished the kingship, and the deposed King Charles was tried, convicted for treason, and executed. Parliament also abolished the aristocratic House of Lords and declared that "supreme authority" resided in the people and their representatives. Anglicanism was formally disestablished, and episcopal ecclesiastical structures were replaced with congregational and presbyterian forms. "Equal and proportional representation" was guaranteed in the election of local representatives. England came under "the democratic rule" of Parliament and the Protectorate of Oliver Cromwell.[208]

After Cromwell died in 1658, the Commonwealth government eventually collapsed. King Charles II, son of Charles I, returned to England, reclaimed the throne in 1660, and restored traditional monarchical government and pre-revolutionary law. This Restoration era was short-lived. When his successor, King James II, the other son of Charles I, began to abuse his royal prerogatives as his father had done, Parliament forced him to abdicate the throne in 1688 in favor of the new dynasty of William and Mary. This was the Glorious Revolution. It established government by the King *in Parliament* and introduced a host of new guarantees to English subjects, notably those set out in the Bill of Rights and the Toleration Act of 1689.[209]

Commonwealth Experiments

The English Revolutions unleashed a torrent of both legal and literary experimentation respecting marriage and the family. Much of this experimentation was outlawed with the Restoration in 1660, but it was prescient of later legal developments and indicative of some of the customs of the English countryside and of the colonies.

In 1653, the Commonwealth Parliament passed a statute that greatly simplified the contracting of marriage and largely removed it from the jurisdiction of the Church of England. Parties of the age of majority (sixteen, boys; fourteen, girls) who wanted to marry had to register with a local parish or justice of the peace. Their banns were to be thrice published at set intervals in the church or in the adjacent marketplace. Thereafter, the couple had to procure a marriage certificate from the same office. If they were under twenty-one years, they also had to procure proof of their parents' or guardians' consent. Weddings were to be performed before a justice of the peace, with two or more witnesses present. The parties were to hold hands and exchange a simple prescribed oath, with no exchange of rings: "I A.B. do here in the presence of God, the searcher of all hearts, take thee C.D. for my wedded Wife [Husband], and do also in the presence of God, and before these witnesses, promise to be unto thee a loving and faithful Husband [loving, faithful, *and obedient* Wife]." The justice of the peace was to pronounce the couple "husband and wife." The signed marriage certificate was to be returned to the parish register. Defiance of any of these steps would render the marriage "void and of none effect."

Local justices of the peace not only conducted weddings in place of priests, but were also given exclusive jurisdiction, in place of church courts, over the "hearing and determining of all matters and controversies touching Contracts and Marriages, and the lawfulness and unlawfulness thereof." They were specifically authorized to seize "the whole estate, real and personal" of "any person" who "by violence or fraud shall steal or take away" another person under twenty-one years of age "with intent to marry."[210] Five years later, Parliament also claimed the power to grant private acts of divorce, with a right to remarry given to the divorced parties.

Much of this 1653 law was repealed during the Restoration of 1660. But marriages that had been contracted before 1660 in accordance with its procedures were validated by statute.[211] Moreover, the practice of granting divorce by private act of Parliament continued. The high costs and cumbersome procedures rendered such acts rare during the next century; there was on average only one divorce every five or six years. But, after 1750, Parliament granted at least one such private act of divorce per year, a rate that slowly increased until the Divorce Reform Acts of 1857 and following years instituted causes of action for divorce in the common law courts.[212]

This legal experimentation with traditional marriage law was matched by even bolder literary speculation. Freed temporarily from censorship laws during the Commonwealth era of 1640–1660, English writers proposed all manner of alternatives to traditional habits and forms of marriage—from the salutary to the prurient. Gerrard Winstanley, the leader of the Diggers, suggested, against prevailing patterns of arranged and male-initiated marriages, that "every man and every woman shall have the free liberty to marry whom they love, if they can obtain the love and liking of that party whom they should marry, and neither birth nor portion shall hinder the match, for we are all of one family mankind." In a further effort to protect women, he urged that a man who impregnated a single woman be forced to marry her, and that convicted rapists and adulterers be executed.[213] A host of writers advocated absolute divorce on proof of cause, with a right to remarriage for both parties. Francis Osborne went further, proposing that marriages be made by annually renewable contracts, rescindable at will by either party. Henry Nevile described a polygamous utopia, which featured "free love" and "open sex." John Hall, among others, advocated open "female nudism," arguing that "nakedness would be less provocative" than current women's fashions.[214] The English world had indeed been "turned upside down."

John Milton and John Locke

It was in this revolutionary context that the great English poet John Milton and the great English philosopher John Locke turned the traditional commonwealth model of marriage "upside down." Traditional formulations treated the domestic commonwealth as a model, even a source, of the political commonwealth. Milton and Locke reversed the analogy. Milton focused on marital dissolution, arguing that failed English marriages, like the failed English commonwealth, should be dissolved and the parties left free to reconstitute themselves. Locke focused on marital formation, arguing that marriages, like commonwealths, must be formed, maintained, and dissolved in accordance with the contract negotiated by a man and woman who are by nature free and equal.

John Milton

John Milton's interpretation of the commonwealth model of marriage was, in part, a personal crusade. His new bride had left him within a month of their wedding in 1642 and repeatedly resisted his attempts at reconciliation. There was no evidence of consanguinity, precontract, or frigidity that could support a case of annulment. There was no right to divorce and remarriage. Milton, his early biographer reports, "could ill bear the disappointment hee mett with by her obstinate absenting: And therefore thought upon a Divorce, that hee might be free to marry another."[215] Invoking "the duty and the right of an instructed Christian," he took his cause to Parliament—addressing four books to them between 1643 and 1646 in an effort to convince them of the *Doctrine and Discipline of Divorce*.[216]

In his Address to Parliament, which opened his first tract in 1643, Milton reversed the conventional commonwealth construction of marriage, pressing an argument for divorce along the same lines as Parliament's argument for revolution:

> He who marries, intends as little to conspire his own ruine, as he that swears Allegiance [to the Crown]: and as a whole people is in proportion to an ill Government, so is one man to an ill marriage. If [Parliament] against any authority, Covnant, or Statute, may by the soveraign edict of charity, save not only their lives, but honest liberties from unworthy bondage, as well may [the married man] against any private Covnant, which hee never enter'd to his mischief, redeem himself from unsupportable disturbances to honest

peace, and just contentment: And much the rather, for that to resist the highest Magistrat though tyrannizing, God never gave us
expresse allowance, only he gave us reason, charity, nature, and
good example to bear us out; but in this domestic misfortune, thus
to demean our selves, besides the warrant of those four great di-
rectors, which doth as justly belong hither, we have an expresse law
of *God*, and such a law, as whereof our Saviour with a solemn threat
forbid the abrogating. For no effect of tyranny can sit more heavily
on the Common-wealth, then this household unhappiness on the
family. And farewell all hope of true Reformation in the state, while
such an evil as this lies undiscerned and unregarded in the
house.[217]

This was Milton's argument in a nutshell. The domestic commonwealth,
like the political commonwealth, may be dissolved if it fails in its fundamental purpose. This is counseled by reason, charity, nature, and experience in the case of political dissolutions. It is further counseled by
the Bible in the case of domestic dissolutions. If such counsel is ignored,
the whole commonwealth will suffer.

The purpose of forming a political commonwealth is to protect liberty, establish order, and secure peace, Milton argued. When one or
more of these purposes is irreconcilably frustrated, the political commonwealth is broken, and either the rulers or the ruled may dissolve
it—by force of arms, if necessary. Thereafter, the parties can reorganize
their political polity in a manner more consistent with the ideal purposes of liberty, order, and peace.[218]

The purpose of forming a domestic commonwealth is to foster love,
create community, deter lust, and procreate children. Of these purposes, marital love is, by far, the most critical. "Mariage is a covnant,"
Milton wrote, echoing familiar sentiments, "the very beeing whereof
consists, not in forc't cohabitation, and counterfeit performance, but un-
fained love and peace . . . and sweet and gladsome society." "[T]he apt
and cheerful conversation of man with woman" is the "chief and noblest
purpose of marriage." "Where love cannot be, there can be left of wedlocke nothing but the empty husk of an outside matrimony"—dry,
shriveled, and dispensable.[219]

Milton underscored this priority of marital love by describing marriage as a threefold society—at once "religious, civill, and corporall." As
a religious society, marriage was "a union of soul, spirit, and mind," between husband and wife—a reflection of the perfect love of Adam and
Eve in Paradise, an expression of the perfect love between Christ and
His Church. As a civil society, marriage was a union "of the couple's person and property," in which each spouse vowed to support and protect

the other in all things "to the death." As a corporal society, marriage was a union of bodies in intercourse to cool passion and to conceive children.

"God appointed the religious society" of marriage as "the highest and most excellent," Milton argued, for it dealt with the essential matters of the soul, the spirit, and the mind. He appointed the "corporall society" of marriage as the "least essential," for this dealt with discretionary matters of the body and its passions. "Wee know that flesh can neither joyn, nor keep together two bodies of it self; what is it then must make them one flesh, but likenes, but fitnes of mind and disposition, which may breed the Spirit of concord, and union between them? . . . For as the unity of minde is neerer and greater than the union of bodies, so doubtles is the dissimilitude greater, and more individuall." Without *agape,* or "soul love," a marriage is dead. Without *eros,* or "carnall love," a marriage can live. Think of the marriage of Mary and Joseph.[220]

Having posited this hierarchy of marital purposes—from the religious to the carnal—Milton thought it "preposterous ignorance and iniquity" that the law of his day should provide remedies "for the rights of the body in mariage but nothing for the wrongs and grievances of the mind." Impotence and frigidity could lead to annulment. But frustration of "the superior and nobler ends both of mariage and the maried persons . . . looses no persons" from marriage. "What courts of conscupiscence are these, wherein fleshly appetite is heard before right reason, lust before love or devotion." If impotence, frigidity, and other frustrations of the base carnal society of marriage can lead to dissolution, then surely incompatability, antagonism, and other frustrations of the higher religious society of marriage should lead to dissolution as well. To hold otherwise is to elevate the needs of the body above those of the soul, to privilege marital sex over marital love.[221]

Milton thus advocated divorce if either the religious or the carnal purposes of marriage were frustrated. Frustration of the religious purposes of marriage because of "irreconcilable incompatibility" provided the more compelling case for divorce, he believed. For the community and concordance of the couple's soul, spirit, and mind was the first and foremost reason God instituted marriage. Adam could not abide isolation, even in the perfection of Paradise; no person can abide it in this vale of tears. And, a person trapped in a marriage with "a mute and spiritles mate" is even lonelier than the unmarried person. The disaffected spouse becomes cold, dark, and sad, growing "not onely in bitterness and wrath, the canker of devotion, but in a desperate and vitious carelessnes," falling victim to "dissimulation, suspicion, fals colours, fals pretences." In such circumstances, divorce is the better course. Who cannot see "how much more Christianly it would be to break by divorce that which is more brok'n by undue and forciable keeping . . . rather then that the whole worship of a Christian mans life should languish and fade away beneath the waight of an immeasurable grief and discouragement."[222]

Frustration of the carnal purposes of marriage should likewise lead to divorce, Milton argued. In some instances, spouses wilfully "betray their bodies" through adultery, cruelty, desertion, drunkenness, incest, sloth, violent crime, or other pathos that destroys any prospects of intimacy with their spouse. In other instances, one spouse suffers permanent impotence, frigidity, contagion, sterility, disfigurement, or similar permanent defect that precludes intercourse or conception. Where married parties cannot reconcile themselves to these conditions, they must be allowed to divorce, Milton argued. For, unless the innocent or capable spouse is "heroically vertuous," he or she inevitably will "despair in vertue and mutin against divine providence"—testing the neighbor's bed, visiting the local brothel, or succumbing to various other "temptations, and occasions to secret adulteries, and unchast roaving." Husbands, eager to perpetuate their family name, might be tempted to concubinage for the sake of having children—a temptation to which even the great patriarch Abraham succumbed to his own misery as well as that of Sarai, Hagar, and Ishmael. And, if the couple already has children, the ills and evils of their marital discord will "undoubtedly redound upon the children . . . and the whole family. It degenerates and disorders the best spirits, leavs them to unsettl'd imaginations, and degraded hopes, careles of themselvs, their household and their fr[ie]nds, unactive to all public service, dead to the Common-weal."[223]

"To injoyn the indissoluble keeping of a mariage found unfit against the good of man both soul and body," Milton concluded, "is to make an Idol of mariage."[224] To be sure, "divorce is not rashly to be made, but reconcilement to be persuaded and endevor'd."[225] But, if such reconciliation cannot be achieved, it is better to take the painful step of divorce, to avoid even worse pain. This is for the good of the couple, their children, and the broader commonwealth. "[P]eace and love, the best subsistence of a Christian family, will return home from whence they are now banisht; places of prostitution wil be lesse haunted, the neighbours bed lesse attempted, the yoke of prudent and manly discipline will be generally submitted to, sober and well order'd living will soon spring up in the Commonwealth." "[T]he constitution and reformation of a commonwealth . . . is, like a building, to begin orderly from the foundation thereof, which is marriage and the family, to set right first whatever is amisse therein." And much is amisse when "the most important freedom that God and Nature hath given us in the family" is compromised by "idolatrous superstitions" against divorce.[226]

Milton did not spell out the legal ramifications of these views on marriage and divorce. He instead reprinted, with his own preface, the legal discussion of marriage and divorce in Martin Bucer's 1550 tract *De Regno Christi*, which we have already seen. He endorsed Bucer's conflation of annulment and divorce, his insistence on the equal rights of husband and wife to petition for divorce on proof of cause, and his call for civil courts to handle all marriage and divorce litigation.[227] He also assembled a rather untidy heap of all manner of liberal divorce laws—from the ancient Judaic to the modern Protestant—to demonstrate the purported anachronism of prevailing English law against divorce.[228] Readers who wanted more on the subject were directed to the systematic legal discussion just published by the English jurist John Selden.[229]

Milton directed his main energies to the theological ramifications of these views of marriage and divorce. He spent a good deal of time deconstructing the conventional theological arguments for the indissolubility of marriage—dismissing them all derisively as "silly superstition," "devilish doctrine," and "hainous barbarisme."[230]

Catholics first called marriage a sacrament because it is permanent, Milton argued, and then later insisted that it is permanent because it is a sacramental sign of Christ's union with His Church. But this sacramental symbolism of marriage only proves that it is the spiritual, rather than corporal, union of marriage that is critical, Milton insisted. "For me I dispute not now whether matrimony bee a mystery or no; if it bee of Christ and his Church, certainly it is not meant of every ungodly and miswedded mariage, but then only mysterious when it is a holy, happy, and peacefull match. . . . Since therefore none but a fit and pious matrimony can signify the union of Christ and his Church, ther cannot be any hindrance of divorce to that wedlock wherein ther can be no good mystery." Milton later gave this argument a more autobiographical twist: "if the Husband must bee as Christ to the Wife, then must the Wife bee as the Church to her Husband. If ther bee a perpetuall contrariety of minde in the Church toward Christ, Christ himself threat'ns to divorce such a Spouse, and hath often don it. If they urge, this was no true Church, I urge again, that was no true Wife."[231]

Continental Protestants argue that marriage is indissoluble because it is a covenant in which God is a party. But this, again, proves only that the spiritual dimensions of marriage are the more pressing, Milton wrote. If marriage is a true covenant among husband, wife, and God, "so much the more it argues the chief society thereof to be in the soul rather then in the body, and the greatest breach thereof to be unfitnes of mind

rather then defect of body, for the body can have less affinity in a covnant more then human." Moreover, to call marriage a covenant is not to
prove its indissolubility. "For equity is understood in every Covnant,
even between enemies, though the terms bee not exprest. If equity therefore made it, extremity may dissolv it. But mariage, they used to say, is
the Covnant of God. Undoubted: and so is any covnant frequently called
in Scripture, wherein God is called as witness. . . . [T]his denomination
adds nothing to the Covnant of Mariage, above any other civil and
solemn contract: nor is it more indissoluble for this reason than any
other against the end of its own ordination. . . . But faith they say must
bee kept in Covnant, though to our dammage. I answer that only holds
true when the other side performs."[232]

Anglicans are even less convincing, Milton charged, for they "dare not
affirm that mariage is either a Sacrament or a mystery, though all those
sacred things give place to man, and yet they invest it with such an aw-
full sanctity, and give it such adamantine chains, to bind with, as if it
were to be worshipt like some *Indian* deity." But this is an "irrationall"
and "silly conformity" to one particular of the Catholic tradition, which
in many other particulars has been rejected.[233]

Both Catholics and Protestants alike argue that marriage is indissoluble because, as Christ commands, "what God has joined together let not
man put asunder." The point of this passage, however, said Milton, is
not the prohibition against man's putting asunder. It is the requirement
that God must join the couple together. "[W]hen is it that God may be
said to joyn, when the parties and their friends consent? No surely; for
that may concurre to leudest ends, or is it when the Church-rites are fin-
isht? Neither; for the efficacy of those depends upon the presupposed
fitness of either party. Perhaps after carnal knowledge? lest of all: for that
may joyn persons whom neither law nor nature dares joyn; tis left, that
only then, when the minds are fitly dispos'd, and enabl'd to maintain a
cherfull conversation, to the solace and love of each other, according as
God intended and promised in the very first foundation of matrimony,
I will make a help meet for him." "So when it shall be found by their apparent unfitnes, that their continuing to be man and wife is against the
glory of God, and their mutuall happiness, it may assure them that God
never joyn'd them."[234]

Having deconstructed traditional Christian arguments about divorce,
Milton set out to reconstruct a biblical argument for divorce. The key
passage, he insisted, was Deuteronomy 24:1. There God proclaimed
through Moses: "When a man hath tak'n a wife and married her, and it
comes to passe that she find no favour in his eyes, because he hath found
some uncleanesse in her, let him write her a bill of divorcement, and

give it in her hand, and send her out of his house," leaving both parties free to remarry thereafter. "Uncleannesse" in this passage, said Milton, means "nakedness or unfitness" of body or of mind. It implicates the whole range of corporal and religious grounds for divorce that he had listed. Religious grounds were the more important, for "what greater nakedness or unfitness of mind then that which hinders ever thee solace and peaceful society of the marital couple." The ancient Hebrews had recognized this and built on this passage a comprehensive doctrine of divorce. Their interpretation was followed by the Greeks, the Romans, the early Christian emperors, and many others. This proves, said Milton, that Deuteronomy 24:1 is no special rule for the Jews. It is a universal moral law, "a grave and prudent Law, full of moral equity, full of due consideration towards nature, that cannot be resisted; a Law consenting with the Laws of wisest men and civilest nations."[235]

Christ did not abrogate this moral law of divorce in his proclamation in Matthew 19:9: "Whosoever shall put away his wife, except it be for fornication, and shall marry another, committeth adultery; and whosoever marrieth her which is put away doth commit adultery."[236] This passage must be understood in context, Milton argued. Christ had already said in Matthew 5:18: "Till heaven and earth pass, one jot or one tittle shall in no wise pass from the law, till all be fulfilled." Moreover, his divorce proclamation was prompted, as Matthew 19:3 reports, by the Pharisees "tempting him, and saying unto him, Is it lawful for a man to put away his wife for every cause?" Christ was giving a direct response to the scheming Pharisees. You, Pharisees, who might "in the hardness of your hearts" abuse the Mosaic law of divorce through inventive interpretation, you may divorce only on grounds of fornication. But others, less hard of heart, may do so on the fuller grounds allowed by Moses. Christ's "rigid sentence against divorce" was designed "not to cut off all remedy from a good man who finds himself consuming away in a disconsolate and uninjoy'd matrimony, but to lay a bridle upon the bold abuses of those overweening Rabbies." Christ's words were not a timeless declaration for the church, but a terse denunciation of the Pharisees.[237]

If Christ's words are so understood, Milton continued, Paul's words can also be understood. In 1 Corinthians 7:15, Paul writes: "if the unbelieving [spouse] depart, let him depart. A brother or a sister is not under bondage in such cases, but God hath called us to peace." Paul is not contradicting Christ by adding desertion or disbelief as another ground for marital dissolution, Milton argued. He is simply confirming the traditional Hebrew practice that where the union of spirit between husband and wife is broken by a form of spiritual "uncleanesse," the marriage is broken and the parties are freed from its bonds.[238] Indeed, Paul goes beyond Moses by granting to both husband and wife alike this freedom to depart from a spiritually broken marriage—a suitable application of Paul's more general teaching that in Christ there is "neither male nor female."[239]

Milton's reconstruction of the commonwealth model of marriage was largely ignored in his day, and when it was recognized it was largely rejected. Even some of the radical writers of the Commonwealth era, who accepted the propriety of divorce and remarriage in cases of adultery and desertion, thought Milton's argument for divorce on the ground of irreconcilable differences proved too much. His books were dismissed for holding the "most dangerous and damnable tenets." If Milton had his way, his critics charged, "the bonds of marriage [will be] let loose to inordinate lust," and men will inevitably "quit of their wives for slight occasions" to the detriment of the couple, the children, the church, and the commonwealth alike. "[W]hat will all the Christian Churches through the world . . . thinke of our wofull degeneration in these deplored times, that so uncouth a designe should be set on foot among us."[240]

Some of this rejection was perhaps a function of Milton's unfortunate choice of titles. By putting *Tetrachordon* and *Colasterion* on his book spines, Milton might have appealed to a stray Graecophile or two, but he could hardly have expected his books to jump into the hands of every passerby.[241] Some of this rejection was doubtless a function of Milton's rather pugnacious and prolix style: five hundred-plus pages of barefisted rhetoric in three years on a tender issue like divorce had to tax even the sympathetic reader. Some of this was doubtless also a function of Milton's iconoclasm. A reader could consider it clever to see one or two counterintuitive constructions of the commonwealth model of marriage. But Milton's gleeful overturning of a whole series of favorite Bible verses and traditional doctrines to support his argument about the nature of marriage and divorce had to have raised suspicions. Particularly since Milton left many of the theological niceties and legal nuances of his argument unexplored, it was easy to dismiss him. Later English reformers, both theological and legal, would look back to Milton as a brilliant prophet who anticipated many of the divorce reforms of 1857 to 1987.[242] But, in his own day, he was a prophet with little honor and little legal influence.

John Locke

John Locke's reconstruction of the commonwealth model of marriage in his *Two Treatises of Government* (1698) had a better immediate reception. In part, this was because Milton and other radical writers of the mid-seventeenth century had prepared the way for him, slowly liberalizing prevailing sentiment about marriage. In part, this was because Locke wrote after the Commonwealth Parliament had experimented quite radically with English marriage law. In part, this was because Locke's reconstruction of marriage was only a by-product of his grand political argument in support of the Glorious Revolution, and what he wrote on marriage in his political writings was amply qualified by his discussion of marriage in his commentaries on the Bible.

In his *Two Treatises,* Locke set out to refute Robert Filmer's monarchical theory of government, which was among the strongest traditional formulations of the commonwealth model. Filmer had argued, as we saw, that God had created the patriarchal domestic commonwealth headed by the paterfamilias as the source of the hierarchical political commonwealth headed by the King. God had created Adam and Eve as founders not only of the first marriage and family, but also of the first state and society. Adam was the first husband, but also the first ruler. Eve was the first wife, but also the first subject. Together with their children, they comprised at once a domestic and a political commonwealth. All persons thereafter were, by birth, subject to the highest male head, descended from Adam.

Locke responded to Filmer first by flatly denying any natural or necessary connection between the political and domestic commonwealths, between the authority of the paterfamilias and of the magistrate. "[T]he Power of a *Magistrate* over a Subject," he wrote, "may be distinguished from that of a *Father* over his Children, a *Master* over his Servant, a *Husband* over his Wife, and a *Lord* over his Slave."[243] The "little Commonwealth" of the family is "very far from" the great commonwealth in England "in its Constitution, Power and End." "[T]he *Master of the Family* has a very distinct and differently limited *Power,* both as to time and extent, over those several Persons that are in it; . . . he has no Legislative Power of Life and Death over any of them, and none too but what a *Mistress of a Family* may have as well as he."[244]

Locke responded next by denying Filmer's patriarchal interpretation of the creation story. God did not create Adam and Eve as ruler and subject, but as husband and wife, said Locke. Adam and Eve were created equal before God. Each had natural rights to use the bounties of Paradise. Each had natural duties to each other and to God. After the Fall into sin, God expelled Adam and Eve from the Garden. He increased man's labor in his use of creation. He increased woman's labor in the bearing of children. He said to Eve: "thy desire shall be to thy husband, and he shall rule over thee" (Gen. 3:16). These words, said Locke, which

Filmer "calls the *Original Grant of Government* were not spoken to *Adam,* neither indeed was there any Grant in them made to *Adam;* they were a Punishment laid upon *Eve.*"[245] These words do not abrogate the natural equality, rights, and duties with which God created Adam and Eve, and all persons after them. They do not render all wives eternally subject to their husbands.[246] And they certainly do not, as Filmer insists, give "a Father or a Prince an Absolute, Arbitrary, Unlimited and Unlimitable Power, over the Lives, Liberties, and Estates, of his Children and Subjects."[247]

Men and women are born free and equal in the state of nature. But "God having made Man such a Creature, that, in his own Judgment, it was not good for him to be alone, put him under strong Obligation of Necessity, Convenience, and Inclination to drive him into *Society,*" Locke argued. A person entered into society by entering into voluntary contracts with other persons of similar inclination. To that extent, the commonwealths of marriage, church, and state might be said to be related, said Locke. Each of these commonwealths was formed by the voluntary agreement of free and equal persons, moving from the state of nature to a social state.

"The first *Society*" to be formed "was between Man and Wife, which gave beginning to that of Parents and Children."[248] This "conjugal society," like every other society, "is made by a voluntary Compact between Man and Woman: and tho' it consists chiefly in such a Communion and Right in one anothers Bodies, as is necessary to its Chief End, Procreation; yet it draws with it mutual Support and Assistance and Communion of Interest too, as necessary not only to unite their Care, and Affection, but also necessary to their common Off-spring, who have a Right to be nourished and maintained by them, till they are able to provide for themselves."[249] Marriage has no necessary form or function beyond this "Chief End" of procreation, Locke argued against traditional understandings. Couples were free to contract about the rest of the relationship as they deemed fit. "*Conjugal society* might be varied and regulated by that Contract, which unites Man and Wife in that Society, as far as may consist with Procreation and the bringing up of Children till they could [provide] for themselves; nothing being necessary to any Society, that is not necessary to the ends for which it is made."[250]

Locke thus combined a contractual and naturalist perspective on marriage. It was a natural right for a man and woman to enter into a marital contract. It was a natural duty for them to render procreation an essential condition of their marital contract. It was the natural right to survival of their child that imposed on parents a further natural duty to remain in their marriage once contracted till their children were self-sufficient. "For the end of *conjunction between Male and Female,* being not barely Procreation, but the continuation of the Species, this conjunction betwixt Male and Female ought to last, even after Procreation, so long as is necessary to the nourishment and support of the young Ones, who are to be sustained by those that got them, till they are able to shift and provide for themselves. . . . [W]hereby the Father, who is bound to take care for those he hath begot, is under an Obligation to continue in Conjugal Society with the same Woman longer than other Creatures, whose young being able to subsist of themselves, before the time of procreation returns again, the Conjugal Bond dissolves of it self, and they are at liberty"[251]

The logical end of Locke's argument was that the childless couple, or the couple whose children were of age, should be free to divorce, unless they had found some other "Communion of Interest" to sustain their contract. Locke dithered on the question of divorce. It was not essential to his political argument to speak definitively on the subject, and he knew the dangers of loose literary speculation on it. In his private diary, he wrote quite brashly: "He that already is married may marry another woman with his left hand. . . . The ties, duration, and conditions of the left hand marriage shall be no other than what is expressed in the contract of marriage between the parties."[252] In his *Two Treatises* and other publications, he only flirted with the doctrine of divorce and remarriage, suggesting delicately that the matter be left to private contractual calculation: "[T]he husband and wife, though they have but one common Concern, yet having different understandings will unavoidably sometimes have different wills too; it therefore being necessary, that the last Determination, i.e., the Rule, should be placed somewhere, it naturally falls to the Man's share, as the abler and the stronger. But the reaching but to the things of their Common Interest and Property, leaves the Wife in the full and free possession of what by Contract is hers by peculiar Right, and gives the Husband no more power over her Life, than she has over his. The *Power of the Husband being* so far from that of an absolute Monarch, that the *Wife* has, in many cases, a Liberty to *separate* from him; where natural Right, or their Contract allows it, whether that Contract be made by themselves in the state of Nature, or by the Customs or Laws of the Countrey they live in; and the Children upon such Separation fall to the Father's or the Mother's Lot, as such Contract does determine."[253]

The other logical end of this argument was that the state had little role to play within marriage and the family. For the state likewise was a voluntary assembly, formed by a governmental contract among like-minded parties. The state was formed after marriage and the family, and was ultimately subordinate to it in priority and right. The marriage contract sets the terms of the agreement between husband and wife, parent and child. The state could intervene only to enforce these contractual rights and duties, and only to vindicate the natural rights and duties of each party within the household. "For all the ends of Marriage being to be obtained under Politick Government, as well as in the state of Nature, the Civil Magistrat doth not abridge this Right, or Power of either naturally necessary to those ends, viz., Procreation and mutual Support and Assistance whilst they are together; but only decides any Controversie that may arise between Man and Wife about them."[254]

Locke did not press this contractarian reconstruction of the commonwealth model to the revolutionary ends that some Enlightenmentarians would reach in the following centuries. Locke was a man of pious Puritan stock who remained firmly devoted to biblical teachings throughout his life. What he gave with his political hand, he took back with his theological hand. His famous *Letters on Toleration* and *The Reasonableness of Christianity* were tracts of deep Christian conviction. In each of them, Locke called church and state to end their unhealthy alliance, to soften their belligerent dogmatism, to return to the simple moral truths of the New Testament. In each of these tracts, he also insisted on coating his doctrine of natural rights and duties with a number of classic Christian conceptions about the natural propriety of heterosexuality, monogamy, procreation, nurture and education of children, and the like. "[H]e that shall collect all the moral rules of the philosophers and compare them with those contained in the New Testament," he wrote, "will find them to come short of the morality delivered by our Saviour, and taught by his apostles. . . . Such a law of morality Jesus Christ hath given us in the New Testament [is] a full and sufficient rule for our direction, and conformable to that of reason."[255]

On the strength of these convictions, Locke endorsed a whole series of biblical teachings on marriage and sex that stood in considerable tension with his more radical statements on marriage in the *Two Treatises*. For example, Locke endorsed Christ's reading of the Commandment against adultery as an injunction not only against "actual uncleanness, but all irregular desires [and] causeless divorces."[256] He endorsed Paul's injunctions against fornication, saying that such conduct "might be so unsuitable to the state of a christian man, that a christian society might have reason to animaadvert upon a fornicator . . . as not comporting with the dignity and principles of that religion, which was the foundation of their society."[257] He glossed Paul's teachings in 1 Corinthians 7 on the relative merits of marriage and celibacy with a matter-of-fact tone that reflects comfortable acceptance of traditional Christian doctrine.

Glossing Paul's statements on the rights and duties of husbands and wives, Locke wrote: "The woman (who in all other rights is inferiour) has here the same power given her over the man's body, that the man has over her's. The reason whereof is plain; because if she had not her man, when she had need of him, as well as the man his woman, when he had need of her, marriage would be no remedy against fornication."[258] He paraphrased, without comment, Paul's requirement that husband and wife remain together till parted by death. He glossed Paul's later requirements that wives must submit to their husbands, and husbands to love their wives thus: "It is from the head that the body receives its vigorous constitution of health and life; this St. Paul pronounces here of Christ, as head of the church, that by that parallel which he makes use of, to represent the relation of husband and wife, he may both show the wife the reasonableness of her subjection to her husband, and the duty incumbent on the husband to cherish and preserve his wife."[259]

Locke stretched the commonwealth model of marriage—and indeed all prior Christian models of marriage—to the breaking point. On the one hand, he was a devout Christian, fully conversant with biblical teachings on marriage and sexuality, but not fully comfortable with their theological exposition or institutional expression in his day. On the other hand, he was a devoted libertarian, fully supportive of the revolutionary reconstruction of the English commonwealth, but not fully satisfied with its philosophical foundation or its legal reification during the Glorious Revolution. From both perspectives, he pressed for a variety of reforms of marriage, family, and sexuality.

Locke the theologian and Locke the political philosopher agreed on many points of marital reform—greater freedom of marital contract, greater equality of husband and wife, greater emphasis on the procreation and education of children, greater restraint on the separation of couples with children, greater protection of wives, children, and servants from abuse. On these twin theological and philosophical foundations, Locke helped to prepare the way for many of the legal reforms in English law, as well as American law, in the next centuries. His views on marriage, like Milton's, had no immediate legal impact, but they proved prescient and prophetic.

Locke the theologian and Locke the political philosopher, however, parted ways on many points as well. Locke the theologian emphasized the biblical norm of marriage as a hierarchical order headed by the husband with subjection by the wife. Locke the philosopher emphasized the voluntary organization of marriage as a negotiated contract between two equal parties. Locke the theologian vested both church and state with a prominent role in the guidance of government of marital and sexual conduct. Locke the philosopher countenanced no role for the church and a minimalist role for the state in policing the conduct of the household. Locke the theologian emphasized the duties of marital love, spiritual companionship, and sexual fidelity for life. Locke the philosopher emphasized the rights of marital equality, procreative capacity, and parental fidelity till children come of age.

Many skeptical readers of his day dismissed Locke as an intellectual schizophrenic, a man incapable of harmonizing his theological convictions and political speculations on marriage, and thus prone to intemperate remarks and indecisive principles on both scores. More sympathetic readers hailed Locke as a methodological genius, a man who liberated the theology and politics of marriage from each other.[260] By distinguishing a natural versus biblical, and a political versus theological discourse on marriage, Locke broke the presumed organic connections between the domestic commonwealth and the political commonwealth, household and state, father and king, child and subject. The household could have its own order and organization based on the marital contract; the state could have its own offices and functions based on the social contract. The church could have its norms for marriage based on biblical revelation; the state could have its norms for marriage based on natural rights. The church could ground its norms of authority and obedience in the Fifth Commandment; the state could ground its norms for authority and obedience in the social contract. A pious Christian could accept the literal truths of the Bible for private life, yet advocate the liberal reforms of the social contract for public law.

To accept Locke's method was to accept the proposition that it was no longer necessary to integrate the spiritual, natural, social, and contractual perspectives on marriage in an organic model—whether the Anglican commonwealth model or any of the other sacramental, social, or covenantal models. With Locke's method, natural and contractual perspectives on marriage could be fully expounded without reference to their religious and social implications. Religious and social perspectives on marriage could be fully defended without reference to their natural or contractual dimensions. Moreover, it was no longer necessary for state, church, or civil society to play an integrated role in the governance of marriage. Marriage was the first society a person entered from the state of nature, and the terms of the marital contract together with the person's natural rights and duties were superior to all other governing norms. If the married person chose to enter into a political, or an ecclesiastical, or a civil society, he or she could subscribe to the marital norms of that particular society. But these sets of norms were independent of each other and subordinate to the natural and contractual norms of the marital contract.

Hugo Grotius, the seventeenth-century Dutch political philosopher on whom Locke partly relied for his philosophical constructions, once ventured the "impious hypothesis" that the law of nature could be valid even if "we should concede that which cannot be conceded without the utmost wickedness, that there is no God, or that the affairs of men are of no concern to him."[261] This idea was hardly original with Grotius and hardly acceptable to the establishment of his day. But Grotius's articulation of it in the midst of the bitter religious warfare and persecution of early seventeenth-century Europe proved propitious. It helped to set afoot the development of a law of nations and a law of the sea that did not depend upon a common theological foundation or necessary role for the church.[262]

A similar claim might be made about Locke's "impious hypothesis" that a law of marriage could be valid even if God were not the founder of the marriage contract, or His Church not an agent in its governance. This idea, too, was hardly original with Locke and hardly acceptable to the establishment of his day. But Locke's articulation of an independent naturalist and contractarian theory of marriage in the midst of the revolutionary upheaval of English society also proved propitious. It helped to set afoot the development of an Anglo-American theory and law of marriage and the family that eventually no longer depended upon established theological doctrines or upon a necessary legal role for the church.

Even cast in its most liberal formulation, the *via media* theology of the Anglican tradition could not ultimately contain Locke's dualistic understanding of marriage. The theological establishment thus steadfastly rejected such naturalist and contractual ideas of marriage, standing alone, for two more centuries. Even stretching traditional doctrines to their breaking point, the English law of marriage could not accommodate the legal reforms contemplated by Locke's more radical asides in his *Two Treatises*. The legal establishment thus resisted such reforms until well into the nineteenth century. It would take the Enlightenment articulation of a purely contractual model of marriage to effectuate these reforms fully. It is to that development that we turn briefly in the next chapter.

5

Marriage as Contract in the Enlightenment Tradition

The laws born of the Catholic and Protestant models of marriage are not the artifacts of an ancient culture to be studied by antiquarians and archivalists alone. Until the twentieth century, this was our law in much of the West, notably in England and America.[1]

At the turn of the twentieth century, leading legal authorities in England and America spoke regularly of marriage as a "state of existence ordained by the Creator," "a consummation of the Divine command to multiply and replenish the earth," "the highest state of existence," "the only stable substructure of social, civil, and religious institutions."[2] They described marriage as "a public institution of universal concern" in which "each individual marriage or its dissolution affects the rights not only of husband and wife, but of all other persons."[3] The United States Supreme Court still spoke regularly of marriage as "more than a mere contract," "a sacred obligation," "a holy estate," "the foundation of the family and society, without which there would be neither civilization nor progress."[4]

At the turn of the twentieth century, English and American legislatures treated marriage much the same way that the Catholic leaders of Trent and the Protestant leaders of Wittenberg, Geneva, and Westminster had done in the sixteenth century. With ample variations, English and American law generally defined marriage as a permanent monogamous union between a fit man and a fit woman of the age of consent, designed for mutual love and support, and for mutual procreation and protection. A typical state law in America required that betrothals be formal and that marriages be contracted with parental consent and witnesses. It required marriage licenses and registration and solemnization before civil and/or ecclesiastical authorities. It prohibited marriages between couples related by various blood or family ties identified in the Mosaic law. It discouraged, and in some states prohibited, marriage where one party was impotent or had a contagious disease that precluded procreation or endangered the other spouse. Couples who sought to divorce had to publicize their intentions, to petition a court, to show adequate cause or fault, to make provision for the dependent spouse and children. Criminal laws outlawed fornication, adultery, sodomy, polygamy, incest, contraception, abortion, and other perceived sexual offenses. Tort laws held third parties liable for seduction, enticement, loss of consortium, or alienation of the affections of one's spouse. The church and broader community were given roles to play in the formation, maintenance, and dissolution of marriage, and in the physical and moral nurture of children.[5]

By contrast, at the turn of the twenty-first century, this traditional lore and law of the family has been largely spurned, notably in America.[6] Today, a contractual view of marriage has come to dominate American law, lore, and life—largely unbuffered by complementary spiritual, social, or natural perspectives, and largely unreceptive to much of a role for the church, state, or broader community. Marriage is viewed increasingly at law and at large today as a private bilateral contract to be formed, maintained, and dissolved as the couple sees fit. Antenuptial, marital, and separation contracts that allow parties to define their own rights and duties within the marital estate and thereafter have gained increasing acceptance. Implied marital contracts are imputed to long-standing lovers, supporting claims for maintenance and support during and after the relationship. Surrogacy contracts are executed for the rental of wombs. Medical contracts are executed for the introduction of embryos or the abortion of fetuses. Requirements of parental consent and witnesses to the formation of marital and related contracts have largely disappeared. No-fault divorce statutes have reduced the divorce proceeding to an expensive formality in most states. Payments of alimony and other forms of postmarital support to dependent spouses and children are giving way to lump sum property exchanges providing a clean break for parties to remarry. Court-supervised property settlements between divorcing spouses are giving way to privately negotiated or mediated settlements often confirmed with little scrutiny by courts. The functional distinctions between the rights of the married and the unmarried couple, the straight and the gay partnership, the legitimate and the illegitimate child have been considerably narrowed by an array of new statutes and constitutional cases. The roles of the church, state, and broader community in marriage formation, maintenance, and dissolution have been gradually truncated in deference to the constitutional principles of sexual autonomy and separation of church and state. Traditional criminal prohibitions against most sexual offenses have become dead letters in most states. Traditional prohibitions against contraception and abortion have been held to violate the constitutional right of privacy. Traditional tort suits for interference with one's spouse or children have become largely otiose.[7]

These exponential legal changes in the course of the twentieth century have been, in part, noble attempts to bring greater equality and equity within marriage and society.[8] These legal changes are also simple reflections of the exponential changes that have occurred in the culture and condition of American families—the stunning advances in reproductive and medical technology, the exposure to vastly different perceptions of sexuality and kinship born of globalization, the explosion of international and domestic norms of human rights, the implosion of the Ozzie and Harriet family born of new economic and professional demands on wives, husbands, and children.[9] A fantastic range of literature—theological, ethical, political, economic, sociological, anthropological, and psychological—has emerged in the past three decades vigorously describing, defending, or decrying these legal changes.[10]

My explanation for these massive legal changes in the course of this century is simple and, by the methodological design of this book, incomplete. What we have also been witnessing in the course of the twentieth century is the gradual rise to legal prominence of an Enlightenment contractarian model of marriage.[11] This model has slowly eclipsed Protestant and Catholic models of marriage and the ideas and institutions that those models have introduced into the Western legal tradition.

Enlightenment thinkers began where John Locke's "impious hypothesis" had ended. In his *Two Treatises of Government* (1698), Locke had ventured the notion that marriage could be seen as a simple, bilateral contract between a man and a woman who stood equal before each other in the state of nature. He had suggested that a natural and contractual perspective on marriage could be defended without necessary reference to spiritual or social perspectives on marriage. He had hypothesized that a law of marriage based on contract could be valid even if God were not viewed as the founder of the marriage contract, nor His Church engaged as an agent in its governance. Locke had not pressed these ideas to their logical or legal conclusions. Indeed, in his theological writings, he had retreated to a literal biblical understanding of marriage without the qualifications he had defended in his *Two Treatises*.[12]

Enlightenment thinkers pressed Locke's "impious hypothesis" to its logical and legal ends, and grounded their sentiments in a new secular theology. The essence of marriage, they argued, was not its sacramental symbolism, nor its covenantal associations, nor its social service to the community and commonwealth, as was traditionally taught. The essence of marriage was the voluntary bargain struck between the two parties. The terms of their marital bargain were not preset by God or nature, church or state, tradition or community. These terms were set by the parties themselves, in accordance with general rules of contract formation and general norms of civil society. Such rules and norms demanded respect for the life, liberty, and property interests of other parties, and compliance with general standards of health, safety, and welfare in the community. But the form and function of their marriage relationship was to be left to the bargain of the parties themselves.[13]

Enlightenment thinkers predicated this understanding of marriage on a new theology of deism, individualism, and rationalism. First, they argued, God was no longer to be viewed as an active agent in the daily affairs of human beings, including their daily marital lives. God had created the human and natural world with its own laws and processes and thereafter left the world to run on its own—occasionally perhaps intervening with acts of miracle or *force majeure*. This theology of deism undercut the traditional notion that God was somehow a necessary party to every marital contract, or that the church was a necessary agent in every scheme of marital governance.

Second, the individual was no longer to be viewed primarily as a sinner seeking eternal salvation or a saint exercising a Godly vocation within the church, state, and household. According to basic Enlightenment theology, each individual was created equal in virtue and dignity, vested with inherent rights of life, liberty, and property, and capable of pursuing independent means and measures of happiness without involvement from any other person or institution. The doctrine of individualism rendered anachronistic the traditional notion that marriage was somehow a spiritual estate or a social calling that demanded the involvement of priests, parents, and peers in its formation and maintenance.

Third, reason was no longer to be viewed as the handmaiden of revelation; rational disputation was no longer to be subordinated to homiletic declaration. The rational process, conducted privately by each individual and collectively in the open marketplace of ideas, was considered to be a sufficient source of private morality and public law.[14] The traditional notion that a law of marriage had to be grounded in scripture and conscience, in nature and custom, or in the law-making functions of church, state, and various mediating structures gave way to a positivist theory of law as the command of the popular or popularly elected sovereign alone.

This basic creed of Enlightenment theology was played out in numerous variations from the eighteenth century onward. It was also brought into numerous combinations with Christian, Judaic, and other theologies. The Enlightenment was no single, unified movement, but a series of diverse ideological movements in various academic disciplines and social circles throughout Europe and North America. For all the variations on its basic themes, however, the Enlightenment contractarian construction of marriage was quite consistent in its formulation and quite insistent on the reformation of traditional marriage laws. It is this Enlightenment contractarian model of marriage that has helped to drive the twentieth-century revolution of Western marriage law.

The Case of
Stephen versus Mill

A convenient introduction to the Enlightenment contractarian model of marriage and its rivalry with traditional forms is offered in a vigorous literary debate in mid-nineteenth century England. The antagonists in the debate were James Fitzjames Stephen, a prominent Anglican jurist and moralist, and John Stuart Mill, a leading libertarian and utilitarian of ample Enlightenment learning. Both were prominent men of letters and occasional legislators. Both spoke for broad constituencies— Stephen for the old order, Mill for a new order.

The setting for much of their debate was the ferment in Parliament for the reform of the traditional English law of marriage inherited from the Reformation; this ferment found equal force in state legislatures in America at the same time.[15] The Stephen-Mill debate was focused by several Parliamentary bills that sought to liberalize marriage and divorce requirements, to liberate children from abusive households, and to provide wives with equal rights over marital property, minor children, and minimal maintenance. For Stephen, the heart of the debate was over the character of marriage and the family: Is this institution "a divine, indissoluble union governed by the *paterfamilias,* or is it a contractual unit governed and dissolved by the wills of the parties?"[16]

James Fitzjames Stephen

Stephen, speaking for the old order, defended the first position.[17] "[T]he political and social changes which have taken place in the world since the sixteenth century have . . . been eminently beneficial to mankind," wrote Stephen.[18] "The terms of the marriage relation as settled by the law and religion of Europe" since that time accord well with scripture, reason, and nature.[19] These sources teach that men are created with superior power, ability, and opportunity in life, which they must discharge with due restraint and accountability to God and to God's representatives in state and church. These sources also teach that women have a special calling to be wives and mothers, teachers and nurturers of children, which calling they must discharge in the household. Our law and religion reflect these divine and natural sentiments, said Stephen, "by prescribing monogamy, indissoluble marriage on the footing of the obedience of the wife to the husband, and a division of labour among men and women with corresponding differences in the matters of conduct, manners, and dress."[20]

Nature is defied if marriage is treated as a simple contract, said Stephen. This notion assumes falsely that men and women are equal. To allow marriage to become "a simple bargained-for contract," without oversight by parents and peers and by church and state, "will inevitably expose women to great abuse." They will have no protection in forming the bargain with naturally superior men, nor protection from men who dismiss them when barren, old, unattractive, troubled, or destitute. "The truth is," Stephen thundered, "that the change of marriage . . . from status to contract," from divine sacrament to simple partnership, "is not favorable to equality" or justice. "Men [and women] are fundamentally unequal, and this inequality will show itself, arrange society [and its law] as you like." "If marriage is to be permanent," and justice and liberty properly guarded, "the government of the family must be put by law and by morals in the hands of the husband."[21]

Nature is also defied if the family is treated as an open society, subject to claims of right by its members. The family, once formed, is an autonomous unit, just like the church and the state. The husband and father is the head of the family, just as the monarch is the head of the church and commonwealth. He must rule the household as God's vice-regent with all benevolence, grace, and Christian devotion. A wife is the husband's co-helper in the family, his "help meet," who must submit to his reasoned judgment in the event of conflict. A child is the father's ward and agent who must obey his every reasonable command.[22]

Stephen was well aware of the potential abuses in this system, given his vaunted expertise in English criminal law. "No one," he writes, "contends that a man ought to have power to order his wife and children about like slaves and beat them if they disobey him." Such conduct must be punished severely through ambitious enforcement of existing criminal laws against assault, battery, child abuse, and the like.[23] These criminal law exceptions, however, cannot unmake other rules governing marriage and family life carefully forged by learned theologians and jurists over the centuries.[24]

John Stuart Mill

Mill attacked Stephen's sentiments with arguments well known in English liberal and literary circles,[25] especially those influenced by Mary Wollstonecraft's writings of the 1790s and thereafter.[26] In part, Mill's attack was directed against the abuses of the traditional system of marriage and family law. Though sometimes the family is marked by "sympathy and tenderness," said Mill, "it is still oftener . . . a school of willfulness, overbearingness, unbounded self-indulgence, and a double-dyed and idealized selfishness" of the husband and father, with the "individual happiness" of the wife and children "being immolated in every shape to his smallest preferences."[27] No system of marriage law that allows such abuses can be justified. Mill himself formally renounced that law when he and Harriet Taylor were married in 1851:

> [I object to] the whole character of the marriage relation as constituted by law . . . for this amongst other reasons, that it confers upon one of the parties to the contract, legal power & control over the person, property, and freedom of action of the other party, independent of her own wishes and will. . . . [H]aving no means of legally divesting myself of these odious powers . . . [I] feel it my duty to put on record a formal protest against the existing law of marriage, in so far as conferring such powers; and a solemn promise never in any case or under any circumstance to use them.[28]

Mill's deeper attack on Stephen's defense of traditional English marriage law was theological—"laying bare the real root of much that is bowed down to as the intention of Nature and the ordinance of God," as Mill put it.[29] The prevailing theology and law of marriage and the family supports a threefold patriarchy, Mill charged. The church dictates to the state its peculiar understanding of nature. The state dictates to the couple the terms of their marital relation and abandons them once the terms are accepted. The man lords over his wife and children, divesting them of all liberty and license in their person and property, thought and belief. "The aim of the law," Mill charged, "is to tie up the soul, the mind, the sense," and the body of the wife and children, together with their "material extensions."[30]

Nature does not teach bondage and subjection of women, said Mill, but the natural liberty and equality of all men and women. "[T]he legal subordination of one sex to the other is wrong and ought to be replaced by a principle of perfect equality with no favour or privilege on the one side nor disability on the other."[31] "What is now called the [inferior] nature of women" and the superior nature of man "is an eminently artificial thing," born of social circumstances, not natural conditions.[32] "If marriage were an equal contract . . . and if [a woman] would find all honourable employments as freely open to her as to men," marriages could be true institutions of liberty and affection, shaped by the preferences of wife and husband, not the prescriptions of church and state.[33]

Nature also does not teach parental tyranny and commodification of children but counsels parental nurture and education of children. Children are not items of property, to be sold on the market of marriage, nor simple conduits through which to pass the family name and fortune. Children are also not slaves or "animals" to be worked and whipped into submission and performance by their parents. "Children below a certain age *cannot* judge or act for themselves; up to a considerably greater age they are inevitably more or less disqualified for doing so—and they need constant nurture, girls as much as boys."[34] If the family were an open unit, where children could seek redress from neglect, abuse, and arbitrary rule, a real family could be realized, and true happiness for all parties involved could be attained. If the paterfamilias does not "fulfill his obligation to feed, nurture, and educate his child with love and patience," said Mill, the *paterpoliticus,* the state as the child's protector under the social contract, "ought to see it fulfilled, at the charge, as far as possible, of the parent."[35]

Mill sought to infuse these contractarian principles of marriage and the family into the common law and public opinion of Victorian England and beyond. In his career as Parliamentarian, philosopher, and journalist, Mill advocated the reform of many familiar institutions of the Western legal tradition of marriage.[36] He urged the abolition of the requirements of parental consent, church consecration, and formal witnesses for marriage.[37] He questioned the exalted status of heterosexual monogamy and supported peaceable polygamy (though he personally found the practice odious).[38] He called for the absolute equality of husband and wife to receive, hold, and alienate property, to enter into contracts and commerce, to participate on equal terms in the workplace, in education, in political life, in social circles.[39] He called for severe punishment of husbands who assaulted, abused, or raped their wives, and for strict prohibitions against prostitution and pornography.[40] He urged fathers to turn from their public vocations and avocations to assist in the care and nurture of their children.[41] He called for equal rights of husband and wives to sue for divorce and remarriage, not only when one spouse committed adultery or desertion, but any time (quoting Milton's words) the couple "become[s] conscious that affection never has existed, or has ceased to exist between them."[42] He castigated the state for leaving annulment and other marital causes to the church and urged that the laws of annulment and divorce be both merged and expanded under exclusive state jurisdiction. He urged that paternal abuse of children be severely punished and that the state intervene where necessary to ensure the proper physical and moral nurture and education of children.[43]

The Transformation of
Anglo-American Marriage Law

This contractarian gospel for the salvation of Western marriage and family law, preached by Mill and many others in the nineteenth century, set out much of the agenda for the transformation of Anglo-American family law along Enlightenment lines. This transformation fell into two phases. The first transformation, from the 1830s forward, was designed to bring greater equality and equity to the traditional family and civil society without denying the basic values of the Western legal tradition of marriage. The second transformation, from the 1960s forward, seems calculated to break the preeminence of the traditional family and the basic values of the Western legal tradition that have sustained it.

Early Legal Reforms
in England

The Enlightenment critique of traditional models of marriage brought many reforms to Anglo-American marriage law, particularly on behalf of women and children. Traditional marriage and family law, under both Catholic and Protestant models, had focused on the contracting and dissolving of marriages. The governance of marriages and families once formed and once dissolved was left largely to the discretion of the husband and father, operating with the counsel of the church and the broader Christian community. In the nineteenth and early twentieth centuries, this pattern shifted dramatically—inspired, in part, by the Enlightenment critique of prevailing norms and practices. Sweeping new laws were passed to reform marriage formalities, divorce, alimony, prenuptial contracts, marital property, wife abuse, child custody and support, and education of minors.

In England, Parliament led the way. In 1835 and 1836, Parliament authorized both religious and civil forms of marriage. Parties who reached the age of consent could marry, as traditionally, in accordance with the ecclesiastical laws of England—featuring the publication of banns and a public wedding in the face of the established church and in the presence of an Anglican priest and at least two witnesses. But now Jewish, Quaker, and (later) Catholic parties could marry in accordance with the religious laws and customs of their own communities, being required only to register their marriages with the Superintendent Registrar's Office after the fact. Moreover, parties could forgo a religious marriage ceremony altogether by swearing a simple oath of marriage before an official in the Superintendent Registrar's Office—much as had been instituted, temporarily, by the 1653 Civil Marriage Act.[44]

Though the method of marrying was pluralized, the rules governing marriage formalities remained rather firm in Victorian and post-Victorian England. Traditional rules regarding affinity, consanguinity, infancy, and polygamy remained in effect, with only a slight relaxation of the traditional impediments of affinity and consanguinity.[45] Traditional laws protecting marital consent remained firm: marriages of minors contracted without parental consent, and marriages procured through force, coercion, drunkenness, or exploitation of the other's mental incapacity were all still voidable and the guilty party subject to civil and criminal penalties. Premarital cohabitation and intercourse were also still subject to strict criminal sanction.[46]

Parliament did, however, gradually relieve children of the costs of their parents' extramarital intercourse. Historically, children conceived out of wedlock bore the brunt of their parents' sexual experimentation. Such children were sometimes aborted *in vitro* or smothered on birth, with the mother incurring rather modest penalties for the offense. If they survived, they were declared illegitimate bastards with severely truncated civil, political, and property rights. In Catholic communities, such illegitimate children often found their way to monasteries, orphanages, and charities run by the church. In Protestant communities, such as England, fewer such systematic forms of charity were generally available, especially outside the main cities. Illegitimate children had to hope for a benevolent official who would remove the traditional obstacles to civil rights and social advance or, as was quite regularly the case, immigrate to one of the colonies. A series of statutes passed in the early twentieth century eased this burden. Abortions and infanticide were subject to firm new criminal prohibitions. Exploitation of (illegitimate) child labor was increasingly restricted and policed. Educational opportunities for illegitimate children, boys and girls alike, were substantially enhanced through the expansion of voluntary (state-funded, religious) schools. Illegitimate children could be more easily legitimated through subsequent marriage of their natural parents and eventually also through adoption by a fit parent, whether or not related. Annulments no longer automatically illegitimated children born of a putative marriage, particularly if the child remained in the custody of one of the two parents.[47]

In 1857, Parliament passed the famous Matrimonial Causes Act, which set afoot a series of changes to traditional English marriage law.[48] The Act introduced three major reforms that had been unsuccessfully advocated in England since the sixteenth-century Reformation. First, the 1857 Act transferred marriage and divorce jurisdiction from the church courts to the common law courts. Only common law courts could now hear cases and order legal relief in disputes over betrothal and marriage, marital cruelty and abuse, paternity and bastardy, petitions for child custody, alimony, and the like. Though the Church of England could maintain an internal body of canon law for voluntary use by its members, the church courts no longer held formal legal authority over English marriage life, and their rulings were subordinated to those of the common law courts.[49]

Second, the 1857 Act authorized private suits for divorce on proof of cause, with a subsequent right to remarry for the innocent party. Parties could still press annulment suits on proof of an impediment of consanguinity, affinity, bigamy, or frigidity, and for separation from bed and board on proof of adultery, desertion, or cruelty. But innocent husbands and wives now also could sue for absolute divorce on proof of the adultery of the other party, with a right to remarry—and be spared the ardor and expense of trying to secure a private act of Parliament for the divorce. Initially, such private suits were procedurally cumbersome and quite expensive. But this new cause of action for divorce did provide a passable road to relief and a fresh start to parties, of some means, who were trapped in marriages with faithless spouses. Through a series of amendments to the 1857 Act—culminating in the Divorce Acts of 1923 and 1937—the procedures for divorce cases were simplified, the costs for divorce suits reduced, and the grounds for divorce expanded to include desertion, cruelty, frigidity, habitual drunkenness, criminal conduct, and other forms of fault. As Lawrence Stone has demonstrated in a pathbreaking study, divorce rates accordingly slowly rose in England. Divorce rates stood at .05 divorces per 1000 marriages in 1870, .22 per 1000 in 1920, 4.7 per 1000 in 1970, to a high of 13.4 per 1000 in 1985. At the same time, separation and annulment rates slowly dropped, with divorce increasingly viewed as the most effective and efficient remedy for broken marriages, particularly after the 1969 Divorce Act introduced divorce on the ground of "irretrievable breakdown," the cause for divorce that John Milton had advocated more than three centuries before.[50]

Third, the 1857 Matrimonial Causes Act ordered that, in cases of annulment or divorce, courts had discretion to place minor children in the custody of that parent who was best suited to care for their maintenance, nurture, and education. This reversed the traditional presumption that child custody belonged to the father—"however promiscuous, venereally diseased, brutal, or drunken" he might be.[51] The Act provided that the wife could claim custody, particularly where the children were of tender years or where the husband was found to be cruel, abusive, or unfit as a caretaker. Courts retained the traditional power to order guilty husbands to pay temporary or permanent alimony to innocent wives. Courts were also newly empowered to make "reasonable" allocations of marital property to the innocent wife and her custodial children. These 1857 provisions, together with subsequent Parliamentary legislation on infant child custody, elementary education, and prevention of cruelty to children, slowly bent the law toward the presumption that custody of a child, particularly a minor, be granted to the mother, and that the father be charged with support payments but entitled to visitation rights until the child reaches the age of majority.[52]

The reforms of marital property introduced by the 1857 Matrimonial Causes Act soon gave rise to more comprehensive legislation on women's rights to property. The Married Women's Property Acts of 1870, 1874, and 1882, and subsequent revisions, slowly released married women from the traditional bonds of coverture that (at least formally) subsumed a woman's person and property into that of her husband. Particularly after the 1882 Act, married women held title and control over the property they brought into the marriage, or acquired after the wedding. They also gained increasing capacities to enter contracts of sale, lease, and mortgage of their properties, and the capacity to execute wills, trusts, and other forms of property disposition—in each case without necessary involvement of their husband and with ample protections against his intermeddling. Women also gained the capacity to sue or be sued in respect of their property. Where such suits placed them in conflict with their husbands, traditional rules of evidence that obstructed wives from testifying against their husbands were somewhat relaxed.[53]

These property law reforms brought ample rights to women who held ample wealth or who worked for more than subsistence wages outside the home. But the reforms were largely irrelevant to the large numbers of women who had no disposable property or who did not work outside the home.[54] Nonetheless, it was these early reforms of marital property law that strengthened the pursuit of the ideal of gender equality. In England at the turn of the twentieth century, property rights were still indispensable to social, economic, and political rights—for women as well as for men. As Millicent Garret Fawcett, a pioneer of women's rights, put it in 1886 with reference to the franchise: "Women's suffrage will not come, when it does come, as an isolated phenomenon; it will come as [a] necessary corollary of other changes which have been gradually and steadily modifying during this century the social history of our country. It will be a political change, not of a very great or extensive character in itself, based upon social, educational, and economic changes which have already take place. It will have the effect of adjusting the political machinery of the country to the altered social conditions of its inhabitants."[55]

This proved to be a prophetic utterance. After their rights to property were enhanced, (married) women were able to gain broader rights and access to higher education, learned societies, trade and commercial guilds and unions, and a variety of professions, occupations, and societies historically closed to them. On the strength of these achievements, women ultimately gained the right to vote and to hold public office in 1918.[56] And, in 1919, the Sex Disqualification (Removal) Act provided: "A person shall not be disqualified by sex or marriage from the exercise of any public function, or from being appointed to or assuming or carrying on any civil profession or vocation, or for admission to any incorporated society [or jury duty]."[57]

These sweeping legal changes in England implemented a number of the reforms advocated by Wollstonecraft, Mill, and a host of other exponents of the Enlightenment contractarian model. The Enlightenment gospel was by no means the only ideological catalyst for these reforms, nor was ideology the only impetus for reform. But it was the Enlightenment contractarian model of marriage that helped to break traditional forms and introduce new reforms in English marriage and family law.

A similar legal transformation took place in America. A comprehensive history of American marriage and family law in this era—from the late colonial period to the New Deal—is still to be written. But the ample studies of selected topics and individual state developments already at hand suggest that American marriage and family law was transformed with equal force in the later nineteenth and early twentieth centuries— fueled in part by American theories of Enlightenment contractarianism, in part by the example of English legal reforms. In nineteenth-century America, Carl Schneider writes, "a family law answering a narrow range of questions about the legal (primarily property) relations of husbands and wives was gradually replaced by a family law that increasingly dealt with the termination of those relations, and that increasingly spoke to the relations between parent and child and between the state and the child. The breadth of this first transformation may be seen in the extraordinary range of family-law subjects that either originated or were wholly reformed in the nineteenth century: the law governing marriage formalities, divorce, alimony, marital property, the division of marital property, child custody, adoption, child support, child abuse and neglect, contraception and abortion."[58]

Other scholars have told various parts of this American story. Mary Ann Glendon and Elaine Tyler May have demonstrated, in rich comparative perspective, the dramatic shifts in American law at the turn of the twentieth century toward greater freedom of contract in the formation and dissolution of marriage.[59] Marylynn Salmon and Michael Grossberg have documented, in exquisite detail, the gradual shifts toward equality of economic opportunity and proprietary capacity for married and unmarried women.[60] Frances Olsen and John Langbein have written at length on the "revolution in family wealth transmission" in early twentieth-century America.[61] Historians of the public school movement and of early twentieth century labor regulations have documented, from different archives, the emerging national concern for the protection and enhancement of children—a concern manifested in comprehensive new laws against child labor and child abuse and a growing recognition of the rights of parents and children to education, health care, and other benefit rights.[62] In some instances, such as divorce reform, American legislatures and courts were ahead of their English counterparts. On other topics, such as women's political and civil rights, the English Parliament blazed the trail.

This first wave of reforms brought many salutary changes to the Western legal tradition of marriage and the family, particularly for women and children. Marriages became easier to contract and easier to dissolve. Courts were more deferential to the wishes of the marital parties. Wives received greater protections in their persons and properties from their husbands, and greater access to and independence in their relationships outside the household. Ironically, the increased emphasis on the contractual nature of marriage also led to an increased solicitude for children—as protected third-party beneficiaries of both the marital contract of their parents and the social contract of their community. Children thus received greater protection from the abuses and neglect of their parents, and greater access to benefit rights of nurture, education, maintenance, and appropriate work. Young women, in particular, received greater freedom to forgo or postpone marriage, and greater access to social, political, and economic opportunities, regardless of their marital status.

Given the explosion of new legislation from the mid-nineteenth century forward, the state also came to replace the church as the principal external authority governing marriage and family life. The Catholic sacramental model of the family governed principally by the extended church, and the Protestant social model of the family governed by the congregation and broader Christian community, gave way to a new model of marriage and the family ruled by the will of the parties subject to the limits of state law. To be sure, parties could still voluntarily subscribe to the internal marriage and family laws of their own religious communities and voluntarily accept the sexual discipline of the clergy. But the state's marriage and family laws were now supreme and would preempt religious laws in cases of conflict. This shift to state law became easy to rationalize in America with the rise to legal prominence of the maxim of "separation of church and state." But in England, too, this preference for state governance of marriage came to dominate early twentieth-century discourse, even though the Church of England remained legally established.

It must be emphasized that this first wave of reforms, catalyzed by the Enlightenment contractarian model, sought to improve the Western legal tradition of marriage more than to abandon it. To be sure, the smug mockery of a Mill and the shattering iconoclasm of some Victorian radicals betrayed ample hostility to the tradition. But this radicalism was needed to fuel the reform movements of the nineteenth century—much as Luther's burning of the canon law books in 1520 was needed to fuel the reforms of canon law in the sixteenth century. Just as Luther and his followers ultimately remained faithful to the Western legal tradition of marriage, so did Mill and other nineteenth-century reformers.

Most Enlightenment reformers accepted the ideal structure of marriage as a presumptively permanent union of a fit man and fit woman of the age of consent. Most accepted the classic definition of the goods and goals of marriage: mutual love and affection, mutual procreation and nurture of children, mutual protection from spiritual and civil harms. The primary goal of these Enlightenment reformers was to purge the traditional household and community of its excessive paternalism, patriarchy, and prudishness, and thus to render the ideal structure and purpose of marriage a greater reality for all. The changes inaugurated in this first wave of reform have been almost universally condoned in the West as salutary. Indeed, with the exception of the law of divorce and remarriage, almost all of these legal changes in Anglo-American common law—and comparable changes in Continental civil law[63]—have now been incorporated into the theological platforms and social policies of Anglican, Protestant, and Catholic communities alike.[64]

Modern Legal Reforms
in America

The same judgment cannot be cast for the second transformation of Anglo-American marriage law currently underway. Since the early 1960s, American reformers have been pressing the Enlightenment contractarian model of marriage to the more radical conclusions that Mill and others had suggested. The same Enlightenment ideals of individualism, freedom, equality, and privacy, which had earlier driven reforms of traditional marriage law, are now being increasingly used to reject traditional marriage laws altogether. The early Enlightenment ideals of marriage as a permanent contractual union designed for the sake of mutual love, procreation, and protection is slowly giving way to a new reality of marriage as a "terminal sexual contract" designed for the gratification of the individual parties.[65]

The Uniform Marriage and Divorce Act—both a "barometer of enlightened legal opinion" and a mirror of conventional custom on marriage[66]—reflects these legal changes. The Uniform Act defines marriage as "a personal relationship between a man and a woman arising out of a civil contract to which the consent of the parties is essential."[67] Historically, valid marriage contracts required the consent of parents or guardians, the attestation of two witnesses, church consecration, and civil licensing and registration. The Uniform Act requires only the minimal formalities of licensing and registration for all marriages, and parental consent for children under the age of majority. Marriages contracted in violation of these requirements are presumptively valid and immune from independent legal attack, unless the parties themselves petition for dissolution within ninety days of contracting marriage.[68] Historically, impediments of infancy, incapacity, inebriation, consanguinity, affinity, sterility, frigidity, bigamy, among several others would nullify the marriage or render it voidable and subject to attack from various parties. It would also expose parties who married in knowing violation of these impediments to civil and criminal sanctions. The Uniform Act makes no provision for sanctions and leaves the choice of nullification to the parties alone. The Act does confirm the traditional impediments protecting consent—granting parties standing to dissolve marriages where they lacked the capacity to contract by reason of infirmity, mental incapacity, alcohol, drugs, or other incapacitating substances, or where there was force, duress, fraud, or coercion into entering a marriage contract.[69] But the Act limits the other impediments to prohibitions against bigamy and marriages between "half or whole blood relatives" or parties related by adoption.[70] And, in many states that have adopted the Uniform Act, all impediments, save the prohibition against bigamy, are regularly waived in individual cases.

These provisions of the Uniform Marriage and Divorce Act reflect a basic principle of modern American constitutional law, first articulated clearly by the Supreme Court in *Loving v. Virginia* (1967): "The freedom to marry has long been recognized as one of the vital personal rights essential to the orderly pursuit of happiness by free men. Marriage is one of the 'basic civil rights of man,' fundamental to our very existence and survival."[71] Using that principle, the Court has struck down, as undue burdens on the right to marry, a state prohibition against interracial marriage, a requirement that noncustodial parents obligated to pay child support must receive judicial permission to marry, and a requirement that a prisoner must receive a warden's permission to marry.[72] This same principle of freedom of marital contract, the draftsmen of the Uniform Act report, has led state courts and legislatures to peel away most of the traditional formalities for marriage formation.

The Supreme Court has expanded this principle of freedom of marital contract into a more general right of sexual privacy within the household. In *Griswold v. Connecticut* (1965), for example, the Supreme Court struck down a state law banning the use of contraceptives by a married couple as a violation of their freedom to choose whether to have or to forgo children.[73] In a 1972 case, the Court stated its rationale clearly: "The marital couple is not an independent entity with a mind and heart of its own, but an association of two individuals, each with a separate emotional and intellectual makeup. If the right of privacy means anything, it is the right of the *individual,* married or single, to be free from unwanted governmental intrusion into matters so fundamentally affecting the person as the decision whether to bear or beget a child."[74] In *Roe v. Wade* the following year, the Court extended this privacy principle to cover the right of abortion by a married or unmarried woman during the first trimester of pregnancy, without interference by the state, her husband, parents, or other third party. Still today, a married woman cannot be required to obtain permission from her husband to have an abortion.[75] In *Moore v. East Cleveland* (1977), the Court struck down a municipal zoning ordinance that impaired members of an extended family from living together in the same household.[76] In *Kirschberg v. Feenstra* (1981), the Court struck down a state statute that gave the husband as "head and master" of the family the right unilaterally to dispose of property held in common with his wife.[77] In all such cases, the private contractual calculus of the parties was considered superior to the general state interest in the health, safety, and welfare of its citizens.

State legislatures and courts have extended these principles of freedom of contact and sexual privacy to other aspects of marriage. Many states, for example, have abandoned their traditional reticence about enforcing prenuptial and marital contracts. The Uniform Premarital Agreement Act, adopted in nearly half the states today, allows parties to contract, in advance of their marriage, all rights pertaining to their individual and common property and "any other matter, including their personal rights and obligations, not in violation of public policy or a statute imposing a criminal penalty."[78] The Act does prohibit courts from enforcing premarital contracts that are involuntary, unconscionable, or based on less than full disclosure by both parties. But, within these broad strictures, marital parties are left free to define in advance their own personal and property rights during marriage or in the event of separation, dissolution, or divorce.

Similarly, many states have left marital parties free to contract agreements on their own, or with a private mediator, in the event of temporary or permanent separation. The Uniform Marriage and Divorce Act provides in §306(a) that "parties may enter into a written separation agreement containing provisions for disposition of property owned by either of them, maintenance of either of them, and support, custody, and visitation of their children." Such agreements are presumptively binding on a court, and, absent a finding of unconscionability, courts will enforce these agreements on their own terms, reserving the right to alter those contract provisions that bear adversely on the couple's children. If the separation ripens into divorce, courts will also often incorporate these separation agreements into the divorce decree, again with little scrutiny of the contents of the agreement.

The same principles of freedom of contract and sexual privacy dominate contemporary American laws of divorce. Until the mid-1960s, a suit for divorce required proof of the fault of one's spouse (such as adultery, desertion, or cruelty), and no evidence of collusion, connivance, condonation, or provocation by the other spouse. Pleadings were public, and proceedings were recorded in public records. If plaintiffs met their burden of proof, the parties could be divorced. The innocent party, particularly the innocent wife, was generally granted custody of minor children. The guilty party, particularly the husband, was sometimes charged with ongoing obligations of alimony payments to the innocent spouse. The guilty party was also usually obligated to make child support payments for dependent children. This law reflected the traditional view that marriage was ideally a perpetual bond of mutual love and support, that reconciliation of estranged spouses was the preferred remedy in cases of mutual fault, and that divorce was designed to relieve the innocent party of the company of a faithless spouse but to preserve at least some of the material benefits of the marriage.[79]

Today, this law of divorce has been abandoned. Every state has now promulgated a "no-fault divorce" statute, and virtually all states allow for divorce on the motion of only one party.[80] The Uniform Marriage and Divorce Act has typical language, allowing for divorce if "both of the parties by petition or otherwise have stated under oath or affirmation that the marriage is irretrievably broken, or one of the parties has so stated and the other has not denied it."[81] Even if the innocent spouse forgives the fault and objects to the divorce, courts must grant the divorce if the plaintiff insists.[82] The Uniform Marriage and Divorce Act and fifteen states have eliminated altogether consideration of the fault of either spouse, even if the fault rises to the level of criminal conduct. The remaining states consider fault only for limited questions of child custody, not for questions of the divorce itself. Husband and wife, in effect, have an unqualified "right to divorce."[83]

Virtually all states have also ordered a one-time division of marital property between the divorced parties. Parties may determine their own property division through prenuptial or separation agreements, which the courts will enforce if the agreements are not unconscionable. But absent such agreements, courts will simply pool the entire assets of the marital household and make an equitable division of the collective property based on numerous factors. The Uniform Marriage and Divorce Act uses typical language: "[T]he court, without regard to marital misconduct, shall . . . equitably apportion between the parties the property and assets belonging to either or both however and whenever acquired, and whether the title thereto is in the name of the husband or wife or both. In making apportionment the court shall consider the duration of the marriage, any prior marriage of either party, antenuptial agreements of the parties, the age, health, station, occupation, amount and sources of income, vocational skills, employability, estate, liabilities, and needs of each of the parties, custodial provisions . . . and the opportunity for each for future acquisition of capital assets and income."[84] These one-time divisions of property have largely replaced traditional forms of alimony and other forms of ongoing support, regardless of the fault, expectations, or needs of either party.[85]

These two reforms of the modern law of divorce serve to protect both the privacy and the contractual freedom of the marital parties. No-fault divorces free marital parties from exposing their marital discords or infidelities to judicial scrutiny and public record. One-time marital property divisions give parties a clean break from each other and the freedom to marry another.[86] Both changes, together, allow parties to terminate their marriages as easily and efficiently as they are able to contract them, without much interference from the state or from the other spouse.

These principles of contractual freedom are qualified in divorce cases involving minor children.[87] The fault of the marital party does still figure modestly in current decisions about child custody. The traditional rule was that custody of children was presumptively granted to the mother, unless she was found guilty of serious marital fault or maternal incompetence. Proof of marital fault by the husband, particularly adultery, homosexuality, prostitution, or sexual immorality, virtually eliminated his chances of gaining custody, even if the wife was also at fault. Today, the court's custodial decisions are guided by the proverbial principle of the "best interests of the child." According to the Uniform Marriage and Divorce Act, courts must consider at once the child's custodial preferences, the parents' custodial interests, "the interrelationship of the child with his [or her] parent or parents," "the child's adjustment to his [or her] home, school, or community," and "the mental and physical health of all parties involved."[88] "The court shall not consider the conduct of a proposed custodian that does not affect his relationship to the child," the Act concludes, setting a high burden of proof for the party who wants to make his or her spouse's marital fault an issue in a contested custody case. Under this new standard, the presumption of maternal custody is quickly softening, and joint and shared custody arrangements are becoming increasingly common.[89]

Where one party is granted sole or principal custody, the noncustodial party is bound to make ongoing support payments—notwithstanding the current preference for a one-time marital property division. Indeed, several federal and state laws now mandate that noncustodial parents pay some 15%–30% of their gross incomes in the form of child support, and punish with unprecedented severity delinquency in payment. Moreover, noncustodial parents are punished for their delinquency in caring for their children. Both federal and state laws punish "deadbeat parents" who shirk responsibilities of visitation and maintenance, neglect or abuse their children during temporary custody, and transport or detain their children against the wishes of the custodial parent.[90]

John Stuart Mill's ideal of marriage as "a private, bargained-for exchange between husband and wife about all their rights, goods, and interests" has become a legal reality in contemporary America. To be sure, courts do not enforce marital contracts as if they are simple commercial contracts. Some states, Milton Regan demonstrates, "will review the substantive fairness of certain antenuptial agreements at the time of enforcement to take account of changes in circumstances since execution. Some states will subject to particularly close scrutiny contract terms dealing with support, impose formalities beyond those required for ordinary contracts, or toll during marriage statutes of limitation relating to claims arising out of antenuptial agreements."[91] But the strong presumption in America today is that adult parties have free entrance into marital contracts, free exercise of marital relationships, and free exit from marriages once their contractual obligations are discharged.[92] Given the erosion of formalities for marriage formation and dissolution, these same freedoms of contract and sexual privacy have been easily extended to various nonmarital heterosexual unions[93] and homosexual relationships as well.[94] To be sure, parties are bound to continue to support their minor children, within and without marriage. But this, too, merely expresses another basic principle of contract law—that parties respect the reliance and expectation interests of their children, who are third-party beneficiaries of their marital or sexual contracts.

James Fitzjames Stephen's warning that private contractualization of marriage will bring ruin to many women and children has also become a reality in America.[95] Premarital, marital, separation, and divorce agreements too often are not arms-length transactions, and too often are not driven by rational calculus alone, however much courts and mediators insist that they are. In the heady romance of budding nuptials, parties are often blind to the full consequences of their bargain. In the emotional anguish of separation and divorce, parties can be driven more by the desire for short-term relief from the other spouse than by the concern for their long-term welfare or that of their children. The economically stronger and more calculating spouse triumphs in these contexts. And in the majority of cases today, that party is still the man, despite the loud egalitarian rhetoric to the contrary.

"Underneath the mantle of equality [and freedom] that has been draped over the ongoing family, the state of nature flourishes," Mary Ann Glendon writes ominously.[96] In this state of nature, contractual freedom and sexual privacy reign supreme, with no real role for the state, church, or broader civil society to play. In this state of nature, married life has become increasingly "brutish, nasty, and short," with women and children bearing the primary costs.[97] In 1970, 13 percent of all households were headed by single mothers; today, the number stands at more than 30 percent, with more than half of these single-mother households below the poverty line. In the 1990s, a quarter of all children conceived are aborted. A third of all children are born to single mothers. One half of all marriages end in divorce. The number of "no parent" households doubles each year. The number of "lost children" in America—born in poverty and in broken households, and more likely than not to drop out of school, out of step, and then out of society altogether—now stands at a staggering fifteen million.[98] The greater the repeal of state regulation of marriage for the sake of marital freedom and sexual privacy, the greater the threat to the true freedom realized for women and children in the first phase of the Enlightenment transformation of marriage.

Perhaps a future generation will look back on the late twentieth century much as we now look back on the late nineteenth century—as the radical phase of a longer revolutionary movement that ultimately brought great benefits to the Western legal tradition. Perhaps we are simply witnessing today the birth pangs of a new marriage order that will feature the final removal of sexual stereotyping and exploitation; the real achievement of distributive justice to women, children, and the poor; the sensible pluralization of Western marriage laws to accommodate new global patterns of sexuality, kinship, and bonding. These are goals to which the Western legal tradition of marriage must surely aspire. And, as Harold Berman reminds us, great legal revolutions always pass through radical phases before they reach an accommodation with the tradition that they had set out to destroy.[99]

It is hard to see the promise of these future benefits, however, in the current phase of the legal revolution of marriage in America. The rudimentary disquisitions on equality, privacy, and freedom offered by courts and commentators today seem altogether too lean to nourish sufficiently the legal revolution of marriage and the family that is now taking place. The elementary deconstructions and dismissals of a millennium-long tradition of marriage and family law and life seem altogether too glib to be taken so seriously. Yet the legal revolution marches on. And the massive social, psychological, and spiritual costs continue to mount up. The wild oats sown in the course of the American sexual revolution have brought forth such a great forest of tangled structural, moral, and intellectual thorns that we seem almost powerless to cut it down. We seem to be living out the grim prophecy that Friedrich Nietzsche offered a century ago: that in the course of the twentieth century, "the family will be slowly ground into a random collection of individuals," haphazardly bound together "in the common pursuit of selfish ends"—and in the common rejection of the structures and strictures of family, church, state, and civil society.[100]

Reflections

The foregoing chapters have recounted the rise of five theological models of marriage and their respective influences on the Western legal tradition: the Catholic sacramental model of the twelfth and thirteenth centuries, the Lutheran social model, the Calvinist covenantal model, the Anglican commonwealth model of early modern times, and the Enlightenment contractarian model of the past century. These five theological models have helped to drive the development of Western marriage and family law.

The foregoing chapters have emphasized the differences among these five models of marriage. *Theologically,* these differences can be traced to the genesis of these models in Catholic sacramental theology, Lutheran two kingdoms doctrines, Calvinist covenantal constructions, Anglican commonwealth theory, and Enlightenment contractarianism, respectively. *Politically,* these differences can be seen in the shifts in marital jurisdiction. Catholics vested exclusive marital jurisdiction in the church. Anglicans left marital jurisdiction to church courts, subject to royal oversight and Parliamentary legislation. Calvinists assigned interlocking marital roles to local consistories and city councils. Lutherans consigned primary marital jurisdiction to the territorial prince or urban council. Enlightenment thinkers reserved authority over marriage to the couple, subject to shrinking state oversight. *Legally,* these differences were most pronounced in the great debates over the form and function, and the length and limits, of rules governing marriage formation, maintenance, and dissolution; sexual alliances, preferences, and expression; spousal roles, rights, and responsibilities; and children's care, custody, and control.

To bring to light these historical Catholic, Protestant, and Enlightenment models is neither to wax nostalgic about a prior golden age of the Western family, nor to write pedantic about arcane antiquities with no modern utility. These are the models that have shaped the Western fam-

ily and the Western legal tradition, for better and for worse. These are
the models that have to be dealt with—critically, constructively, and
comprehensively—by jurists and theologians, preachers and politicians,
activists and academics alike.

At minimum, it might be instructive to note that family crises on a
comparable scale to those we face today have been faced before. And bitter jeremiads about the end of civil society and the dissolution of all social order have been voiced before—by Chrysostom and Augustine in
the fifth century, by Aquinas and Hugh of St. Victor in the thirteenth
century, by Luther and Calvin in the sixteenth century. Indeed, in some
respects, the Western legal tradition of marriage in the past millennium
has simply come full circle. Secret and private marriages were tolerated
at the beginning of this millennium, were condemned by Catholic and
Protestant leaders in the middle of this millennium, but have now returned to prominence under Enlightenment theories of privacy. The
single life was the celibate ideal of Catholics at the beginning of this millennium, was condemned by Protestants in the middle of this millennium, and has now returned to social prominence under the inspiration
of Enlightenment individualism. Sexual pathos was prominent at the
opening of this second millennium with widespread concubinage, prostitution, voyeurism, polygamy, adultery, fornication, sodomy, wife and
child abuse, teenage pregnancy, abortion, and much else. Sexual pathos
has returned with equal pungency at the close of this second millennium.

More fully conceived, these five traditional models, particularly those
of Catholic and Protestant stock, have provided many enduring prescriptions for marriage that need to be pondered even in our day. From
different perspectives, both Catholic and Protestant traditions have seen
that marriage is at once a natural, religious, social, and contractual unit;
that in order to survive and flourish, this institution must be governed
both externally by legal authorities and internally by moral authorities.
From different perspectives, these traditions have seen that the family is
an inherently communal enterprise in which marital couples, magistrates, and ministers must all inevitably cooperate. After all, marital contracts are of little value without courts to interpret and enforce them.
Marital properties are of little use without laws to protect and value
them. Marital laws are of little consequence without canons to inspire
and legitimate them. Marital customs are of little cogency without natural norms and narratives to ground them.

The Western tradition has learned, through centuries of experience, to
balance the norms of marital formation, maintenance, and dissolution.
There was something cruel in a medieval canon law that countenanced

easy contracting of marriage but provided for no escape from a marriage once properly contracted. The Council of Trent responded to this inequity by establishing several safeguards to the legitimate contracting of marriage. The lesson in this is that rules governing marriage formation and dissolution must be comparable in their stringency. Stern rules of marital dissolution require stern rules of marital formation. Loose formation rules demand loose dissolution rules, as we see today. To fix "the modern problem of divorce" will require reforms of rules at both ends of the marital process. There was something equally cruel in Calvin's rigid insistence on reconciliation of all married couples save those few who could successfully sue for divorce. Later Protestants responded to this inequity by reinstituting the remedy of separation from bed and board for miserable couples incapable of either reconciliation or divorce. The lesson in this is that rules of marriage require equitable application; general principles of marriage law cannot decide all concrete cases.[1] And to strike this balance between rule and equity, principle and precept, demands the active involvement of trained judges and jurists.

The Western tradition has recognized that the family has multiple forms and that it can change over time and across cultures. The celebrated nuclear family of husband and wife, and of daughter and son, is only one model that the Western tradition has cherished. It was common in the past to extend the theological and legal concept of the family to other kinds of units: the single household with one parent alongside children, stepchildren, adopted children, or grandchildren; the extended household embracing servants, students, and sojourners or embracing three or four generations of relatives with obligations of mutual care and nurture among them; the communal household of siblings or friends, single or widowed, with or without children; the spiritual household of brothers and sisters joined in the cloister, chantry, or charity, and dedicated to service of God, neighbor, and each other.

The Western tradition has also recognized that marriage and the family have multiple goods and goals. This institution might well be rooted in the natural order and in the will of the parties. Participation in it might well not be vital, or even conducive, to a person's salvation. But the Western tradition has seen that marriage and the family are indispensable to the integrity of the individual and the preservation of the social order.

In Catholic and Anglican parlance, marriage has three inherent goods, which Augustine identified as *fides, proles, et sacramentum*. Marriage is an institution of *fides*—faith, trust, and love between husband and wife, and parent and child, that goes beyond the faith demanded of any other temporal relationship. Marriage is a source of *proles*—children who carry on the family name and tradition, perpetuate the human species, and fill God's church with the next generation of saints. Marriage is a form of *sacramentum*—a symbolic expression of Christ's love for his church, even a channel of God's grace to sanctify the couple, their children, and the broader community.

In Lutheran and Calvinist parlance, marriage has both civil and spiritual uses in this life. On the one hand, the family has general "civil uses" for all persons, regardless of their faith. Marriage deters vice by furnishing preferred options to prostitution, promiscuity, pornography, and other forms of sexual pathos. Marriage cultivates virtue by offering love, care, and nurture to its members, and by holding out a model of charity, education, and sacrifice to the broader community. Marriage enhances the life of a man and a woman by providing them with a community of caring and sharing, of stability and support, of nurture and welfare. It might take other communities to sustain a husband or wife, such as churches, clubs, unions, and the welfare state. But, for most people, these are no substitutes for marriage. Marriage enhances the life of the child by providing it with a chrysalis of nurture and love, with a highly individualized form of socialization and education. It might take a whole village to raise a child properly, but it takes a marriage to make one.

On the other hand, the family has specific "spiritual uses" for believers—ways of sustaining and strengthening them in their faith. The love of wife and husband can be among the strongest symbols we can experience of Yahweh's love for His elect, of Christ's love for His Church. The sacrifices we make for our spouses and children can be among the best reflections we can offer of the perfect sacrifice of Golgotha. The procreation of children can be among the most important Words we have to utter.[7]

Notes

Notes to the Introduction

1. H. Richard Niebuhr, *Christ and Culture* (New York: Harper & Row, 1951), 39–40.
2. See Henry Sumner Maine, *Ancient Law* (1861); id., *Village Communities in the East and the West* (1871); id., *Early History of Institutions* (1875); id., *Early Law and Custom* (1883). See studies in Paul Vinogradoff, *The Teaching of Sir Henry Maine* (Oxford: Oxford University Press, 1904); R.C.J. Cocks, *Sir Henry Sumner Maine: A Study in Victorian Jurisprudence* (Cambridge: Cambridge University Press, 1988).
3. Maine, *Ancient Law,* 121.
4. Kenneth Bock, "The Moral Philosophy of Sir Henry Sumner Maine," *Journal of History of Ideas* 37 (1976):147, 149. See also criticisms in sources cited in note 2; and Henry Orenstein, "The Ethnological Theories of Henry Sumner Maine," *American Anthropologist* 70 (1968):264; Mark Francis, "Henry Sumner Maine: Victorian Evolution and Political Theory," *History of European Ideas* 19 (1994):753.
5. See esp. James A. Brundage, *Law, Sex, and Christian Society in Medieval Europe* (Chicago: University of Chicago Press, 1987); R.H. Helmholz, *Marriage Litigation in Medieval England* (Cambridge: Cambridge University Press, 1974); id., *The Spirit of the Classical Canon Law* (Athens: University of Georgia Press, 1996); John T. Noonan, Jr., *Contraception: A History of Its Treatment by the Catholic Theologians and Canonists* (Cambridge, Mass.: Belknap Press, 1965); id., *The Power to Dissolve: Lawyers and Marriages in the Courts of the Roman Curia* (Cambridge, Mass.: Belknap Press, 1972). For further references to their work, see chapters 1 and 4, below.
6. See esp. Mary Ann Glendon, *Abortion and Divorce in Western Law* (Chicago: University of Chicago Press, 1988); id., *The Transformation of Family Law: State, Law, and Family in the United States and Western Europe* (Chicago: University of Chicago Press, 1989); id., *The New Family and the New Property* (Toronto: Butterworths, 1981); Max Rheinstein, *Marriage Stability, Divorce, and the Law* (Chicago: University of Chicago Press, 1971); Lawrence Stone, *The Family, Sex, and Marriage in England, 1500–1800* (New York: Harper & Row, 1979); id., *Road to Divorce: England 1530–1987* (Oxford: Oxford University Press, 1990). For further references, see chapters 4 and 5, below.
7. Mary Ann Glendon, *State, Law, and Family: Family Law in Transition in the United States and Western Europe* (Boston/Dordrecht: Martinus Nijhoff Publishers, 1977), 1.
8. See discussion in chapter 2, below.
9. The notable exceptions are the work of Steven Ozment, *When Fathers Ruled: Family Life in Reformation Europe* (Cambridge and London: Harvard University Press, 1983); Robert M. Kingdon, *Adultery and Divorce in Calvin's Geneva* (Cambridge and London: Harvard University Press, 1995); and Cornelia Seeger, *Nullité de mariage divorce et séparation de corps a Genève, au temps de Calvin: Fondements doc-*

trinaux, loi et jurisprudence (Lausanne: Mémoires et documents publiés par la société d'histoire de la suisse romande, 1989), discussed in chapter 3, below.
10. See sources in chapter 4, below.
11. The phrase is from Jean Bethke Elshtain, "Marriage in Civil Society," *Family Affairs* 7 (Spring 1996):1–5. See also Council on Families, *Marriage in America: A Report to the Nation* (New York: Institute for American Values, 1995).

Notes to Chapter 1:
Marriage as Sacrament in the Roman Catholic Tradition

1. See also Mark 10:29–31; 13:12–13; and Luke 12:51–53.
2. The Gospel of Mark, which is generally taken as an earlier text, largely repeats this language, but without the allowance of divorce in the case of the wife's unchastity. See Mark 10:2–10. The same absolute language appears more briefly in Luke 16:18.
3. 2 Cor. 11:2; see also Matt. 9:15; Rev. 19:7–8, 21:2.
4. See also Col. 3:18–21; 1 Tim. 2:11–15.
5. 1 Cor. 7:8–39; 1 Tim. 5:3–16.
6. See also 1 Cor. 5:1; 6:9, 15–20; Eph. 5:3–4; Col. 3:5–6; 1 Tim. 2:9–10; 3:2.
7. *The Teaching of the Twelve Apostles, Didache, or The Oldest Church Manual,* Philip Schaff, trans. and ed., 3d rev. ed. (New York: Funk & Wagnalls, 1889), 161, 168, 172; *Didascalia Apostolorum,* R. Hugh Connolly, trans. (Oxford: Clarendon Press, 1929), chaps. 2, 3, 4, and 14.
8. See illustrative provisions in Philip Schaff and Henry Wace, eds., *The Seven Ecumenical Councils,* repr. ed. (Grand Rapids: Wm. B. Eerdmans Publishing Co., 1952), 11, 46–51, 70, 73, 79, 81–82, 92, 95, 98, 129, 149, 156, 157, 279, 280, 452, 460–462, 569–570, 604 613. See thorough discussion in David Balch and Carolyn Osiek, *Families in the New Testament World* (Louisville: Westminster John Knox Press, 1997).
9. See sources and analysis in Philip L. Reynolds, *Marriage in the Western Church: The Christianization of Marriage During the Patristic and Early Medieval Periods* (Leiden: E.J. Brill, 1994), 121–240.
10. See esp. Tertullian, *Apologeticus* and *De Spectaculis,* in *Tertullian,* Gerald H. Rendall, trans. and ed. (New York: G.P. Putnam's Sons, 1931), 32, 35–48, 79, 105, 179, 274–281 (on criticizing Roman institutions); id., *Against Marcion,* in Alexander Roberts and James Donaldson, eds., *The Ante-Nicene Fathers,* repr. ed. (Buffalo: The Christian Literature Publishing Co., 1885), 3:294, 385–387 (on procreative good of marriage); Clement, *The Instructor,* in *Ante-Nicene Fathers,* 2:212–222 (on believers as children of God), 250–253 (on proper relations of men and women), 259–263 (on the lawful use of marriage); id., *Stromata* in *Ante-Nicene Fathers,* 2:377–379 (on marital goods).
11. See Jean Gaudemet, "Les transformations de la vie familiale au bas empire et l'influence du christianisme," *Romanitas* 4 (1962):58–85; id., "Tendances nouvelles de la legislation familiale aux ivme siècle," *Antiquitas* 1 (1978):187–207; John T. Noonan, Jr., "Novel 22," in W.J. Bassett, ed., *The Bond of Marriage: An Ecumenical and Interdisciplinary Study* (Notre Dame and London: University of Notre Dame Press, 1968), 41–90; Engbert J.J. Jonkers, *Invloed van het Christendom op de romeinsche wetgeving betreffende het concubinaat en de echtscheiding* (Wageningen: H. Veenman, 1938).

12. Ambrose, *Concerning Widows*, chap. 4.23, in Philip Schaff and Henry Wace, eds., *A Select Library of Nicene and Post-Nicene Fathers of the Christian Church, Second Series*, repr. ed. (Grand Rapids: Wm. B. Eerdmans Publishing Co., 1952), 10:395 [hereafter *Fathers Library*]. See also Gregory of Nyssa, *On Virginity*, in *Fathers Library*, 5:342–371; Jerome, *Letters*, in *Fathers Library*, 6:22–42, 66–79, 102–111, 141–148, 260–272, and id., *Against Jovianus*, in *Fathers Library*, 6:346–386. See also the classic discussion of Peter Brown, *The Body and Society: Men, Women, and Sexual Renunciation in Early Christianity* (New York: Columbia University Press, 1988).

13. For reasons and examples, see Theodore Mackin, *Marriage in the Catholic Church: What Is Marriage?* (New York: Paulist Press, 1982), 38–80.

14. John Chrysostom, *Sermon on Marriage*, in *St. John Chrysostom on Marriage and Family Life* (Crestwood, N.J.: St. Vladimir's Press, 1986), 85.

15. Ibid., 81.

16. Id., *Homily 20 on Ephesians 5:22–33*, in *Chrysostom on Marriage and Family Life*, 54–55.

17. Id., *Homily on Matthew*, in *Fathers Library*, 10:443–444. See also id., *Homilies on the Acts of the Apostles and the Epistle to the Romans*, in *Fathers Library*, 11:140–141, 295–296 (warning against marrying for money and status).

18. Id., *How to Choose a Wife*, in *Chrysostom on Marriage and Family Life*, 89–114, at 97.

19. Id., *Homily 20*, 43, 44. See also id., *Homilies on the Epistles of Paul to the Corinthians*, in *Fathers Library*, 12:70 ("marriage is a solemn thing and that which recruits our race and the cause of numerous blessings").

20. Id., *Homily 20*, 53.

21. See generally John T. Noonan, Jr., *Contraception: A History of Its Treatment by the Catholic Theologians and Canonists* (Cambridge, Mass.: Belknap Press, 1965), 126–139; Reynolds, *Marriage*, 241–314.

22. Augustine, *City of God*, XIV.10, 21, 22.

23. Id., *Sermons on New Testament Lessons*, Sermon I. 22, in *Fathers Library*, 6:253; see also *City of God*, XIV.18.

24. Id., *City of God*, XV.16; XIX.7, 14.

25. Ibid., XIX.16.

26. See esp. id., *De bono coniugali*, in R.J. Deferrari, ed., *Saint Augustine: Treatises on Marriage and Other Subjects* (New York: Fathers of the Church, Inc., 1955), 9–51.

27. Id., *On Original Sin*, chap. 39 [xxxiv], in *Fathers Library*, 5:251.

28. Id., *De bono coniugali*, chaps. 4–7.

29. Id., *On Marriage and Concupiscence*, chaps. 11 [x] and 19 [xvii] in *Fathers Library*, 5:261, 271.

30. Id., *De bono coniugali*, chap. 15.

31. Noonan, *Contraception*, 128–129.

32. Harold J. Berman, *Law and Revolution: The Formation of the Western Legal Tradition* (Cambridge, Mass.: Harvard University Press, 1983).

33. Hugh of St. Victor, *On the Sacraments of the Christian Faith*, Part II, R. Deferrari, trans. (Cambridge, Mass.: Harvard University Press, 1951).

34. Petrus Lombardus, *Libri IV sententiarum*, 2d rev. ed. (Florence: Collegio di San Bonaventura, 1916), bk. 4, dist. 26–42 (1150). Lombard's discussion of marriage was so famous that Erasmus later quipped: "There are as many commentaries on the sentences of Peter Lombardus as there are theologians." Letter to Vozius, 1518, quoted in Elizabeth F. Rogers, *Peter Lombard and the Sacramental System* (New York: n.p., 1917), 77.

35. Thomas Aquinas, *Summa Theologiae*, Part III (Supp.), qq. 41–68, in *Sancti Thomae Aquinatis, Opera Omnia*, ed. Leonina (Rome: 1918–1930), vols. 4–12, and *The*

Summa Theologiae, English trans. by English Dominican Fathers (London: 1912–1936), 22 vols.

36. See collection in Emil Friedberg, ed., *Corpus Iuris Canonici,* 2 vols. (Lipsiae: ex officina Bernhardi Tauchnitz, 1879–1881). See a list of later canon law titles in Helmut Coing, *Handbuch der Quellen und Literatur der neueren europäischen Privatrechtsgeschichte* (München: Beck, 1977), 1:1011ff., with excerpts in Rudolf Weigand, ed., *Die Naturrechtslehre der Legisten und Dekretisten von Irnerius bis Accursius und von Gratian bis Johannes Teutonicus* (München: Max Hueber Verlag, 1967), 283ff. The best analysis of these texts is in James A. Brundage, *Law, Sex, and Christian Society in Medieval Europe* (Chicago: University of Chicago Press, 1987), 176–550.

37. Lombard, *Sentences,* bk. 4, dist. 26.2; Aquinas, *Summa Theol.,* Pt. II–II, qq. 151–156; Pt. III, q. 41, art. 1; Hugh of St. Victor, *Sacraments,* 325–329. For a later summary, see William Hay, *Lectures on Marriage* (1533–35), trans. J. Barry (Edinburgh: Stair Society, 1967), 19, 39–41.

38. Lombard, *Sentences,* bk. 4, dist. 26.3–4; Aquinas, *Summa Theol.,* Pt. III, q. 41, art. 2. See further sources and texts in Joseph Friesen, *Geschichte des kanonischen Eherechts bis zum Verfall der Glossenliteratur,* 2d ed, repr. ed. (Aalen: Scientia Verlag, 1963), 25ff.

39. Lombard, *Sentences,* bk. 4, dist. 26.3.

40. See sources and discussion in Christopher N.L. Brooke, "The Cult of Celibacy in the Eleventh and Twelfth Centuries," in id., *The Medieval Idea of Marriage* (Oxford and New York: Oxford University Press, 1991), 61–92.

41. Aquinas, *Summa Theol.,* Pt. III, q. 41, art. 2.

42. See John T. Noonan, Jr., "Marital Affection in the Canonists," *Studia Gratiana* 12 (1967):489; Jean Leclercq, *Monks on Marriage: A Twelfth Century View* (New York: Seabury Press, 1982), 12–39, 72–81. But cf. Rudolf Weigand, "Liebe und Ehe bei den Dekretisten des 12. Jahrhunderts," in id., *Liebe und Ehe im Mittelalter* (Goldbach: Keip Verlag, 1993), 60–79 (showing the paucity of the theme of love in the writings of twelfth century canonists).

43. See texts in Weigand, *Naturrechtslehre,* 283–298.

44. Lombard, *Sentences,* bk. 4, dist. 28.4. Gratian had earlier focused on consent to sexual intercourse, but this view was spurned by later canonists and decretists. For reasons, see Brundage, *Law, Sex, and Christian Society,* 235–242, 260–278.

45. Lombard, *Sentences,* bk. 4, dist. 27.2.

46. Quoted by Mackin, *What Is Marriage?* 186. See other views in Dieter Schwab, *Grundlagen und Gestalt der staatlichen Ehegesetzgebung in der Neuzeit bis zum Beginn des 19. Jahrhunderts* (Bielefeld; Verlag Ernst und Werner Gieseking, 1967), 34–40.

47. Hugh of St. Victor, *De beatae Mariae Virginis Virginitate,* in *Patrologia Latinae* 176:859, quoted and discussed in Mackin, *What is Marriage?* 155.

48. See Harold J. Berman, "The Religious Sources of General Contract Law," in id., *Faith and Order: The Reconciliation of Law and Religion* (Atlanta: Scholars Press, 1993), 187, 190–196, on the "moral theory of contract" in the twelfth and thirteenth centuries.

49. See John T. Noonan, Jr., "Power to Choose," *Viator* 4 (1973):419–434.

50. Respectively, X.4.1.29; C. 31, q. 2, c. 1; and Hostiensis, *Summa aurea,* quoted by R.H. Helmholz, *The Spirit of the Classical Canon Law* (Athens: University of Georgia Press, 1996), 237.

51. See sources in ibid., 238–241; Michael M. Sheehan, "Theory and Practice: Marriage of the Unfree and Poor in Medieval Society," *Mediaeval Studies* 50 (1988): 457–487; Charles J. Reid, "The Canonistic Contribution to the Western Rights Tradition," *Boston College Law Review* 33 (1991):37, 73–80.

52. See Rudolf Weigand, *Die bedingte Eheschliessung im kanonischen Recht* (München: Max Hueber Verlag, 1963); Karl Michealis, *Das abendlandische Eherecht im Übergang Vum Spätenmittelalter zur Neuzeit* (Göttingen: Vandehoeck & Ruprecht, 1990), 13–35.

53. On the theological debate whether the sacrament of marriage was instituted by Christ or had already been instituted in Paradise in the creation of man and woman, see Jaroslav Pelikan, *Reformation of Church and Dogma (1300–1700)* (Chicago: University of Chicago Press, 1984), 51ff; and Brundage, *Law, Sex, and Christian Society,* 430ff. On the gradual acceptance of Aquinas's view that Christ had instituted marriage as a sacrament in *Summa Theol.,* Pt. III, q. 42, see S.P. Heaney, *The Development of the Sacramentality of Marriage from Anselm of Laon to Thomas Aquinas* (Washington, D.C.: Catholic University of America Press, 1963); Ralph J. Lawrence, *The Sacramental Interpretation of Ephesians 5:32 from Peter Lombard to the Council of Trent* (Washington, D.C.: Catholic University of America Press, 1963).

54. Hay, *Lectures on Marriage,* 31.

55. See esp. Mackin, *What Is Marriage?* 20–22, 31–33, 332–333.

56. Gratian, *Decretum,* C.27.q.2; Vincentius Hispanus, Lectura ad X.1.21.5, quoted by Brundage, *Law, Sex, and Christian Society,* 433n; Albert the Great, *Commentary on the Sentences,* bk. 4, dist. 26.11 and dist. 31.37, discussed in Noonan, *Contraception,* 286–288.

57. See generally Dyan Elliott, *Spiritual Marriage: Sexual Abstinence in Medieval Wedlock* (Princeton, N.J.: Princeton University Press, 1993).

58. John Duns Scotus, *Quaestiones in IV libros Sententiarum,* bk. 4, dist. 26.14, in id., *Opera Omnia,* repr. ed. (Farnbourgh: Gregg, 1969), 19:168.

59. Aquinas, *Summa Theol.* Pt. II–II, q. 100, art. 2; Alexander III, *Cum Locum,* X.4.1.14. See discussion in Charles Donahue, Jr., "The Policy of Alexander the Third's Consent Theory of Marriage," *Proceedings of the Fourth International Congress of Medieval Canon Law* (Vatican City, 1976), 251–281.

60. Thomas Aquinas, *Summa contra Gentiles,* bk. 4, chap. 78, in *Sancti Thomae Aquinatis, Opera Omnia,* ed. Leonina (Rome: 1918–1930), quoted in Lawrence, *Sacramental Interpretation,* 71nn. See further quotes and discussion in Theodore Mackin, *Marriage in the Catholic Church: Divorce and Remarriage* (New York: Paulist Press, 1984), 224–365.

61. Aquinas, *Commentary on the Sentences,* quoted by Mackin, *Divorce and Remarriage,* 342.

62. Ibid.

63. Joseph Martos, *Doors to the Sacred: A Historical Introduction to Sacraments in the Catholic Church* (Garden City, N.Y.: Image Books, 1982), 430–432.

64. See, e.g., the attack of the Cathars in the thirteenth century discussed in Brundage, *Sex, Law, and Christian Society,* 431–432; and of Marsilius of Padua, *Defensor Pacis,* disc. 2, chaps. 10, 25, 26, in Alan Gewirth, *Marsilius of Padua: The Defender of the Peace,* vol. 2: *The Defensor Pacis Translated with an Introduction* (New York: Columbia University Press, 1956).

65. See, e.g., Mackin, *What Is Marriage?* 225–327; Karl Rahner, "Marriage as Sacrament," in id., *Theological Investigations,* D. Bourke, trans. (New York: Herder & Herder, 1973), 10:199–221; E. Schillebeeckx, *Marriage: Human Reality and Saving Mystery* (New York: Sheed & Ward, 1965).

66. On the medieval concept of jurisdiction, see generally Berman, *Law and Revolution,* 221ff., 260ff.; Udo Wolter, "Amt und Officium in mittelalterlichen Quellen von 13. bis 15. Jahrhunderts," *Zeitschrift der Savigny-Stiftung (Kan. Ab.)* 105

(1988):246; M. van de Kerckhove, "La notion de jurisdiction dans la doctrine des décrétistes et premiers décrétalistes," *Études franҫiscanes* 49 (1937):420.

67. On the development of the *Corpus Iuris Canonici* (so named for the first time in 1671), see Knut Wolfgang Nörr, "Die Entwicklung des Corpus Iuris Canonici," in Coing, *Handbuch*, 1:835–846.

68. See, e.g., R.H. Helmholz, *Marriage Litigation in Medieval England* (Cambridge: Cambridge University Press, 1974), 112–164; John T. Noonan, Jr., *The Power to Dissolve: Lawyers and Marriage in the Courts of the Roman Curia* (Cambridge, Mass.: Harvard University Press, 1972); Rudolf Weigand, "Zur mittelalterlichen kirchlichen Ehegerichtsbarkeit: Rechtsvergleichende Untersuchung," *Zeitschrift der Savigny-Stiftung (Kan. Ab.)* 67 (1981):218–247.

69. The following brief overview of the medieval canon law of marriage is drawn from the entries on marriage in Friedberg, ed., *Corpus Iuris Canonici* and from the following secondary sources: Brundage, *Law, Sex, and Christian Society,* 229–550; Helmholz, *Marriage Litigation,* 25–111; Friesen, *Geschichte des kanonischen Eherechts,* 227ff.; Rudolph Sohm, *Das Recht der Eheschliessung aus dem deutschen und kanonischen Recht geschichtlich entwickelt* (Aalen: Scientia Verlag, 1966), 107–186; Adhémar Esmein, *Le mariage en droit canonique,* 2d ed., 2 vols. (Paris: Sirrey, 1929–1935); L. van Apeldoorn, *Geschiedenis van het nederlandsche huwelijksrecht voor de invoering van de fransche wetsgeving* (Amsterdam: Uitgeversmaatschappij, 1925), 36–70.

70. According to some recent studies, this was the "secret" or "clandestine" marriage against which the late medieval church railed. Secret marriages, in the sense of privately contracted unions formed between parties who were legally to be married, were imprudent but not sinful. It was better to seek the company of witnesses, the consent of parents, and the consecration of a priest, but failure to involve these parties did not nullify the marriage prior to Council of Trent. But secret marriages, in the sense of parties keeping secret their impediment and proceeding with marriage (publicly or privately), were both imprudent and sinful. Case studies in France and Germany suggest that it was this second form of secret marriage that was heavily litigated in church courts. See Klaus M. Linder, *Courtship and the Courts: Marriage and Law in Southern Germany, 1350–1550* (Th.D. Diss., Harvard, 1988), esp. 126ff.; Beatrice Gottlieb, "The Meaning of Clandestine Marriage," in Robert Wheaton and Tamara K. Hareven, eds., *Family and Sexuality in French History* (Philadelphia: University of Pennsylvania Press, 1980), 53; Reinhard Lettmann, *Die Diskussion über die klandestinen Ehen und die Einführung einer zur Gültigkeit verpflichtenden Eheschliessung auf dem Konzil von Trent* (Münster: Aschendorff, 1967).

71. See analysis in chapter 4.

72. Winfried Trusen, "Forum internum und gelehrten Rechts im spätmittelalter Summae confessorum und Traktate" also "Wegsbereiter der Rezeption," *Zeitschrift der Savigny-Stiftung (Kan. Ab.)* 57 (1971):83.

73. The most influential confessional books on marriage included *Summa Raymundi de Penaforti de poenitentia et matrimonio* (c. 1280), *Summa pisana casuum conscientiae* (c. 1338), and *Summa angelica de casibus conscientiae* (1486). See G. Ziegler, *Die Ehelehre der Pönitentialsummen von 1200–1350* (Regensburg: Verlag Friedrich Pustet, 1956); Thomas N. Tentler, *Sin and Confession on the Eve of the Reformation* (Princeton, N.J.: Princeton University Press, 1977).

74. See good examples in Helmholz, *Marriage Litigation,* 74–111.

75. Quoted by Mackin, *Divorce and Remarriage,* 293.

76. H.J. Schroeder, *Councils and Decrees of the Council of Trent* (St. Louis: B. Herder Book Co., 1941), 1, 10.

77. "Decree Concerning the Opening of the Council," First Session (December 13, 1545), in ibid., 11.

78. "Doctrine of the Sacrament of Matrimony," Twenty-Fourth Session (November 11, 1563), in ibid., 180.

79. Canons 1–12, in ibid., 181–182. See also "Decree Concerning Reform" (November 11, 1563), Chapter XX, in ibid., 211 (on matrimonial jurisdiction).

80. Chapters I, X, in ibid., 183–185, 189–190.

81. Chapters II–V, in ibid., 185–187.

82. Chapter IX, in ibid., 189.

83. Chapter VI, in ibid., 187–188.

84. Chapter VIII, in ibid., 188–189.

85. Quoted in Introduction to *Catechism of the Council of Trent for Parish Priests,* trans. John A. McHugh and Charles J. Callan (Rockford, Ill.: Tan Books and Publishers, 1982), xxiii. The following quotations are based on this authorized translation.

86. "Decree Concerning Reform" (November 11, 1563), chapter VII, in Schroeder, *Councils and Decrees,* 197–198; cf. also ibid., 255.

87. All quotes are from the Catechism, 338–55.

88. See Brundage, *Sex, Law, and Christian Society,* 572–574, 608–617; Noonan, *Power to Dissolve;* Hans Christoph Schaefer, *Der Einfluss des kanonischen Eherechts auf die moderne staatliche Ehegesetzgebung* (Inaugural Diss., Heidelberg, 1963).

Notes to Chapter 2:
Marriage as Social Estate in the Lutheran Reformation

1. On Henry VIII, see chapter 4, below. On Philip of Hesse, see discussion and sources in Paul Mikat, *Die Polygamiefrage in der frühen Neuzeit* (Opladen: Westdeutscher Verlag, 1988), 13ff.; Hasting Eells, *The Attitude of Martin Bucer Toward the Bigamy of Philip of Hesse* (New Haven: Yale University Press, 1924).

2. I have not included Anabaptist contributions to the Western legal tradition of marriage, in part because they were by design not so politically influential, in part because the subject has been authoritatively analyzed in George Huntston Williams, *The Radical Reformation,* 3d ed. (Kirksville, Mo.: Sixteenth Century Essays & Studies, 1992), 756–798.

3. The case is recounted in Theodore Muther, *Doctor Johann Apell. Ein Beitrag zur Geschichte der deutschen Jurisprudenz* (Königsberg, 1861), 14ff. Excerpts from the pleadings and court records are included in *Politische Reichshandel. Das ist allerhand gemeine Acten Regimentssachen und weltlichen Discursen* (Frankfurt am Main: Bey Johann Bringern, 1614), 785–795. All quotes from the case record are taken from this source, unless otherwise noted. The record also touches on a companion case involving Apel's fellow Würzburg canon and advocate, Friedrich Fischer, which I do not analyze.

4. See generally Karl Heinz Burmeister, *Das Studium der Rechte im Zeitalter des Humanismus im deutschen Rechtsbereich* (Wiesbaden: G. Pressler, 1974), 73ff., 287ff.

5. Johann Apel, *Defensio Johannis Apelli ad Episcopum Herbipolensem pro svo conivgio* (Wittemberge, 1523). See also Luther's correspondence in *D. Martini Luthers Werke: Kritische Gesamtausgabe* repr. ed. (Weimar: Hermann Bohlaus, 1964–68) [hereafter WA], Briefe, 2:353, 354, 357. On the long publication history of Apel's tract, see Muther, *Doctor Johann Apell,* 72ff.

6. Lazarus Spengler, *Eyn kurtzer ausszug aus dem Bebstlichen rechten der Decret und Decretalen, in den artickeln, die ungeverlich Gottes Wort gemess sein* (Wittenberg: I.

Club, 1530). From the *Decretum* (c. 1140), Spengler selected abbreviated versions of 30 of the 101 *distinctions* in Part I; cryptic paraphrases of 21 of the 36 *causae* in Part II as well as an excerpt from the *Tractatus de Poenitentia;* and excerpts and brief commentary on all 5 distinctiones of the discussion *de Consecratione* in Part III. Of the six major cases of marriage in Part II of the *Decretum,* however, Spengler was very selective, including only paraphrases and commentaries on C.27, q.1; C.30, q.5; C. 32, q.4; and C. 33, q. 2 — a total of 2 pages from a section of the *Decretum* that fills fifty-seven pages in a modern edition. From the Decretals of Gregory IX (1234), Spengler selected excerpts from twenty-one titles total, but none from the titles on marriage in Book IV of the Decretals. Spengler included nothing from the later books that comprised the *Corpus Iuris Canonici.*

7. See Luther, *Tidschreden,* WA, 62:219, and discussion in Roderich von Stintzing, *Das Sprichwort "Juristen böse Christen" in seinen geschichtlichen Bedeutung* (Bonn: Verlag von Rud. Besser, 1875); Karl Köhler, *Luther und die Juristen. Zur Frage nach dem gegenseitigen Verhältnis des Rechtes und Sittlichkeit* (Gotha: Verlag von L. Hübner, 1873).

8. Johann Apel, *Methodica dialectices ratio ad jurisprudentiam accommodata* (1535), and id., *Isagoge per dialogum in quatuor libros Institutionum D. Justiniani Imperatoris* (1540). On the history and influence of these two publications, see Roderich von Stintzing, *Geschichte der deutschen Rechtswissenschaft, Erste Abteilung* (München: Oldenbourg, 1880), 287–296.

9. This section of the chapter is adapted from John Witte, Jr., "The Transformation of Marriage Law in the Lutheran Reformation," in John Witte, Jr., and Frank S. Alexander, eds., *The Weightier Matters of the Law: Essays on Law and Religion* (Atlanta: Scholars Press, 1988), 57–98.

10. Martin Luther, *Uom eelichen Leben [On Married Life]* (1522), in WA, 10/2:275, translated in Jaroslav Pelikan and Helmut T. Lehmann, eds., *Luther's Works* (Philadelphia: Muhlenberg Press, 1955–1986) [hereafter LW], 45/II:17, 36–37.

11. See generally Steven F. Ozment, *When Fathers Ruled: Family Life in Reformation Europe* (Cambridge and London: Harvard University Press, 1983), 3–24; id., *Protestants: The Birth of a Revolution* (New York: Doubleday, 1992), 151–158. For comparable sentiments in the pamphleteers, see sources and discussion in Scott Hendrix, "Masculinity and Patriarchy in Reformation Germany," *Journal of the History of Ideas* 56 (1995):177.

12. See sources in John Witte, Jr., "The Civic Seminary: The Origins of Public Education in Reformation Germany," *Journal of Law and Religion* 12 (1996):173, 174–176.

13. Martin Luther's writings on marriage and family law include: *Ein Sermon von dem eelichen Stand* (1519), in WA, 2:162; LW, 44:3; *Uom eelichen Leben* (1522), in WA, 10/2:275, LW, 45:11; *Commentary on First Corinthians 7* (1523), in WA, 12:97; LW, 28:9; *An die herrn deutschs ordens, das sie falsche keuscheyt meyden und zur rechten eelichen keuscheyt greyffen Ermanung* (1523), in WA, 12:228; LW, 45:131; *Von de Ehesachen* (1530), in WA, 30/III:198; LW, 46:261; "Counsel in Questions of Marriage and Sex," in Theodore G. Tappert, ed., *Luther: Letters of Spiritual Counsel* (Philadelphia: Westminster Press, 1955).

For Philip Melanchthon's views, see *De arbore consanguinitatis et affinitatis* (1540), in Josef Clug, *Von Ehesachen* (Wittenberg, 1540, 1541), and in G. Bretschneider, ed., *Corpus Reformatorum,* 28 vols. (Brunsvigae: Apud C.A. Schwetschke et Filium, 1864–) [hereafter CR], 16:509; *De coniugio piae commonefactiones* (Wittenberg, 1551), published in revised, expanded form under the title *Disputatio de conjugio* (Wittenberg, 1556), in *Loci praecipui theologici . . . cum appendice Disputationis de coniugio* (Lipsiae, 1556); *Defensio coniugii sacerdotum pia et erudita* (n.d.), in CR, 23:673; *De divortio Henrici VIII* (1531), in CR, 2:520–530; *De casu matrimonilia* (1542), in CR, 4:777–779; *Iudicium in causa matrimoniali* (1544), in CR, 5:306–308; *Decretum Consistorii in eo casu, quod quis antea stupratum duxit* (1552), in CR, 7:1002–4.

Martin Bucer's views are collected in D.F. Wright, ed., *Common Places of Martin Bucer* (Appleford: The Sutton Courtenay Press, 1972), chap. 15; *De Regno Christi* (1550), bk. 2, chaps. 15–27, in *Martini Buceri Opera Latina* (Paris: Presses Universitaires de France, 1954), vol. 15, with partial English translation in W. Pauck, ed., *Melanchthon and Bucer* (Philadelphia: Westminster Press, 1969). Bucer's views are discussed at some length in chapter 4, below.

For Johannes Bugenhagen's views, see *Von dem ehelich en Stande der Bischofe vnd Daiken* (Wittenberg, 1525), revised as *De coniugio episcoporum & diacorum* (Argentorati: I. Knoblochus, 1526); *Vom ehebruch und weglauffen* (Wittenberg, 1539, 1541), bound with Basilius [Erasmus] Sarcerius, *Corpus iuris matrimonialis. Vom Ursprung, Anfang und Herkomen des Heyligen Ehestandts* (Frankfurt am Main: P. Schmidt, 1566, 1569), and with Joachim von Beust, *Tractatus de iure connubiorum et dotium* (Frankfurt am Main: P. Schmidt, 1591).

For Johannes Brenz's views, see *Wie in Eesachen vnnd den fellen so sich derhalben zutragen nach Götlichem billichem rechten christenlich zu handeln* (Nürnberg: Jobst Gutknecht, 1529), reprinted, with revisions, under the title *Wie in Ehesachen und inn den fellen so sich derhalben zu tragen nach götlichen billichen Rechten Christlich zu handeln sey. Mit vorrhede Mart. Luthers* (Wittenberg, 1531); *Libellus casuum quorundam matrimonialium elegantissimus* (Basilae: apud Baptholomaeum Vuisthemorum, 1536); *Operum reverendi et clarissimi theologi D. Ioannis Brentii* (Tubingae: Excudebat Georgius Gruppenbachius, 1576–1594), 8:590–618 (on marriage), 677–694 (on monastic vows). For modern editions, see the collection of excerpts on marriage, sexuality, divorce, and celibacy in Johannes Brenz, *Frühschriften,* ed. Martin Brecht, Gerhard Schäfer and Frieda Wolf, 2 vols. (Tübingen: J.C.B. Mohr, 1970–1974), 2:58–63, 118–121, 213–296, and in Julius Hartmann and Karl Jäger, *Johannes Brenz nach gedruckten und ungedruckten Quellen* (Hamburg: F. Petrus, 1840), 1:342ff.

Good summaries of the reformers' positions are also provided in the early Lutheran confessions, collected in *Triglott Concordia: The Symbolic Books of the Ev. Lutheran Church German-Latin-English* (St. Louis: Concordia Publishing, 1921) [hereafter TC]. See Augsburg Confession (1530), art. 23 ("Of the Marriage of Priests"), art. 27 ("Of Monastic Vows"), in TC, 61ff., 75ff.; Apology of the Augsburg Confession, art. 23 ("Of the Marriage of Priests"), art. 27 ("Of Monastic Vows"), in TC, 363ff., 419ff.; Smalcald Articles, art. 11 ("Of the Marriage of Priests"), art. 15 ("Of Monastic Vows"), in TC, 499, 501.

14. For discussion of the new evangelical theology of marriage, see, e.g., Emil A. Friedberg, *Das Recht der Eheschliessung in seiner geschichtlichen Entwicklung,* repr. ed. (Aalen: Scientia Verlag, 1968), 153–240; Walter Köhler, "Luther als Eherichter," *Beiträge zur sachsischen Kirchengeschichte* 47 (1947):18; Hans Liermann, "Evangelisches Kirchenrecht und staatliches Eherecht in Deutschland, Rechtsgeschichtliches-Gegenwartsprobleme," in Thomas Wurtenberger, ed., *Existenz und Ordnung: Festschrift für Erik Wolf* (Frankfurt am Main: Klostermann, 1962), 43ff.; Karl Michaelis, "Ueber Luthers eherechtliche Anschauungen und deren Verhaltnis zum mittelalterlichen und neuzeitlichen Eherecht," in *Festschrift für Erich Ruppel zum 65. Geburtstag* (Hannover: Lutherhaus, 1968), 43; Reinhard Seeberg, "Luthers Anschauung von dem Geschlechtsleben der Ehe und ihre geschichtliche Stellung," *Luther-Jahrbuch* 7 (1925): 77; Klaus Suppan, *Die Ehelehre*

Martin Luthers. Theologische und rechtshistorische Aspekte des reformatorischen Eheverständnisses (Salzburg: Universitätsverlag A. Pustet, 1971).

15. Luther writes that a truly Christian home and family is "a real church, an elect cloister, yea, a paradise, for the father and mother here become like God, because they are the rulers, bishops, pope, doctor, pastors, preacher, schoolmaster, judge, and lord." Quoted by Gustav M. Bruce, *Luther as an Educator* (Westport, Conn.: Greenwood Press, 1979), 123.

16. *Loci communes* (1555), in C.L. Manschreck, ed., *Melanchthon on Christian Doctrine* (New York: Oxford University Press, 1965), 323–324.

17. Justin Göbler, *Der Rechten Spiegel* (Frankfurt am Main, 1550), quoted by Gerald Strauss, *Law, Resistance, and the State: The Opposition to Roman Law in Reformation Germany* (Princeton, N.J.: Princeton University Press, 1986), 118.

18. WA, 34:73; WA, 50:651–652; LW, 41:176–177; TC, 393.

19. See above, chapter 1, on Chrysostom and Tertullian.

20. See Apel, *Defensio*, folios A11–13.

21. LW, 45:18–22; 28:9–12, 27–31. See also quotes in Inge Mager, "'Es is nicht gut dass der Mensch allein sei' (Gen 2, 18): Zum Familienleben Philipp Melanchthons," *Archiv für Reformationsgeschichte* 81 (1990):120–137.

22. See, e.g., Martin Luther, *De votis monasticis Martini Lutheri iudicium* (1521), in WA, 8:564; LW, 44:243; Martin Luther, *Anwort auf etliche Fragen, Klostergelübde belangend. . . .* (1526), in WA, 19:283; LW, 46:139; Pauck, ed., *Melanchthon and Bucer,* 59; Bugenhagen, *Von dem ehelich en Stande der Bischofe vnd Duiken;* id., *Was man vom Closter leben halten sol* (Wittenberg: G. Rhaw, 1529); TC, 363ff., 419ff. A powerful indictment of monasticism was also issued by Johann Apel, *Defensio,* and by another leading jurist, Johann von Schwarzenberg, the author of the new criminal codes, the Bambergensis (1507) and the Carolina (1532). See Johann von Schwarzenberg, *Ain schöner Sendbreyff . . . Darin er treffenliche und Christliche ursache anzaigt, wie und warumb er sein Tochter daselbst . . . hinweg gefurt und wider under sein Afterlichen Schutz und Oberhand sich genommen had. Ain vorred A. Osiander* (Augsburg: M. Ramminger, 1524). For secondary literature, see, e.g., Berhard Lohse, "Die Kritik am Mönchtum bei Luther und Melanchthon," in Vilmos Vatja, ed., *Luther und Melanchthon: Referate und Berichte des Zweiten Internationalen Kongresses für Lutherforschung Münster, 8 -13. August 1960* (Gottingen: Vandenhoeck & Ruprecht, 1960), 129–145; id., *Mönchtum und Reformation: Luthers Auseinandersetzung mit dem Mönchsideal des Mittelalters* (Göttingen: Vandenhoeck & Ruprecht, 1963).

23. See, e.g., the Smalcald Articles (1537), arts. 11, 14, in TC, 499, 501: "To prohibit marriage, and to burden the divine order of priests with perpetual celibacy, they have had neither authority nor right [to do], but have acted like antichristian, tyrannical, desperate scoundrels, and have thereby caused all kinds of horrible, abominable, innumerable sins of unchastity, in which they still wallow . . . Therefore, we are unwilling to assent to their abominable celibacy, nor will we tolerate, but we wish to have marriage free as God has instituted it. . . . [Furthermore,] [a]s monastic vows conflict with the first chief article [on God the Creator's divine majesty], they must be absolutely abolished . . . For he who makes a vow to live as a monk believes that he will enter upon a mode of life holier than ordinary Christians lead, and wishes to earn heaven by his own work not only for himself, but also for others; this is to deny Christ."

24. This is the heart of Luther's 1521 diatribe against monastic vows in LW, 44:243, 46:139. See also Melanchthon, CR, 1:195; Apel, *Defensio*, folios A11–12.

25. WA, 28:10. A further collection of passages by Luther to the same effect is

assembled in Seeberg, "Luthers Anschauung," 94ff. See also August Franzen, *Zölibat und Priesterehe in der Auseinandersetzung der Reformationszeit und der katholische Reform des 16. Jahrhunderts* (Münster: Aschendorff, 1969).

26. Ibid. See also Apel, *Defensio,* A11–12.

27. Melanchthon, *Loci communes* (1521), in Pauck, ed., *Melanchthon and Bucer,* 60–61; TC, 501.

28. LW, 45:47.

29. Johannes Brenz, "Sermo de matrimonio," in Brenz, *Frühschriften,* 2:119; Brenz, "De matrimonio, viduitate et virginitate," in ibid., at 58–63.

30. See sources in Harold J. Berman and John Witte, Jr., "The Transformation of Western Legal Philosophy in Lutheran Germany," *Southern California Law Review* 62 (1989):1573, 1585–1595.

31. LW, 21:93.

32. LW, 46:265. See similar views in Bucer, *De Regno Christi,* chap. 15, with further discussion in Hartwig Dieterich, *Das protestantische Eherecht in Deutschland bis zur Mitte des 17. Jahrhunderts* (München: Claudius Verlag, 1970), 80ff.; Walter Köhler, *Zürcher Ehegericht und Genfer Konsistorium* (Leipzig: Verlag von M. Heinsius Nachfolger, 1942), 2:427ff.

33. On the three uses of the law doctrine, see John Witte, Jr., and Thomas C. Arthur, "The Three Uses of the Law: A Protestant Source of the Purposes of Criminal Punishment?" *Journal of Law and Religion* 10 (1994):433 and sources cited therein. Though the early theologians did not speak of the "uses of marriage," there are striking parallels in their description of the functions of marriage and of the uses of law. See, e.g., LW, 45:38–49, which was synthesized by later evangelical writers. See, e.g., Cyriacus Spangenberg, *Ehespiegel: Das ist Alles was vom heyligen Ehestande nützliches, nötiges, und tröstliches mag gesagt werden* (Strassburg: Samuel Emmel, 1563).

34. For Luther's doctrine of the sacraments, see esp. LW, 36:11; see also TC, 310ff. See also discussion in Jaroslav Pelikan, *Spirit Versus Structure: Luther and the Institutions of the Church* (New York: Harper & Row, 1968), 17–31, 113–138.

35. John Dillenberger, ed., *Martin Luther: Selections from His Writings* (Garden City, N.Y.: Doubleday, 1961), 326.

36. Ibid., 331. Early in his career, Luther tentatively accepted penance as a third sacrament, but later rejected this position. See generally Pelikan, *Spirit Versus Structure.*

37. LW, 21:95.

38. See esp. Wolfgang Fabricius Capito, *Responsio de missa matrimonio & iure magistratus in religionem* (Argentorati: Per Vu. Rihelium, 1537). See further Dieterich, *Das protestantische Eherecht,* 44ff., 81ff.; Seeberg, "Luthers Anschauung," 93ff.

39. See Dieterich, *Das protestantische Eherecht,* 47, 86; Roland Kirstein, *Die Entwicklung der Sponsalienlehre und der Lehre vom Eheschluss in der deutschen protestantischen Eherechtslehre bis zu J.H. Bohmer* (Bonn: Rohrscheid, 1966), 39ff.; Walter Köhler, "Die Anfänge des protestantischen Eherechtes," *Zeitschrift der Savigny-Stiftung (Kan. Ab.)* 74 (1941):271, 278ff.

40. Among numerous legal tracts, see esp. Apel, *Defensio*; Joachim von Beust, *Tractatus connubiorum praestantiss, iuris consultorum* (vol. 1, Jena, 1606; vols. 2–3, Frankfurt, 1617, 1618, 1742) (bound with tracts by Mauser and Schneidewin); see also the earlier edition, *Tractatus de iure connubiorum et dotium* (bound with tracts by Melanchthon and Bugenhagen); Nicolaus Hemming, *Libellus de conjugio, repudio, et divortio* (Leipzig, 1578); Konrad Mauser, *Explicatio erudita et utilis X. tituli inst. de nuptiis* (Jena, 1569); Melchior Kling, *Matrimonialium causarum tractatus, methodico ordine scriptus* (Frankfurt am Main: apud Eigenolph., 1553); Basilius Monner, *Tractatus duo. I. De matrimonio. II. De clandestinis conjugiis,* 2d ed. (Jena, 1604);

Johannes Oldendorp, *Collatio iuris civilis et canonici, maximam adferens boni & aequi cognitionem* (Coloniae: Ioannes Cymnicus excudebat, 1541), 38–40, 46–48, 77–79; Sarcerius, *Corpus juris matrimonialis;* Johannes Schneidewin, *In institutionum imperialium titulum X. De nuptiis . . .* (Frankfurt, 1571), bound with von Beust, *Tractatus* (1606 ed.), vol. 1; Bernard Walther, *Von den Legitimationen und Bewisung der Siptschafft* (Leipzig, 1558), in Max Rantelen, ed., *Bernard Walters privatrechtliche Traktate aus dem 16. Jahrhunderts* (Leipzig, 1937), 120. Among convenient later summaries provided by Reformation jurists, see esp. Johannes Althusius, *De matrimonio: theses aliquot resp. Rugerus à Rhemen* (1589); Johannes Althusius, *De matrimonio contrahendo et dissolvendo, resp. Wesselus Hemessen* (1593); Iusti Henning Boehmeri, *Ivs ecclesiasticvm protestantivm vsvm modernvm ivxta seriem decretalium ostendens & ipsis rerum argumentiis illustrans* (Halae: Litteris et impendsis Orphanotrophei, 1714), vol. 3. For a good overview of the sixteenth-century literature, see Alfred Söllner, "Die Literatur zum gemeinen und partikularen Recht in Deutschland, Oesterreich, den Niederlanden und der Schweiz," in Helmut Coing, ed., *Handbuch der Quellen und Literatur der neueren europäischen Privatrechtsgeschichte* (München: Beck, 1977), 2/1:501, 585ff.

41. See Judith W. Harvey, *The Influence of the Reformation on Nürnberg Marriage Laws, 1520–1535* (Ph.D. Diss., Ohio State University, 1972), 96–112 (on Nürnberg); Karl Kock, *Studium Pietatis: Martin Bucer als Ethiker* (Neukirchen-Vluyn: Neukirchener Verlag, 1962), 139ff. (on Strasbourg); W. Haalk, "Die Rostocker Juristenfakultat als Spruchskollegium," *Wissenschaftliche Zeitschrift der Universität Rostock* 3 (1958):401, 414ff. (on Rostock); Wilhelm Ebel, *Studie über ein Goslarer Ratsurteilsbuch des 16. Jahrhunderts nebst einem Urkundenanhang* (Göttingen: O. Schwartz, 1961), 37ff., 53ff. (on Goslar). See also the function of *Schoppenstühl* in marital adjudication as described by Adolf F. Stölzel, *Die Entwicklung des gelehrten Richtertums in den deutschen Territorien* (Aalen: Scientia Verlag, 1964), 1:388ff.; John P. Dawson, *The Oracles of the Law* (Ann Arbor: University of Michigan Press, 1968), 198–213, 240–241; and Ebel, *Studie über ein Goslarer Ratsurteilsbuch,* 530ff.

42. See Guido Kisch, *Consilia: Eine Bibliographie der Juristischen Konsiliensammlungen* (Basel: Helbingi Lichtenhahn, 1970); Heinrich Gehrke, *Die Rechtsprechungs- und Konsilienliteratur Deutschland bis zum Ende des alten Reichs* (Frankfurt am Main, Univ. Fachber. Rechtwissen. Diss., 1972).

43. See examples of these in Melanchthon, CR, 4:777–779; 5:306–308; 7:1002–1004; Capito, *Responsio de missa matrimonio;* Johannes Brenz, "Ehegutachten," in Brenz, *Frühschriften,* 2:253–296; and discussion of Luther's marriage opinions in Köhler, "Luther als Eherichter."

44. On Schürpf and his relationship with Luther and other reformers, see generally Wiebke, Schaich-Klose, *D. Hieronymous Schürpf: Leben und Werk des Wittenberger Reformationsjuristen, 1481–1554* (Trogen: F. Meilli, 1967). It was Schürpf's example most of all, Luther wrote late in his life, "that inspired me [in 1517] to write of the great effort of the Catholic Church." Melanchthon, *Oratio de vita clarissimi Hieronymi Schurffi* (1556), in CR, 12:86.

45. Schürpf's *consilia* are collected in Hieronymous Schürpff, *Consilia seu reponsa iuris centuria I–III* (Frankfurt, 1556, 1564). See discussion in Theodore Muther, *Aus dem Universitäts- und Gelehrtenleben im Zeitalter der Reformation* (Erlangen: A. Deichert, 1866), 186ff.; Otto Mejer, "Zur Geschichte des ältesten protestantischen Fherechts, inbesondere der Ehescheidungsfrage," *Zeitschrift für Kirchenrecht* 16 (1881):35.

46. I have translated the term "polizei" (which today means literally "police") with the phrase "public policy," to reflect contemporary usage. "Polizei" had a twofold meaning in circa 1500: (1) a condition of good order in the public realm; and (2)

the legal provisions directed at producing that order. Adalbert Erler and Ekkehard Kaufmann, eds., *Handwörterbuch zur deutschen Rechtsgeschichte* (Berlin:
E. Schmidt Verlag, 1984), 3:cols. 1800–1803. These two meanings of the term
were effectively conflated during the Lutheran Reformation to connote the notion
of the state's public policy designed to foster the general welfare and common
good (*Gemeinnutz*). See, for example, the classic political manual of the Lutheran
jurist Johann Oldendorp, *Von Rathschlagen, Wie man gute Policey und Ordnung in
Stedten und Landen erhalten möge [Of Political Matters: How to Maintain Good Policy
and Order in Cities and Towns]* (Excudebat Christophorus Reusnerus, 1597; fascimilie reprint Glashütten im Taunus, 1971). See discussion in R.W. Scribner, "Police
and the Territorial State in Sixteenth Century Württemberg," in E.I. Kouri and
Tom Scott, eds., *Politics and Society in Reformation Europe* (New York: St. Martin's
Press, 1987), 103ff.

47. The best collections of this new legislation are in Arthur Kern, ed., *Deutsche Hofordnungen des 16. und 17. Jahrhunderts,* 2 vols. (Berlin: Weidmann, 1905); Aemilius L.
Richter, *Die evangelischen Kirchenordnungen des sechszehnten Jahrhunderts,* repr. ed.,
2 vols. (Nieuwkoop: B. DeGraaf, 1967); Emil Sehling ed., *Die evangelischen
Kirchenordnungen des 16. Jahrhunderts* (Leipzig: O.R. Reisland, 1902–1913), vols.
1–5, continued under the same title (Aalen: Scientia Verlag, 1955–), vols. 6–16.
Within the vast literature on the promulgation and enforcement of this new legisla-
tion, see, besides sources already cited, Martin Brecht, "Anfänge reformatorischen
Kirchenordnungen bei Johannes Brenz," *Zeitschrift der Savigny-Stiftung (Kan. Ab.)* 96
(1969):322; B. Gesschen, *Zur ältesten Geschichte und ehegerichtslichen Praxis des
Leipziger Konsistoriums* (Leipzig, 1894); Ernst-Wilhelm Kohls, "Martin Bucers Anteil
und Anleigen bei der Auffassung der Ulmer Kirchenordnung in Jahre 1531,"
Zeitschrift für evangelischen Kirchenrecht 15 (1970):333; Thomas Max Safley, *Let No
Man Put Asunder: The Control of Marriage in the German Southwest: A Comparative
Study, 1550–1600* (Kirksville, Mo: Sixteenth Century Journal Publications, 1984),
41ff.; Gottfried Seebass, *Das reformatorische Werk des Andreas Osiander* (Nürnberg:
Verein für bayerische Kirchengeschichte, 1967), 184ff; Anneliese Sprengler-
Ruppenthal, "Zur Rezeption des römischen Rechts in Eherecht der Reformation,"
Zeitschrift der Savigny-Stiftung (Kan. Ab.) 112 (1978):363, 392ff.; Gerold Tietz, *Ver-
lobung, Trauung, und Hochzeit in den evangelischen Kirchenordnungen des 16. Jahrhunderts* (Tübingen, Phil. Fak. Diss., 1969); François Wendel, *Le mariage à Strasbourg à
l'époque de la réforme 1520–1692* (Strasbourg: Imprimerie Alsacienne, 1928), 77ff.

48. See Kurd Schulz, "Bugenhagen als Schöpfer der Kirchenordnungen," in *Johann Bugenhagen. Beiträge zu seinem 400. Todestag* (Berlin: Evangelische Verlagsanstalt,
1958), 51; Eike Wolgast, "Bugenhagen in den politischen Krisen seiner Zeit," in
Hans-Gunter Leder, ed., *Johannes Bugenhagen: Gestalt und Wirkung* (Bonn: Evangelische Verlagsanstalt, 1984); Anneliese Sprengler-Ruppenthal, "Bugenhagen
und das kanonische Recht," *Zeitschrift der Savigny-Stiftung (Kan. Ab.)* 75 (1989):
375.

49. LW, 45:11ff., 274ff. See also Brenz, *Wie in Ehesachen,* chap. 2; Pauck, ed.,
Melanchthon and Bucer, 320. See discussion in Sohm, *Das Recht der Eheschliessung,*
138–139, 197–198; Kirstein, *Die Entwicklung,* 28ff. The promises are ambiguous
because the verbs "will" and "sollst," though commonly understood to be in the
present tense, can also be interpreted as future verbs.

50. LW, 46:205ff. See Dieterich, *Das protestantische Eherecht,* 93–96.

51. LW, 46:268ff.

52. LW, 53:110ff. See discussion in Kirstein, *Die Entwicklung,* 734; Köhler, "Die Anfänge," 292.

53. Ibid. For further discussion of the Lutheran reformers' heavy emphasis on the requisite public character of marriage and its relation to Lutheran theological beliefs, see Michaelis, "Ueber Luthers eherechtliche Anschauungen," 51ff.

54. Dieterich, *Das protestantische Eherecht*, 121.

55. Sohm, *Das Recht der Eheschliessung*, 198.

56. See ibid., at 233ff., and a good contemporary catalogue of views in von Beust, *Tractatus de iure connubiorum et dotium*, folio 5a–5b.

57. See the Church Ordinances of Zürich (1529), Brandenburg-Nürnberg (1533), Württemberg (1536), Kassell (1539), Schwabisch-Hall (1543), Cologne (1543), and Tecklenberg (1588), as well as the Consistory Ordinance of Brandenberg (1573) in Richter, *Kirchenordnungen*, 1:135ff., 209ff., 270ff., 304ff.; 2:16ff., 47ff., 476ff., and 381ff.

58. See the Goslar Consistory Ordinance (1555) and the Declaration of the Synod of Emden (1571) in Richter, *Kirchenordnungen*, 2:166ff., 340. See also the Opinions of the Wittenberg Court quoted in Sohm, *Das Recht der Eheschliessung*, 199–200.

59. See overview in Tietz, *Verlobung, Trauung, und Hochzeit*.

60. See the quotations collected in Dieterich, *Das protestantische Eherecht*, 123–127.

61. See Marriage Ordinance of Württemberg (1537) in Richter, *Kirchenordnungen*, 1:280. The Wittenberg marriage court apparently also took this rigid stance, though absolute parental consent was not prescribed in the Wittenberg statute. See Dieterich, *Das protestantische Eherecht*, 156–157.

62. See, e.g., the Church Ordinances of Basel (1529) and Brandenburg (1573) and the Declarations of the Synod of Emden (1571) in Richter, *Kirchenordnungen*, 1:125; 2:376, 340. See also the Reformation Ordinance of Hesse (1526), Marriage Ordinance of Württemberg (1553), and the Schauenburg Policy Ordinance (1615), quoted in Gustav Schmelzeisen, *Polizeiordnung und Privatrecht* (Münster/Koln, 1955), 33–34.

63. See the Constitution of the Wittenberg Consistory Ordinance (1542), the Church Ordinance of Cellische (1545), the Marriage Ordinance of Dresden (1556), the Territorial Ordinance of Prussia (1577), the Marriage Ordinance of Kurpf (1582), and the Schauenburg Policy Ordinance (1615) in Sehling, *Kirchenordnungen*, 1:20ff., 292ff., 343ff., and Schmelzeisen, *Polizeiordnung und Privatrecht*, 36. See also illustrative cases in von Beust, *Tractatus de iure connubiorum et dotium*, folios 82b–86a.

64. See, e.g., the Church Ordinance of Goslar (1555) in Richter, *Kirchenordnungen*, 2:165. The age of majority in that jurisdiction was 20 for men, 18 for women; in some jurisdictions, the age of majority was as high as 27 for men and 25 for women; see Schmelzeisen, *Polizeiordnung und Privatrecht*, 35.

65. The Marriage Ordinance of Zürich (1525), copied in several south German cities, was the first to declare void *ab initio* all unwitnessed marriages. See Köhler, "Die Anfänge," 74ff. The more typical early statutes are the Church Ordinance of Ulm (1531) and the Marriage Ordinance of Württemberg (1537) in Richter, *Kirchenordnungen*, 1:158, 280.

66. Marriage Ordinance of Württemberg (1553) and Church Ordinance of Goslar (1555) in Richter, *Kirchenordnungen*, 2:129, 165. See discussion in Köhler, "Die Anfänge," 292.

67. See, e.g., Church Ordinance of Ulm (1531) in Richter, *Kirchenordnungen*, 1:159.

68. See the Zürich Chorgericht Ordinance (1525) and the Church Ordinances of Basel (1530), Kassel (1530), Ulm (1531), Strasbourg (1534), and the numerous later statutes quoted and discussed in Friedberg, *Das Recht Eheschliessung*, 213–217, and Schmelzeisen, *Polizeiordnung und Privatrecht*, 45–46.

69. See the Ordinances of Nürnberg (1537), Augsburg (1553), and Ulm (1557) described in Ozment, *When Fathers Ruled*, 36 and Köhler, "Die Anfänge," 296ff.

70. See the Marriage Ordinance of Württemberg (1553) in Richter, *Kirchenordnungen*, 2:128, and the Church Ordinance of Palatine on the Rhine (1563), in Sehling, *Kirchenordnungen*, 6·133.

71. See above, chapter 1.

72. LW, 45:22, criticizing the eighteen impediments set out in the *Summa angelica de casibus conscientiae* (1486). This was among the books that Luther burned, along with the canon law books, in 1520.

73. Andreas Osiander, *Gutachten über die Zeremonien* (1526), 69, quoted by Harvey, *The Influence*, 232. For further discussion of Osiander's views, see Seebass, *Das reformatorische Werk*, 191ff.

74. Dillenberger, ed., *Selections*, 330–331.

75. Ibid. See also LW, 45:22–30; Bucer, *De Regno Christi*, chap. 17; and discussion of other views in Dieterich, *Das protestantische Eherecht*, 97–98.

76. Ibid.

77. See generally ibid., LW, 45:22ff., 66ff., 102ff., 128ff., and discussion in Friedberg, *Das Rechtder Eheschliessung*, 212ff.; Kirstein, *Die Entwicklung*, 28ff., 57ff.; Köhler, "Die Anfänge," 375ff. For statutory examples, see, e.g., the Consistory Ordinances of Brandenburg (1573) and Prussia (1584) in Richter, *Kirchenordnungen*, 2:383ff., 466ff. (on impediments to protect free consent); Kurbrandenburg Church Ordinance (1540) in ibid., 1:323ff. (on the impediment respecting errors of quality).

78. See, e.g., LW, 35:138, 45:28; Bucer, *Common Places*, 406ff., and discussion of other reformers' views in Dieterich, *Das protestantische Eherecht*, 78ff., 110ff. Conservative jurists, such as Kling and Schürpf, however, rejected this impediment with great hesitation; Schürpf, in fact, by 1536, considered the children of clerics to be illegitimate and recommended that legacies and inheritances not be bequeathed to them. See Stintzing, *Geschichte*, 275.

79. Church Ordinances of Northeim (1539), Kurbrandenburg (1540), Braunschweig-Wolfenbüttel (1543), as well as the Consistory Ordinance of Wittenberg (1542) in Richter, *Kirchenordnungen*, 1:287ff., 323ff., 367ff., and 2:56ff.

80. Dillenberger, ed., *Selections*, 335.

81. The early writers who adopted this position—Brenz, Kling, Clammer, Mauser, and Monner—accepted the traditional doctrine as a restriction on marriage; they advocated annulment of consummated marriages only if the parties were related by blood to the second degree. To support their position, these early writers cited scripture (Lev. 18:6–13) for the first degree; Roman law (D. 23, 2, 53, 68) and scripture for the second; canon law and Germanic law for the third; and canon law for the fourth. See Dieterich, *Das protestantische Eherecht*, 131–135. It should be noted that strict enforcement of the impediment of consanguinity to the fourth degree eliminated for one person several hundred people as prospective marriage partners—a not insignificant restriction for those who lived in small, isolated communities. See Rudolph Weigand, "Ehe- und Familienrecht in der mittelalterlichen Stadt," in Alfred Haverkamp, ed., *Haus und Familie in der spätmittelalterlichen Stadt* (Tübingen: J.C.B. Mohr, 1984), 173; Richard Koebner, "Die Eheauffassung des ausgehenden deutschen Mittelalters," *Archiv für Kulturgeschichte* 9 (1911):136.

82. See a convenient table in Melanchthon, *De arbore consanguinitatis et affinitatis*, folios aii–bii. For Osiander's position, see Harvey, *The Influence*, 250: "Osiander proposed four rules by which one could determine which degrees of relationship were forbidden: whatever wife is forbidden to me, the same woman's brother or spouse is forbidden to my sister; female and male sex makes no difference in the degrees of blood relationship; whatever is forbidden in the ascending line is also forbid-

den in the descending line; whatever man my wife cannot marry after my death because she has been my wife, the same man's wife is forbidden to me after his death." Impediments of consanguinity to the third degree were accepted by the Württemberg Marriage Ordinance (1537), the Cellisches Ehebedenken (1545), the Mecklenburg Church Ordinance (1557), the Hessen Reformation Ordinance (1572), the Mecklenburg Policy Ordinance (1572), the Lübeck Ordinance (1581), respectively, in Richter, *Kirchenordnungen,* 1:280; Sehling, *Kirchenordnungen,* 1:296; 5:212; Schmelzeisen, *Polizeiordnung und Privatrecht,* 50ff. Impediments of consanguinity to the second degree were accepted by the Saxon General Articles (1557) in Richter, *Kirchenordnungen,* 2:178ff.

83. See esp. LW, 45:3ff., 23ff.; Bucer, *Common Places,* 410ff. The Levitical law of impediments of consanguinity was adopted by later statutes, e.g., the Brandenburg Ordinance (1694) and the Prussian Cabinet Order (1740), quoted and discussed in Schmelzeisen, *Polizeiordnung und Privatrecht,* 51–52.

84. See Dieterich, *Das protestantische Eherecht,* 135–36.

85. Ibid., 100, 161.

86. Ibid., 100, 136. Though most statutes silently ignore the spiritual impediments, a few later statutes explicitly deny their validity. See, e.g., the Church Ordinance of Lower Saxony (1585) and the Braunschweiger Policy Ordinance (1618), quoted and discussed in Schmelzeisen, *Polizeiordnung und Privatrecht,* 53.

87. This impediment was retained by a few early reformers such as Kling, Schürpf, and Brenz. Many later jurists who rejected the impediment still insisted that the adopted child be granted the full rights of protection and inheritance accorded the natural child. See Dieterich, *Das protestantische Eherecht,* 101, 137.

88. See the Cellisches Ehebedenken (1545), the Consistory Ordinance of Goslar (1555), and the Marriage Ordinance of Dresden (1556), in Sehling, *Kirchenordnungen,* 1:295; Richter, *Kirchenordnungen,* 2:166; Sehling, *Kirchenordnungen,* 1:343.

89. Dieterich, *Das protestantische Eherecht,* 68, 102.

90. LW, 45:26.

91. See R.H. Helmholz, *The Spirit of the Classical Canon Law* (Athens: University of Georgia Press, 1996), 240–241, and further discussion in chapter 1.

92. The reformers often quoted Genesis 2:24 and Matthew 19:5 in support of their view: "Therefore a man leaves his father and mother and cleaves to his wife, and the two become one flesh." The reformers set forth their views on divorce and remarriage in a variety of tracts. See, e.g., LW, 46:276ff.; Melanchthon, CR, 7:487; 21:1079ff.; Bugenhagen, *Vom ehebruch und weglauffen,* folios 171ff.; Brenz, *Wie in Ehesachen,* folios 185ff.; Schneidewin, *In institutionum,* 484ff.; Mauser, *Explicatio,* 335ff.; Monner, *Tractatus,* 203ff. For general discussions, see Hans Hesse, *Evangelisches Ehescheidungsrecht in Deutschland* (Bonn: H. Bouvier, 1960); F. Albrecht, *Verbrechen und Strafen als Ehescheidungsgrund nach evangelischen Kirchenrecht* (Ph.D. Diss., München, 1903); J. Grabner, *Ueber Desertion und Quasi-desertion als Scheidungsgrund nach dem evangelischen Kirchenrecht* (Ph.D. Diss., Leipzig, 1882); Aemilius Richter, *Beiträge zur Geschichte des Ehescheidungsrecht in der evangelischen Kirche* (Aalen: Scientia Verlag, 1958).

93. Bucer, "The Judgment of Martin Bucer Touching Divorce," 465.

94. Bucer, *Common Places,* 416–417; LW, 46:275–281.

95. LW, 45:30–31.

96. Quoted by Ozment, *When Fathers Ruled,* 84.

97. Theodosian Code 3.16.1,2; Justinian Code 5.17.8,9,10. Divorce by mutual consent, permitted by Emperor Anastasius in 497, was rejected some forty years later in Justinian's Novella 117.8–14. See Susan Treggiari, *Roman Marriage: Iusti*

Coniuges from the Time of Cicero to the Time of Ulpian (Oxford: Clarendon Press, 1991), 435ff.; P. Corbett, *The Roman Law of Marriage* (Oxford: Clarendon Press, 1930), 218ff.

98. Engbert J.J. Jonkers, *Invloed van het Christendom op de romeinsche wetgeving betreffende het concubinaat en de echtscheiding* (Wageningen: H. Veenman, 1938). For the reformers' recounting of this history, see Dieterich, *Das protestantische Eherecht,* 105–108, 143–146, 163–166.

99. LW, 21:94ff.; Bucer, *Common Places,* 411ff.; and the views of Brenz and Bugenhagen discussed by Ozment, *When Fathers Ruled,* 89ff.; Sprengler-Ruppenthal, "Zur Rezeption," 395ff.

100. LW, 21:94; see also Bucer, *Common Places,* 411–412, and discussion of other reformers in Richter, *Beiträge,* 32ff.; Ozment, *When Fathers Ruled,* 89.

101. Bugenhagen, *Vom ehebruch und weglauffen,* folios miii-oiii.

102. See the numerous church ordinances and other statutes quoted and discussed by Hans Dietrich, *Evangelisches Ehescheidungsrecht nach den Bestimmungen der deutschen Kirchenordnungen des 16. Jahrhunderts* (Berlin, 1892), 12–14, 164; Hesse, *Evangelisches Ehescheidungsrecht,* 31–33; Albrecht, *Verbrechen und Strafen,* 43–46. The Church Ordinance of Lübeck (1531) and Marriage Ordinance of Württemberg (1537), drafted by Brenz, as well as the Marriage Ordinance of Pfalz (1563) and Church Ordinance of Huttenberg (1555), cite Roman law prominently alongside scripture in support of this ground for divorce. See Sehling, *Kirchenordnungen,* 5:356; Richter, *Kirchenordnungen,* 1:280; 2:257, 163. Melanchthon and Kling refer several times to earlier canonical and patristic writings in their discussions of adultery. See CR, 21:103, and Kling, *Matrimonialium causarum tractatus,* folio 101v. See also Richter, *Beiträge,* 29–30, on Kling's views.

103. LW, 45:32. See discussion in Ozment, *When Fathers Ruled,* 85ff.; Hesse, *Evangelisches Ehescheidungsrecht,* 32.

104. *Bambergensis Halsgericht und rechtliche Ordnung,* art. 145 (1507), repeated with revisions in *Constitutio Criminalis Carolina,* art. 120 (1532), in Josef Köhler and Willy Scheel, eds., *Die peinliche Gerichtsordnung Kaiser Karls V. Constitutio Criminalis Carolina* (Aalen: Scientia Verlag, 1968), 63.

105. See, e.g., Bugenhagen, *Vom ehebruch und weglauffen,* folios oiii-piii.

106. Bugenhagen's *Vom ehebruch und weglauffen.*

107. See, e.g., Dillenberger, ed., *Selections,* 32–33; Bucer, *Common Places,* 410–411. On the reaction of the civil authorities thereto, see Dieterich, *Das protestantische Eherecht,* 105ff.; Harvey, *The Influence,* 113ff.; Kock, *Studium Pietatis,* 141ff. The Bambergensis and Carolina, however, ordered "death by the sword" as criminal punishment for adultery; these statutes further provided that innocent spouses who, on discovery of the philandering parties, immediately killed one or both of them, were not subject to penalty. Such provisions, which had been part of Germanic law for centuries, were only rarely enforced by the end of the sixteenth century. Even where the adulterer was spared, however, he or she was denied the right to remarry and was subject to severe penalty when prosecuted for subsequent acts of prostitution, homosexuality, and other sexual crimes. See Schmelzeisen, *Polizeiordnung und Privatrecht,* 53–54.

108. This was the view of, e.g., Ambrosius Blarer and Johannes Oecolampadus, among theologians, and Schürpf, Schneidewin, Kling, and the draftsmen of the Church Ordinances of Schwabisch-Hall (1531) and of Lower Saxony (1585), among jurists. Johannes Brenz initially permitted divorce only on this ground, but later expanded the grounds for divorce. Even in this later period, however, Brenz permitted remarriage only to victims of adultery, and exacted ecclesiastical penalties against church members who divorced for reasons other than adultery. See

Köhler, "Die Anfänge," 302; Hesse, *Evangelisches Ehescheidungsrecht,* 32–33; Albrecht, *Verbrechen und Strafen,* 14–16; Schmelzeisen, *Polizeiordnung und Privatrecht,* 61.

109. Bugenhagen, *Vom ehebruch und weglauffen,* folios oiii–piii. See Church Ordinances of Pomerania (1535) and Lippische (1538), in Richter, *Kirchenordnungen,* 1:250ff.; 2:499ff., and other statutes quoted and discussed in Hesse, *Evangelisches Ehescheidungsrecht,* 33–35; Dietrich, *Evangelisches Ehescheidungsrecht,* 17–25; Grabner, *Ueber Desertion,* 63ff.; Schmelzeisen, *Polizeiordnung und Privatrecht,* 60–61.

110. See, e.g., the Church Ordinances of Goslar (1531) and Cellisches Ehebedenken (1545) and the Consistory Ordinance of Mecklenberg (1571) in Richter, *Kirchenordnungen,* 1:156; Sehling, *Kirchenordnungen,* 1:295ff.; 5:239ff.

111. LW, 45:33–34. See also Dietrich, *Evangelisches Ehescheidungsrecht,* 25–31.

112. Church Ordinances of Lippische (1538), Göttingen (1542), Mecklenberg (1552), the Württemberg Marriage Ordinance (1553), and the Consistory Ordinance of Prussia (1584), in Richter, *Kirchenordnungen,* 1:365; 2:120, 130, 466, 499.

113. Ozment, *When Fathers Ruled,* 93.

114. See the numerous statutory provisions listed in Dietrich, *Evangelisches Ehescheidungsrecht,* 31ff.; Hesse, *Evangelisches Ehescheidungsrecht,* 35ff.; Köhler, "Die Anfänge," 303ff. See a contemporary catalogue in von Beust, *Tractatus de iure connubiorum,* folios 54b–59.

115. See the Church Ordinances of Hannover (1536) and Huttenberg (1555), and the Marriage Ordinance of Pfalz (1563), quoted in Dietrich, *Evangelisches Ehescheidungsrecht,* 31–32. A similar provision is recommended by Sarcerius, *Corpus jurio matrimonialis,* folio 216.

116. See, e.g., LW, 36:102ff., 45:30ff., 46:311ff. See comparable practices in Switzerland described in Thomas Max Safley, "Canon Law and Swiss Reform. Legal Theory and Practice in the Marital Courts of Zurich, Bern, Basel, and St. Gall," in R.H. Helmholz, ed., *Canon Law in Protestant Lands* (Berlin: Duncker & Humblot, 1992), 187.

117. Witness the conservative practices of the courts of Nürnberg, Zurich, and Basel as described in Harvey, *The Influence,* 153ff.; Ozment, *When Fathers Ruled;* Adrian Staehelin, *Die Einführung der Ehescheidung in Basel zur Zeit der Reformation* (Basel: Helbing & Lichtenhahn, 1957), 101ff.

118. See, e.g., cases collected in von Beust, *Tractatus de iure connubiorum.* In the cases and commentaries, von Beust draws eclectically from Protestant, Catholic, and Roman authorities. In instances of conflict of laws, authorities are generally listed side by side, with Protestant sources generally preferred to Catholic, and legal opinions preferred to theological opinions. A catalogue of authorities lists more than twenty canonists, including such leading lights as Gratian, Hostiensis, Innocent III, Innocent IV, Jason de Maino, Johannes Andreae, Joannes de Imola, Panormitanus, and Paulus de Castro.

119. See, e.g., Johann Oldendorp, *Lexicon Iuris* (Francforti: apud Chr. Egenolphum, 1546/1553), 138–139; id., *Collatio iuris civilis et canonici,* entry on "Matrimonio." See broader discussion in Friedrich Merzbacher, "Johann Oldendorp und das kanonischen Recht," in id., *Recht–Staat–Kirche: ausgewählte Aufsätze,* ed. Gerhard Koebler (Wien: Bohlau, 1989), 246–274; Johannes Heckel, "Das Decretum Gratiani und das deutsche evangelische Kirchenrecht," *Studia Gratiana* 3 (1955): 483; Rudolf Schäfer, "Die Geltung des kanonischen Rechts in der evangelischen Kirche Deutschland von Luther bis zur Gegenwart," *Zeitschrift der Savigny-Stiftung (Kan. Ab.)* 49 (1915):165; Hans Liermann, "Das kanonische Recht als Gegenstand des gelehrten Unterrichts an den protestantischen Universitäten Deutschlands in den ersten Jahrhunderten nach der Reformation," in id., *Der Jurist und die Kirche:*

Ausgewählte kirchenrechtliche Aufsätze und Rechtsgutachten, ed. Martin Heckel et al. (München: Beck, 1973), 108–131.

120. Kling, *Matrimonialium causarum tractatus.*
121. Ibid., proemium, A2–A3.
122. In this 44-folio page tract, Kling cited Hostiensis fourteen times, Panormitanus thirty-one times, and Johannes Andreae six times. There is not one direct citation to any Lutheran theologian or jurist.

Notes to Chapter 3:
Marriage as Covenant in the Calvinist Tradition

1. Rudolf Sohm, *Das Recht der Eheschliessung aus dem deutschen und kanonischen Recht geschichtlich entwickelt* (Aalen: Scientia Verlag, 1966), 266.
2. *Du contrat social* (1762), bk. 2, chap. 7n., reprinted in Jean- Jacques Rousseau, *The Social Contract and the Discourse on the Origin of Inequality,* Lester G. Crocker, ed. (New York: Washington Square Press, 1967), 44n. For comparable and contrary evaluations of Calvin's reformation, see quotations and sources in John Witte, Jr., "Moderate Religious Liberty in the Theology of John Calvin," *Calvin Theological Journal* 31 (1996):359–361.
3. "Letter d'une dame inconnue à la Compagnie des Pasteurs. De France, 24 juin 1555," in Jean-Francois Bergier and Robert M. Kingdon, eds., *Registres de la compagnie des pasteurs de Genève au temps de Calvin* (Geneva: Droz, 1964), 1:138–140. The editors speculate that the woman was Madame de Cany, with whom Calvin had corresponded several times before.
4. "Résponse de la Compagnie à la lettre précédente Genève, 22 juillet 1552," in ibid., 140–141, reprinted from G. Baum et al., eds., *Ioannis Calvini opera quae supersunt omnia* (Brunsvigae: C.A. Schwetschke et filium, 1892), 10:239–241 [hereafter CO]. Though the opinion is unsigned, it bears Calvin's unmistakable tone and content.
5. See comparable sentiments in "Letter to Madame de Pons (November 20, 1553)," in Jules Bonnet, ed., *Letters of John Calvin,* repr. ed. (New York: Burt Franklin, 1972), 2:436; "Letter to Madame de Rentigny (April 10, 1558)," ibid., 3:416–418; "Letter to Unknown Woman (June 4, 1559)," CO, 17:539; two undated consilia, in CO, 10: 255–258, 264–266. See discussion in Charmarie J. Blaisdell, "Calvin's Letters to Women: The Courting of Ladies in High Places," *Sixteenth Century Journal* 13 (1982):3. Nancy L. Roelker, "The Appeal of Calvinism to French Noblewomen in the Sixteenth Century," *Journal of Interdisciplinary Studies* 2 (1970–71):405. For a list of these letters, see Charmarie J. Blaisdell, "Calvin's and Loyola's Letters to Women: Politics and Spiritual Counsel in the Sixteenth Century," in Robert V. Schnucker, ed., *Calviniana: Ideas and Influence of John Calvin* (Ann Arbor: University of Michigan Press, 1988), 235, 248–250.
6. See, e.g., Consilium (December 30, 1557), in CO, 10:242–244: "So many people ask my advice that I am not always free to comply with all their requests, but I am not so capricious as to be displeased by their pious concerns."
7. On Calvin's general views of civil disobedience, see, e.g., *Ioannis Calvini Institutio Religionis Christianae* (Basel, 1536), chap. 6.13, in CO, 1:1–251 [hereafter *Institutes* (1536)]; Comm. Dan. 6:22; Comm. Deut. 5:16, with discussion and sources in Witte, "Moderate Religious Liberty," nn 65 and 134. On the analogy between marital and civic relations, see CO, 29:549, 636–638, with discussion in Josef Bohatec,

Calvins Lehre von Staat und Kirche mit besonderer Berücksichtigung des Organismus-gedankens (Aalen: Scientia Verlag, 1968), 652–653.

8. John T. McNeill, *The History and Character of Calvinism* (New York: Oxford University Press, 1954), 93–158; A. Ganoczy, *Le jeune Calvin. Genèse et evolution de la vocation réformatorice* (Wiesbaden: F. Steiner, 1966); Walter Köhler, *Zürcher Ehegericht und Genfer Konsistorium* (Leipzig: Verlag von M. Heinsius Nachfolger, 1942), 2:505–540 [hereafter Köhler, *Genfer Konsistorium*]. See church ordinances in Aemilius Richter, ed., *Die evangelischen Kirchenordnungen des sechszehnten Jahrhunderts. I: Vom Anfange der Reformation bis . . . 1542* (Nieuwkoop: B. DeGraaf, 1967).

9. See Josef Bohatec, *Budé und Calvin: Studien zur Gedankenwelt des französichen Früh-humanismus* (Graz: H.B. Ohlaus Nachfolge, 1950), 127–148; Quirinius Breen, *John Calvin: A Study in French Humanism* (Grand Rapids: Wm. B. Eerdmans Publishing Co., 1931), 40–66, 86–99.

10. See sources and discussion in Harold J. Berman and John Witte, Jr., "The Transformation of Western Legal Philosophy in Lutheran Germany," *Southern California Law Review* 62 (1989):1573, 1585–1595.

11. Calvin, *Institutes* (1536), chap. 6.13. See also ibid., 6.14, 6.35.

12. Ibid., chap. 1.19, 1.22.

13. Ibid., chap. 4.1, 5.68–71.

14. Ibid., chap. 5.68–71, 6.25.

15. Geneva adopted a formal "résolution de vivre selon la loi évangelique" on May 21, 1536, triggering a series of shifts in jurisdiction from clergy to magistracy within a few years. See Emile Rivoire and Victor van Berchem, eds., *Les sources du droit du canton de Genève* (Aarau: Sauerländer, 1927–1935), vol. 2, item no. 701 [hereafter *Les sources du droit du canton de Genève*]. Ironically, a decade before, the city council had unequivocally confirmed its support for the church's jurisdiction over marriage. See "Statute of December 20, 1528," in ibid., item no. 621; see also ibid., item no. 571 (a November 13, 1521, confirmation of ecclesiastical jurisdiction by Charles II, Duke of Savoy). See general discussion in Köhler, *Genfer Konsistorium*, 2:514–515, 541–555; Cornelia Seeger, *Nullité de mariage divorce et séparation de corps a Genève, au temps de Calvin: Fondements doctrinaux, loi et jurisprudence* (Lausanne: Mémoires et documents publiés par la société d'histoire de la suisse romande, 1989), 22–29, 188–189, 200 [hereafter Seeger, *Mariage*].

16. *Institutes* (1536), chap. 6.17, 6.20.

17. See ibid., dedicatory epistle, and chap. 6.4, 6.14–32; Geneva Catechism (1536), item 17.

18. Ibid., chap. 5.71.

19. Ibid., chap. 5.71, 6.25, 6.31; "Articles concernant l'organisation de l'Église et du culte á Genève, proposés au Conseil par les ministres le 16 janvier 1537," CO, 10:5, 13.

20. "Les Ordonnances ecclesiastiques de l'Église de Genève (1541)," in Bergier and Kingdon, eds., *Registres de la compagnie des pasteurs*, 1:1. A slightly altered version appears in *Les sources du droit du canton de Genève*, vol. 2, item no. 794. A truncated version was issued in 1547 for rural areas and is reprinted in CO, 10:51–58.

21. Quote from Köhler, *Genfer Konsistorium*, 188. See studies in Seeger, *Mariage*, 199–304; Carl A. Cornelius, "De Gründung der calvinischen Kirchenverfassung in Genf, 1541," in id., *Historische Arbeiten, vornehmlich zur Reformationszeit* (Leipzig, 1899), 251; Robert M. Kingdon, *Adultery and Divorce in Calvin's Geneva* (Cambridge and London: Harvard University Press, 1995), 7–30; E. William Monter, *Studies in Genevan Government (1536–1605)* (Geneva: Droz, 1964), 57–83.

22. Robert M. Kingdon, "Calvin and the Family: The Work of the Consistory of Geneva," in Richard C. Gamble, ed., *Calvin's Work in Geneva* (New York and London: Garland Publishing Co., 1992), 93, 95.

23. Oaths were formally required only in 1556, though several earlier consistory cases show that the practice antedated the requirement. See Bergier and Kingdon, eds., *Registres de la compagnie des pasteurs,* 2:68, for the requirement.

24. Les Ordonnances ecclesiastiques, in Bergier and Kingdon, eds., *Registres de la compagnie des pasteurs,* 1:9, 13.

25. *Institutes* (1536), 6.47 (quoting in part from Cicero's *Laws*).

26. See the statutes of 1481–1536 collected in *Les sources du droit du canton de Genève,* vol. 2, items no. 290, 294, 297, 300, 302, 345, 373, 398, 405, 420, 447, 485, 496, 510, 524, 562, 580.

27. See statutes of 1539–1544 in ibid., items no. 756, 757, 775, 786, 795, 813. What survives of Calvin's efforts to pass a criminal code for Geneva (as well as ordinances on civil procedure, evidence, taxation, inheritance, contracts, and administrative law) is in CO, 10:125–146. See discussion in Josef Bohatec, *Calvin und das Recht,* 2d ed., repr. ed., (Aalen: Scientia Verlag, 1991), 209–279.

28. The Ordinance was completed on November 5, 1545; it was presented to the Small Council on November 10 and to twelve representatives of the General Council on November 13. It was commended but not formally approved, and was circulated thereafter among ministers and magistrates of Geneva and beyond in slightly varying drafts. On November 11, 1549, another committee, again led by Calvin, was convened to study existing marriage law and to recommend improvements to the Marriage Ordinance. Calvin presented his report on November 25, but complained on January 30, 1550, that still no official position had been taken on the ordinance. On May 1, 1551, Calvin again complained to the Council that the lack of clear guidelines led to much confusion over questions of marriage. It was not until 1561 that the ordinance finally received formal endorsement, now with a few more amendments (CO, 10:33n). The 1545 version is in CO, 10:33; a 1547 version in Bergier and Kingdon, eds., *Registres de la compagnie des pasteurs,* 30; the final 1561 version is incorporated in Les Ordonnances ecclesiastiques (1561) in CO, 10:91, and Richter, *Kirchenordnungen,* 1:342. The following analysis and quotations are based on provisions common to all three drafts, unless otherwise noted.

29. See statute of June 4, 1537, in *Les sources du droit du canton de Genève,* vol. 2, item no. 732 (requiring a one-year waiting period).

30. The 1545 version set the age of majority as 24 for men, 20 for women.

31. See also statute of January 18, 1541, in *Les sources du droit du canton de Genève,* vol. 2, item no. 785 (requiring churches to keep civil marriage registers); Les ordonnances ecclesiastiques, in Bergier and Kingdon, eds., *Registres de la compagnie des pasteurs,* 1:9 (regarding church announcements of banns).

32. Desertion by fiancés was addressed first in the 1547 version, more fully in the 1561 version.

33. See also statutes of September 19, 1547, and July 22, 1549, in *Les sources du droit du canton de Genève,* vol. 2, items 845 and 862.

34. CO, 6:203.

35. The statute prohibited betrothal and marriage for parties related by these degrees of consanguinity: (1) father and daughter, mother and son, "and all other descendents sequence, inasmuch as this contravenes the propriety of nature and is forbidden both by the law and God and by the civil laws"; (2) uncle and niece or great-niece, aunt and her nephew or great-nephew, and so on in sequence, "inasmuch as the uncle represents the father and the aunt is in the place of the mother";

(3) brother and sister or half brother and half sister; and (4) first cousins, saying that "while marriage is forbidden neither by the law of God nor by the civil law of the Romans, nevertheless for the avoidance of scandal (since for a long time it has not been customary), and for fear lest the Word of God should be blasphemed by the ignorant, marriage should not be contracted between first cousins until such time as we give a different ruling. There shall be no impediment to the other degrees."

The statute further prohibited betrothal and marriage between parties related by these degrees of affinity: (1) a man with his son's or grandson's widow, or a woman with her daughter's or granddaughter's husband, "and so on with other relations in a direct line"; (2) a man with his wife's daughter or granddaughter; (3) a woman with her husband's son or grandson; (4) a man with the divorced wife of his nephew or great nephew, or a woman with her niece or great-niece's husband; and (5) a man with the widow of his brother and no woman with the widower of her sister. Moreover, the statute concludes: "When it comes to notice that a man has committed adultery with another man's wife he may not take her in marriage because of the scandal and the dangers connected with it."

36. Calvin elaborated on this issue of property division at some length. What survives of his effort is in a "Fragment d'un projet d'ordonnance en matière matrimoniale," in CO, 10:143–144, and "Deuxiéme fragment d'un projet d'ordonnance sur la procédure civile," in CO, 10:139, 141.

37. For the criminal law in action, see E. William Monter, "Crime and Punishment in Calvin's Geneva, 1562," *Archiv für Reformationsgeschichte* 64 (1973): 281. Monter reports that an "almost complete and consecutively numbered list of all criminal arrests and trials, from February, 1562 to February, 1563" includes 197 criminal cases. Of these cases, forty-one dealt with extramarital sex (adultery, rape, fornication, and sodomy). Of these, three defendants were convicted and executed for raping children; three convicted adulterers and six fornicators were banished; two convicted homosexuals were executed.

38. Collected in *Registres du Consistoire de Genève*, vol. 2, with a few cases also reported in Bergier and Kingdon, eds., *Registres de la compagnie des pasteurs,* the clerical bench of the consistory. A microfilm of the original 21-volume *Registres du Consistoire de Genève* is available at the Meeter Center for Calvin Studies at Calvin College. The register has been transcribed in (thankfully readable!) French by Robert M. Kingdon and others. The cases discussed hereafter are drawn from the transcript of volume 2, prepared by Professor Kingdon and Jeffrey R. Watt.

The consistory record of 1542–1545 has only a few cases on marriage, family, and sexuality. See, e.g., in vol. 1:11 (inquires into care for illegitimate child); 1:15 (reprimands husband for spiritual delinquency of wife); 1:19 (refers question of legitimacy of Catholic wedding ceremony to the law of the magistrate); 1:192 (approves use of aunt's consent in place of parent's consent to marriage); 2:2 (mediates conflict between abandoned wife and her son over use of property left by deserter); 2:12–13 (hears character testimony in a divorce case that was later approved).

39. Case of Francoys Bastard, November 18, 1546, in ibid., 2:92.

40. Case of the Servants of Girad Perlet, December 16, 1546, in ibid., 2:98.

41. Case of Pierre Dolen, October 28, 1546, in ibid., 2:86.

42. Case of Jehanne, Daughter of Pierre Beyard, November 18, 1546, in ibid., 2:92.

43. Case of Jehanne, Maid of Lady Batezarde, January 7, 1546, in ibid., 2:24.

44. Case of Don Lergier Joly, November 18, 1546, in ibid., 2:92.

45. Case of Jehanne Fontanna and His Wife, June 24, 1546, in ibid., 2:68.

46. Case of Jacques Gruent, April 20, 1546, in ibid., 2:51. Gruent compounded his

problems by "slandering Sir Calvin for saying in his sermons that dancers are de-
bauchers. Sir Calvin answered him that he has said it differently in his sermons—
that dancing leads to debauchery." Moreover, the notary notes, Gruent was found
"drunk that evening and caused scandal."

47. Case of Ayme Ploncon, June 24, 1546, in ibid., 2:67.
48. Case of the Widow [Relaissé] of Jehan Debeyre, June 17, 1546, in ibid., 2:66.
49. Case of "the Lacques," January 28, 1546, in ibid., 2:28.
50. February 18, 1546, ibid., 2:34. On Favre's reputation and relationship with
    Calvin, see Kingdon, *Adultery and Divorce,* 181ff.; McNeill, *The History,* 169ff.
51. Divorce of François Favre, October 30, 1548, in Bergier & Kingdon, eds., *Registres
    de la compagnie des pasteurs,* 1:41.
52. See Kingdon, *Adultery and Divorce,* 182; id., "Anticlericalism in the Registers of the
    Geneva Consistory, 1542–1564," in Peter A. Dykema and Heiko A. Oberman,
    eds., *Anticlericalism in Late Medieval and Early Modern Europe* (Leiden: E.J. Brill,
    1993), 617.
53. See *Registres du Consistoire de Genève,* vols. 3–7; Frédéric-August Cramer, ed.,
    Notes extraites des registres du Consistoire de l'Église de Genève, 1541–1814 (Geneva,
    1853), with a rapid-fire distillation of relevant cases from Cramer's collection in
    Köhler, *Genfer Konsistorium,* 2:580ff.
54. The most colorful such cases are captured in Kingdon, *Adultery and Divorce.*
55. See also Seeger, *Mariage,* 135–182.
56. See Köhler, *Genfer Konsistorium,* 2:642–645, who traces some of these Genevan
    "innovations" to the laws of Zurich (1525) and Basel (1529). These prototypical
    laws are reprinted in Richter, *Kirchenordnungen,* 1:21, 120, and analyzed in Köh-
    ler's first volume, and in Thomas Max Safley, "Canon Law and Swiss Reform: Le-
    gal Theory and Practice in the Marital Courts of Zurich, Bern, Basel, and St. Gall,"
    in R.H. Helmholz, ed., *Canon Law in Protestant Lands* (Berlin: Duncker & Hum-
    blot, 1992), 187.
57. André Biéler, *L'Homme et la femme dans la morale Calviniste* (Geneva: Labor et
    Fides, 1963), 36, with sources and discussion in E. William Monter, "Women in
    Calvinist Geneva (1550–1800)," *Signs: Journal of Women in Culture and Society* 6
    (1980):189; Roger Stauffenegger, "Le Mariage à Genève vers 1600," *Mémoires de
    la société pour l'histoire de droit et des institutions de anciens pays bourguignons, com-
    tois et romands* 27 (1966):317.
58. See, e.g., Der Erbaren Stadt Brunswig Christliche Ordeninge (1528), in Richter,
    Kirchenordnungen, 1:106, drafted by the Lutheran leader Johannes Bugenhagen
    and a model for some two dozen polities in Germany and Scandinavia; Ordnung
    so ein Ersame Staat Basel (1529), in ibid., 1:120, drafted by Ulrich Zwingli and a
    model for several Swiss cities; Württembergische Eheordnung (1553), in ibid.,
    2:128, drafted by Johannes Brenz and a model for southern German cities.
59. CO, 17:238.
60. Case of Phillibert of Beauxliex, May 20, 1546, in *Registres du Consistoire de Genève,*
    2:55.
61. Entry on December 16, 1546, in ibid., 2:98.
62. See generally Kingdon, "Anticlericalism," 617–623.
63. Ibid. For a good example of such scorn and contempt, see, e.g., Case of Lady
    Grante, March 22, 1548, in *Registres du Consistoire de Genève,* 4:11. Lady Grante
    apparently had already appeared a few times before the consistory for various
    moral and marital peccadillos. In this instance, the notary reports that the "woman
    told the ministers that she did not like to come to the Consistory, even if it was re-
    quired by the church." When Calvin told her of the new charges, and that her be-
    havior before the consistory that day was contemptuous, "she retorted that he was

not telling the truth. All the assistants were shocked at her audacity, and even though everybody tried to reprimand her, she continued to say outrageous things against Calvin—that he came to Geneva to bring trouble and war, and since he had come there was neither good nor peace. When she was reprimanded [by Calvin] that what she said was wrong, she responded . . . that he does not practice what he preaches, nor is there any love in him, only hatred, nor has a word of consolation ever come from his mouth." The woman's audacity, the notary reports, resulted in her ban from the Lord's Supper. For other instances, see references and discussion in Kingdon, "Anticlericalism."

64. See, e.g., Comm. Lev. 20:10, 22:22–27; Serm. Deut. 5:18; 22:5–8, 13–25; Serm. Eph. 5:28–30, 31–33; "Contra la Secte des Libertines," in CO, 7:212ff.

65. For a chart of Calvin's preaching schedule, see T.H.L. Parker, *The Oracles of God: An Introduction to the Preaching of John Calvin* (London and Redhill: Lutterworth Press, 1947), 160–162, with sermons collected in CO and in *Supplementa Calvinia* (Neukirchen: Kreis Moers Neukirchener Verlag der Buchhandlung, 1961–). Calvin's biblical commentaries, all written after 1547 (save his *Commentary on Romans*, which has little discussion of marriage), are collected in CO, with translations in *Calvin's Commentaries*, 47 vols. (Edinburgh: Oliver & Boyd, 1843–1859). His letters are collected in CO and in Bonnet, *Letters of John Calvin*. In what follows, I have used the CO and *Supplementa Calvinia* editions, unless otherwise noted.

66. *Institutes* (1536), chap. 5.68. But cf. *Institutes* (1559), bk. 4, chap. 19.34, where Calvin repeats this language verbatim—and indeed the entire 1536 discussion of the section on marriage as a "false sacrament." This language stood in considerable tension with that of his sermons and commentaries discussed below.

67. Irenaeus, *Against Heretics*, bk. 4.

68. See sources and discussion in Daniel J. Flazar, *Covenant and Commonwealth: From Christian Separation Through the Protestant Reformation* (New Brunswick, N.J.: Transaction Publishers, 1996); and John Witte, Jr., "Blest Be the Ties that Bind: Covenant and Community in Puritan Thought," *Emory Law Journal* 36 (1987): 579, 580–581.

69. See *Institutes* (1559), bk. 2, chaps. 10–11; bk. 4, chaps. 15–16. For the covenant doctrines of other early reformers, see J. Wayne Baker, *Heinrich Bullinger and the Covenant: The Other Reformed Tradition* (Athens: Ohio University Press, 1980), 1–26, 181–216; Kenneth Hagen, "From Testament to Covenant in the Early Sixteenth Century," *Sixteenth Century Journal* 3 (1972):1–24; Max L. Stackhouse, *Covenant and Commitments: Faith, Family, and Economic Life* (Louisville, Ky.: Westminster John Knox Press, 1997), 147ff. Stackhouse's entire book is an ingeniously crafted manifesto for a modern covenantal theology and ethic of family life.

70. See, e.g., Comm. Eph. 5:22.

71. Comm. Mal. 2:14. See also Serm. Eph. 5:22–26 ("Marriage is not a thing ordained by men. We know that God is the author of it, and that it is solemnized in his name. The Scripture says that it is a holy covenant, and therefore calls it divine."); Serm. Deut. 5:18: ("[M]arriage is called a covenant with God, . . . meaning that God presides over marriages").

72. Comm. Lev. 19:29; Serm. Deut. 5:16; Comm. 1 Cor. 7:36, 38; Serm. 1 Cor. 7:36–38; Comm. Eph. 6:1–3.

73. Comm. 1 Thess. 4:3; Comm. 1 Peter 2:9; *Institutes* (1559), bk. 4, chap. 18:16–17.

74. Serm. Eph. 5:31–33.

75. CO, 45:529 and discussion in Seeger, *Mariage*, 94–95.

76. *Institutes* (1559), bk. 2, chap. 7.1, 8.1; bk. 4, chap. 20.15.

77. Among many other references, see *Institutes* (1559), bk. 2, chaps. 2.22, 7.3–4, 10,

8.1–2; bk. 3, chap. 19.15–16; bk. 4, chap. 20.3, 15, 16; Comm. Rom. 2:14–15; Serm. Deut. 4:44–6:4, 19:14–15. See discussion in Bohatec, *Calvin und das Recht,* 1–93; Jürgen Baur, *Gott, Recht und weltliches Regiment im Werke Calvins* (Bonn: H. Bouvier, 1965), 26–75; I. John Hesselink, *Calvin's Concept of the Law* (Allison Park, Pa.: Pickwick Publishers, 1992), 18–24, 51–85.

78. Comm. Gen. 2:18; Comm. Deut. 24:1–4; Comm. Mal. 2:15; Comm. Matt. 19:3–9 and Mark 10:2–12; Consilium in CO, 10:239–241.

79. Comm. Gen. 1:27, 1:28, 2:18, 2:21, 2:22; Comm. 1 Cor. 9:11; Comm. Eph. 5:30–32; Serm. Eph. 5:28–30.

80. Comm. Gen. 1:27.

81. Comm. Gen. 2:18, 22.

82. Comm. Gen. 2:18. See also Comm. 1 Cor. 9:8, 11:4–10.

83. Comm. Gen. 2:18.

84. Comm. Gen. 2:22, 2:25, 3:16; Serm. 1 Cor. 11:4–10; Comm. 1 Cor. 3:1–4, 6, 7:1, 9:10; Comm. Eph. 5:22–26, 28–30; Serm. Eph. 5:31–33; Comm. 1 Tim. 2:13, 5:13, 14; Serm. Titus 2:3–5. For analysis, see Claude-Marie Baldwin, "John Calvin and the Ethics of Gender Relations," *Calvin Theological Journal* 26 (1991):133; Bohatec, *Calvins Lehre von Staat und Kirche,* 655–659; Biéler, *L'Homme et la Femme,* 35–42; Willis P. DeBoer, "Calvin on the Role of Women," in David E. Holwerda, ed., *Exploring the Heritage of John Calvin* (Grand Rapids: Baker Book House, 1976), 236–272.

85. See, e.g., Comm. 1 Tim. 2:9 (deprecating women's vain apparel); Comm. Titus 2:3 (castigating women outside the home as "prattlers and rumormongerers"); Serm. Eph. 5:3–5, 22–26 (bemoaning the "audacity" of women's dress, speech, and manner outside the home); Comm. 1 Pet. 3:3 (same).

86. Comm. Gen. 2:18; Serm. Deut. 24:1–4; Lect. Ezek. 26:25, 26; Serm. Eph. 5:28–30.

87. Comm. Gen. 2:18; Comm. Gen. 29:18; Comm. Lev. 20:10, 22:22–27; Comm. Dan. 11:38–39; Comm. 1 Cor. 7:3, 9:11.

88. Comm. Gen. 2:18 (arguing that this equality is implicit in the concept of Eve being "a help meet for Adam"). But cf. Comm. 1 Cor. 11:4 ("For in his home, the father of the family is like a king. Therefore he reflects the glory of God, because of the control which is in his hands."); Serm. Eph. 5:22–26 (arguing that "husbands are advanced to the honor of superiority on condition that they should not be cruel toward their wives"). See discussion in DeBoer, "Calvin on the Role of Women," 236–256.

89. Comm. 1 Cor. 7:3. See also Comm. Matt. 19:9; Serm. 1 Cor. 7:3–5; Serm. Deut. 24:5–6.

90. Serm. Deut. 21:18–21; Comm. Gen. 2:18.

91. See sources and discussion in Witte, "Moderate Religious Liberty," 378–382; John Witte, Jr., and Thomas C. Arthur, "The Three Uses of the Law: A Protestant Source of the Purposes of Criminal Punishment?" *Journal of Law and Religion* 10 (1994): 433.

92. Though Calvin had adumbrated this theory of the uses of the law already in the mid-1530s, his full elaboration came in his 1559 edition of the *Institutes.* There he distinguished a "civil use of the moral law" (that yielded civil morality through coercion), a "theological use" (condemning persons in their sin to repent), and an "educational use" (teaching those who have repented spiritual morality). See *Institutes* (1559), bk. 2, chap. 7.6–13. The fullest exposition of the doctrine before 1559 came in his *Sermons on Deuteronomy* of the mid-1550s, where Calvin was interpreting the Jewish laws of marriage, divorce, polygamy, adultery, and the like. See, e.g., Serm. Deut. 5:18, 21; 21:15–17; 22:25–30; 24:1–4. Here, Calvin gener-

ally distinguished only the civil use and educational use (he called it "spiritual" use), touching lightly on the "theological use" only in Serm. Deut. 5:21. My discussion, therefore, distinguishes only the first two uses. Cf. discussion of the "three uses of marriage" in the Lutheran tradition, discussed in chapter 2, and references to the uses doctrine in "Reflections," below.

93. *Institutes* (1559), bk. 2, chap. 7.10. See also serm. Deut. 24:1–4.
94. Ibid. See also *Institutes* (1559), bk. 4, chap. 20.3.
95. Ibid., bk. 2, chap. 8.6–10; Serm. Deut. 5:18, 21, 21:15–17.
96. *Institutes* (1559), bk. 2, chap. 7.12.
97. Ibid., bk. 2, chap. 8.6.
98. The terms are from Lon L. Fuller, *The Morality of Law,* rev. ed. (New Haven, Conn.: Yale University Press, 1964). Calvin spoke of "civil morality" versus "spiritual morality." See *Institutes* (1559), bk. 2, chap. 7.10; bk. 4, 20.3; Serm. Deut. 21:15–17.
99. See *Institutes* (1559), bk. 4, chap. 11.3–16; bk. 4, chap. 20.1–2; Witte, "Moderate Religious Liberty," 383–399.
100. Comm. Lev. 18:22; Serm. Deut. 22:13–24.
101. Comm. Lev. 18 and 20 passim; Comm. Gen. 29:27; Serm. Deut. 22.25–30. See also Consilium, in CO, 10:231–323, and Consilium in CO, 10:235–238 (regarding the right of a man to marry his dead brother's widow in Lev. 18:18—by that point a cause célèbre occasioned by Henry VIII's marriage to Katherine of Aragon, the widow of Henry VII); Consilium, in CO, 10:233–235 (on a man marrying his deceased wife's sister).
102. Consilium, in CO, 10:235–238. See also Serm. Deut. 22:25–30.
103. Comm. Lev. 18:6–18; Consilia, in CO, 10:231–232, 233–235, 235–238.
104. Building on Calvin's doctrine, Beza elaborated these Levitical impediments at length in his *De Repudiis et Divortiis* (1563), reprinted in Theodore Beza, *Tractationum Theologicarum,* 2d ed. (Eusthatii Vignon, 1582), 50, 53–68.
105. See generally Paul Mikat, *Die Polygamiefrage in der frühen Neuzeit* (Düsseldorf: Westdeutscher Verlag, 1987); John Cairncross, *After Polygamy Was Made a Sin: The Social History of Christian Polygamy* (London: Routledge & Kegan Paul, 1974). The most notorious instance was Saxon Prince Philip of Hesse's bigamy, which Luther and Bucer had accepted as a necessary "lie" to avoid greater evil. See Hasting Eells, *The Attitude of Martin Bucer Toward the Bigamy of Philip of Hesse* (New Haven: Yale University Press, 1924). Polygamy was also a plank in the platform of several Anabaptists. See John L. Thompson, "Patriarchs, Polygamy, and Private Resistance: John Calvin and Others on Breaking God's Rules," *Sixteenth Century Journal* 35/1 (1994):3, 7–15.
106. Comm. Gen. 1:27, 29:27; Comm. Matt. 19:3–9 and Mark 10:2–12.
107. Serm. Deut. 21:15–17; Comm. Mal. 2:15.
108. Comm. Gen. 2:24.
109. Comm. Gen. 1:27, 2.24. See, e.g., Comm. Gen. 29:27 (re: Jacob and Leah); Serm. 2 Sam. 3:1–11 (re: Abner's polygamy); 5:13–21 (re: David's polygamy); 11:16 (re: David's adultery and polygamy with Bathsheba).
110. Comm. Mal. 2:14–15; Comm. 1 Sam. 1:6–8; Consilium, in CO, 10:231.
111. Ibid.; Serm. Deut. 21:15–17.
112. Comm. Matt. 19:3–9 and Mark 10:2–12. See also Comm. 1 Tim. 3:2 (condemning use of polygamy by bishops or other clergy); Comm. Mal. 2:16 (dismissing as "gross ignorance" traditional Catholic teachings that remarriage by widows or widowers was a form of "serial polygamy").
113. See Theodore Beza, *De polygamia* (c. 1569), in Theodore Beza, *Tractationum Theologicarum,* 2d ed. (Eusthatii Vignon, 1582), 1–49.

114. Serm. Eph. 5:31–33.
115. *Institutes* (1559), bk. 2, chap. 8.41; Comm. Exod. 20:14.
116. Comm. Lev. 20:10, 22:22–27.
117. Serm. Deut. 5:18. See also Serm. Deut. 22:25–30; Serm. 2 Sam. 5:13–21; Comm. 1 Cor. 7:11.
118. Serm. Eph. 5:22–26.
119. Serm. Deut. 22:13–19.
120. Ibid. The quoted passage is from Beza, *De Repudiis et Divortiis*, 100.
121. Comm. Lev. 20:10, 22–27.
122. Comm. Deut. 23:24–25, 24:1–4; Comm. Matt. 19:9 and discussion in Biéler, *L'Homme et la Femme*, 69–73. See also Beza, *De Repudiis et Divortiis*, 89: After adultery, "the bond of marriage, if it persists, is kept united by the will of the innocent spouse, and can be made strong again by the will of the innocent spouse."
123. Comm. Matt. 19:3–9 and Mark 10:2–12.
124. Ibid. See also Beza, *De Repudiis et Divortiis*, 90.
125. Serm. Deut. 24:1–4. See also Serm. Deut. 21:15–17.
126. Comm. Matt. 19:3–9 and Mark 10:2–12. See also Comm. Gen. 2:24 ("Those who, for slight causes, rashly allow for divorces, violate, in one single particular, all the laws of nature and reduce them to nothing.").
127. Ibid.
128. Calvin did, however, periodically recognize the legitimacy of divorce to avoid greater sins, such as incest and polygamy. Commenting on Laban's manipulation of Jacob into marrying both Leah and Sarah, he wrote: "In this truly he grieviously sins, that he not only involves his nephew in polygamy, but pollutes both him and his own daughters by incestuous nuptials. . . . The Lord, through Malachi, pronounces divorce to be more tolerable than polygamy. Laban, blinded by avarice, so sets his daughters together, so that they spend their whole lives in mutual hostility. He also perverts all the laws of nature by casting two sisters into one marriage bed." Comm. Gen. 29:27; see also Comm. Mal. 2:14; Serm. Deut. 24:1–4.
129. Ibid.
130. Letter by Charles d'Epseville (a pseudonym for Calvin), in CO, 10:255–258 (emphasis added). Beza, *De Repudiis et Divortiis*, 88–89, repeated this counsel, arguing that the divorce and remarriage of both parties could occur without any involvement of the magistrate.
131. Consilium, in CO, 10:231.
132. Serm. Deut. 22:13–19.
133. *Institutes* (1559), bk. 2, chap. 7.44.
134. Comm. 1 Cor. 7:11. See also Serm. Deut. 24:1–4.
135. Consilium, December 30, 1561, in CO, 10:242–244.
136. Ibid; Comm. 1 Cor. 7:11.
137. Serm. Deut. 24:1–4. See also Comm. 1 Cor. 9:11 ("If they be separated, they are like the mutilated members of the mangled body. Let them, therefore, be connected with each other by this tie of mutual aid and amicableness.").
138. Comm. 1 Cor. 7:11; Consilium, December 30, 1561, in CO, 10:242–244.
139. Ibid.
140. Ibid. See also Comm. Matt. 19:9; Comm. 1 Cor. 7:11.
141. Comm. 1 Cor. 7:12.
142. See cases in Seeger, *Mariage*, 380–403.
143. Comm. 1 Cor. 7:11.
144. Beza, *De Repudiis et Divortiis*, 95–99.
145. *Institutes* (1559), bk. 2, chap. 8.41, 44; Comm. Lev. 20:10, 22:22–27.

146. Serm. Deut. 5:18.
147. "Contra la secte Libertines," CO, 7:212ff.
148. In 1563, Geneva adopted the rule that when fornicating couples appear at the church for their wedding ceremony, "the minister make public declaration of their fault, which they ought also to recognize to undo the scandal." *Les sources du droit du canton de Genève,* vol. 3, item no. 1042. Four months later, the penalty against fornication was raised from six days to nine, plus a fine; recidivists had also to appear before the sermon and make public confession of their sin and reparation to the shamed parties and families. Ibid., vol. 3, item no. 1946.
149. Serm. Deut. 22:25–30, 28:25–29, 59–64; Comm. Lev. 20:10, 22:22–27; Lect. Ezek. 16:9, 20; Comm. 1 Cor. 6:18; Serm. Eph. 5:3–5.
150. Quoted and discussed in Georgia Harkness, *John Calvin: The Man and His Ethics* (New York: Henry Holt, 1931), 130.
151. Serm. Deut. 22:5–8, 25–30; Serm. Eph. 5:3–5; Comm. 1 Pet. 3:3; Serm. Titus 2:3–5.
152. See Biéler, *L'Homme et la Femme,* 124–126, 138–145; W. Fred Graham, *The Constructive Revolutionary: John Calvin and His Socio-Economic Impact* (Atlanta: John Knox Press, 1978), 110–115.
153. Consilium in CO, 10:231.
154. Ibid.
155. Ibid. See also Beza, *De repudiis et divortiis,* 72–73, 109–110; Seeger, *Mariage,* 116–118.
156. See, e.g., Letter to Lelius Socinus (c. 1549), CO, 13:307–311 (condemning marriage between a reformed man and a Catholic woman); Letter to Lelius Socinus (December 7, 1549), CO, 13:484–487 (condemning marriage between a Christian and a Turk).
157. See Comm. 1 Cor. 7:12, 14; Anonymous Letter (April 28, 1556), in CO, 10:264–266.
158. Serm. Deut. 21:10–14. See also Letter to Lelius Socinus, CO, 13:487.
159. Comm. Gen. 6:2.
160. Ibid. See also Comm. 1 Thess. 4:3.
161. See Comm. Gen. 29:18, where Calvin writes that there is nothing wrong with Jacob's loving Rachel more than Leah because Rachel was prettier.
162. Comm. Gen. 6:2. See also Biéler, *L'Homme et la Femme,* 81–88, on Calvin's views of female beauty.
163. Letter to Farel (May 19, 1539), in Calvin, *Letters,* 1:139, 141.
164. McNeill, *The History and Character of Calvinism,* 156.
165. See Richard Stauffer, *L'humanité de Calvin* (Neuchatel: Delachaux et Niestlé, 1964), 19ff.; Williston Walker, *John Calvin* (New York: Schocken Books, 1960), 357ff.
166. Comm. 1 Tim. 5:11.
167. Ibid.; Comm. 1 Cor. 7:1.
168. Comm. 1 Cor. 7:9. See also Comm. 1 Cor. 7:36; Comm. 1 Tim. 5:14.
169. Ibid. See also the annulment of a betrothal of a woman over 70 to a man of 27 or 28 in the Case of Jean Hachart (December 31, 1556), in *Registres du Consistoire de Genève,* 11:93; and ibid. (January 5, 1557), in Bergier and Kingdon, eds., *Registres de la compagnie des pasteurs,* 2:71, with brief discussion in Köhler, *Genfer Konsistorium,* 2:631.
170. Letter to Ministers of Neuchâtel (September 26, 1558), in Calvin, *Letters,* 3:473 (writing that "poor Master William has been for once so ill-advised for his weakness" in wishing to contract marriage at 68 years old); Letter to Farel (September

1558), in ibid., 3:475 (excusing himself from Farel's wedding). In this instance, the consistory disagreed with Calvin and approved Farel's wedding, much to Calvin's chagrin. See CO, 21, 703, and Köhler, *Genfer Konsistorium,* 631.

171. Serm. Deut. 5:18.
172. Serm. Deut. 22:13–19.
173. Serm. Deut. 5:18. See also Comm. 1 Cor. 7:6 ("Marriage is a veil by which the fault of immoderate desire is covered over, so that it no longer appears in the sight of God.").
174. Serm. Deut. 22:13–19, 24:5–6.
175. Comm. 1 Cor. 7:3, 7:5; Serm. Deut. 22:13–19; Comm. Matt. 19:3–9 and Mark 10:2–12.
176. CO, 7:212. See also Beza, *De repudiis et divortiis,* 82–83. For background, see Dyan Elliott, *Spiritual Marriage: Sexual Abstinence in Medieval Wedlock* (Princeton, N.J.: Princeton University Press, 1993).
177. Comm. Gen. 1:28; Comm. Psalms 127:3, 128:3; Comm. 1 Tim. 5:14.
178. Comm. Gen. 16:1–6; Comm. Matt. 19:9. See also Beza, *De repudiis et divortiis,* 108.
179. Comm. Gen. 16:1–6. See also Beza, *De repudiis et divortiis,* 105–106.
180. Comm. 1 Cor. 7:11. See also Comm. Mal. 2:14.
181. See Beza, *De repudiis et divortiis,* 71–73, and cases summarized in Seeger, *Mariage,* 353–355.
182. Comm. Matt. 19:9.
183. Consilium, December 2, 1561, in CO, 10:241–242. But cf. Comm. Matt. 19:9 (where Calvin argues that a husband should not touch a leprous wife, but "I do not pronounce him at liberty to divorce").
184. CO, 10:242.
185. See, e.g., Letter of Monsieur de Falais (May 1, 1547), in Calvin, *Letters* 2:110–111 (where Calvin expressed great dismay that a woman asked a man for marriage "rather than wait to be asked," and expressed confidence that "a judge will soon put an end to the matter"). See also other instances where Calvin engaged in virtual bride-hunts for (the sons of) distinguished friends and parishioners, even to the point of brokering one such relationship between a couple sight unseen. See, e.g., Letter to Monsieur de Falais (July 4, 1546), in Calvin, *Letters,* 2:63; Letters to Viret (July 13, 15, and 25, 1546), in ibid., 2:65–69; Letter to Monsieur de Falais (May 1, 1547), ibid., 2:110; Letter to Monsieur de Falais (July 17, 1548), ibid., 2:173; Letter to Viret (September 1, 1548), ibid., 4:409. To be sure, in this, Calvin was following the customary practice of any well-meaning aristocrat or pastor of the day. But note that, for the sake of biblical truth, he was quite willing to break the custom and the common law on other issues of gender equality.
186. See, e.g., William J. Bouwsma, *John Calvin: A Sixteenth-Century Portrait* (New York: Oxford University Press, 1988).
187. Comm. Gen. 2:21, 2:24, 6:2; Serm. Deut. 21:10–14; Comm. Mal. 2:14, 16; Comm. Matt. 19:11; Comm. 1 Cor. 7:14, 9:11; "Contra la Secte des Libertines," in CO, 7:212ff.
188. Comm. Gen. 2:18. But cf. *Institutes* (1559), bk. 4, chap. 19 (where Calvin criticizes sharply Catholic sacramental views that regarded "carnal copulation" as an indispensable part of the sacrament of marriage).
189. Serm. 2 Tim. 5; CO, 53:492.
190. Lect. 44–47 on Ezekiel 16; Comm. Mal. 2:14–15; Lect. Hos. 2:2; Serm. Deut. 21:10–14.
191. Serm. Eph. 5:28–30, 31–33; Comm. Eph. 5:30–32.
192. Serm. Eph. 5:28–30; Lect. Ezek. 16:9, 17; Lect. Hos. 2:2; Serm. Deut. 21:10–14.

193. *Institutes* (1559), bk. 4, chap. 19.34. This repeats verbatim what Calvin had written in *Institutes* (1536), chap. 5.69.

194. Comm. Gen. 29:27; see also Comm. Gen. 2:18; Serm. Eph. 5:22–26; Consilium in CO, 10:231–232.

195. CO, 51:763ff. For Calvin's general views of contract, such as they are, see his "Fragments des travaux de Calvin relatifs à la Législation civile et politique," in CO, 10:126, 130–132, 139, with brief discussion of commercial contracts in Bohatec, *Calvins Lehre von Staat und Kirche,* 687–700.

196. Comm. 1 Cor. 7:11.

197. See *Institutes* (1559), bk. 2, chap. 8.42; bk. 4, chap. 19.34–37; Comm. Gen. 2:18, 2:22; Comm. Matt. 19:11 ("the choice to marry is not put in our own hands, as if we were to deliberate on the matter"); Comm. 1 Cor. 7:7–8, 25–28; Comm. 1 Tim. 5:13. See also correspondence in CO, 5:330; 7:42, 670.

198. Serm. Deut. 22:25–30.

199. CO, 7:212ff. See also Comm. Gen. 2:24.

200. Serm. Deut. 5:18.

201. For Calvin's later uses of the two kingdoms theory, see Witte, "Moderate Religious Liberty," nn. 24, 75, 114.

202. One such embellishment was that Calvin prioritized the father's consent over that of the mother, basing this on the headship of man to woman after the fall into sin. See, e.g., Consilium, CO, 10:231–232, 238–239; Serm. Eph. 5:3–5. The Marriage Ordinance of 1545 also gives priority to the consent of fathers or male guardians.

203. See esp. Heinrich Bullinger, *Der christlich Eestand* (Zurich, 1540), discussed in chapter 4, below. Though Calvin and Bullinger corresponded regularly, I have found no evidence that Calvin used Bullinger's marriage tract in formulating his theology of marriage, let alone that Calvin had any influence on Bullinger's formulations. It is evident that Uldaricus Zwingli, an important earlier reformer of marriage in Zurich, had at least adumbrated a comparable covenantal theology of marriage that both Bullinger and Calvin knew. See his *De vera et falsa religione commentarius* (1525), in *Huldreich Zwinglis Sämtliche Werke* (Zürich: Theologischer Verlag, 1982), 3:590, at 762–763 (brief section on marriage), with discussion and sources in Charles S. McCoy and J. Wayne Baker, *Foundation of Federalism: Heinrich Bullinger and the Covenantal Tradition* (Louisville: Westminster/John Knox Press, 1991).

204. See George Huntston Williams, *The Radical Reformation,* 3d ed. (Kirksville, Mo.: Sixteenth Century Essays & Studies, 1992), 755–798.

205. Seeger, *Mariage,* 97–101.

206. See generally William G. Naphy, *Calvin and the Consolidation of the Genevan Reformation* (Manchester and New York: Manchester University Press, 1994).

207. "L'authoritaté du Consistoire confirmée," in Bergier and Kingdon, eds., *Registres de la compagnie des pasteurs,* 2:59.

208. See generally, Pierre Anciaux, *The Sacrament of Penance* (New York: Sheed & Ward, 1962); Karl Rahner, *Theological Investigations,* C. Ernest, trans. (Baltimore: Helicon Press, 1963), 2:135ff.

209. See *Institutes* (1559), bk. 4, chap. 17.40, and sources and discussion in John Witte, Jr., "The Catholic Origins and Calvinist Orientation of Dutch Reformed Church Law," *Calvin Theological Journal* 28 (1993):328, 338–49.

210. Köhler, *Genfer Konsistorium,* 2:504ff.

211. See Seeger, *Mariage,* 286–95, in general, and Kingdon, *Adultery and Divorce,* passim, for several such examples. On the use of torture by judicial tribunals in this period, see generally John H. Langbein, *Torture and the Law of Proof* (Cambridge: Harvard University Press, 1974).

212. Reported in Köhler, *Genfer Konsistorium,* 2:631.
213. Case of Jeanne, Daughter of the Late Roz Favre of Avully (February 18, 1557), in *Registres du Consistoire de Genève,* 12:5.
214. Case of Antoine Gozet (March 4, 1557), in ibid., 12:12.
215. Ibid., 12:14.
216. Case of Pierre Clerc of Bonne (February 25, 1557), in ibid., 12:8. See also Case of Francoys Longey (August 30, 1557), in ibid., 12:91 (father of a daughter reprimanded for not seeking consent to marriage of his future son-in-law's father).
217. Case of Sir DuBoys (February 18, 1557), in ibid., 12:5.
218. Case of Laurens Corbet and Pierrine Quitaine, (February 18, 1557), in ibid., 12:5.
219. Case of Jean Tissier et al. (August 12 and 19, 1557), in ibid., 12:86, 89.
220. Case of Philiberte, Daughter of the Late Guillaume the Chapuis (May 27, 1557), in ibid., 12:52.
221. Ibid., 12:62.
222. Case of Francoys Chastellain (January 2, 1556), in ibid., 10:81.
223. Case of Nycolas Millet (May 13 and 20, 1557), ibid., 12:45. The notary seems to have grouped the two days of proceedings together. Moreover, the first "supplication" by Nycolas and other documents are dated "July 27, 1559." Either this case was backdated and interpolated to May, 1557, or Nycolas's initial filing was misdated—by him or by the notary who transcribed it.
224. Order (May 20, 1557), in ibid., 12:48.
225. Case of Bartholmye et Ducreson (December 31, 1556), in ibid., 11:93.
226. Case of Thomas Lambert and Jehanne Marie (April, 1557), in ibid., 12:38.
227. Case of the Widow of Jean Achard (January, 1557), in Bergier and Kingdon, eds., *Registres de la compagnie des pasteurs,* 2:71, with further discussion in Köhler, *Genfer Konsistorium,* 2:631.
228. Ibid. See also CO, 21:703.
229. Case of Henri Clement et al. (January 9, 1556), in *Registres du Consistoire de Genève,* 10:83 (January 23, 1556); in ibid., 10:88 (March 5, 1556); in ibid., 11:7 (March 4, 1557); in ibid., 12:15.
230. Case of Jacques Regnault (March 4, 1557), ibid., 12:12. The consistory ruled similarly in the Case of Claude Myerge (July 22, 1557), in ibid., 12:77, when a fiancé, who had left the city, sought to return and have his engagement restored.
231. Case of Jacques Regnault (March 18, 1557), in ibid., 12:18.
232. Case of Claude of the Crouse et al. (March 4, 1557), in ibid., 12:13.
233. Case of Francoys Rosset and His Wife Mathée (March 18, 1557), in ibid., 12:17.
234. Case of Étienne DeFaye (May 6, 1557), in ibid., 12:41 (approving as "true, good, and legitimate" the marriage of an aristocrat that was celebrated in "Christian church" in France, and certified in a sealed certificate); Case of Claude of St. Mahet and Estienne of St. Mahet (August 30, 1557), in ibid., 12:92 (a man, privately charged with being illegitimately married, was given three months to get his "marriage attestation"); Case of Arnault Casaubon and Meugyne Rosseau (September 9, 1557), in ibid., 12:96 (consistory confirms marriage on production of marriage attestation and testimony of the two corroborating witnesses); Case of Estienne Claude Marie Legreste (September 9, 1557), ibid., 12:96 (same).
235. Case of Bernard Martin and Pernette His Wife (March 11, 1557), in ibid., 12:12.
236. Case of Pierre DuBuisson (April 22, 1557), in ibid., 12:36.
237. Case of Jehan Dosteus of Colombier (June 3, 1557), in ibid., 12:62.
238. Case of André Peronnet (January 21, 1557), in ibid., 11:100.
239. Case of the Wife of Jehan Piedmontoys (June 3, 1557), in ibid., 12:60; (June 10, 1557), in ibid., 12:62. See also Case of Antoine Phillipin (December 31, 1556), in ibid., 11:93 (single man caught drunk in a married woman's bedroom questioned

about fornication, but not charged); Case of Mermet Foudral (July 29, 1557), in ibid., 12:81 (man reprimanded for continuing to visit a married woman, in violation of the Council's order); Case of Jehan Bron (September 2, 1557), in ibid., 12:93 (man reinstated to communion, after being banned for frequenting a married woman's house and "causing scandal for the neighbors").

240. Case of Jehan Pascart of Sollignier (April 15, 1557), in ibid., 12:32. He was readmitted to communion a few months later, after confessing his wrong and being admonished. Case of Jehan Pascart of Sillingy [sic] (September 2, 1557), in ibid., 12:92.

241. Case of Master Symon Thyven and Janne, Widow of Jehan Liborne (September 2, 1557), in ibid., 12:93.

242. Case of Girault of Lespinasse et al. (March 4, 1557), in ibid., 12:8.

243. Case of Jehan Grangier of Laconex (April 22, 1557), in ibid., 12:35. See also Case of André Dominique (May 20, 1557), ibid., 12:48. Once banned from the Lord's Supper for alleged fornication, he asked for the ban to be lifted. "He was asked to confess his faults, but he did not like to do so. For that reason, he was asked not to come back to the consistory, since he did not like to repent."

244. Case of Jehanton des Boys (September 2, 1557), in ibid., 12:93. See also Case of Bernardine (September 2, 1557), in ibid., 12:94 (woman reinstated to communion after confessing her adultery).

245. Case of Claude, Daughter of Francoyse Bastard of Chastellaine (May 6, 1557), in ibid., 12:41.

246. Case of Claude Blanchet and Claude, Daughter of Francoys Bastard of Chastellaine (May 20, 1557), in ibid., 12:46.

247. Case of Michael Gilbert (March 25, 1557), in ibid., 12:21 (the notary crossed out· "decided, first, that the Lord's Supper should be forbidden to him").

248. Case of Pernette, Daughter of Bernard Dentan of Meynier (March 25, 1557), in ibid., 12:21.

249. Case of Jacquema, Sister of Audrey Quad (August 12 and 19, 1557), in ibid., 12:85, 89.

250. Case of the Maid of Pierre Mutin (May 20, 1557), in ibid., 12:46.

251. Case of Ameyd Doctet and Pernette, Wife of Pierre Troiller (June 1, 1557), in ibid., 12:52. See also Case of Barbe, Wife of Robert Maillard (September 16, 1557), in ibid., 12:96 (case involving detailed but conflicting testimony over her alleged adultery referred to Council for disposition).

252. Case of Michel Poincteau (September 23, 1557), in ibid., 12:99.

253. Case of Jehan Griffon and Bernarde, Widow of Jaques Verdon (March 25, 1557), in ibid., 12:21.

254. (May 20, 1557), in ibid., 12:48.

255. Case of Hudry Roiod (April 15, 1557), in ibid., 12:29.

256. Case of Master Jean Fabri, Minister (March 5, 1556), in ibid., 11:7.

257. Case of Jehan Favre (January 21, 1557), in ibid., 11:99.

258. Case of Jacqueline Obod (May 6, 1557), in ibid., 12:41.

259. Case of Bernardine of Falcon, Italian, et al. (February 6, 1556), in ibid., 10:89; and (September 9, 1557), in ibid., 12:101.

260. Case of Janne Cavette and Sir Jaques Marcelli (July 8, 1557), in ibid., 12:72.

261. Kingdon, *Adultery and Divorce,* 71–97. For earlier descriptions, see Köhler, *Genfer Konsistorium,* 2:628–630; Seeger, *Mariage,* 406–407.

262. See Case of Antoine Calvin (September 27, 1548), in *Registres du Consistoire de Genève,* 4:62, with analysis of these and other proceedings in Kingdon, *Adultery and Divorce,* 74–78; Köhler, *Genfer Konsistorium,* 2:629–630.

263. Case of Antoine Calvin (January 7, 1557), in *Registres du Consistoire de Genève,*

11:95. In a letter to Viret, sent the same day, Calvin again reported "great grief." "For when that abandoned woman, who was then my brother's wife, lived in my house, we discovered that she had committed adultery with the hunchbacked Peter. The only consolation that we have is that my brother will be freed from her by a divorce." Calvin, *Letters* 3:308. See also Calvin's later reflections in CO, 16, 382.

264. Kingdon, *Adultery and Divorce*, 79–93.

265. Ibid., passim; Köhler, *Genfer Konsistorium*, 2:626–645 (using cases in Cramer, *Notes extraites*, passim); Seeger, *Mariage*, 305–450.

266. See generally E. William Monter, "The Consistory of Geneva: 1559–1569," *Bibliothèque d'Humanisme et Renaissance* 38 (1976):467–484.

267. Seeger, *Mariage*, 305–331.

268. Ibid., 332–374.

269. Ibid., 464–465.

270. Ibid., 417; Kingdon, *Adultery and Divorce*, 176.

271. Ibid. See also Stauffenegger, "Le mariage à Genève vers 1600," 317; P. Bels, "La formation du lien de mariage dans l'église protestante française (XVIe et XVIIe siècle)," in ibid., 331; Jeffrey R. Watt, "The Control of Marriage in Reformed Switzerland, 1550–1800," in W. Fred Graham, ed., *Sixteenth Century Essays and Studies—Later Calvinism: International Perspectives* (Kirksville, Mo.: Sixteenth Century Journal Publishers, 1994), 29; Lawrence Stone, *Road to Divorce: England 1530–1987* (Oxford: Oxford University Press, 1990).

272. See McNeill, *History and Character of Calvinism,* 237ff.; Menna Priest, ed., *International Calvinism* (Oxford: Clarendon Press, 1985).

273. See sources and broader discussion in chapter 4.

274. See George Elliott Howard, *A History of Matrimonial Institutions* (Chicago: University of Chicago Press, 1904), 2:121–226, 328–366; Edmund S. Morgan, *The Puritan Family: Religion and Domestic Relations in Seventeenth Century New England* (New York: Harper & Row, 1966); John Demos, *A Little Commonwealth: Family Life in Plymouth Colony* (New York: Oxford University Press, 1970).

275. See sources and discussion in Witte, "The Catholic Origins," 328–351.

276. The most influential on marriage included "Plakkaat, betreffende huwelijk, echtbreuk enz., (1574)," in *Nederlands archief voor kerkgeschiedenis (n.s.)* 39 (1952/3):121; Politieke ordonnantie van Holland (1580), items 1–28, in A. De Blecourt en N. Japiske, *Klein plakkaatboek van Nederland* (Groningen: J.B. Wolters, U.M., 1919), 126; Politieke ordonnantie van Zeeland (1583), items 6–23, in *Klein plakkaatboek,* 129; *Egtreglement, Over de Steden, ende ten platten Lande, in de Heerlijkheden en Dorpen, staande onder de Generaliteit* (s'Gravenhage: Hillebrandt van Wouw, 1664).

277. For a good summary of the contemporary learned law, see Hugo Grotius, *The Jurisprudence of Holland,* trans. and ed. R.W. Lee (Oxford: Clarendon Press, 1926), bk. 1, chaps. v–xii. For a more exhaustive treatment, see Hendrik Brouwer, *De Jure Connubiorum, libri duo* (Delphis: Adrianum Beman, 1714). The best collection of cases is in C. van Bijnkerkshoek, *Observationes tumultuariae,* 4 vols., E.M. Meijers et al., eds. (Haarlem, 1926–1962). See further sources in John Witte, Jr., "The Plight of Canon Law in the Early Dutch Republic," in Helmholz, ed., *Canon Law in Protestant Lands,* 135–164.

278. For good overviews, see L. van Apeldoorn, *Geschiedenis van het nederlandsche huwelijksrecht voor de invoering van de fransche wetsgeving* (Amsterdam: Uitgeversmaatschappij, 1925), 84–122, 126–170, 180–188, 195–198; H.F.W.D. Fischer, "De gemengde huwelijken tussen Katholiken en Protestanten in de Nederlanden van de XVIe tot de XVIIe eeuw," *Tijdschrift voor Rechtsgeschiedenis/Revue d'Histoire*

due Droit 31 (1963):463–485; Els Kloek, "Seksualiteit, huwelijk en gezinsleven ti-jdens de lange zestiende eeuw, 1450–1650," in Ton Zwaan, ed., *Familie, huwelijk en gezin in West-Europa. Van Middeleeuwen tot moderne tijd* (Amsterdam: Boom/ Open Universiteit, 1993), 107–138.

279. A.J.M. van Overveldt, *De dualiteit van kerkelijk en burgerlijk huwelijk* (Tilburg, 1953). For a good example of comparable English Puritan reforms, see the marriage reforms in the 1552 Reformation of Ecclesiastical Law and 1653 Parliamentary Act discussed in chapter 4, below, at nn. 110–118, 208, and accompanying texts. For New England, see Morgan, *The Puritan Family,* 29ff.

280. Herman van den Brink, "The Married Life of Jan Klaasen en Katrijn," in id., *The Charm of Legal History* (Amsterdam: Adolf M. Hakkert, 1974), 189, 198–199.

Notes to Chapter 4:
Marriage as Commonwealth in the Anglican Tradition

1. William Perkins, *Christian Oeconomy or a Short Survey of the Right Manner of Erecting and Ordering a Family According to the Scriptures* (c. 1590), reprinted in Ian Breward, ed., *The Work of William Perkins* (Appleford: The Sutton Courtenay Press, 1970), 3:418–419.

2. Robert Cleaver, *A Godly Form of Householde Gouernment* (London: Thomas Creede, 1598), 1.

3. John Donne, *The Works,* ed. Henry Alford (Cambridge: Cambridge University Press, 1839), 4:485. See discussion on the concept of *via media* theology in Charles H. George and Katherine George, *The Protestant Mind of the English Reformation: 1570–1640* (Princeton, N.J.: Princeton University Press, 1961), 375–418.

4. See John F. New, *Anglican and Puritan* (Stanford: Stanford University Press, 1964) (criticizing the Georges for an unduly ecumenical reading of early modern English theology). See further sources and discussion in Ian Breward, "Introduction," to Perkins, *Christian Oeconomy,* 1:1–33, 116–120.

5. See Barbara Shapiro, *Probability and Certainty in Seventeenth Century English Thought* (Princeton, N.J.: Princeton University Press, 1983).

6. In the vast literature, see esp. Henry Ansgar Kelly, *The Matrimonial Trials of Henry VIII* (Stanford: Stanford University Press, 1976); and more recent discussion and sources in A.A. Chibi, "The Interpretation and Use of Divine and Natural Law in the First Marriage Crisis of Henry VIII," *Archiv für Reformationsgeschichte* 85 (1994):265–286; Diarmand MacCulloch, *Thomas Cranmer: A Life* (New Haven and London: Yale University Press, 1996), 41–78; V. Murphy, "The Literature and Propaganda on Henry's Divorce," in Diarmand MacCulloch, ed., *The Reign of Henry VIII: Politics, Policy and Piety* (Basingstoke: MacMillan, 1995), chap. 6; G. Bedouelle and P. LeGal, *Le Divorce du Roi Henry VIII: Études et Documents* (Geneva: Travaux d'Humanisme et Renaissance, 1987).

7. Quoted by Kelly, *Matrimonial Trials,* 169.

8. 24 Henry VIII, c. 12.

9. 25 Henry VIII, c. 22.

10. 26 Henry VIII, c. 1.

11. See Chilton L. Powell, *English Domestic Relations 1487–1653: A Study of Matrimony and Family Life in Theory and Practice as Revealed by the Literature, Law, and History of the Period* (New York: Columbia University Press, 1917), 207–224.

12. See Joan Lockwood O'Donovan, *The Theology of Law and Authority in the English Reformation* (Atlanta: Scholars Press, 1991), 11–80.

13. See a list of titles in George E. Howard, *A History of Matrimonial Institutions* (Chicago: University of Chicago Press, 1907), 1:364–370, and discussion in Frederick J. Smithen, *Continental Protestantism and the English Reformation* (London: James Clarke & Co., n.d.), 43–135; Eric Josef Carlson, *Marriage and the English Reformation* (Oxford: Blackwell, 1994), 3–9, 67–87.

14. See *The Early Works of Thomas Becon, S.T.P.,* ed. J. Ayre for the Parker Society, 3 vols. (Cambridge: University Press, 1843). This collection duplicates much from an earlier collection of Becon's writings, *The First Part of the Bokes, which Thomas Becon made* (London: J. Day, 1560–1564), save one title, *The Booke of Matrimonie both Profitable and Comfortable for all Them that Entende Quietly and Godly to lyue in the Holy State of Honorable Wedlocke* (c. 1560), in ibid., I, bk. 12 (STC 1710), a tract of 236 folio pages. See discussion of Becon's views on marriage in D.S. Bailey, *Thomas Becon and the Reformation in England* (Edinburgh: Oliver and Boyd, 1952), 22, 57–58, 96, 111–115, with a list of his writings on marriage in ibid., 140–147. See also Powell, *English Domestic Relations,* 75, 111–114, 125–129, 155–158, 244. *Becon's Booke of Matrimonie* must not be confused with Heinrich Bullinger's *The Golde Boke of Christen Matrimonye* (1542), which was frequently reprinted under Becon's pen name, Theodore Basille. Becon's tract includes many of the same themes as Bullinger's tract and a virtually identical preface, but the two works are quite distinct. Becon devotes more than half of the work to polemics against the canon law and scholastic theology, which find virtually no place in Bullinger's. See esp. Becon, *Booke of Matrimonie,* Second Part, folios DCxvi–DCxlviii.

15. Ibid., folio CCCCClxxv.

16. Ibid., folios CCCCClx, CCCClxiii.

17. Becon, *Early Works,* 3:198. See also Becon, *Booke of Matrimonie,* folio DClxxviff.

18. Becon, *Booke of Matrimonie,* folios CCCCClxxv–Dxxii.

19. Ibid., folio CCCCClxiii.

20. Becon, *Early Works,* 2:532–533 (I have revised the order slightly); see also ibid., 3:198–199, 235–236. For a prototype of this Christ versus Anti-Christ dialectic, see William Tyndale, *Doctrinal Treatises and Introduction to Different Portions of the Holy Scripture,* ed. H. Walter for the Parker Society (Cambridge: University Press, 1848), 232–246.

21. See, e.g., Tyndale, *Doctrinal Treatises,* 23, 169–170, 199; *The Sermons of Edwin Sandys,* ed. J. Ayre for the Parker Society (Cambridge: University Press, 1842), 2:50–51, 281, 325–326, 434, 455; *Early Writings of John Hooper,* ed. S. Carr for the Parker Society (Cambridge: University Press, 1843), 126, 137–138, 149; *Sermons of Hugh Latimer,* ed. G.E. Corrie for the Parker Society (Cambridge: University Press, 1844), 169–170. For later Anglican views on parental consent, see Richard L. Greaves, *Society and Religion in Elizabethan England* (Minneapolis: University of Minnesota Press, 1981), 155–177.

22. *The Remains of Edmund Grindal,* ed. W. Nicholson for the Parker Society (Cambridge: University Press, 1843), 127, 143, 189; Hooper, *Early Writings,* 138. For later Anglican views, which were quite discordant on this point, see Greaves, *Society and Religion,* 177–190.

23. *Miscellaneous Writings and Letters of Thomas Cranmer,* ed. J.E. Cox for the Parker Society (Cambridge: University Press, 1846), 94–95, 328–329, 359–360; Grindal, *Remains,* 127, 143, 175; John Jewell, *Works,* ed. J. Ayre for the Parker Society (Cambridge: University Press, 1845–1850), 3:1243–1245.

24. Cranmer, *Miscellaneous Writings,* 168–169; T. Cooper, *An Answer in Defense of the Truth Against the Apology of Private Mass* (1562), ed. W. Goode for the Parker So-

ciety (Cambridge: University Press, 1850), 171; *Remains of Myles Coverdale,* ed. George Pearson for the Parker Society (Cambridge: University Press, 1846), 483–485; William Fulke, *A Defence of the Sincere and True Translations of the Holy Scriptures into the English Tongue,* ed. C.H. Hartshorne for the Parker Society (Cambridge: University Press, 1843), 71–72, 115–117, 471–491; id., *Stapleton's Fortress Overthrown,* ed. R. Gibbings for the Parker Society (Cambridge: University Press, 1848), 93–104; Jewell, *Works,* 2:727–728, 882–883, 989, 1128–29, 3:390–411, 805–810; Nicholas Ridley, *The Works of Nicholas Ridley,* ed. H. Christmas for the Parker Society (Cambridge: University Press, 1843), 302–305; William Tyndale, *An Answer to Sir Thomas More's Dialogue,* ed. H. Walter for the Parker Society (Cambridge: University Press, 1850), 29, 52–53, 151–160. See also John Ponet, *A Defence for Mariage of Priestes* (London: 1549) and its rejoinder by Thomas Martin, *Traictise Declarying and Plainly Provyng That the Pretensed Mariage of Priestes and Professed Persones is no Marriage* (London: 1554).

25. Hooper, *Early Writings,* 378–387.
26. Jewell, *Works,* 3:390–392. For later Anglican views, see Greaves, *Society and Religion,* 191–201.
27. Even in his *Booke of Matrimonie,* folio DCxlix.b, prepared after the Thirty-Nine Articles, Becon wrote of marriage as the man and woman "coupled in most hie love, in permixtion of bodies, in the confederate bond of the sacrament, and finally in the felowship of all chaunces."
28. See, e.g., Tyndale, *Doctrinal Treatises,* 1:254; Cranmer, *Miscellaneous Writings,* 115–116; Jewell, *Works,* 2:1125. Two decades later, this position was taken in the Thirty-Nine Articles, inspiring a torrent of homilies and commentaries on the subject. See, e.g., Thomas Rogers, *The Catholic Doctrine of the Church of England: An Exposition of the Thirty-Nine Articles,* ed. J.J.S. Perowne for the Parker Society (Cambridge: University Press, 1844), 260ff. See summary in Carlson, *Marriage and the English Reformation,* 37–45.
29. Thomas Becon, Preface to [Heinrich Bullinger,] *The Golde Boke of Christen Matrimonie* (1542) (STC 1723), folios A.ii.b., Aiii. For other Tudor Anglican views on the relative merits of marriage and celibacy, see Greaves, *Society and Religion,* 119–130; Carlson, *Marriage and the English Reformation,*49–66.
30. Becon, *Booke of Matrimonie,* folio DCxvi.
31. Ibid., folio DCxvi.b.
32. But cf. ibid., folio Dcxi, where he writes: "Who knoweth not, that the principall ende, for which God instituted Matrimony, is to be frutefull, & to avoyde fornication." This off-hand comment was corrected by a later section of more than thirty folio pages devoted to exposition of all three causes of marriage.
33. Ibid., folios DCxlviii–xlix.
34. See long discussions of marital love in ibid., folios DCxxvi, DCxlvi.b–xlviii, DCl, DClxvi–DClxvi.b.
35. Ibid., folios DCl.b–li.
36. Ibid., folio DCliv.b.
37. Becon, *Early Works,* 1:272. Cf. ibid., 371 (on marital faithfulness). Becon did offer a more substantial digest of domestical duties grounded in the familiar passages of Paul and Peter. His four hundred-page *A New Catechism* (1560) devotes some thirty pages to the exposition of household duties—"Husbands Toward Their Wives," "Wives Toward Their Husbands," "Fathers and Mothers Toward Their Children," "Children Toward Their Parents," "Masters or Householders Toward Their Servants"—followed by sections on the offices and duties of widows, unmarried young men, maids and young unmarried women. Becon, *Early Works,*

2:344–377, with summary in ibid., 3:130–135. He summarizes this section on duties in his *Booke of Matrimonie*, DClxiiii–lxxviii. But this contribution was largely derivative and duplicative of Tyndale's and Bullinger's work, discussed below.

38. Becon, *Booke of Matrimonie*, folios DClxxiiii.b, DClxiiii–DClxxviii.

39. For later Anglican formulations, see Greaves, *Society and Religion*, 204–213, 228–236.

40. Becon, *Early Works*, 2:104, 97.

41. Ibid., 2:99.

42. Ibid., 3:5–6; "A Homily of Whoredome and Unclennesse," in *Certayne Sermons, or Homilies, Appointed by the Kynges Maiestie* (London: Richard Grafton, 1547), c.i–e.iii (STC 13639); Preface to Bullinger's *The Golde Boke*, folios A.iiii.b–B.vi.b. For Becon's related jeremiads against clerical abuses, sumptuousness, and economic exploitation, see Bailey, *Thomas Becon*, 58–67.

43. Becon, *Booke of Matrimonie*, folios DCxlii–DClxxxii provides a long discussion of Catholic and Continental Protestant views, quoting at length from several Church Fathers and Councils, and then Erasmus, Luther, Bucer, Melanchthon, Calvin, Bullinger, Brenz, and others.

44. Heinrich Bullinger, *Der christlich Eestand* (Zurich, 1540), translated as *The Christen State of Matrimonye* (London, 1541) (STC 4045), by Myles Coverdale, one of the early translators of the Bible into English, and as *The Golde Boke of Christen Matrimonye* (London, 1542) (STC 1723) under Thomas Becon's pseudonym, Theodore Basille.

45. Martin Bucer, *De Regno Christi* (1550), in *Martini Buceri Opera Latini*, ed. François Wendel (Paris, 1955), vol. 25, with partial English translation in *Melanchthon and Bucer*, ed. Wilhelm Pauck (Philadelphia: Westminster Press, 1969), 155, 315–333 (bk. 2, chaps. 16–21, 47 on marriage); and in *The Judgement of Martin Bucer Concerning Divorce* (1644), in *The Complete Prose Works of John Milton* (New Haven: Yale University Press, 1959), 2:416–479 (bk. 2, chaps. 15–47 with some omissions).

46. Bullinger, *The Golde Boke*, folio v.

47. Ibid., folios i.b–ii, iii.

48. Ibid., folios xxi.b, xxiii, xxxvi.b, lxxvii.b–lxxviii. The chapter commending clerical marriage (and criticizing mandatory celibacy and chastity, with typical Protestant arguments) is included only in the 1541 edition at 27.b–31.

49. Ibid., folios bv–v.b.

50. Ibid., folios xix, xxi.b.

51. See, e.g., *The Decades of Henry Bullinger: The First and Second Decades*, ed. Thomas Harding for the Parker Society (Cambridge: University Press, 1849), Second Decade, Tenth Sermon, 397–398: "the first cause why matrimony was instituted is man's commodity, that thereby the life of man might be the pleasanter and more commodious."

52. Bullinger, *The Golde Boke*, folios iii.b–iiii. Bullinger returns to these themes of marital love in folios xxii–xxiiii, xxxvi.b–xxxviii. Contemporaneous Tudor divines sometimes offered similar sentiments on the purposes of marriage, with an emphasis on marital affection, love, and companionship. See, e.g., Sandys, *Sermons*, 315–316: "Marriage is honourable in respect of the causes for which it was ordained. . . . The first is mutual society, help, and comfort. And this were a cause sufficient to esteem of marriage if there were no other. . . . The second cause . . . is increase and propagation. . . . Another cause . . . is a remedy against uncleanness." Sandys then went on to expound "the duties of love" couples owe to each other. Ibid., 316–324, 329. See also Edmund Tilney, *A Brief and Pleasant Discourse*

of Duties in Marriage, Called the Flower of Friendshippe (London, 1571), folios
Biiibv–Biiic, Biiia (calling marriage a "true, and perfect love").

53. Bullinger, *The Golde Booke,* folios vi, vii.

54. Ibid., folios vi–vi.b, xv–xviii. Elsewhere he writes: "[T]he holy Scripture diligently
teacheth all men to have a special care, that they contract matrimony devoutly, ho-
lily, soberly, wisely, lawfully, and in the fear of God; and that no evil disposition
or covetousness, desire of promotion, or fleshly lust, may lead and provoke them;
and that wedlock be not entered into otherwise than either the laws of man or of
God permit." *The Decades of Henry Bullinger: The Fifth Decade,* ed. Thomas Harding for the Parker Society (Cambridge: University Press, 1852), Tenth Sermon,
510.

55. Bullinger, *The Golde Boke,* folios vii–x. Bullinger includes among prerequisites:
"faith, Gods glorye, gods seruyce, understandynge or knoledge, prudence, truth,
sobernesse, righteousness, lyberalyte, chastite, humblenesse, honestye, and nour-
tour, synglenesse and dilgence, and such lyke vertues." Ibid., folio xlii–xliii.b.

56. This chapter was dropped from the 1542 edition, but included in the 1541 edition, 12–20.

57. Ibid., folios x–xv.

58. Ibid., folio xlvi.b. See generally folios xlvi–l.b.

59. Ibid., folio l.b.

60. Ibid., folio l.b.

61. Quotes from ibid., folios liii, lv.b.

62. Ibid., folios liii–lv, lxii–lxiii.b.

63. Ibid., folios lv–lvi.

64. Ibid., folios lxv.b–lxvii.

65. William Gouge, *Of Domesticall Duties: Eight Treatises* (London: John Haviland, c.
1622) (STC 12119).

66. See, e.g., Becon, *Early Works,* 2:344–377 and 3:130–135. For earlier prototypes—
from John Wycliff's *Of Weddid Men and Wifis and of Here Children also,* in the later
fourteenth century, to the section in Tyndale, *Doctrinal Treatises,* 168–200—see
Powell, *English Domestic Relations,* 101–114. For later forms, see ibid., 129–146
and James T. Johnson, *A Society Ordained by God: English Puritan Marriage Doctrine
in the First Half of the Seventeenth Century* (Nashville: Abingdon Press, 1970). Powell says that Bullinger's book "is by far the most important both for its content and
its influence." Ibid., 114. See also George Hunston Williams, *The Radical Reformation,* 3d ed. (Kirksville, Mo.: Sixteenth Century Essays & Studies, 1992), 773,
arguing that Bullinger's tract "stablized Reformed ideas of husbands and wives and
household management."

67. Bullinger, *The Golde Boke,* folios xxiiii–xxxvi.b.

68. 1541 ed., folio lxxvi.b.

69. Bullinger, *The Golde Boke,* folio lxxvii.b.

70. See editor's notes in Bullinger, *The Fifth Decade,* xviii–xix. 31 Henry VIII c. 14
(1539), prescribed, inter alia, maintenance of clerical celibacy and vows of
chastity. This was repealed by 1 Edward VI c. 12 (1547), as well as subsequent
legislation mandating the Thirty-Nine Articles.

71. Becon, *Early Works,* 1:29.

72. The work is summarized in Bullinger, *The Second Decade,* 393–435. In the 1586
Convocation, Archbishop Whitgift directed the lower clergy to study Bullinger's
Decades as part of their theological training. Alec R. Vidler, *Christ's Strange Work:
An Exposition of the Three Uses of God's Law,* rev. ed. (London: SCM Press, 1963),
34.

73. Becon, Preface to *The Golde Boke,* folio Aiiii.b.

74. See also Becon, *Booke of Matrimonie,* folio DCxlix: "For being that a city standeth of houses, and the common weal of private things, and of ruling of a household and family, the discipline to govern a common weal is ordained: how shall he rule a citye that hath not learned to rule a house: how shall he govern a common weal that never knew his private and familier businesse . . . For truly matrimony geveth a great exercise to morall Philosophe. For it hathe a certain householde common weale annexed, in rulinge that whyche a manne may sone learne and have experience of wisdom, temperaunce, love to god and his kinne, and al other vertues." Ibid., folios CCCClxcvii–CCCClxcvix: "The order of wedlocke . . . maketh kyngdomes populous greate. . . . [It] bringeth forthe children, sonnes and daughters, to the common weale . . . whiche at all times are not only ready to do good to the common weale but also to dy for the conservation of the same. . . . [T]hey refuse no labour, no payne, to shewe their obedience towarde their Superiors, . . . to do good to all men, . . . to do God's good will & pleasure, in labouring, in calling upon God, in thanking God for his benefites, in mortifieng the fylthy lustes of the fleshe, in wearing suche apparell, as becometh godlynes, in relieving the poore and the needye, in visiting the sicke, in dyeng unto synne and lyving unto righteousnes."

75. See C.H. Smith, *Cranmer and the Reformation Under Edward VI* (Cambridge: University Press, 1926), 155–177. Bucer was especially influential on Archbishop Whitgift of Canterbury in his disquisitions over marriage questions with Cartwright. See, e.g., The *Works of John Whitgift,* ed. J. Ayre for the Parker Society (Cambridge: University Press, 1852), 3:353–359. For Bucer's influence in England more generally, see Wilhelm Pauck, *Das Reich Gottes auf Erden. Utopie und Wirklichkeit. Eine Untersuchung zu Butzers De Regno Christi und der englischen Staatskirche des 16. Jahrhunderts* (Berlin: Dunker & Humblot, 1928); Constantin Hopf, *Martin Bucer and the English Reformation* (Oxford: Basil Blackwell, 1946).

76. Bucer, *De Regno Christi,* bk. 2, chaps. 15–16.

77. Ibid., bk. 2, chaps. 18, 19, 26, 38.

78. Ibid., bk. 2, chap. 38.

79. Ibid., bk. 1, chaps. 2, 5; bk. 2, chaps. 15, 21, 28, 47.

80. Ibid., bk. 2, chaps. 38, 39.

81. Ibid., bk. 2, chap. 26.

82. Ibid., bk. 2, chap. 40. On the earlier Roman law of divorce, see Susan Treggiari, *Roman Marriage: Iusti Coniuges from the Time of Cicero to the Time of Ulpian* (Oxford: Clarendon Press, 1991), 435–482.

83. Bucer, *De Regno Christi,* bk. 2, chap. 37, with fuller exposition in chaps. 40–44.

84. Ibid., bk. 1, chaps. 8–9; bk. 2, chaps. 1–2.

85. Ibid., bk. 2, chaps. 1, 15.

86. Ibid., bk. 2, chap. 40.

87. Ibid., bk. 2, chap. 47.

88. See Johnson, *A Society Ordained by God,* 51–120 (on Puritan views); Lawrence Stone, *The Family, Sex, and Marriage in England, 1500–1800* (New York: Harper & Row, 1979), 217–253 (on affective individualism). For a comparable emphasis in Calvin's writings of the mid-sixteenth century, see chapter 3, above. For medieval Catholic prototypes, see John T. Noonan, Jr., "Marital Affection in the Canonists," *Studia Gratiana* 12 (1967):489.

89. See Johnson, *A Society Ordained by God;* William and Malleville Haller, "The Puritan Art of Love," *Huntington Library Quarterly* 5 (1941–1942):235–272; Edmund Leites, *The Puritan Conscience and Modern Sexuality* (New Haven: Yale University Press, 1986).

90. 24 Henry VIII, c. 12. See also 25 Henry VIII c. 19.
91. 26 Henry VIII, c. 1.
92. 25 Henry VIII, c. 19; 27 Henry VIII, c. 15; 35 Henry VIII, c. 16.
93. 32 Henry VIII, c. 38 (repealing 25 Henry VIII c. 22 and 28 Henry VIII, c. 7); 1 Eliz. c. 1 s. 3. Archbishop Parker issued a table of forbidden degrees in 1563, which was adopted by the 99th Canon of 1604. See also the summary of accepted impediments in *The King's Book, or A Necessary Doctrine and Erudition for Any Man,* 1543 (London: S.P.C.K., 1932), 58–59.
94. Ibid., c. 22.
95. 32 Henry VIII c. 38, repealed by 2 & 3 Edward VI, c. 3, and 1 & 2 Mary c. 8 (both of which allowed for full enforcement of precontract impediments), partly revived by 1 Eliz. c. 1 s. 12 (which was read to allow consideration of precontract impediments only if the present couple had no children).
96. Howard, *Matrimonial Institutions,* 1:360–363 (quoting a 1538 injunction of Thomas Cromwell, repeated in 1547 by Edward VI).
97. 32 Henry VIII, c. 10, 19; 2 & 3 Edward VI, c. 21. See also 1 Edward VI, c. 12, repealing 35 Henry VIII, c. 5 (the statute calling for enforcement against clergy of the Six Articles of Religion, 31 Henry VIII, c. 14, which included a prohibition against the preaching or practice of clerical marriage).
98. 25 Henry VIII, c. 21.
99. See 25 Henry VIII, c. 6; 2 & 3 Edward VI, c. 29; 5 Eliz. c. 17.
100. 3 & 4 Edward VI, c. 10; 5 & 6 Edward VI, c. 1, repealed by 1 Mary 2 c. 2.
101. 1 Eliz. c. 1.
102. "Form of Solemnization of Matrimony," in *The Book of Common Prayer 1559,* ed. John E. Booty (Charlottesville: University of Virginia Press, 1976), 290–291.
103. Promulgated by the Synod of Westminster (1200) for England and the Fourth Lateran Council (1215) for the Church universal, with subsequent canons providing that if any clergyman celebrated a marriage without banns or license he would be suspended for a year. One could also get a dispensation from the Bishop, permitting the marriage to take place without publication of banns. This license, authorized already in the fourteenth century, was confirmed by 25 Henry VIII, c. 21.
104. 32 Henry VIII, c. 38 (repealing 25 Henry VIII c. 22 and 28 Henry VIII, c. 7), and 1 Eliz., c. 1, s. 3. Archbishop Parker issued a table of forbidden degrees in 1563, which was adopted by the 99th Canon of 1603.
105. 1 Eliz. c. 2.
106. See Richard Burn, *Ecclesiastical Law,* 6th ed. (London: A. Stahan, 1797), 3:232–274; Ronald A. Marchant, *The Puritans and the Church Courts in the Diocese of York* (London: Longmans, 1960), 1–25. See acts against Catholic and sectarian dissenters in 13 Eliz. c. 2; 27 Eliz. c. 2: 35 Eliz. c. 1, 2.
107. *The Thirty-Nine Articles of Religion of the Church of England, Published A.D. 1571,* Art. XXIII, in Philip Schaff, *The Creeds of Christendom* (New York: Harper and Brothers, 1877), 3:486, 502–503, following *Articles agreed on by the Bishoppes, and other learned menne in the Synod at London . . . M.D.LII.,* Art. 31, in Edward Cardwell, ed., *Synodalia: A Collection of Articles of Religion, Canons, and Proceedings of Convocations in the Province of Canterbury* (Oxford: University Press, 1842), 1:18, 29–30.
108. 1571 Articles, Art. XXV, following the language of the 1562 *Articles* in Cardwell, ed., *Synodalia,* 1:66. This doctrinal innovation was very recent. A statement of Convocation in 1557 (Cardwell, ed., *Synodalia,* 2:448, 452) had unequivocally confirmed "the seven sacraments of the church." *The King's Book,* 57–65, in 1543 defended the sacrament of matrimony at some length. (For earlier English texts from 1530 onward that denied or deprecated the sacramental quality of marriage, see Carlson, *Marriage and the English Reformation.*)

109. 1571 Articles, Art. XXV.

110. See Praefatio of John Foxe to the 1571 Reformation, in Edward Cardwell, ed., *The Reformation of the Ecclesiastical Laws* (Oxford: University Press, 1850), vii–viii, xxx, with a listing of Commission members in James C. Spalding, ed., *The Reformation of the Ecclesiastical Laws of England, 1552* (Kirksville, Mo: Sixteenth Century Essays & Studies, 1992), 37–38. For the Commission's empowering legislation, see 25 Henry VIII, c. 19; 27 Henry VIII, c. 15; 35 Henry VIII, c. 16.

111. Reprinted and translated in Spalding, ed., *1552 Reformation,* with relevant provisions "Concerning Marriage," "Concerning Degrees Prohibited in Marriage," "Concerning Adultery and Divorce," in ibid., 87–106. See also Cardwell, ed., *1571 Reformation,* 39–58, with identical provisions on marriage, impediments, and divorce.

112. Spalding, ed., *1552 Reformation,,* "Concerning Matrimony," chap. 1. A later article, "Concerning Sacraments," recognizes only Eucharist and Baptism.

113. Ibid., "Concerning Marriage," chap. 9. See also "Concerning Adultery and Divorce," chaps. 2, 4 (regarding adultery by married clergy); "Concerning the Church, and the Ministers and Their Duties," chaps. 4–6, 13 (referring to wives and families of clergy).

114. Ibid., chaps. 2, 4–5. See also "On Sacraments," chap. 7 (on "solemn rites of marriage before the eyes of the whole church with the greatest gravity and fidelity").

115. Ibid., "Concerning Matrimony," chap. 7.

116. Ibid., "Concerning Adultery and Divorce," chap. 14.

117. Ibid., "On Crimes."

118. A.G. Dickens, *The English Reformation* (New York: Schocken Books, 1964), 244–254; Ralph Houlbrooke, *Church Courts and the People During the English Reformation 1520–1570* (Oxford: Oxford University Press, 1979), 16–19.

119. This was confirmed by Acts and Proceedings of Convocation (1604), Canon 99, 102, in Cardwell, ed., *Synodalia,* 1:245, 304–305.

120. R.H. Helmholz, *Roman Canon Law in Reformation England* (Cambridge: Cambridge University Press, 1990), 69–79; id., "Canon Law in Post-Reformation England," in id., ed., *Canon Law in Protestant Lands* (Berlin: Duncker & Humblot, 1992), 203, 213–214; Houlbrooke, *Church Courts,* 18–19.

121. As Zurich reformer Perceval Wiburn reported glumly from England in circa 1571: "The greater part of the Canon law is still in force there, and all ecclesiastical censures are principally taken from it." *The Zurich Letters,* ed. H. Robinson for the Parker Society (Cambridge: University Press, 1842), 359.

122. See generally J. Hurstfield, *The Queen's Wards: Wardship and Marriage Under Elizabeth I* (Cambridge: Cambridge University Press, 1958).

123. William Harrington, *In this boke are conteyned the comendacions of matrimonye/the manner & fourme of contractyng solempnysynge and lyvyng in the same etc.* (London, 1528), a tract written circa 1513, provides a good summary of canon law impediments on the eve of the Tudor Reformation. For the law at the end of the Tudor Reformation, see Henry Swinburne, *A Treatise of Spousals or Matrimonial Contracts* (written circa 1591) (London: S. Roycroft, 1686), 45–108; *The Lavves Resolutions of Womens Rights, or, The Lavves Provision for Women* (London: Assigns of John More, Esq., 1632), 51–115; *Baron and Feme. A Treatise of the Common Law Concerning Husbands and Wives* (London: Assigns of Richard and Edward Atkyns, Esq., 1700), 28–50.

124. See 1597 Constitutions and Canons Ecclesiastical in Cardwell, ed., *Synodalia,* 1:152–155, 161–163, with discussion in John Godolphin, *Repertorium Canonicum,* 3d ed. (London: Assigns of R. & E. Atkins, 1687). On the medieval en-

forcement of these impediments, see R.H. Helmholz, *Marriage Litigation in Medieval England* (Cambridge: Cambridge University Press, 1974), 74–100.

125. Sir Edward Coke, *The First Part of the Institutes of the Lawes of England* (London, 1628), folios 32, 33v, 235; id., *The Third Part of the Institutes of the Lawes of England* (London, 1644), 93. See also discussion in Martin Ingram, *Church Courts, Sex and Marriage in England, 1570–1640* (Cambridge: Cambridge University Press, 1987), 145.

126. Burn, *Ecclesiastical Law*, 1:118–135.

127. 1 James c. 11.

128. See a contemporary critique in W[illiam] H[eale], *An Apologie for Women, or Opposition to Mr. Dr. G. his Assertion . . . That it was Lawful for Husbands to Beate Their Wives* (Oxford: Joseph Barnes, 1609), and discussion in J.M. Biggs, *The Concept of Matrimonial Cruelty* (London: University of London Press, 1962).

129. Some of these were anticipated in two canons: "De moderandis indulgentiis pro celebratione matrimonii absque trina bannorum denunciatione" and "De sententiis divortii non temere ferendis," in Cardwell, ed., *Synodalia*, 1:147, 152–155.

130. Quoted by Ingram, *Church Courts*, 135.

131. Canons 100, 101, in Cardwell, ed., *Synodalia*, 1:305. The age of consent for marriage was twelve for girls, fourteen for boys. Swinburne, *A Treatise of Spousals*, 45–54.

132. See Acts and Proceedings of Convocation (1604), item VI, in Cardwell, ed., *Synodalia*, 2:580, 583 (only chancellors granted licenses for marriage). This was a different use of the marriage license than encountered in chapter 3, on Calvinism. In Geneva, and later Protestant polities, all betrothed parties had to procure a license from the magistrate and deliver it to the church to trigger publication of the banns. Procurement of the license was a prerequisite to any legitimate marriage, not an alternative to ecclesiastical marriage.

133. Canons 101, 103. Per Canon 104, no parental consent was required for the marriage of an emancipated widow or widower.

134. See "Constitutions and Canons Ecclesiastical (1640)," Canon 16, in Cardwell, ed., *Synodalia*, 1:380, 412 (requiring that licenses be issued only by an authorized official from the region in which one of the parties has been resident for at least a month); "Representation from the Lower House of Convocation to the House of Bishops (1702)," in ibid., 2:707, 711–712 (complaining of frequent abuses of granting licenses and solemnizing marriages without parental consent; spurious distribution of licenses by surrogate clergy; and failures to celebrate marriages in church); "Acts and Proceedings of Convocation (1710)," in ibid., 2:724, 731 (calling for closer restrictions of licensed marriages); "Proposals of the Lower House of Convocation About Matrimonial Licenses (1712)," ibid., 2:770; "Draught of canons for regulating matrimonial licenses, in order to the more effectual preventing of clandestine marriages," in ibid., 2:794 (attempted systematic revision and expansion of the 1604 Canons).

135. For a picture of this practice by a later jurist, see Henry John Stephen, *New Commentaries on the Laws of England* (London: Henry Butterworth, 1842), 2:286–287.

136. 26 Geo. II, c. 33. See Lawrence Stone, *Road to Divorce; A History of the Making and Breaking of Marriage in England* (New York and Oxford: Oxford University Press, 1995), 96–1, 37.

137. Cardwell, ed. *Synodalia*, 2:579–580. See also 1597 Constitutions and Canons Ecclesiastical, in ibid., 1:152–155, 161–163.

138. Canons 105–106.

139. Canon 107.

140. Canon 108.
141. 1 James c. 11. In cases of unaccountable desertion for more than seven years, a party could remarry with immunity from the statute, on the presumption that the ex-spouse had died. Godolphin, *Repertorium Canonicum,* 507–508.
142. Ibid., 494–498, 504–507. On the celebrated divorce cases of the Marquess of Northampton (1552) and Sir John Stawell (1572), which had granted the plaintiff rights of remarriage, see Sir Lewis Dibden and Sir Charles Chadwick Healey, *English Church Law and Divorce* (London: J. Murray, 1912), 62–69, 83–92. Just before promulgation of the 1604 Canons, Star Chamber had held that, at English law, divorce even for adultery entails only separation from bed and board alone. *Rye v. Fuljambe* (1602), in Edmund Gibson, *Codex Iuris Ecclesiastici Anglicani,* 2 vols., 2d ed. (London: J. Baskett, 1713), 1:466.
143. See summary in William Blackstone, *Commentaries on the Law of England* (Oxford: Clarendon Press, 1765–1769), 1:430, and discussion in Marylynn Salmon, *Women and the Law of Property in Early America* (Chapel Hill and London: University of North Carolina Press, 1986), 14–57.
144. *Baron and Feme,* 89–90, 336–344. See modern discussion and sources in Susan Staves, *Married Women's Separate Property in England, 1660–1833* (Cambridge, Mass.: Harvard University Press, 1990).
145. Helmholz, *Roman Canon Law,* 77.
146. Ibid., 77–79; Godolphin, *Repertorium,* 508–513.
147. Ibid.
148. Helmholz, *Roman Canon Law,* 79.
149. Ibid., 69–70. For studies, see ibid., 70–79; Ingram, *Church Courts;* Ronald A. Marchant, *The Church Under the Law: Justice, Administration, and Discipline in the Diocese of York 1560–1640* (Cambridge, England: Cambridge University Press, 1969), passim; Carlson, *Marriage and the English Reformation,* 105–180. A compilation of some relevant statutes and cases is also provided in Burn, *Ecclesiastical Law,* 2:433–512; Godolphin, *Repertorium Canonicum,* 492–513.
150. Ingram, *Church Courts,* 367.
151. See, e.g., Richard Hooker, *Laws of Ecclesiastical Polity,* bk. 5, chap. 73.1 ("single life be a thing more angelical and divine," but marriage was needed to increase citizens and saints) in *The Work of Mr. Richard Hooker in Eight Books of the Laws of Ecclesiastical Polity with Several Other Treatises,* 3 vols., ed. Isaac Walton (London: W. Clark, 1821); George Herbert, *The Works,* ed. F.E. Hutchinson (Oxford: Oxford University Press, 1941), 236–237; John Cosin, *The Works,* ed. J. Sansom (Oxford: Oxford University Press, 1843–1845), 1:48, 56.
152. For a listing of procreation, deterrence, and mutual society and love, see, e.g., Perkins, *Christian Oeconomy,* 419–420; William Ames, *The Marrow of Theology,* 3d ed. (1629), John D. Eusden, trans. and ed. (Boston: Pilgrim Press, 1968), 319–320, items 39, 42–43; William Gouge, *Of Domesticall Duties: Eight Treatises,* 2d ed. (London: John Beale, 1626), bk. I, 122–123 (same). For a listing that begins with marital love, see, e.g., Thomas Gataker, *A Good Wife, God's Gift* (London: John Haviland, 1623), 9–13, 27–40 and discussion of Milton below. See Johnson, *A Society Ordained by God,* 51–119. Johnson, in my view, makes too much of the novelty and priority of seventeenth-century Puritan discussions of marital love. The theme of marital love was already emphasized by sixteenth-century divines such as Becon, Bullinger, and Bucer, and indeed by Continental Protestants and Catholics before them.
153. See Swinburne, *Treatise of Spousals;* Matthew Griffith, *Bethel; or A Forme for Families* (London: J. Days, 1633).
154. See, e.g., Hooker, *Laws,* bk. 5, chap. 73 (describing the controversy and defend-

ing the Anglican position); William Bradshaw, *A Marriage Feast: A Sermon on the Former Part of the Second Chapter of the Evangelist* (London: Edward Griffin, 1620) (defending church celebration and wedding feasts as the modern equivalent of the marriage feast of Cana where Christ performed his first miracle).

155. See, e.g., Lancelot Andrewes, *Against Second Marriage After Sentence of Divorce with a Former Match, the Party Then Living* (c. 1610), reprinted in James Bliss, ed., *Library of Anglo-Catholic Theology* (Oxford: J.H. Parker, 1854), 106–110, and discussion of other writers in D.S. Bailey, *Sexual Relations in Christian Thought* (New York: Harper & Bros., 1959), 215–231; A.R. Winnett, *Divorce and Remarriage in Anglicanism* (New York: St. Martin's Press, 1958), 60–78.

156. See summary in *The King's Book*, 64–65.

157. For Anglican critique, see John Cosin, *Argument Proving that Adultery Works a Dissolution of the Marriage* (c. 1670), reprinted in J. Sansom, ed., *Works: Library of Anglo-Catholic Theology* (Oxford: [s.n.], 1843), 4:489ff. For Anglo-Puritan critique, see John Rainolds, *A Defence of the Judgement of the Reformed Churches. That a man may lawfullie not onlie put awaie his wife for her adulterie, but also marrie another* (n.p. 1609) (STC 20607). See discussion in Bailey, *Sexual Relations*, 215ff.; Winnett, *Divorce and Remarriage*, 79–117.

158. Edmund Bunny, *Of Divorce for Advlterie, and Marrying Againe: That There is no Sufficient Warrant so to do* (Oxford: Joseph Barnes, 1610).

159. Andrewes, *Against Second Marriage*, 108–109.

160. See Mary L. Shanley, "Marriage Contract and Social Contract in Seventeenth Century English Political Thought," *Western Political Quarterly* 32 (1979):79–91; Susan Dwyer Amussen, *An Ordered Society. Gender and Class in Early Modern England* (Oxford: Basil Blackwell, 1988), 34–66, 134–179.

161. Becon, *Booke of Matrimonie*, folio DCxlix.

162. Perkins, *Works*, 3:418–419. See paraphrase in Robert Pricke, *The Doctrine of Superioritie, and of Subjection, contained in the Fifth Commandment of the Holy Law of Almightie God* (London: Ephraim Dawson & T. Downe, 1609), A8–9.

163. Cleaver, *A Godly Form of Householde Gouernment*, 1. Cleaver's book was reprinted at least eight times by 1630 and reprinted several times again in the eighteenth century. Haller and Haller, "The Puritan Art of Love," 241n.

164. William Gouge, *Of Domesticall Duties: Eight Treatises* (London: John Haviland, 1622), 17, 27, Epistle, sig. 2v.

165. Daniel Rogers, *Matrimoniall Honour* (London: Philip Nevil, 1642), 17.

166. Amussen, *An Ordered Society*, 38.

167. Dudley Fenner, *Sacra theologica, sive veritas quae est secundum pietatem* (London: T. Dawson, c. 1585), bks. 4–8 (on the divine, political, ecclesiastical, and familial covenant commonwealths). See also id., *The Artes of Logike and Rhetorike . . . Together with Examples of the same for Methode, in the gouernment of the Familie* (Middleburg: R. Shiders, 1584), folio A (on the parallel internal duties and structures of "the familie, Church, or commonwealth"), folios B–C (discussing "the common state of the familie" that serves "to further the peace and tranquillitie of the commonwealth but also of Religion and true holyness"). See more generally E.M.W. Tillyard, *The Elizabethan World Picture* (New York: Vintage Books, 1944) on the theories of the hierarchical natural, social, political, and domestic order in early modern English literature.

168. Pricke, *The Doctrine of Superioritie;* the quote is the subtitle of the book. See also Cosin, *Works*, 1:48, 56 ("marriage is an honorable estate in all men, a state ordained by God himself in paradise, a state without which there can be no society in this world durable"); Gataker, *A Good Wife*, 27 ("[T]he Societie of Man and Wife [is] the main Root, Source, and Originall of all other Societies").

169. John Dod and Robert Cleaver, *A Plaine and Familiar Exposition of the Ten Commandments, with a methodicall short Catechisme, Containing Briefly all the Principall Grounds of Christian Religion* (London: Thomas Man, 1604), 181 (STC 6968).

170. Cleaver, *Householde Gouernment*, 6–7.

171. Ibid., 92, 114, 159ff., 202ff.; Dod and Cleaver, *Plaine and Familiar Exposition*, 24, 226–228.

172. Cleaver, *Householde Gouernment*, 9–42.

173. Ibid., 52–91, 203–222; Dod and Cleaver, *Plaine and Familiar Exposition*, 221–222.

174. Cleaver, *Householde Gouernment*, 188–191, 243ff.; Dod and Cleaver, *Plaine and Familiar Exposition*, 174–222.

175. Ibid., 186.

176. Cleaver, *Householde Gouernment*, 174–175.

177. Ibid., Preface, A4.

178. Ibid., 4–5.

179. Gouge, *Of Domesticall Duties* (1622), 17, 27.

180. Richard Baxter, *A Christian Directory* (1673), quoted by Shanley, "Marriage Contract," 79.

181. Pricke, *The Doctrine of Superioritie*, B2.

182. Rogers, *Matrimoniall Honour*, 17.

183. Robert Filmer, *Patriarcha and other Political Works*, ed. Peter Laslett (Oxford: Oxford University Press, 1949). See similar formulations in John Wing, *The Crovvn Conjugall; or, The Spouse Royall* (London: John Beale for R. Mylbourne, 1632) (STC 25845); Dudley Digges, *The Unlawfulnesse of Subjects taking up Armes Against their Soveraigne* (s.l., s.n., 1644); William Lawrence, *Marriage by the Morall Law of God Vindicated [and] The Right of Primogeniture in Succession to the Kingdoms of England and Scotland* (London, 1681). See James Daly, *Sir Robert Filmer and English Political Thought* (Toronto: University of Toronto Press, 1979); G.J. Schochet, *Patriarchalism in Political Thought: The Authoritarian Family and Political Speculation and Attitudes Especially in Seventeenth Century England* (New York: Basic Books, 1975).

184. Filmer, *Patriarcha*, chaps. I, VII. See also id., *Observations upon Aristotles Politiques Touching Forms of Government Together with Directions for Obedience to Governours in Dangerous and Doubtfull Times*, in Laslett, ed., *Patriarcha and Other Works*, 185, 188 ("Adam was Father, King, and Lord over his Family").

185. Sir Robert Filmer, *Directions for Obedience to Government in Dangerous or Doubtful Times*, in ibid., 231, 232.

186. Filmer, *Patriarcha*, chap. V.

187. Ibid., chap. VII.

188. Ibid., chap. VI.

189. Gataker, *A Good Wife*, 27, listing the "purposes of marriage" as "societie," "assistance," "comfort and solace," "issue," and "remedie against incontinence." Ibid., 31–38. See also Thomas Gataker, *A Good Wife: God's Gift: and A Wife Indeed. Two Marriage Sermons* (London: John Haviland, 1623), 5 (STC 11659): "Husband and wife are neerer than Friends. . . ingrafted into the other, and so fastened together, they cannot again be sundered."

190. Rogers, *Matrimoniall Honour*, 146, 150, 157, 184.

191. Jeremy Taylor, *The Measures and Offices of Friendship*, 3d ed. (London: R. Royston, 1662), 79.

192. Gouge, *Of Domesticall Duties*, 356.

193. William Whately, *A Bride-Bush, or A Wedding Sermon: Compendiously Describing the Duties of Married Persons: By Performing Whereof, Marriage shall be to them a Great*

Help, Which Now Finde it a Little Hell (London: William Jaagard for Nicholas Bourne, 1617) (STC 25296). See also Ingram, *Church Courts,* 144–145.

194. See Haller and Haller, "The Puritan Art of Love"; Johnson, *A Society Ordained by God;* Leites, *Puritan Conscience,* 75–104.

195. *The King's Book,* 57, 63.

196. See Powell, *English Domestic Relations,* 179–206; Kathleen M. Davies, "Continuity and Change in Literary Advice on Marriage," in R.B. Outhwaite, ed., *Marriage and Society: Studies in the Social History of Family* (New York: St. Martin's Press, 1981), 58–80.

197. See illustrative sermons in *Sermons or Homilies Appointed to be Read in the Churches in the Time of Queen Elizabeth* (Liverpool, 1799), with discussion in Ingram, *Church Courts,* 142–145.

198. See the treatment of marital love in Calvin in chapter 3 above, and in the Catholic tradition in chapter 1 above.

199. W[illiam] H[eale], *An Apologie for Women, or Opposition to Mr. Dr. G. his Assertion . . . That it was Lawful for Husbands to Beate their Wives,* 2d ed. (Oxford: Joseph Barnes, 1614), 105.

200. See esp. Cleaver, *Householde Gouernment,* 111–138; Swinburne, *Treatise on Spousals,* 11–14, 222–240.

201. See, e.g., Cleaver, *Householde Gouernment,* 154: "if they be wel and vertuously brought up, God is greatly honoured by them, the common wealth is aduanced: yea their Parents and all other, fare the better for them."

202. Jeremy Taylor, *Eniautos,* 2d ed. (London: Richard Royston, 1655), 2:224–225.

203. William Whately, *A Care-Cloth: or a Treatise of the Cumbers and Troubles of Marriage* (London: Felix Kyngston for Thomas Man, 1624), A2 (STC 25299).

204. Heale, *An Apologie for Women,* 10–11.

205. Andrewes, *Works,* 2:233–234. See also Ames, *Marrow,* 319, items 34–35, arguing: "The perpetuity of marriage does not depend only upon the will and covenant of the persons contracting, for then by consent of both a covenant so begun might be broken, as is the case between master and servant. Rather, the rule and bond of this covenant is the institution of God . . . which establishes the individual companionship of husband and wife [and] looks toward the good of mankind and its rightful conservation and their hereditary succession."

206. On hierarchical order in English society, see Louis B. Wright, *Middle Class Culture in Elizabethan England* (Chapel Hill: University of North Carolina Press, 1953).

207. Christopher Hill, *The World Turned Upside Down: Radical Ideas During the English Revolution* (New York: Viking Press, 1972). See also id., *The Century of Revolution, 1603–1714* (New York: W.W. Norton, 1961); Lawrence Stone, *The Causes of the English Revolution, 1529–1642* (New York: Harper & Row, 1972).

208. See documents in C.H. Firth and R.S. Rait, eds., *Acts and Ordinances of the Interregnum 1642–1660,* 3 vols. (London: H.M. Stationery Printing Office, 1911), 2:18, 24, 120, 122, 813.

209. 1 William & Mary, st. 2, c. 2, c. 18.

210. "How Marriages shall be Solemnized and Registered . . ." (1653), in H. Scobell, ed., *A Collection of Acts and Ordinances of General Use Made in the Parliament* (London: Henry Hills and John Field, 1658), Pt. II, 236–238, confirmed in 1656, in ibid., at 389.

211. 12 C. II, c. 33.

212. See Stone, *Family, Sex, and Marriage,* 34–35, indicating that between 1670 and 1750, there were only 17 such acts; between 1750 and 1799, there were 114. No woman received a private act of divorce until 1801. Salmon, *Women and the Law*

of Property, 60. For the cumbersome procedures, see Allen Horstman, *Victorian Divorce* (New York: St. Martin's Press, 1985), 20ff.

213. Gerrard Winstanley, *The Law of Freedom in a Platform, or True Magistracy Restored,* ed. R.W. Kenny (New York: Schocken Books, 1941), 146.

214. Quoted in Hill, *The World Turned Upside Down,* 313–314.

215. Quoted in "Introduction" to Milton, *Works,* 2:137–183, at 138.

216. Milton's main tracts on marriage are: *The Doctrine and Discipline of Divorce, Restored to the Good of Both Sexes, from the Bondage of Canon Law* (London, 1643), 2d ed. (London, 1644), in *Works,* 2:217–356; *Tetrachordon: Expositions upon the foure chief places in Scripture, which treat of Mariage . . .* (London, 1644/1645), in *Works,* 2:571–718; *Colasterion: A Reply to a Nameless Answer Against the Doctrine and Discipline of Divorce* (London, 1645), in *Works,* 2:719–758. He also provided a glossed translation of Bucer's chapters on marriage and divorce under the title *The Judgement of Martin Bucer, Concerning Divorce* (London, 1644), in *Works,* 2:416–479 (with preface at 430–440). See discussion of these works in the editor's introduction, *Works,* 2:137–164; Johnson, A *Society Ordained by God,* 121–152; William Haller, *Liberty and Reformation in the Puritan Revolution* (New York: Columbia University Press, 1955), 78–99.

217. Milton, *Works,* 2:229.

218. Ibid. Milton expounded this view in *Areopagitica* (1645) and *The Tenure of Kings and Magistrates* (1649).

219. Milton, *Works,* 2:235, 246, 254, 256.

220. Ibid., 2:268–269, 605–609.

221. Ibid., 2:239–240, 248–250, 599.

222. Ibid., 2:251–252, 259–260, 589–591, 630–631.

223. Ibid., 2:254, 632. Milton adds at 631: "One of the chief matrimonial ends is said to seek a holy seed. But where an unfit mariage administers continual cause of hatred and distemper . . . much unholiness abide. . . . God therfore knowing how unhappy it would bee for children to bee born in such a family, gives the Law either as a prevention, that beeing an unhappy pair, they should not adde to bee unhappy parents, or els a remedy that if ther be children, while they are fewest, they may follow either parent, as shall bee agreed, or judg'd, from the house of hatred and discord, to a place of more holy and peaceable education."

224. Ibid., 2:276.

225 Ibid., 2:680.

226. Ibid., 2:230, 431, 438–439.

227. See Ibid., 2:343, calling it illegimate and rapacious for the church "to pluck the power & arbitrement of divorce from the master of the family, into whose hands Christ so left it, preaching only to the conscience, and not authorizing a judiciall Court to tosse about and divulge the unaccountable and secret reasons of disaffection between man & wife."

228. Ibid., 2:692–718.

229. Ibid., 2:350 (and 1:403, 10:513), referring to John Selden, *De iure naturali et gentium, juxta disciplinam Ebraeorum libri septem* (London: Excudebat Richardus Bishopus 1640), bk. V, chap. vii (STC 22168). See further Eivion Owen, "Milton and Selden on Divorce," *Studies in Philology* 43 (1946): 233–257.

230. Milton, *Works,* 2:235, 238, 248.

231. Ibid., 2:236–237, 591, 601–602, 607, 630–631, 732.

232. Ibid., 2:245, 275–276, 624.

233. Ibid., 2:277.

234. Ibid., 2:274–277, 328, 650–651.

235. Ibid., 2:239–244, 306.

236. In a later text, Milton added the argument that the the word "fornication" means "a constant alienation and disaffection of mind," or "the continuall practise of disobedience and crossnes from the duties of love and peace." Ibid., 2:673.

237. Ibid., 2:283, 621, 636, 661–662.

238. Ibid., 2:681–683, adducing Exod. 34:16; Deut. 7:3, 6; Neh. 13:24, 26 to support his argument for the propriety of divorce of a Gentile or infidel.

239. Ibid., 2:339.

240. Quotes from sources excerpted in William R. Parker, *Milton's Contemporary Reputation* (Columbus: Ohio State University Press, 1940), 74–79. See also ibid., 170–217, a facsimilie reprint of an anonymous pamphlet, *An Answer to a Book, Intituled, The Doctrine and Discipline of Divorce* (London: William Lee, 1644), to which Milton responded in *Colasterion* (1645), in *Works*, 2:719–758.

241. See Parker, *Milton's Contemporary Reputation*, 17–24.

242. See references to Milton in Lawrence Stone, *Road to Divorce: England 1530–1987* (Oxford: Oxford University Press, 1990), 348–351, 407 and discussion on the Divorce Reform Acts in ibid., 368–422.

243. John Locke, *Two Treatises of Government* (1698), ed. Peter Laslett (Cambridge: Cambridge University Press, 1960), II.2. For analysis, see sources and discussion in A. John Simmons, *The Lockean Theory of Rights* (Princeton, N.J.: Princeton University Press, 1992), 167–221.

244. Ibid., II.86.

245. Ibid., I.47.

246. In ibid., I.47, Locke did allow the thought that if Eve is understood "as the representative of all other Women," God's words "will at most concern the Female Sex only, and import no more but that Subjection they should ordinarily be in to their Husbands." But, he immediately added, that such subjection is not necessary "if the Circumstances either of her Condition or Contract with Her Husband should exempt her from it."

247. Ibid., I.9. See also I.98: "Paternal Power, being a Natural Right rising only from the relation of Father and Son, is as impossible to be inherited as the Relation itself, and a Man may pretend as well to Inherit the Conjugal Power the Husband, whose Heir he is, had over his Wife, as he can to Inherit the Paternal Power of a Father over his Children. For the Power of the Husband being founded on Contract, and the Power of the Father founded on *Begetting*, he may as well Inherit the Power obtained by the conjugal contract, which was only Personal, as he may the Power obtained by Begetting, which could reach no farther then the Person of him, that does not beget."

248. Ibid., II.77.

249. Ibid., II.78.

250. Ibid., II.83.

251. Ibid., II.79–80.

252. Diary Entry, 1678, 1679, quoted in editor's note to ibid., II, 81, in Laslett, ed., *Two Treatises* (paperback ed.), at 364.

253. Ibid., II.82.

254. Ibid., II.83.

255. John Locke, *The Reasonableness of Christianity*, in *The Works of John Locke*, 12th ed. (London: C.& J. Rivington et al., 1824), 6:140–143. See also ibid., 11–15, and the fuller account in his *Essay on the Law of Nature*, trans. and ed. W. von Leyden, (Oxford: Oxford University Press, 1954).

256. Locke, *Reasonableness of Christianity*, 115.

257. John Locke, *A Paraphrase and Notes on St. Paul's First Epistle to the Corinthians*, in Locke, *Works*, 7:118–119 (notes on 1 Cor. 6:12–13).

258. Ibid., 7:122–123 (notes on 1 Cor. 7:1–4).
259. Locke, *A Paraphrase and Notes on St. Paul's Epistle to the Ephesians*, in *Works*, 7:488 (notes on Eph. 5:23).
260. See generally J.W. Gough, *The Social Contract: A Critical Study of Its Development* (Oxford: Clarendon Press, 1936), 119–153.
261. Hugo Grotius, *De Jure Belli ac Pacis* (1625), Prolegommena, 11.
262. See Brian Tierney, *The Idea of Natural Rights: Studies on Natural Rights, Natural Law and Church Law 1150–1625* (Atlanta: Scholars Press, 1997), 317–324.

Notes to Chapter 5:
Marriage as Contract in the Enlightenment Tradition

1. See esp. Mary Ann Glendon, *State, Law, and Family: Family Law in Transition in the United States and Western Europe* (Boston/Dordrecht: Martinus Nijhoff Publishers, 1977).
2. W.C. Rodgers, *A Treatise on the Law of Domestic Relations* (Chicago: T.H. Flood, 1899); Joel Bishop, *New Commentaries on Marriage, Divorce, and Separation* (Chicago: T.H. Flood, 1891), 1:3–7.
3. Ibid., 2:217.
4. *Maynard v. Hill*, 125 U.S. 190, 210–11 (1888); *Reynolds v. United States*, 98 U. S. 145, 165 (1878); *Murphy v. Ramsey*, 11 U.S. 15, 45 (1885).
5. See generally Max Rheinstein, *Marriage Stability, Divorce, and the Law* (Chicago: University of Chicago Press, 1971), chaps. 1–2; Milton C. Regan, Jr., *Family Law and the Pursuit of Intimacy* (New York: New York University Press, 1993), chap. 1. For an English overview, see R.H. Graveson and F.R. Crane, eds., *A Century of Family Law: 1857–1957* (London: Sweet & Maxwell, Ltd., 1957).
6. For analysis of European developments, see Mary Ann Glendon, *The Transformation of Family Law: State, Law, and Family in the United States and Europe* (Chicago: University of Chicago Press, 1989).
7. See sources and discussion in Regan, *Family Law*, chaps. 2, 5; Carl E. Schneider, "Moral Discourse and the Transformation of American Family Law," *Michigan Law Review* 83 (1985):1803; Lee E. Teitelbaum, "The Last Decade(s) of American Family Law," *Journal of Legal Education* 46 (1996):546.
8. See Jean Bethke Elshtain, *Public Man, Private Woman: Women in Social and Political Thought* (Princeton, N.J.: Princeton University Press, 1981), 100–146, 201–297.
9. See discussion and sources in Lisa Sowle Cahill, *Sex, Gender, and Christian Ethics* (Cambridge, Mass.: Cambridge University Press, 1996); Ted Peters, *For the Love of Children: Genetic Technology and the Future of the Family* (Louisville: Westminster John Knox Press, 1996); Don S. Browning et al., *From Culture Wars to Common Ground: Religion and the American Family Debate* (Louisville: Westminster John Knox Press, 1997); Max L. Stackhouse, *Covenant and Commitments: Faith, Family, and Economic Life* (Louisville: Westminster John Knox Press, 1997); Christopher Lasch, *Haven in a Heathen World: The Family Besieged* (New York: Basic Books, 1977).
10. See the overview of recent literature in Don S. Browning, "Christian Ethics and the Family Debate: An Overview," *The Annual of the Society of Christian Ethics* (1996): 1–12; id., "Egos Without Selves: A Theological-Ethical Critique of the Family Theory of the Chicago School of Economics," *The Annual of the Society of Christian Ethics* (1994):127–144.
11. For similar arguments, see, e.g., Regan, *Family Law*, 2–3, 35–42, 118–153; Carl

E. Schneider, "Moral Discourse and Family Law," 1805–1808, 1828–1833, 1839–1845; id., "Marriage, Morals, and the Law: No-Fault Divorce and Moral Discourse," *Utah Law Review* (1994): 503; Lee Teitelbaum, "Moral Discourse and Family Law," *Michigan Law Review* 84 (1985):430.

12. See sources and discussion in chapter 4, above.

13. For later uses of Locke, see sources and discussion in Carole Pateman, *The Sexual Contract* (Stanford, Calif.: Stanford University Press, 1988).

14. See esp. Ernst Cassirer, *The Philosophy of the Enlightenment* (Princeton, N.J.: Princeton University Press, 1951); Henry F. May, *The Enlightenment in America* (New York: Oxford University Press, 1976).

15. Among numerous sources, see, e.g., Mary Lyndon Shanley, *Feminism, Marriage, and the Law in Victorian England, 1850–1895* (Princeton, N.J.: Princeton University Press, 1989); Lawrence Stone, *Road to Divorce: A History of the Making and Breaking of Marriage in England* (New York and Oxford: Oxford University Press, 1995); Graveson and Crane, eds., *A Century of Family Law*; Marylynn Salmon, *Women and the Law of Property in Early America* (Chapel Hill and London: University of North Carolina Press, 1986).

16. James Fitzjames Stephen, *Liberty, Equality and Fraternity*, ed. Stuart D. Warner (Indianapolis: Liberty Fund, 1993), 151.

17. See ibid., with other references in Sir C.P. Ilbert, "Sir James Fitzjames as a Legislator," *Law Quarterly Review* 10 (1894):222; Sir Leslie Stephen, *Life of Sir James Fitzjames Stephen* (London: Smith, Elder & Co., 1895); James A. Colaiaco, *James Fitzjames Stephen and the Crisis of Victorian Thought* (New York: St. Martin's Press, 1983).

18. Stephen, *Liberty, Equality and Fraternity*, 15.

19 Ibid., 150. See also ibid., 15: "Mr. Mill and his disciples would be the last persons in the world to say that the political and social changes which have taken place in the world since the sixteenth century [Reformation] have not on the whole been eminently beneficial to mankind."

20. Ibid., 142.

21. Ibid., 138–141, 150–153.

22. Ibid., 107–108, 141–142.

23. See references scattered throughout his classic tract, James Fitzjames Stephen, *A History of the Criminal Law of England*, 3 vols. (London: MacMillan, 1883).

24. Ibid., 141.

25. See especially several tracts in *Collected Works of John Stuart Mill*, ed. John M. Robson, repr. ed. (Toronto: University of Toronto Press, 1984), vol. 21; *On Liberty* (1859), chap. 5, in John Stuart Mill, *Utilitarianism, On Liberty, Essay on Bentham*, ed. Mary Warnock (New York: New American Library, 1974). See discussion in Gail Tulloch, *Mill and Sexual Equality* (Hertfordshire and Boulder: Lynne Reinner Publishers, 1989); Susan Mendus, "The Marriage of True Minds: The Ideal Marriage in the Philosophy of John Stuart Mill," in Susan Mendus and Jane Rendall, eds., *Sexuality and Subordination: Interdisciplinary Studies of Gender in the Nineteenth Century* (London and New York: Routledge and Kegan Paul, 1989), 171–191.

26. Mary Wollstonecraft, *A Vindication of the Rights of Women* [1792], ed. Charles W. Hagelman, Jr., (New York: W.W. Norton, 1967). See analysis in Elshtain, *Public Man, Private Woman*, 228ff.; Virginia Saprio, *A Vindication of Political Virtue: The Political Theory of Mary Wollstonecraft* (Chicago: University of Chicago Press, 1992), 144ff. For Wollstonecraft's more general literary influence, see Shirley Foster, *Victorian Women's Fiction: Marriage, Freedom, and the Individual* (London: Croom Helm, 1985).

27. Mill, *Collected Works,* 21:288–289.
28. Quoted and discussed in Shanley, *Feminism, Marriage, and the Law,* 3. See also F.A. Hayeck, *John Stuart Mill and Harriet Taylor: Their Friendship and Subsequent Marriage* (London: Routledge & Kegan Paul, 1951).
29. Mill, *Collected Works,* 21:263.
30. Ibid., 21:37.
31. Ibid., 21:261.
32. Ibid., 21:263.
33. Ibid., 21:298.
34. Mill, *Principles of Political Economy,* in ibid., 3:952–953. See also ibid., 16:1470; 17:1624, 1668–1669; 19:401.
35. Mill, *On Liberty,* chap. 5, at 126, 238–239. See also the article of Harriet Taylor and J.S. Mill, in Mill, *Collected Works,* 25:1172–1176 (decrying child abuse and "domestic ruffianism").
36. See the collection of excerpts from his formal and informal writings in Ann P. Robson and John M. Robson, eds., *Sexual Equality: Writings by John Stuart Mill, Harriet Taylor Mill, and Helen Taylor* (Toronto: University of Toronto Press, 1994).
37. Mill, *Collected Works,* 21:46.
38. See, e.g., Mill, *On Liberty,* chap. 5, at 223–225.
39. Mill, *Collected Works,* 21:287ff. See also collection of excerpts in Robson and Robson, eds., *Sexual Equality,* 103–304.
40. Mill, *Collected Works,* 17:1692–1694.
41. Ibid., 21:299–322.
42. See collection of statements in Robson and Robson, eds., *Sexual Equality,* 28–34, 53–102. Quote is from Mill's article on Henri Saint-Simon, in ibid., 23, and Mill, *Collected Works,* 23:677–680.
43. Mill, *Collected Works,* 25:1172–1176; Mill, *On Liberty,* chap. 5, at 238–239.
44. 5 & 6 Will. 4 c. 54.
45. These rules were only marginally reformed in the early twentieth century and remain more or less unchanged on the books still today. See, e.g., the reforms of impediment laws in Deceased Brother's Widow Act, 11 & 12 Geo. 5 c. 24; Marriage (Prohibited Degrees of Relationship Act), 21 & 22 Geo. 5 c. 31 (1931). See generally Glendon, *The Transformation of Family Law,* 35–84, comparing English, American, German, French, and Swedish law on marital formation.
46. See T.E. James, "The English Law of Marriage," in Graveson and Crane, eds., *A Century of Family Law,* 20–36. The provisions of the 1836 Act and its progeny were confirmed in the Marriage Act of 1949, 12, 13, & 14 Geo. 6 c. 76.
47. See, e.g., 8 & 9 Vict. c. 10; 33 & 34 Vict. c. 75; 35 & 36 Vict. c. 12; 2 Edw. 7 c. 42; 15 & 16 Geo. 5 c. 45; 16 & 17 Geo. 5 c. 60; 22 & 23 Geo. 5 c. 46; 1 & 2 Geo. 6 c. 25; 7 & 8 Geo. 6 c. 31, with later confirmation in 12, 13, 14 Geo. 6 c. 76, and 14 Geo. 6 c. 25. See discussion in T.E. James, "The Illegitimate and Deprived Child," in Graveson and Crane, eds., *A Century of Family Law,* 39–55.
48. 20 & 21 Vict. c. 85. See amendments in 21 & 22 Vict. c. 108; 22 & 23 Vict. c. 61; 23 & 24 Vict. c. 144; 27 & 28 Vict. c. 44; 28 & 29 Vict. c. 43; 29 Vict. c. 32; 30 Vict. c. 11; 41 & 42 Vict. c. 19; 7 Edw. 7 c. 12. For analysis of the formation of the Act and its inherent limitations, see Shanley, *Feminism, Marriage, and the Law,* 22–48. For subsequent reforms that expanded and equalized the rights of divorce, see Stone, *Road to Divorce,* 368–422.
49. For details, see A.K.R. Kiralfy, "Matrimonial Tribunals and Their Procedure," in Graveson and Crane, eds., *A Century of Family Law,* 289–310.
50. Stone, *Road to Divorce,* 437–438. See also Rheinstein, *Marriage Stability, Divorce, and the Law,* 311–352.

51. Stone, *Road to Divorce,* 388.

52. See, e.g., 33 & 34 Vict. c. 75; 39 & 40 Vict. c. 79; 49 & 50 Vict. c. 27; 52 & 53 Vict. c. 44; 54 & 55 Vict. c. 3; 15 & 16 Geo. 5 c. 45. See discussion in Shanley, *Feminism, Marriage, and the Law,* 131–55; P.H. Pettit, "Parental Control and Guardianship," in Graveson and Crane, eds., *A Century of Family Law,* 56–87. For analogous American developments, see, e.g., S. Randall Humm et al., eds., *Child, Parent, and State: Law and Policy Reader* (Philadelphia: Temple University Press, 1994).

53. See esp. 33 & 34 Vict. c. 93; 45 & 46 Vict. c. 75; 49 & 50 Vict. c. 52; 56 & 57 Vict. c. 71. See Shanley, *Feminism, Marriage, and the Law,* 103–130. For antecedent developments, see Susan Staves, *Married Women's Separate Property in England, 1660–1833* (Cambridge, Mass.: Harvard University Press, 1990).

54. Glendon, *The Transformation of Family Law,* 111ff.; see also generally id., *The New Family and the New Property* (Toronto: Butterworths, 1981).

55. Quoted by Norman St. John-Stevas, "Women in Public Law," in Graveson and Crane, eds., *A Century of Family Law,* 256–257.

56. See esp. Sandra Stanley Holton, *Feminism and Democracy: Women's Suffrage and Reform Politics in Britain, 1900–1918* (New York: Cambridge University Press, 1986).

57. 9 & 10 Geo. 6, c. 71.

58. Schneider, "Moral Discourse and Family Law," 1805.

59. See Glendon, *The Transformation of Family Law; Elaine Tyler May, Great Expectations: Marriage and Divorce in Post-Victorian America* (Chicago: University of Chicago Press, 1980). See also Rheinstein, *Marriage Stability, Divorce, and the Law.*

60. Salmon, *Women and the Law of Property;* Michael Grossberg, *Governing the Hearth: Law and the Family in Nineteenth Century America* (Chapel Hill: University of North Carolina Press, 1985).

61. See, e.g., Frances Olsen, "The Family and the Market: A Study of Ideology and Legal Reform," *Harvard Law Review* 96 (1983):1497; John H. Langbein, "The Twentieth Century Revolution in Family Wealth Transmission," *Michigan Law Review* 86 (1988):722.

62. See sources in John Witte, Jr., "The Civic Seminary: The Sources of Modern Public Education in the Lutheran Reformation of Germany," *Journal of Law and Religion* 12 (1996):173–223, at 219ff.

63. Cf. the more radical developments and repeals during the French Revolution, as discussed in Monique Cuillieron, "Les causes matrimoniales des officialités de Paris au siècle des lumières, 1726–1789," *Revue historique de droit français èt etranger* 66 (1988):527, and James F. Traer, *Marriage and the Family in Eighteenth Century France* (Ithaca, N.Y.: Cornell University Press, 1980). The French revolutionaries had sought to treat marriage as any other private contract, to be formed and dissolved by mutual consent alone, with severe restrictions on the traditional superior legal status of the paterfamilias. France largely spurned these revolutionary reforms in the Napoleanic Code of 1804, but this revolutionary program continued to work its influence in nineteenth-century Belgium and the Netherlands. See Rheinstein, *Marriage Stability, Divorce, and the Law,* 194–221; L. van Apeldoorn, *Geschiedenis van het nederlandsche huwelijksrecht voor de invoering van de fransche wetsgeving* (Amsterdam: Uitgeversmaatschappij, 1925).

64. See sources and discussion in Phyllis D. Airhart and Margaret Lamberts Bendroth, eds., *Faith Traditions and the Family* (Louisville: Westminster John Knox Press, 1996).

65. The phrase is from Pateman, *The Sexual Contract.*

66. Schneider, "Moral Discourse and Family Law," 1811.

67. See, e.g., Uniform Marriage and Divorce Act, s. 201 [hereafter UMDA]. The Act is

duplicated in Walter O. Weyrauch, Sanford N. Katz, and Frances Olsen, *Cases and Materials on Family Law* (St. Paul: West Publishing Co., 1994), 1092–1110.

68. UMDA, ss. 202–206. Parents or guardians may seek dissolution of the marriage of their minor child or ward, provided the action is brought before the child reaches the age of majority. Ibid., s. 208.

69. Ibid., ss. 207–208.

70. Ibid., s. 207.

71. *Loving v. Virginia,* 388 U.S. 1, 12 (1967), quoting in part *Skinner v. Oklahoma,* 316 U.S. 535, 541 (1942). See also dicta in *Meyer v. Nebraska,* 262 U.S. 390, 399 (1930), and Universal Declaration of Human Rights (1948), art. 16–1: "Men and women of full age, without any limitation due to race, nationality, or religion, have the right to marry and found a family." For comparative discussion, see Glendon, *The Transformation of Family Law,* 75–82.

72. Respectively, *Loving v. Virginia; Zablocki v. Redhail,* 434 U.S. 374 (1978); *Turner v. Safely,* 482 U.S. 78 (1987).

73. 381 U.S. 479 (1965). The same principle has been extended to protect access of unmarried couples, and even minors, to contraceptives. See *Eisenstadt v. Baird,* 405 U.S. 438 (1972); *Carey v. Population Services International,* 431 U.S. 678 (1977).

74. *Eisenstadt,* 405 U.S. at 453.

75. 410 U.S. 113 (1973). In its last abortion case, *Planned Parenthood v. Casey,* 112 S.Ct. 2791 (1992), the Court upheld the right of abortion and struck down a state requirement of notification of one's spouse or the natural father as an "undue burden" upon this right.

76. 431 U.S. 494 (1977).

77. 450 U.S. 455 (1981).

78. Uniform Premarital Agreement Act, s. 3. The Act is duplicated in Weyrauch et al., *Family Law,* 1111–1113.

79. See good summary in Harry Krause, *Family Law in a Nutshell,* 3rd ed. (St. Paul: West Publishing Co., 1995), 333–352.

80. See the history of this "liberal breakthrough," which began in New York and California in the late 1960s, in Rheinstein, *Marriage Stability, Divorce, and the Law,* 317–366.

81. UMDA, s. 305; see also ibid., ss. 302–303.

82. See e.g., *Desrochers v. Desrochers,* 347 A. 2d 150 (N.H. 1975), with summary in Linda D. Elrod and Robert G. Spector, "A Review of the Year in Family Law," *Family Law Quarterly* 29 (1996):741. See also the treatment of religious divorce, and religious aversions to civil divorce, in Lawrence C. Marshall, "The Religion Clauses and Compelled Religious Divorces: A Study in Marital and Constitutional Separations," *Northwestern University Law Review* 80 (1985):204.

83. See, e.g., *Boddie v. Connecticut,* 401 U.S. 371 (1971) (outlawing filing fees for divorce) and discussion in Bruce Hafen, "The Constitutional Status of Marriage, Kinship, and Sexual Privacy: Balancing the Individual and State Interests," *Michigan Law Review* 81 (1983):463.

84. UMDA, s. 307 (Alternative A).

85. See ibid., s. 308, regarding temporary maintenance. See generally Carl E. Schneider, "Rethinking Alimony: Marital Decisions and Moral Discourse," *Brigham Young Law Review* (1991):197.

86. See sources and discussion in Regan, *Family Law,* 137–143, and Lenore J. Weitzmann and Ruth B. Dixon, "The Alimony Myth: Does No-Fault Divorce Make a Difference?" *Family Law Quarterly* 14 (1980):141.

87. See the critical essays in Stephen D. Sugarman and Herma Hill Kay, eds., *Divorce Reform at the Crossroads* (New Haven, Conn.: Yale University Press, 1990).

88. UMDA, s. 402. See critical analysis in Humm et al., eds., *Child, Parent, and State,* 3–67.

89. See summary in Teitelbaum, "The Last Decade(s) of American Family Law," 546–549, and an excellent case study in Eleanor E. Maccoby and Robert H. Mnookin, *Dividing the Child: Social and Legal Dilemmas of Custody* (Cambridge, Mass.: Harvard University Press, 1992).

90. See, e.g., Uniform Child Custody Jurisdiction Act; Parental Kidnapping Prevention Act, 28 U.S.C.A. 1738A (1982), and further sources and discussion in Schneider, "Moral Discourse in Family Law," 1812–1817 and Krause, *Family Law,* 225–332. The two acts are in Weyrauch et al., *Family Law,* 1114–1125.

91. Regan, *Family Law,* 38. See also ibid., 148–152; Glendon, *The Transformation of Family Law,* 135ff.; and Homer H. Clark, Jr., "Antenuptial Contracts," *University of Colorado Law Review* 50 (1979):141.

92. See, e.g., Martha Minow, "The Free Exercise of Families," *University of Illinois Law Review* (1991):925.

93. See, e.g., *Marvin v. Marvin,* 18 Cal. 3d 660, 134 Cal. Rptr. 815 (1976) (imputing a marital relationship to unmarried lovers and sustaining duties for marital property division), with discussion of its wide-ranging progeny in Krause, *Family Law,* 71–87.

94. See *Baehr v. Lewin,* 852 P.2d 44 (Haw., 1993), and broader analysis in Lynn D. Wardle, "A Critical Analysis of Constitutional Claims for Same-Sex Marriage," *Brigham Young University Law Review* (1996): and David Orgon Coolidge, *Same-Sex Marriage?* (Crossroads Monograph Series on Faith and Public Policy, 1996).

95. See Lenore J Weitzmann, *The Marriage Contract: Spouses, Lovers, and the Law* (New York: Free Press, 1991), and further sources and discussion in Glendon, *The Transformation of Family Law,* 135–147; Regan, *Family Law,* 143–152.

96. Glendon, *The Transformation of Family Law,* 146.

97. See generally Lenore J. Weitzmann, *The Divorce Revolution: The Unexpected Social and Economic Consequences for Women and Children in America* (New York: Free Press, 1985).

98. See statistical summaries in Krause, *Family Law,* 1–2; Jonathan Alter, "Powell's New War," *Newsweek* (April 28, 1997):28–31; Laura Gatland, "Putting the Blame on No-Fault," *ABA Journal* (April 1997):50–54.

99. Harold J. Berman, *Law and Revolution: The Formation of the Western Legal Tradition* (Cambridge, Mass.: Harvard University Press, 1983).

100. Letter of August 1886, quoted in Friederich Merzbacher, *Liebe, Ehe, und Familie* (Berlin: Duncker & Humblot, 1958), 113.

Notes to Reflections

1. Cf. *Lochner v. New York,* 198 U.S. 45, 76 (1905) (Holmes, J., dissenting): "General propositions do not decide concrete cases."

2. Cf. John E. Coons, "The Religious Rights of Children," in John Witte, Jr., and Johan van der Vyver, eds., *Religious Human Rights in Global Perspective: Religious Perspectives* (The Hague and Boston: Martinus Nijhoff Publishers, 1996), 172: "In a faint echo of the divine, children are the most important Word most of us will utter."

Bibliography

Airhart, Phyllis D., and Margaret Lamberts Bendroth, eds. *Faith Traditions and the Family* (Louisville: Westminster John Knox Press, 1996).

Albrecht, F. *Verbrechen und Strafen als Ehescheidungsgrund nach evangelischen Kirchenrecht* (Ph.D. Diss., München, 1903).

Alter, Jonathan. "Powell's New War," *Newsweek* (April 28, 1997):28.

Althusius, Johannes. *De matrimonio contrahendo et dissolvendo, resp. Wesselus Hemessen* (1593).

———. *De matrimonio: theses aliquot resp. Rugerus à Rhemen* (1589).

Ambrose of Milan. *Concerning Widows,* in Philip Schaff and Henry Wace, eds., *A Select Library of Nicene and Post-Nicene Fathers of the Christian Church, Second Series,* repr. ed. (Grand Rapids: Wm. B. Eerdmans Publishing Co., 1952), vol. 10.

Ames, William. *The Marrow of Theology,* 3d ed. (1629), trans. and ed. John D. Eusden (Boston: Pilgrim Press, 1968).

Amussen, Susan Dwyer. *An Ordered Society: Gender and Class in Early Modern England* (Oxford: Basil Blackwell, 1988).

An Answer to a Book, Intituled, The Doctrine and Discipline of Divorce (London: William Lee, 1644).

Anciaux, Pierre. *The Sacrament of Penance* (New York: Sheed & Ward, 1962).

Andrewes, Lancelot. *Against Second Marriage After Sentence of Divorce with a Former Match, the Party Then Living* (c. 1610), reprinted in James Bliss, ed., *Library of Anglo-Catholic Theology* (Oxford: J.H. Parker, 1854).

Apel, Johann. *Defensio Johannis Apelli ad Episcopum Herbipolensem pro svo conivgio* (Wittemberge, 1523).

———. *Isagoge per dialogum in quatuor libros Institutionum D. Justiniani Imperatoris* (1540).

———. *Methodica dialectices ratio ad jurisprudentiam accommodato* (1535).

Aquinas, Thomas. *Sanctie Thomae Aquinatis, Opera Omnia,* ed. Leonina (Rome: 1918–1930), vols. 4–12; and *The Summa Theologiae,* English trans. by English Dominican Fathers (London: 1912–1936), 22 vols.

Augustine. *De bono coniugali,* in R.J. Deferrari, ed., *Saint Augustine. Treatises on Marriage and Other Subjects* (New York: Fathers of the Church, 1955).

————. *The City of God Against the Pagans,* 7 vols., trans. William M. Green (Cambridge, Mass.: Harvard University Press, 1963).

————. *On Marriage and Concupiscence,* in Philip Schaff and Henry Wace, eds., *A Select Library of Nicene and Post-Nicene Fathers of the Christian Church, Second Series,* repr. ed. (Grand Rapids: Wm. B. Eerdmans Publishing Co., 1952), vol. 5.

————. *On Original Sin,* in ibid.

————. *Sermons on New Testament Lessons,* in Philip Schaff and Henry Wace, eds., *A Select Library of Nicene and Post-Nicene Fathers of the Christian Church, Second Series,* repr. ed. (Grand Rapids: Wm. B. Eerdmans Publishing Co., 1952), vol. 6.

Bailey, D.S. *Sexual Relations in Christian Thought* (New York: Harper & Bros., 1959).

————. *Thomas Becon and the Reformation in England* (Edinburgh: Oliver and Boyd, 1952).

Baker, J. Wayne. *Heinrich Bullinger and the Covenant: The Other Reformed Tradition* (Athens, Ohio: University Press, 1980).

Balch, David, and Carolyn Osiek. *Families in the New Testament World* (Louisville: Westminster John Knox Press, 1997).

Baldwin, Claude-Marie. "John Calvin and the Ethics of Gender Relations," *Calvin Theological Journal* 26 (1991):133.

Baron and Feme. A Treatise of the Common Law Concerning Husbands and Wives (London: Assigns of Richard and Edward Atkyns, Esq., 1700).

Bassett, W.J., ed. *The Bond of Marriage: An Ecumenical and Interdisciplinary Study* (Notre Dame and London: University of Notre Dame Press, 1968).

Baur, Jürgen. *Gott, Recht und weltliches Regiment im Werke Calvins* (Bonn: H. Bouvier, 1965).

Becon, Thomas. *The Booke of Matrimonie both Profitable and Comfortable for all Them that Entende Quietyly and Godly to lyue in the Holy State of honorable Wedlocke* (c.1560), in Thomas Becon, *The First Part of the Bokes, which Thomas Becon made* (London: J. Day, 1560–1564), vol. 1 (STC 1710).

————. *The Early Works of Thomas Becon, S.T.P.,* ed. J. Ayre for the Parker Society, 3 vols. (Cambridge: University Press, 1843).

————. "A Homily of Whoredome and Unclennesse," in *Certayne Sermons, or Homilies, Appointed by the Kynges Maiestie* (London: Richard Grafton, 1547) (STC 13639).

————. *A New Catechism,* in Thomas Becon, *The Early Works of Thomas Becon, S.T.P.,* ed. J. Ayre for the Parker Society, 3 vols. (Cambridge: University Press, 1843), 2:344.

————. Preface to [Heinrich Bullinger], *The Golde Boke of Christen Matrimonye* (1542) (STC 1723).

Bedouelle, G. and P. LeGal. *Le Divorce du Roi Henry VIII: Études et Documents* (Geneva: Travaux d'Humanisme et Renaissance, 1987).

Bels, P. "La formation du lien de mariage dans l'église protestante française (XVIe et XVIIe siècle)," in *Mémoires de la société pour l'histoire de droit et des institutions de anciens pays bourguignons, comtois et romands* 27 (1966):331.

Bergier, Jean-François, and Robert M. Kingdon, eds. *Registres de la compagnie des pasteurs de Genève au temps de Calvin,* 2 vols. (Geneva: Droz, 1964).

Berman, Harold J. *Faith and Order: The Reconciliation of Law and Religion.* Emory University Studies in Law and Religion, no.3 (Atlanta: Scholars Press, 1993).

―――. *Law and Revolution: The Formation of the Western Legal Tradition* (Cambridge, Mass.: Harvard University Press, 1983).

―――. "The Religious Sources of General Contract Law," in Harold J. Berman, *Faith and Order: The Reconciliation of Law and Religion* (Atlanta: Scholars Press, 1993), 187.

Berman, Harold J. and John Witte, Jr. "The Transformation of Western Legal Philosophy in Lutheran Germany," *Southern California Law Review* 62 (1989):1573.

Beschle, Donald L. "God Bless the Child? The Use of Religion as a Factor in Child Custody and Adoption Proceedings," *Fordham Law Review* 58 (1989):383.

Beust, Joachim von. *Tractatus connubiorum praestantiss, iuris consultorum* (vol. 1, Jena, 1606; vols. 2–3, Frankfurt, 1617, 1618, 1742).

―――. *Tractatus de iure connubiorum et dotium* (Frankfurt am Main: P. Schmidt, 1591).

Beza, Theodore. *De polygamia* (c. 1569), in Theodore Beza, *Tractationum Theologicarum,* 2d ed. (Eusthatii Vignon, 1582), 1.

―――. *De Repudiis et Divortiis* (1563), in Theodore Beza, *Tractationum Theologicarum,* 2d ed. (Eusthatii Vignon, 1582), 50.

Biéler, André. *L'Homme et la femme dans la morale Calviniste* (Geneva: Labor et Fides, 1963).

Biggs, J.M. *The Concept of Matrimonial Cruelty* (London: University of London Press, 1962).

Bishop, Joel. *New Commentaries on Marriage, Divorce, and Separation,* 2 vols. (Chicago: T.H. Flood, 1891).

Blackstone, William. *Commentaries on the Law of England,* 4 vols. (Oxford: Clarendon Press, 1765–1769).

Blaisdell, Charmarie J. "Calvin's and Loyola's Letters to Women: Politics and Spiritual Counsel in the Sixteenth Century," in Robert V. Schnucker, ed., *Calviniana: Ideas and Influence of John Calvin* (Ann Arbor: University of Michigan Press, 1988), 235.

―――. "Calvin's Letters to Women: The Courting of Ladies in High Places," *Sixteenth Century Journal* 13 (1982):3.

Bliss, James, ed. *Library of Anglo-Catholic Theology* (Oxford: J.H. Parker, 1854).

Bock, Kenneth. "The Moral Philosophy of Sir Henry Sumner Maine," *Journal of History of Ideas* 37 (1976):147.

Boehmeri, Iusti Henning. *Ivs ecclesiasticvm protestantivm vsvm modernvm ivxta seriem decretalium ostendens & ipsis rerum argumentiis illustrans,* 3 vols. (Halae: Litteris et impendsis Orphanotrophei, 1714).

Bohatec, Josef. *Budé und Calvin: Studien zur Gedankenwelt des franzöischen Frühhumanismus* (Graz: H.B. Ohlaus Nachfolge, 1950).

———. *Calvin und das Recht,* 2d ed., repr. ed. (Aalen: Scientia Verlag, 1991).

———. *Calvins Lehre von Staat und Kirche mit besonderer Berücksichtigung des Organismusgedankens* (Aalen: Scientia Verlag, 1968).

The Book of Common Prayer [1559], ed. John E. Booty (Charlottesville: University of Virginia Press, 1976).

Boswell, John. *Same-Sex Union in Premodern Europe* (New York: Villard Books, 1994).

Bouwsma, William J. *John Calvin: A Sixteenth-Century Portrait* (New York: Oxford University Press, 1988).

Bradshaw, William. *A Marriage Feast: A Sermon on the Former Part of the Second Chapter of the Evangelist* (London: Edward Griffin, 1620).

Brecht, Martin. "Anfänge reformatorischen Kirchenordnungen bei Johannes Brenz," *Zeitschrift der Savigny-Stiftung (Kan. Ab.)* 96 (1969):322

Breen, Quirinius. *John Calvin: A Study in French Humanism* (Grand Rapids: Wm. B. Eerdmans Publishing Co., 1931).

Brenz, Johannes. *Frühschriften,* ed. Martin Brecht, Gerhard Schäfer, and Frieda Wolf, 2 vols. (Tübingen, J.C.B. Mohr, 1970–1974).

———. *Libellus casuum quorundam matrimonialium elegantissimus* (Basilae: apud Bartholomaeum Vuisthemorum, 1536).

——— *Operum reverendi et clarissimi theologi D. Ioannis Brentii* (Tubingae: Excudebat Georgius Gruppenbachius, 1576–1594).

———. *Wie in Eesáchen vnnd den fellen so sich derhalben zutragen nach Götlichem billichem rechten christenlich zu handeln* (Nürnberg: Jobst Gutknecht, 1529), reprinted, with revisions, under the title *Wie in Ehesachen und inn den fellen so sich derhalben zu tragen nach götlichen billichen Rechten Christlich zu handeln sey. Mit vorrhede Mart. Luthers* (Wittenberg, 1531).

Brooke, Christopher N.L. *The Medieval Idea of Marriage* (Oxford and New York: Oxford University Press, 1991).

Brouwer, Hendrik. *De Jure Connubiorum, libri duo* (Delphis: Adrianum Beman, 1714).

Brown, Peter. *The Body and Society: Men, Women, and Sexual Renunciation in Early Christianity* (New York: Columbia University Press, 1988).

Browning, Don S. "Christian Ethics and the Family Debate: An Overview," *The Annual of the Society of Christian Ethics* (1996):1–12.

———. "Egoes Without Selves: A Theological-Ethical Critique of the Family Theory of the Chicago School of Economics," *The Annual of the Society of Christian Ethics* (1994):127.

Browning, Don S., et al. *From Culture Wars to Common Ground: Religion and the American Family Debate* (Louisville: Westminster John Knox Press, 1997).

Bruce, Gustav M. *Luther as an Educator* (Westport, Conn.: Greenwood Press, 1979).

Brundage, James A. *Law, Sex, and Christian Society in Medieval Europe* (Chicago: University of Chicago Press, 1987).

Bucer, Martin. *Common Places of Martin Bucer,* ed. D. F. Wright (Appleford: The Sutton Courtenay Press, 1972).

———. *De Regno Christi* (1550), in *Martini Buceri Opera Latina,* vol. 15 (Paris: Presses Universitaires de France, 1954, 1955); translated in Wilhelm Pauck, ed., *Melanchthon and Bucer* (Philadelphia: Westminster Press, 1969).

Bugenhagen, Johannes. *Vom ehebruch und weglauffen* (Wittenberg, 1539, 1541).

———. *Von dem ehelich en Stande der Bischofe vnd Daiken* (Wittenberg, 1525); revised as *De coniugio episcoporum & diacorum* (Argentorati: I. Knoblochus, 1526).

———. *Was man vom Closter leben halten sol* (Wittenberg: G. Rhaw, 1529).

Bullinger, Heinrich. *Der christlich Eestand* (Zurich, 1540); translated as *The Christen State of Matrimonye* (London, 1541) (STC 4045), by Myles Coverdale, and as *The Golde Boke of Christen Matrimonye* (London, 1542) (STC 1723), under Theodore Basille.

———. *The Decades of Henry Bullinger: The Fifth Decade,* ed. Thomas Harding for the Parker Society (Cambridge: University Press, 1852).

———. *The Decades of Henry Bullinger: The First and Second Decades,* ed. Thomas Harding for the Parker Society (Cambridge: University Press, 1849).

Bunny, Edmund. *Of Divorce for Advlterie, and Marrying Againe: That There is no Sufficient Warrant so to do* (Oxford: Joseph Barnes, 1610).

Burmeister, Karl Heinz. *Das Studium der Rechte im Zeitalter des Humanismus im deutschen Rechtsbereich* (Wiesbaden: G. Pressler, 1974).

Burn, Richard. *Ecclesiastical Law,* 6th ed., 4 vols. (London: A. Stahan, 1797).

Cahill, Lisa Sowle. *Sex, Gender, and Christian Ethics* (Cambridge, Mass.: Cambridge University Press, 1996).

Cairncross, John. *After Polygamy Was Made a Sin: The Social History of Christian Polygamy* (London: Routledge & Kegan Paul, 1974).

Calvin, John. *Calvin's Commentaries,* 47 vols. (Edinburgh: Oliver & Boyd, 1843–1859).

———. *Ioannis Calvini opera quae supersunt omnia,* G. Baum et al., eds., 59 vols. (Brunsvigae: C.A. Schwetschke et filium, 1892).

———. *Letters of John Calvin,* ed. Jules Bonnet, repr. ed., 4 vols. (New York: Burt Franklin, 1972).

————. *Supplementa Calvinia* (Neukirchen: Kreis Moers Neukirchener Verlag der Buchhandlung, 1961–).

Capito, Wolfgang Fabricius. *Responsio de missa matrimonio & iure magistratus in religionem* (Argentorati: Per Vu. Rihelium, 1537).

Carlson, Eric Josef. *Marriage and the English Reformation* (Oxford: Blackwell, 1994).

Cardwell, Edward, ed. *The Reformation of the Ecclesiastical Laws* (Oxford: University Press, 1850).

————, ed. *Synodalia: A Collection of Articles of Religion, Canons, and Proceedings of Convocations in the Province of Canterbury* (Oxford: University Press, 1842).

Cassirer, Ernst. *The Philosophy of the Enlightenment* (Princeton, N.J.: Princeton University Press, 1951).

Catechism of the Council of Trent for Parish Priests, trans. John A. McHugh and Charles J. Callan (Rockford, Ill.: Tan Books and Publishers, 1982).

Chibi, A.A. "The Interpretation and Use of Divine and Natural Law in the First Marriage Crisis of Henry VIII," *Archiv für Reformationsgeschichte* 85 (1994): 265.

Choisy, Eugène, *La théocratie à Genève au temps de Calvin* (Geneva: Droz, 1897).

Chrysostom, John. *Homilies on the Acts of the Apostles and the Epistle to the Romans*, in Philip Schaff and Henry Wace, eds., *A Select Library of Nicene and Post-Nicene Fathers of the Christian Church, Second Series,* repr. ed. (Grand Rapids: Eerdmans, 1952), vol. 11.

————. *Homilies on the Epistles of Paul to the Corinthians,* in Philip Schaff and Henry Wace, eds., *A Select Library of Nicene and Post-Nicene Fathers of the Christian Church, Second Series,* repr. ed. (Grand Rapids: Wm. B. Eerdmans Publishing Co., 1952), vol. 12.

————. *Homily on Matthew,* in Philip Schaff and Henry Wace, eds., *A Select Library of Nicene and Post-Nicene Fathers of the Christian Church, Second Series,* repr. ed. (Grand Rapids: Wm. B. Eerdmans Publishing Co., 1952), vol. 10.

————. *St. John Chrysostom on Marriage and Family Life* (Crestwood, N.J.: St. Vladimir's Press, 1986).

Clark, Homer H., Jr. "Antenuptial Contracts," *University of Colorado Law Review* 50 (1979):141.

————. *The Law of Domestic Relations in the United States,* 2d ed. (St. Paul, Minn.: West Publishing Co., 1988).

Cleaver, Robert. *A Godly Form of Householde Gouernment* (London: Thomas Creede, 1598).

Clement. *The Instructor,* in Alexander Roberts and James Donaldson, eds., *The Ante-Nicene Fathers,* repr. ed. (Buffalo: The Christian Literature Publishing Co., 1885), vol. 2.

————. *Stromata,* in ibid.

Cocks, R.C.J. *Sir Henry Sumner Maine: A Study in Victorian Jurisprudence* (Cambridge, England: Cambridge University Press, 1988).

Coing, Helmut, ed. *Handbuch der Quellen und Literatur der neueren europäischen Privatrechtsgeschichte,* 4 vols. (München: Beck, 1977).

Coke, Sir Edward. *The First Part of the Institutes of the Lawes of England* (London, 1628).

———. *The Third Part of the Institutes of the Lawes of England* (London, 1644).

Colaiaco, James A. *James Fitzjames Stephen and the Crisis of Victorian Thought* (New York: St. Martin's Press, 1983).

Colley, Linda. *Britons, Forging the Nation 1707–1837* (New Haven: Yale University Press, 1992).

Comment. "Homosexuals Rights to Marry: A Constitutional Test and a Legislative Solution," *University of Pennslyvania Law Review* 128 (1979):193.

Coolidge, David Orgon. *Same-Sex Marriage?* (Crossroads Monograph Series on Faith and Public Policy, 1996).

Cooper, Thomas. *An Answer in Defense of the Truth Against the Apology of Private Mass* (1562), ed. W. Goode for the Parker Society (Cambridge: University Press, 1850).

Corbett, P. *The Roman Law of Marriage* (Oxford: Clarendon Press, 1930).

Cornelius, Carl A. *Historische Arbeiten, vornehmlich zur Reformationszeit* (Leipzig, 1899).

Cosin, John. *The Works,* ed. J. Sansom (Oxford: Oxford University Press, 1843–1845).

Council on Families. *Marriage in America: A Report to the Nation* (New York: Institute for American Values, 1995).

Coverdale, Myles. *Remains of Myles Coverdale,* ed. George Pearson for the Parker Society (Cambridge: University Press, 1846).

Crabites, Pierre. *Clement VII and Henry VIII* (London: George Routledge & Sons, Ltd., 1936).

Cramer, Frédéric-August, ed. *Notes extraites des registres du Consistoire de l'Église de Genève, 1541–1814* (Geneva, 1853).

Cranmer, Thomas. *Miscellaneous Writings and Letters of Thomas Cranmer,* ed. J.E. Cox for the Parker Society (Cambridge: University Press, 1846).

Cuillieron, Monique. "Les causes matrimoniales des officialités de Paris au siècle des lumières, 1726–1789," *Revue historique de droit français et étranger* 66 (1988):527.

Daly, James. *Sir Robert Filmer and English Political Thought* (Toronto: University of Toronto Press, 1979).

Davies, Kathleen M. "Continuity and Change in Literary Advice on Marriage," in R.B. Outhwaite, ed., *Marriage and Society: Studies in the Social History of Family* (New York: St. Martin's Press, 1981), 58.

Dawson, John P. *The Oracles of the Law* (Ann Arbor: University of Michigan Press, 1968).

De Blecourt, A. and N. Japiske. *Klein plakkaatboek van Nederland* (Groningen: J.B. Wolters, U.M., 1919).

DeBoer, Willis P. "Calvin on the Role of Women," in David E. Holwerda, ed., *Exploring the Heritage of John Calvin* (Grand Rapids: Baker Book House, 1976), 236.

Demos, John. *A Little Commonwealth: Family Life in Plymouth Colony* (New York: Oxford University Press, 1970).

Dibden, Sir Lewis, and Sir Charles Chadwick Healey. *English Church Law and Divorce* (London: J. Murray, 1912).

Dickens, A.G. *The English Reformation* (New York: Schocken Books, 1964).

Didascalia Apostolorum, trans. R. Hugh Connolly (Oxford: Clarendon Press, 1929).

Dieterich, Hartwig. *Das protestantische Eherecht in Deutschland bis zur Mitte des 17. Jahrhunderts* (München: Claudius Verlag, 1970).

Dietrich, Hans. *Evangelisches Ehescheidungsrecht nach den Bestimmungen der deutschen Kirchenordnungen des 16. Jahrhunderts* (Berlin, 1892).

Digges, Dudley. *The Unlawfulnesse of Subjects taking up Armes Against their Soveraigne* (s.l., s.n., 1644).

Dod, John, and Robert Cleaver. *A Plaine and Familiar Exposition of the Ten Commandments, with a methodicall short Catechisme, Containing Briefly all the Principall Grounds of Christian Religion* (London: Thomas Man, 1604) (STC 6968).

Donahue, Charles, Jr. "The Policy of Alexander the Third's Consent Theory of Marriage," *Proceedings of the Fourth International Congress of Medieval Canon Law* (Vatican City, 1976), 251.

Donne, John. *The Works,* 6 vols., ed. Henry Alford (Cambridge: Cambridge University Press, 1839).

Duns Scotus, John. *Opera Omnia,* repr. ed (Farnbourgh: Gregg, 1969).

Dykema, Peter A., and Heiko A. Oberman, eds. *Anticlericalism in Late Medieval and Early Modern Europe* (Leiden: E.J. Brill, 1993).

Ebel, Wilhelm. *Studie über ein Goslarer Ratsurteilsbuch des 16. Jahrhunderts nebst einem Urkundenanhang* (Göttingen: O. Schwartz & Co., 1961).

Eells, Hasting. *The Attitude of Martin Bucer Toward the Bigamy of Philip of Hesse* (New Haven: Yale University Press, 1924).

Egtreglement, Over de Steden, ende ten platten Lande, in de Heerlijkheden en Dorpen, staande onder de Generaliteit (s'Gravenhage: Hillebrandt van Wouw, 1664).

Elazar, Daniel J. *Covenant and Commonwealth: From Christian Separation Through the Protestant Reformation* (New Brunswick, N.J.: Transaction Publishers, 1996).

Elliott, Dyan. *Spiritual Marriage: Sexual Abstinence in Medieval Wedlock* (Princeton, N.J.: Princeton University Press, 1993).

Elrod, Linda D., and Robert G. Spector. "A Review of the Year in Family Law," *Family Law Quarterly* 29 (1996):741.

Elshtain, Jean Bethke. "Marriage in Civil Society," *Family Affairs* 7 (Spring 1996):1.

————. *Public Man, Private Woman: Women in Social and Political Thought* (Princeton: Princeton University Press, 1981).

Erler, Adalbert, and Ekkehard Kaufmann, eds. *Handwörterbuch zur deutschen Rechtsgeschichte* (Berlin: E. Schmidt Verlag, 1984).

Esmein, Adhémar. *Le mariage en droit canonique,* 2d ed., 2 vols. (Paris: Sirrey, 1929–1935).

Fenner, Dudley. *The Artes of Logike and Rhetorike . . . Together with Examples of the same for Methode, in the gouernment of the Familie* (Middleburg: R. Shiders, 1584).

————. *Sacra theologica, sive veritas quae est secundum pietatem* (London: T. Dawson, c. 1585).

Filmer, Robert. *Patriarcha and other Political Works,* ed. Peter Laslett (Oxford: Oxford University Press, 1949).

Firth, C.H., and R.S. Rait, eds. *Acts and Ordinances of the Interregnum 1642–1660,* 3 vols. (London: H.M. Stationery Printing Office, 1911).

Fischer, H.F.W.D. "De gemengde huwelijken tussen Katholiken en Protestanten in de Nederlanden van de XVIe tot de XVIIe eeuw," *Tijdschrift voor Rechtsgeschiedenis/Revue d'Histoire due Droit* 31 (1963):463.

Foster, Shirley. *Victorian Women's Fiction: Marriage, Freedom, and the Individual* (London: Croom Helm, 1985).

Francis, Mark. "Henry Sumner Maine: Victorian Evolution and Political Theory," *History of European Ideas* 19 (1994):753.

Franzen, August. *Zölibat und Priesterehe in der Auseinandersetzung der Reformationszeit und der katholische Reform des 16. Jahrhunderts* (Münster: Aschendorff, 1969).

Freed, Doris Jonas, and Henry H. Foster. "Divorce in the Fifty States," *Family Law Quarterly* 14 (1981):229.

Friedberg, Emil, ed. *Corpus Iuris Canonici,* 2 vols. (Lipsiae: ex officina Bernhardi Tauchnitz, 1879–1881).

————. *Das Recht der Eheschliessung in seiner geschichtlichen Entwicklung,* repr. ed. (Aalen: Scientia Verlag, 1968).

Friesen, Joseph. *Geschichte des kanonischen Eherechts bis zum Verfall der Glossenliteratur,* 2d ed., repr. ed. (Aalen: Scientia Verlag, 1963).

Fulke, William. *A Defence of the Sincere and True Translations of the Holy Scriptures into the English Tongue,* ed. C.H. Hartshorne for the Parker Society (Cambridge: University Press, 1843).

————. *Stapleton's Fortress Overthrown,* ed. R. Gibbings for the Parker Society (Cambridge: University Press, 1848).

Fuller, Lon L. *The Morality of Law,* rev. ed. (New Haven, Conn.: Yale University Press, 1964).

Gamble, Richard C., ed. *Calvin's Work in Geneva* (New York and London: Garland Publishing Co., 1992).

Ganoczy, A. *Le jeune Calvin. Genèse et evolution de la vocation réformatorice* (Wiesbaden: F. Steiner, 1966).

Gataker, Thomas. *A Good Wife: God's Gift: and A Wife Indeed. Two Marriage Sermons* (London: John Haviland, 1623) (STC 11659).

Gatland, Laura. "Putting the Blame on No-Fault," *ABA Journal* (April 1997):50.

Gaudemet, Jean. "Les transformations de la vie familiale au bas empire et l'influence du christianisme," *Romanitas* 4 (1962):58.

————. "Tendances nouvelles de la legislation familiale aux ivme siècle," *Antiquitas* 1 (1978):187.

Gehrke, Heinrich. *Die Rechtsprechungs- und Konsilienliteratur Deutschland bis zum Ende des alten Reichs* (Frankfurt am Main, Univ. Fachber. Rechtwissen. Diss., 1972).

George, Charles H., and Katherine George. *The Protestant Mind of the English Reformation: 1570–1640* (Princeton, N.J.: Princeton University Press, 1961).

Gesschen, B. *Zur ältesten Geschichte und ehegerichtslichen Praxis des Leipziger Konsistoriums* (Leipzig, 1894).

Gewirth, Alan. *Marsilius of Padua: The Defender of the Peace,* vol. 2. *The Defensor Pacis Translated with an Introduction* (New York: Columbia University Press, 1956).

Gibson, Edmund. *Codex Iuris Ecclesiastici Anglicani,* 2nd ed. 2 vols., (London: J. Baskett, 1713).

Glendon, Mary Ann. *Abortion and Divorce in Western Law* (Chicago: University of Chicago Press, 1988).

————. *The New Family and the New Property* (Toronto: Butterworths, 1981).

————. *State, Law, and Family: Family Law in Transition in the United States and Western Europe* (Boston and Dordrecht: Martinus Nijhoff Publishers, 1977).

————. *The Transformation of Family Law: State, Law, and Family in the United States and Western Europe* (Chicago: University of Chicago Press, 1989).

Godolphin, John. *Repertorium Canonicum,* 3d ed. (London: Assigns of R. & E. Atkins, 1687).

Gottlieb, Beatrice. "The Meaning of Clandestine Marriage," in Robert Wheaton and Tamara K. Hareven, eds., *Family and Sexuality in French History* (Philadelphia: University of Pennsylvania Press, 1980), 53.

Gouge, William. *Of Domesticall Duties: Eight Treatises* (London: John Haviland, c. 1622) (STC 12119); 2d ed. (London: John Beale, 1626).

Gough, J.W. *The Social Contract: A Critical Study of Its Development* (Oxford: Clarendon Press, 1936).

Grabner, J. *Ueber Desertion und Quasi-desertion als Scheidungsgrund nach dem evangelischen Kirchenrecht* (Ph.D. Diss., Leipzig, 1882).

Graham, W. Fred. *The Constructive Revolutionary: John Calvin and His Socio-Economic Impact* (Atlanta: John Knox Press, 1978).

———, ed. *Sixteenth Century Essays and Studies—Later Calvinism: International Perspectives* (Kirksville, Mo.: Sixteenth Century Journal Publishers, 1994).

Graveson, R.H., and F.R. Crane, eds. *A Century of Family Law: 1857–1957* (London: Sweet & Maxwell, 1957).

Greaves, Richard L. *Society and Religion in Elizabethan England* (Minneapolis: University of Minnesota Press, 1981).

Gregory of Nyssa. *On Virginity,* in Philip Schaff and Henry Wace, eds., *A Select Library of Nicene and Post-Nicene Fathers of the Christian Church, Second Series,* repr. ed. (Grand Rapids: Eerdmans, 1952), vol. 5.

Grey, Thomas C. *The Legal Enforcement of Morality* (New York: Knopf, 1983).

Griffith, Matthew. *Bethel; or A Forme for Families* (London: J. Days, 1633).

Grindal, Edmund. *The Remains of Edmund Grindal,* ed. W. Nicholson for the Parker Society (Cambridge: University Press, 1843).

Grossberg, Michael. *Governing the Hearth: Law and the Family in Nineteenth Century America* (Chapel Hill: University of North Carolina Press, 1985).

Grotius, Hugo. *De Jure Belli ac Pacis* (1625).

———. *The Jurisprudence of Holland,* trans. and ed. R.W. Lee (Oxford: Clarendon Press, 1926).

Haalk, W. "Die Rostocker Juristenfakultat als Spruchskollegium," *Wissenschaftliche Zeitschrift der Universität Rostock* 3 (1958):401.

Hafen, Bruce. "The Constitutional Status of Marriage, Kinship, and Sexual Privacy: Balancing the Individual and State Interests," *Michigan Law Review* 81 (1983):463.

Hagen, Kenneth. "From Testament to Covenant in the Early Sixteenth Century," *Sixteenth Century Journal* 3 (1972):1.

Haller, William. *Liberty and Reformation in the Puritan Revolution* (New York: Columbia University Press, 1955).

Haller, William, and Malleville Haller. "The Puritan Art of Love," *Huntington Library Quarterly* 5 (1941–1942):235.

Harkness, Georgia. *John Calvin: The Man and His Ethics* (New York: Henry Holt, 1931).

Harrington, William. *In this boke are conteyned the comendacions of matrimonye/the manner & fourme of contractyng solempnysynge and lyvyng in the same etc.* (London, 1528).

Hartmann, Julius, and Karl Jäger. *Johannes Brenz nach gedruckten und ungedruckten Quellen,* 2 vols. (Hamburg: F. Petrus, 1840).

Harvey, Judith W. *The Influence of the Reformation on Nürnberg Marriage Laws, 1520–1535* (Ph.D. Diss., Ohio State University, 1972).

Haskell, Paul G. "Premarital Estate Contract and Social Policy," *North Carolina Law Review* 57 (1979):415.

Haverkamp, Alfred, ed. *Haus und Familie in der spätmittelalterlichen Stadt* (Tübingen: J.C.B. Mohr, 1984).

Hay, William. *Lectures on Marriage* (1533–35), trans. J. Barry (Edinburgh: Stair Society, 1967).

Hayeck, F.A. *John Stuart Mill and Harriet Taylor: Their Friendship and Subsequent Marriage* (London: Routledge & Kegan Paul, 1951).

H[eale], W[illiam]. *An Apologie for Women, or Opposition to Mr. Dr. G. his Assertion . . . That it was Lawful for Husbands to Beate Their Wives* (Oxford: Joseph Barnes, 1609); 2d ed. (Oxford: Joseph Barnes, 1614).

Heaney, S.P. *The Development of the Sacramentality of Marriage from Anselm of Laon to Thomas Aquinas* (Washington, D.C.: Catholic University of America Press, 1963).

Heckel, Johannes. "Das Decretum Gratiani und das deutsche evangelische Kirchenrecht," *Studia Gratiana* 3 (1955):483.

Helmholz, R.H., ed. *Canon Law in Protestant Lands* (Berlin: Duncker & Humblot, 1992).

———. "Canon Law in Post-Reformation England," in R.H. Helmholz, ed., *Canon Law in Protestant Lands* (Berlin: Duncker & Humblot, 1992), 203.

———. *Marriage Litigation in Medieval England* (Cambridge: Cambridge University Press, 1974).

———. *Roman Canon Law in Reformation England* (Cambridge: Cambridge University Press, 1990).

———. *The Spirit of the Classical Canon Law* (Athens: University of Georgia Press, 1996).

Hemming, Nicolaus. *Libellus de conjugio, repudio, et divortio* (Leipzig, 1578).

Hendrix, Scott. "Masculinity and Patriarchy in Reformation Germany," *Journal of the History of Ideas* 56 (1995):177.

Herbert, George. *The Works*, ed. F.E. Hutchinson (Oxford: Oxford University Press, 1941).

Hesse, Hans. *Evangelisches Ehescheidungsrecht in Deutschland* (Bonn: H. Bouvier, 1960).

Hesselink, I. John. *Calvin's Concept of the Law* (Allison Park, Pa.: Pickwick Publishers, 1992).

Hill, Christopher. *The Century of Revolution, 1603–1714* (New York: W.W. Norton, 1961).

———. *The World Turned Upside Down: Radical Ideas During the English Revolution* (New York: Viking Press, 1972).

Hoffmann, H. *Das Kirchenverfassung der niederländischen Reformierten bis zum*

Beginne der dordrechter Nationalsynode von 1618/1619, 2d ed. (Tübingen: J.C.B. Mohr, 1907).

Holton, Sandra Stanley. *Feminism and Democracy: Women's Suffrage and Reform Politics in Britain, 1900–1918* (New York: Cambridge University Press, 1986).

Holwerda, David E., ed. *Exploring the Heritage of John Calvin* (Grand Rapids: Baker Book House, 1976).

Hooker, Richard. *The Work of Mr. Richard Hooker in Eight Books of the Laws of Ecclesiastical Polity With Several Other Treatises,* 3 vols., ed. Isaac Walton (London: W. Clark, 1821).

Hooper, John. *Early Writings of John Hooper,* ed. S. Carr for the Parker Society (Cambridge: University Press, 1843).

Hopf, Constantin. *Martin Bucer and the English Reformation* (Oxford: Basil Blackwell, 1946).

Horstman, Allen. *Victorian Divorce* (New York: St. Martin's Press, 1985).

Houlbrooke, Ralph. *Church Courts and the People During the English Reformation 1520–1570* (Oxford: Oxford University Press, 1979).

Howard, George Elliott. *A History of Matrimonial Institutions,* 3 vols. (Chicago: University of Chicago Press, 1904, 1907).

Hugh of St. Victor. *De beatae Mariae Virginis Virginitate,* in *Patrologia Latinae,* vol. 176.

———. *On the Sacraments of the Christian Faith,* trans. R. Deferrari (Cambridge, Mass.: Harvard University Press, 1951).

Humm, S. Randall, et al., eds. *Child, Parent, and State: Law and Policy Reader* (Philadelphia: Temple University Press, 1994).

Hurstfield, J. *The Queen's Wards: Wardship and Marriage Under Elizabeth I* (Cambridge: Cambridge University Press, 1958).

Ilbert, Sir C.P. "Sir James Fitzjames as a Legislator," *Law Quarterly Review* 10 (1894):222.

Ingram, Martin. *Church Courts, Sex and Marriage in England, 1570–1640* (Cambridge: Cambridge University Press, 1987).

Jerome. *Against Jovianus,* in Philip Schaff and Henry Wace, eds. *A Select Library of Nicene and Post-Nicene Fathers of the Christian Church, Second Series,* repr. ed. (Grand Rapids: Wm. B. Eerdmans Publishing Co., 1952), vol. 6.

———. *Letters,* in Philip Schaff and Henry Wace, eds., *A Select Library of Nicene and Post-Nicene Fathers of the Christian Church, Second Series,* repr. ed. (Grand Rapids: Wm. B. Eerdmans Publishing Co., 1952), vol. 6.

Jewell, John. *Works,* 4 vols., ed. J. Ayre for the Parker Society (Cambridge: University Press, 1845–1850).

Johnson, James T. *A Society Ordained by God: English Puritan Marriage Doctrine in the First Half of the Seventeenth Century* (Nashville: Abingdon Press, 1970).

Jonkers, Engbert J.J. *Invloed van het Christendom op de romeinsche wetgeving betreffende het concubinaat en de echtscheiding* (Wageningen: H. Veenman, 1938).

Karst, Kenneth L. "The Freedom of Intimate Association," *Yale Law Journal* 89 (1980):624.

Kelly, Henry Ansgar. *The Matrimonial Trials of Henry VIII* (Stanford, Calif.: Stanford University Press, 1976).

Kern, Arthur, ed. *Deutsche Hofordnungen des 16. und 17. Jahrhunderts,* 2 vols. (Berlin: Weidmann, 1905).

Kingdon, Robert M. *Adultery and Divorce in Calvin's Geneva* (Cambridge and London: Harvard University Press, 1995).

————. "Anticlericalism in the Registers of the Geneva Consistory, 1542–1564," in Peter A. Dykema and Heiko A. Oberman, eds., *Anticlericalism in Late Medieval and Early Modern Europe* (Leiden: E.J. Brill, 1993): 617.

————. "Calvin and the Family: The Work of the Consistory of Geneva," in Richard C. Gamble, ed., *Calvin's Work in Geneva* (New York and London: Garland Publishing Co., 1992): 93.

————, et al., ed. *Registres du Consistoire de Genève,* 21 vols. (unpublished), in Meeter Center, Calvin College.

The Kings Book, or A Necessary Doctrine and Erudition for Any Man, 1543 (London: S.P.C.K., 1932).

Kirstein, Roland. *Die Entwicklung der Sponsalienlehre und der Lehre vom Eheschluss in der deutschen protestantischen Eherechtslehre bis zu J.H. Bohmer* (Bonn: Rohrscheid, 1966).

Kisch, Guido. *Consilia: Eine Bibliographie der Juristischen Konsiliensammlungen* (Basel: Helbingi Lichtenhahn, 1970).

Kling, Melchior. *Matrimonialium causarum tractatus, methodico ordine scriptus* (Franc. apud Chr. Egenolphum, 1543, 1553).

Kloek, Els. "Seksualiteit, huwelijk en gezinsleven tijdens de lange zestiende eeuw, 1450–1650," in Ton Zwaan, ed., *Familie, huwelijk en gezin in West-Europa. Van Middeleeuwen tot moderne tijd* (Amsterdam: Boom/Open Universiteit, 1993), 107.

Knutson, Donald C. *Homosexuality and the Law* (New York: Haworth Press, 1980).

Kock, Karl. *Studium Pietatis: Martin Bucer als Ethiker* (Neukirchen-Vluyn: Neukirchener Verlag, 1962).

Koebner, Richard. "Die Eheauffassung des ausgehenden deutschen Mittelalters," *Archiv für Kulturgeschichte* 9 (1911):136.

Köhler, Josef, and Willy Scheel, eds. *Die peinliche Gerichtsordnung Kaiser Karls V. Constitutio Criminalis Carolina* (Aalen: Scientia Verlag, 1968).

Köhler, Karl. *Luther und die Juristen. Zur Frage nach dem gegenseitigen Verhältnis des Rechtes und Sittlichkeit* (Gotha: Verlag von L. Hübner, 1873).

Köhler, Walter. "Die Anfänge des protestantischen Eherechtes," *Zeitschrift der Savigny-Stiftung (Kan. Ab.)* 74 (1941):271.

————. "Luther als Eherichter," *Beiträge zur sächsischen Kirchengeschichte* 47 (1947):18.

———. *Zürcher Ehegericht und Genfer Konsistorium,* 2 vols. (Leipzig: Verlag von M. Heinsius Nachfolger, 1942).

Kohls, Ernst-Wilhelm. "Martin Bucers Anteil und Anleigen bei der Auffassung der Ulmer Kirchenordnung in Jahre 1531," *Zeitschrift für evangelischen Kirchenrecht* 15 (1970):333.

Kouri, E.I., and Tom Scott, eds. *Politics and Society in Reformation Europe* (New York: St. Martin's Press, 1987).

Krause, Harry. *Family Law in a Nutshell,* 3rd ed. (St. Paul, Minn.: West Publishing Co., 1995).

———. "The Twentieth Century Revolution in Family Wealth Transmission," *Michigan Law Review* 86 (1988):722.

Langbein, John H. *Torture and the Law of Proof* (Cambridge, Mass.: Harvard University Press, 1974).

Lasch, Christopher. *Haven in a Heathen World: The Family Besieged* (New York: Basic Books, 1977).

Latimer, Hugh. *Sermons of Hugh Latimer,* ed. G.E. Corrie for the Parker Society (Cambridge: University Press, 1844).

The Lavves Resolutions of Womens Rights, or, The Lavves Provision for Women (London: Assigns of John More, Esq., 1632).

Lawrence, Ralph J. *The Sacramental Interpretation of Ephesians 5:32 from Peter Lombard to the Council of Trent* (Washington, D.C.: Catholic University of America Press, 1963).

Lawrence, William. *Marriage by the Morall Law of God Vindicated [and] The Right of Primogeniture in Succession to the Kingdoms of England and Scotland* (London, 1681).

Leclercq, Jean. *Monks on Marriage: A Twelfth Century View* (New York: Seabury Press, 1982).

Leder, Hans-Gunter, ed. *Johannes Bugenhagen: Gestalt und Wirkung* (Bonn: Evangelische Verlagsanstalt, 1984).

Leites, Edmund. *The Puritan Conscience and Modern Sexuality* (New Haven, Conn.: Yale University Press, 1986).

Lettmann, Reinhard. *Die Diskussion über die klandestinen Ehen und die Einführung einer zur Gültigkeit verpflichtenden Eheschliessung auf dem Konzil von Trent* (Münster: Aschendorff, 1967).

Liermann, Hans. "Das kanonische Recht als Gegenstand des gelehrten Unterrichts an den protestantischen Universitäten Deutschlands in den ersten Jahrhunderten nach der Reformation," in id., *Der Jurist und die Kirche: Ausgewählte kirchenrechtliche Aufsätze und Rechtsgutachten,* ed. Martin Heckel et al. (München: Beck, 1973), 108.

———. "Evangelisches Kirchenrecht und staatliches Eherecht in Deutschland, Rechtsgeschichtliches-Gegenwartsprobleme," in Thomas Wurtenberger, ed., *Existenz und Ordnung: Festschrift für Erik Wolf* (Frankfurt am Main: Klostermann, 1962), 43.

Linder, Klaus M. *Courtship and the Courts: Marriage and Law in Southern Germany, 1350–1550* (Th.D. Diss., Harvard, 1988).

Locke, John. *Essay on the Law of Nature,* trans. and ed. W. von Leyden (Oxford: Oxford University Press, 1954).

———. *Two Treatises of Government* (1698), ed. Peter Laslett (Cambridge: Cambridge University Press, 1960).

———. *The Works of John Locke,* 12th ed., 9 vols. (London: C. & J. Rivington et al., 1824).

Lohse, Berhard. "Die Kritik am Mönchtum bei Luther und Melanchthon," in Vilmos Vajtas, ed., *Luther und Melanchthon: Referate und Berichte des Zweiten Internationalen Kongresses für Lutherforschung Münster, 8.–13. August 1960* (Göttingen: Vandenhoeck & Ruprecht, 1960), 129.

———. *Mönchtum und Reformation: Luthers Aufeinandersetzung mit dem Mönchsideal des Mittelalters* (Göttingen: Vandenhoeck & Ruprecht, 1963).

Lombardus, Petrus. *Libri IV sententiarum,* 2d rev. ed. (Florence: Collegio di San Bonaventura, 1916), bk. 4, dist. 26–42 (1150).

Luther, Martin. "Counsel in Questions of Marriage and Sex," in Theodore G. Tappert, ed., *Luther: Letters of Spiritual Counsel* (Philadelphia: Westminster Press, 1955).

———. *D. Martini Luthers Werke: Kritische Gesamtausgabe,* repr. ed. (Weimar: Hermann Bohlaus, 1964–68).

———. *Luther's Works,* 65 vols., trans. and ed. Jaroslav Pelikan and Helmut T. Lehmann (Philadelphia: Muhlenberg Press, 1955–1986).

——— *Martin Luther: Selections from His Writings,* ed. John Dillenberger (Garden City, N.Y.: Doubleday, 1961).

Maccoby, Eleanor E., and Robert H. Mnookin. *Dividing the Child: Social and Legal Dilemmas of Custody* (Cambridge, Mass.: Harvard University Press, 1992).

MacCulloch, Diarmand, ed. *The Reign of Henry VIII: Politics, Policy and Piety* (Basingstoke: MacMillan, 1995).

———. *Thomas Cranmer: A Life* (New Haven and London: Yale University Press, 1996).

Mackin, Theodore. *Marriage in the Catholic Church: Divorce and Remarriage* (New York: Paulist Press, 1984).

———. *Marriage in the Catholic Church: What Is Marriage?* (New York: Paulist Press, 1982).

Mager, Inge. "'Es is nicht gut dass der Mensch allein sei' (Gen 2, 18): Zum Familienben Philipp Melanchthons," *Arichiv für Reformationsgeschichte* 81 (1990):120.

Marchant, Ronald A. *The Church Under the Law: Justice, Administration, and Discipline in the Diocese of York 1560–1640* (Cambridge: Cambridge University Press, 1969).

———. *The Puritans and the Church Courts in the Diocese of York* (London; Longmans, 1960).

Marshall, Lawrence C. "The Religion Clauses and Compelled Religious Divorces: A Study in Marital and Constitutional Separations," *Northwestern University Law Review* 80 (1985):204.

Marsilius of Padua. *Defensor Pacis,* in Alan Gewirth, *Marsilius of Padua. The Defender of the Peace,* vol. 2: *The Defensor Pacis Translated with an Introduction* (New York: Columbia University Press, 1956).

Martin, Thomas. *Traictise Declarying and Plainly Provyng That the Pretensed Mariage of Priestes and Professed Persones is no Marriage* (London, 1554).

Martos, Joseph. *Doors to the Sacred: A Historical Introduction to Sacraments in the Catholic Church* (Garden City, N.Y.: Image Books, 1982).

Maurer, Wilhelm. "Reste des kanonischen Rechtes im Frühprotestantismus," *Zeitschrift der Savigny-Stiftung (Kan. Ab.)* 95 (1965):190.

Mauser, Konrad. *Explicatio erudita et utilis X. tituli inst. de nuptiis* (Jena, 1569).

May, Elaine Tyler. *Great Expectations: Marriage and Divorce in Post-Victorian America* (Chicago: University of Chicago Press, 1980).

May, Henry F. *The Enlightenment in America* (New York: Oxford University Press, 1976).

McCoy, Charles S., and J. Wayne Baker. *Foundation of Federalism: Heinrich Bullinger and the Covenantal Tradition* (Louisville, KY: Westminster John Knox Press, 1991).

McNeill, John T. *The History and Character of Calvinism* (New York: Oxford University Press, 1954).

Mejer, Otto. "Zur Geschichte des ältesten protestantischen Eherechts, inbesondere der Ehescheidungsfrage," *Zeitschrift für Kirchenrecht* 16 (1881):35.

Melanchthon, Philip. *De arbore consanguinitatis et affinitatis* (1540), in Josef Clug, *Von Ehesachen* (Wittenberg, 1540, 1541).

———. *De coniugio piae commonefactiones* (Wittenberg, 1551), published in revised, expanded form under the title *Disputatio de conjugio* (Wittenberg, 1556), in *Loci praecipui theologici . . . cum appendice Disputationis de coniugio* (Lipsiae, 1556).

———. *Loci communes* (1521), in W. Pauck, ed., *Melanchthon and Bucer* (Philadelphia: Westminster Press, 1969).

———. *Loci communes* (1555), in C.L. Manschreck, ed., *Melanchthon on Christian Doctrine* (New York: Oxford University Press, 1965).

———. *Werke,* in G. Bretschneider, ed., *Corpus Reformatorum,* 28 vols. (Brunsvigae: Apud C.A. Schwetschke et Filium, 1864–).

Mendus, Susan. "The Marriage of True Minds: The Ideal Marriage in the Philosophy of John Stuart Mill," in Susan Mendus and Jane Rendall, eds., *Sexuality and Subordination: Interdisciplinary Studies of Gender in the Nineteenth Century* (London and New York: Routledge & Kegan Paul, 1989), 171.

Merzbacher, Friederich. "Johann Oldendorp und das kanonischen Recht," in id., *Recht-Staat-Kirche: ausgewählte Aufsätze,* ed. Gerhard Koebler (Wien: Bohlau, 1989), 246.

————. *Liebe, Ehe, und Familie* (Berlin: Duncker & Humblot, 1958).

Michaelis, Karl. *Das abendländische Eherecht im Übergang vum spätenmittelalter zur Neuzeit* (Gottingen: Vandenhoeck and Ruprecht, 1990).

————. "Ueber Luthers eherechtliche Anschauungen und deren Verhältnis zum mittelalterlichen und neuzeitlichen Eherecht," in *Festschrift für Erich Ruppel zum 65. Geburtstag* (Hannover: Lutherhaus, 1968), 43.

Mikat, Paul. *Die Polygamiefrage in der frühen Neuzeit* (Opladen: Westdeutscher Verlag, 1988).

Mill, John Stuart. *Collected Works of John Stuart Mill,* repr. ed. John M. Robson, (Toronto: University of Toronto Press, 1984).

————. *Utilitarianism, On Liberty, Essay on Bentham,* ed. Mary Warnock (New York: New American Library, 1974).

Milton, John. *The Complete Prose Works of John Milton* (New Haven, Conn.: Yale University Press, 1959).

Minow, Martha. "The Free Exercise of Families," *University of Illinois Law Review* (1991):925.

Monner, Basilius. *Tractatus duo. I. De matrimonio. II. De clandestinis conjugiis,* 2d ed. (Jena, 1604).

Monter, E. William. "The Consistory of Geneva: 1559–1569," *Bibliothèque d'Humanisme et Renaissance* 38 (1976):467.

————. "Crime and Punishment in Calvin's Geneva, 1562," *Archiv für Reformationsgeschichte* 64 (1973):281.

————. *Studies in Genevan Government (1536–1605)* (Geneva: Droz, 1964).

————. "Women in Calvinist Geneva (1550–1800)," *Signs: Journal of Women in Culture and Society* 6 (1980):189.

Morgan, Edmund S. *The Puritan Family: Religion and Domestic Relations in Seventeenth Century New England* (New York: Harper & Row, 1966).

Murphy, V. "The Literature and Propaganda on Henry's Divorce," in Diarmand MacCulloch, ed., *The Reign of Henry VIII: Politics, Policy and Piety* (Basingstoke: MacMillan, 1995), chap. 6.

Muther, Theodore. *Aus dem Universitäts- und Gelehrtenleben im Zeitalter der Reformation* (Erlangen: A. Deichert, 1866).

————. *Doctor Johann Apell. Ein Beitrag zur Geschichte der deutschen Jurisprudenz* (Köningsberg, 1861).

Naphy, William G. *Calvin and the Consolidation of the Genevan Reformation* (Manchester and New York: Manchester University Press, 1994).

New, John F. *Anglican and Puritan* (Stanford, Calif.: Stanford University Press, 1964).

Niebuhr, H. Richard. *Christ and Culture* (New York: Harper & Row, 1951).

Noonan, John T., Jr. *Contraception: A History of Its Treatment by the Catholic Theologians and Canonists* (Cambridge, Mass.: Belknap Press, 1965).

———. "The Family and the Supreme Court," *Catholic University of America Law Review* 23 (1973):255.

———. "Marital Affection in the Canonists," *Studia Gratiana* 12 (1967):489.

———. "Novel 22," in W.J. Bassett, ed., *The Bond of Marriage: An Ecumenical and Interdisciplinary Study* (Notre Dame and London: University of Notre Dame Press, 1968), 41.

———. "Power to Choose," *Viator* 4 (1973): 419.

———. *The Power to Dissolve: Lawyers and Marriages in the Courts of the Roman Curia* (Cambridge, Mass.: Belknap Press, 1972).

———. *A Private Choice: Abortion in America in the Seventies* (New York: Free Press, 1979).

Nörr, Knut Wolfgang. "Die Entwicklung des Corpus Iuris Canonici," in Helmut Coing, *Handbuch der Quellen und Literatur der neueren europäischen Privatrechtsgeschichte* (München: Beck, 1977), 1:835–846.

Note. "Developments in the Law—The Constitution and the Family," *Harvard Law Review* 93 (1980):1156.

O'Donnell, William J., and David A. Jones. *The Law of Marriage and Marriage Alternatives* (Lexington, Mass.: Lexington Books, 1982).

O'Donovan, Joan Lockwood. *The Theology of Law and Authority in the English Reformation.* Emory University Studies in Law and Religion, No.1(Atlanta: Scholars Press, 1991).

Oldendorp, Johannes. *Collatio iuris civilis et canonici, maximam adferens boni & aequi cognitiionem* (Coloniae: Ioannes Gymnicus excudebat, 1541).

———. *Lexicon Iuris* (Francforti: apud Chr. Egenolphum, 1546/1553).

———. *Von Rathschlagen, Wie man gute Policey und Ordnung in Stedten und Landen erhalten möge* (Excudebat Christophorus Reusnerus, 1597; fascimilie reprint Glashütten im Taunus, 1971).

Olsen, Frances. "The Family and the Market: A Study of Ideology and Legal Reform," *Harvard Law Review* 96 (1983):1497.

Orenstein, Henry. "The Ethnological Theories of Henry Sumner Maine," *American Anthropologist* 70 (1968):264.

Outhwaite, R.B., ed. *Marriage and Society: Studies in the Social History of Family* (New York: St. Martin's Press, 1981).

Owen, Eivion. "Milton and Selden on Divorce," *Studies in Philology* 43 (1946): 233.

Ozment, Steven E. *Protestants: The Birth of a Revolution* (New York: Doubleday, 1992).

———. *When Fathers Ruled: Family Life in Reformation Europe* (Cambridge and London: Harvard University Press, 1983).

Parker, T.H.L. *The Oracles of God: An Introduction to the Preaching of John Calvin* (London and Redhill: Lutterworth Press, 1947).

Parker, William R. *Milton's Contemporary Reputation* (Columbus: Ohio State University Press, 1940).

Pateman, Carole. *The Sexual Contract* (Stanford, Calif: Stanford University Press, 1988).

Pauck, Wilhelm. *Das Reich Gottes auf Erden. Utopie und Wirklichkeit. Eine Untersuchung zu Butzers De Regno Christi und der englischen Staatskirche des 16. Jahrhunderts* (Berlin: Duncker & Humblot, 1928).

———, ed. *Melanchthon and Bucer* (Philadelphia: Westminster Press, 1969).

Pelikan, Jaroslav. *Reformation of Church and Dogma (1300–1700)* (Chicago: University of Chicago Press, 1984).

———. *Spirit Versus Structure: Luther and the Institutions of the Church* (New York: Harper & Row, 1968).

Perkins, William. *The Work of William Perkins*, 3 vols., ed. Ian Breward (Appleford: The Sutton Courtenay Press, 1970).

Peters, Ted. *For the Love of Children: Genetic Technology and the Future of the Family* (Louisville: Westminster John Knox Press, 1996).

Politische Reichshandel. Das ist allerhand gemeine Acten Regimentssachen und weltlichen Discursen (Frankfurt am Main: Bey Johann Bringern, 1614).

Ponet, John. *A Defence for Mariage of Priestes* (London, 1549).

Powell, Chilton L. *English Domestic Relations 1487–1653: A Study of Matrimony and Family Life in Theory and Practice as Revealed by the Literature, Law, and History of the Period* (New York: Columbia University Press, 1917).

Pricke, Robert. *The Doctrine of Superioritie, and of Subjection, contained in the Fifth Commandement of the Holy Law of Almightie God* (London: Ephraim Dawson, 1609) (STC 20337).

Priest, Menna, ed. *International Calvinism* (Oxford: Clarendon Press, 1985).

Rahner, Karl. *Theological Investigations*, trans. D. Bourke (New York: Herder & Herder, 1973), vol. 10; trans. C. Ernest (Baltimore: Helicon Press, 1963), vol. 2.

Rainolds, John. *A Defence of the Judgement of the Reformed Churches. That a man may lawfullie not onlie put awaie his wife for her adulterie, but also marrie another* (n.p. 1609) (STC 20607).

Rantelen, Max, ed. *Bernard Walters privatrechtliche Traktate aus dem 16. Jahrhundert* (Leipzig, 1937).

The Reformation of the Ecclesiastical Laws of England, 1552 ed. James C. Spalding (Kirksville, Mo.: Sixteenth Century Essays & Studies, 1992).

Regan, Milton C., Jr. *Family Law and the Pursuit of Intimacy* (New York: New York University Press, 1993).

Reid, Charles J. "The Canonistic Contribution to the Western Rights Tradition," *Boston College Law Review* 33 (1991):37.

Reynolds, Philip L. *Marriage in the Western Church: The Christianization of Marriage During the Patristic and Early Medieval Periods* (Leiden: E.J. Brill, 1994).

Rheinstein, Max. *Marriage Stability, Divorce, and the Law* (Chicago: University of Chicago Press, 1971).

Richter, Aemilius. *Beiträge zur Geschichte des Ehescheidungsrecht in der evangelischen Kirche* (Aalen: Scientia Verlag, 1958).

―――, ed. *Die evangelischen Kirchenordnungen des sechszehnten Jahrhunderts,* repr. ed., 2 vols. (Nieuwkoop: B. DeGraaf, 1967).

Ridley, Nicholas. *The Works of Nicholas Ridley,* ed. H. Christmas for the Parker Society (Cambridge: University Press, 1843).

Rivoire, Emile, and Victor van Berchem, eds. *Les sources du droit du canton de Genève,* 4 vols. (Aarau: Sauerländer, 1927–1935).

Roberts, Alexander, and James Donaldson, eds. *The Ante-Nicene Fathers,* repr. ed. (Buffalo: The Christian Literature Publishing Co., 1885).

Robinson, H., ed. *The Zurich Letters,* 2 vols. (Cambridge: University Press, 1842).

Robson, Ann P., and John M. Robson, eds. *Sexual Equality: Writings by John Stuart Mill, Harriet Taylor Mill, and Helen Taylor* (Toronto: University of Toronto Press, 1994).

Rodgers, W.C. *A Treatise on the Law of Domestic Relations* (Chicago: T.H. Flood, 1899).

Roelker, Nancy L. "The Appeal of Calvinism to French Noblewomen in the Sixteenth Century," *Journal of Interdisciplinary Studies* 2 (1970–71):405.

Rogers, Daniel. *Matrimoniall Honour* (London: Philip Nevil, 1642).

Rogers, Elizabeth F. *Peter Lombard and the Sacramental System* (New York: n.p., 1917).

Rogers, Thomas. *The Catholic Doctrine of the Church of England: An Exposition of the Thirty-Nine Articles,* ed. J.J.S. Perowne for the Parker Society (Cambridge: University Press, 1844).

Rousseau, Jean-Jacques. *The Social Contract and the Discourse on the Origin of Inequality,* ed. Lester G. Crocker (New York: Washington Square Press, 1967).

Safley, Thomas Max. "Canon Law and Swiss Reform: Legal Theory and Practice in the Marital Courts of Zurich, Bern, Basel, and St. Gall," in R.H. Helmholz, ed., *Canon Law in Protestant Lands* (Berlin: Duncker & Humblot, 1992), 187.

―――. *Let No Man Put Asunder: The Control of Marriage in the German Southwest: A Comparative Study, 1550–1600* (Kirksville, Mo.: Sixteenth Century Journal Publications, 1984).

Salmon, Marylynn. *Women and the Law of Property in Early America* (Chapel Hill and London: University of North Carolina Press, 1986).

Sandys, Edwin. *The Sermons of Edwin Sandys*, ed. J. Ayre for the Parker Society (Cambridge: University Press, 1842).

Sansom, J., ed. *Works: Library of Anglo-Catholic Theology* (Oxford: [s.n.], 1843).

Saprio, Virginia. *A Vindication of Political Virtue: The Political Theory of Mary Wollstonecraft* (Chicago: University of Chicago Press, 1992).

Sarcerius, Basilius [Erasmus]. *Corpus juris matrimonialis. Vom Ursprung, Anfang und Herkomen des Heyligen Ehestandts* (Frankfurt am Main: P. Schmidt, 1569).

Schaefer, Hans Christoph. *Der Einfluss des kanonischen Eherechts auf die moderne staatliche Ehegesetzgebung* (Inaugural Diss., Heidelberg, 1963).

Schäfer, Rudolf. "Die Geltung des kanonischen Rechts in der evangelischen Kirche Deutschland von Luther bis zur Gegenwart," *Zeitschrift der Savigny-Stiftung (Kan. Ab.)* 49 (1915):165.

Schaff, Philip. *The Creeds of Christendom*, 3 vols. (New York: Harper and Brothers, 1877).

Schaff, Philip, and Henry Wace, eds. *The Seven Ecumenical Councils*, repr. ed. (Grand Rapids: Wm. B. Eerdmans Publishing Co., 1952).

———. *A Select Library of Nicene and Post-Nicene Father of the Christian Church*, Second Series, repr. ed. (Grand Rapids: Wm. B. Eerdmans Publishing Co., 1952.)

Schaich-Klose, Wiebke. *D. Hieronymous Schürpf: Leben und Werk des Wittenberger Reformationsjuristen, 1481–1554* (Torgen. F. Meilli, 1967).

Schillebeeckx, E. *Marriage: Human Reality and Saving Mystery* (New York: Sheed & Ward, 1965).

Schmelzeisen, Gustav. *Polizeiordnung und Privatrecht* (Munster/Köln, 1955).

Schneider, Carl E. "Marriage, Morals, and the Law: No-Fault Divorce and Moral Discourse," *Utah Law Review* (1994):503.

———. "Moral Discourse and the Transformation of American Family Law," *Michigan Law Review* 83 (1985):1803.

———. "Rethinking Alimony: Marital Decisions and Moral Discourse," *Brigham Young Law Review* (1991):197.

Schneidewin, Johannes. *In institutionum imperialium titulum X. De nuptiis. . . .* (Frankfurt, 1571).

Schnucker, Robert V., ed. *Calviniana: Ideas and Influence of John Calvin* (Ann Arbor: University of Michigan Press, 1988).

Schochet, G.J. *Patriarchalism in Political Thought: The Authoritarian Family and Political Speculation and Attitudes Especially in Seventeenth Century England* (New York: Basic Books, 1975).

Schroeder, H.J. *Councils and Decrees of the Council of Trent* (St. Louis: B. Herder Book Co., 1941).

Schulz, Kurd. "Bugenhagen als Schöpfer der Kirchenordnungen," in *Johann Bugenhagen. Beiträge zu seinem 400. Todestag* (Berlin: Evangelische Verlagsanstalt, 1958), 51.

Schürpff, Hieronymous. *Consilia seu reponsa iuris centuria I–III* (Frankfurt, 1556, 1564).

Schwab, Dieter. *Grundlagen und Gestalt der staatlichen Ehegesetzgebung in der Neuzeit bis zum Beginn des 19. Jahrhunderts* (Bielefeld: Verlag Ernst und Werner Gieseking, 1967).

Schwarzenberg, Johann von. *Ain schöner Sendbreyff . . . Darin er treffenliche und Christliche ursache anzaigt, wie and warumb er sein Tochter daselbst . . . hinweg gefurt und wider under sein Afterlichen Schutz und Oberhand sich genommen had. Ain vorred A. Osiander* (Augsburg: M. Ramminger, 1524).

Scobell, H., ed. *A Collection of Acts and Ordinances of General Use Made in the Parliament* (London: Henry Hills and John Field, 1658).

Scribner, R.W. "Police and the Territorial State in Sixteenth Century Württemberg," in E.I. Kouri and Tom Scott, eds., *Politics and Society in Reformation Europe* (New York: St. Martin's Press, 1987), 103.

Seebass, Gottfried. *Das reformatorische Werk des Andreas Osiander* (Nürnberg: Verein für bayerische Kirchengeschichte, 1967).

Seeberg, Reinhard. "Luthers Anschauung von dem Geschlechtsleben der Ehe und ihre geschichtliche Stellung," *Luther-Jahrbuch* 7 (1925):77.

Seeger, Cornelia. *Nullité der mariage divorce et séparation de corps a Genève, au temps de Calvin: Fondements doctrinaux, loi et jurisprudence* (Lausanne: Mémoires et documents publiés par la société d'histoire de la suisse romande, 1989).

Sehling, Emil, ed. *Die evangelischen Kirchenordnungen des 16. Jahrhunderts* (Leipzig: O.R. Reisland, 1902–1913), vols. 1–5, continued under the same title (Aalen: Scientia Verlag, 1955–), vols. 6–16.

Selden, John. *De iure naturali et gentium, juxta disciplinam Ebraeorum libri septem* (London: Excudebat Richardus Bishopus 1640) (STC 22168).

Sermons or Homilies Appointed to be Read in the Churches in the Time of Queen Elizabeth (Liverpool, 1799).

Shanley, Mary. *Feminism, Marriage, and the Law in Victorian England, 1850–1895* (Princeton, N.J.: Princeton University Press, 1989).

———. "Marriage Contract and Social Contract in Seventeenth Century English Political Thought," *Western Political Quarterly* 32 (1979):79.

Shapiro, Barbara. *Probability and Certainty in Seventeenth Century English Thought* (Princeton, N.J.: Princeton University Press, 1983).

Sheehan, Michael M. "Theory and Practice: Marriage of the Unfree and Poor in Medieval Society," *Mediaeval Studies* 50 (1988):457.

Simmons, A. John. *The Lockean Theory of Rights* (Princeton, N.J.: Princeton University Press, 1992).

Smith, C.H. *Cranmer and the Reformation Under Edward VI* (Cambridge: University Press, 1926).

Smithen, Frederick J. *Continental Protestantism and the English Reformation* (London: James Clarke & Co., n.d.).

Sohm, Rudolf. *Das Recht der Eheschliessung aus dem deutschen und kanonischen Recht geschichtlich entwickelt* (Aalen: Scientia Verlag, 1966).

Söllner, Alfred. "Die Literatur zum gemeinen und partikularen Recht in Deutschland, Oesterreich, den Niederlanden und der Schweiz," in Helmut Coing, ed., *Handbuch der Quellen und Literatur der neueren europäischen Privatrechtsgeschichte* (München: Beck, 1977), 2/1:501.

Spangenberg, Cyriacus. *Ehespiegel: Das ist Alles was vom heyligen Ehestande nützliches, nötiges, und tröstliches mag gesagt werden* (Strassburg: Samuel Emmel, 1563).

Spengler, Lazarus. *Eyn kurtzer ausszug aus dem Bebstlichen rechten der Decret und Decretalen, in den artickeln, die ungeverlich Gottes Wort gemess sein* (Wittenberg: I. Club, 1530).

Sprengler-Ruppenthal, Anneliese. "Bugenhagen und das kanonische Recht," *Zeitschrift der Savigny-Stiftung (Kan. Ab.)* 75 (1989):375.

———. "Zur Rezeption des römischen Rechts in Eherecht der Reformation," *Zeitschrift der Savigny-Stiftung (Kan. Ab.)* 112 (1978):363.

Stackhouse, Max L. *Covenant and Commitments: Faith, Family, and Economic Life* (Louisville: Westminster John Knox Press, 1997).

Staehelin, Adrian. *Die Einführung der Ehescheidung in Basel zur Zeit der Reformation* (Basel: Helbing & Lichtenhahn, 1957).

Stapleton, William. *Stapleton's Fortress Overthrown,* ed. Richard Gibbings for the Parker Society (Cambridge: University Press, 1848).

Stauffenegger, Roger. "Le Mariage a Genève vers 1600," in *Mémoires de la société pour l'histoire de droit et des institutions de anciens pays bourguignons, comtois et romands* 27 (1966):317.

Stauffer, Richard. *L'humanité de Calvin* (Neuchatel: Delachaux et Niestlé, 1964).

Staves, Susan. *Married Women's Separate Property in England, 1660–1833* (Cambridge, Mass.: Harvard University Press, 1990).

Stephen, Henry John. *New Commentaries on the Laws of England,* 4 vols. (London: Henry Butterworth, 1842).

Stephen, James Fitzjames. *A History of the Criminal Law of England,* 3 vols. (London: MacMillan, 1883).

———. *Liberty, Equality and Fraternity,* ed. Stuart D. Warner (Indianapolis: Liberty Fund, 1993).

Stephen, Sir Leslie. *Life of Sir James Fitzjames Stephen* (London: Smith, Elder & Co., 1895).

Stintzing, Roderich von. *Das Sprichwort "Juristen böse Christen" in seinen geschichtlichen Bedeutung* (Bonn: Verlag von Rud. Besser, 1875).

Stölzel, Adolf F. *Die Entwicklung des gelehrten Richtertums in den deutschen Territorien,* 2 vols. (Aalen: Scientia Verlag, 1964).

Stone, Lawrence. *The Causes of the English Revolution, 1529–1642* (New York: Harper & Row, 1972).

———. *The Family, Sex, and Marriage in England, 1500–1800* (New York: Harper & Row, 1979).

———. *Road to Divorce: England 1530–1987* (Oxford: Oxford University Press, 1990).

———. *Road to Divorce: A History of the Making and Breaking of Marriage in England* (New York and Oxford: Oxford University Press, 1995).

Strauss, Gerald. *Law, Resistance, and the State: The Opposition to Roman Law in Reformation Germany* (Princeton, N.J.: Princeton University Press, 1986).

Sugarman, Stephen D., and Herma Hill Kay, eds. *Divorce Reform at the Crossroads* (New Haven, Conn.: Yale University Press, 1990).

Suppan, Klaus. *Die Ehelehre Martin Luthers. Theologische und rechtshistorische Aspekte des reformatorischen Eheverständnisses* (Salzburg: Universitätsverlag A. Pustet, 1971).

Swinburne, Henry. *A Treatise of Spousals or Matrimonial Contracts* (c. 1591) (London: S. Roycroft, 1686).

Taylor, Jeremy. *Eniautos,* 2d ed. (London: Richard Royston, 1655).

———. *The Measures and Offices of Friendship,* 3d ed. (London: R. Royston, 1662).

The Teaching of the Twelve Apostles, Didache, or The Oldest Church Manual, trans. and ed. Philip Schaff, 3d rev. ed. (New York: Funk & Wagnalls, 1889).

Teitelbaum, Lee E. "The Last Decade(s) of American Family Law," *Journal of Legal Education* 46 (1996):546.

———. "Moral Discourse and Family Law," *Michigan Law Review* 84 (1985): 430.

Tentler, Thomas N. *Sin and Confession on the Eve of the Reformation* (Princeton, N.J.: Princeton University Press, 1977).

Tertullian. *Against Marcion,* in Alexander Roberts and James Donaldson, eds., *The Ante-Nicene Fathers,* repr. ed. (Buffalo: The Christian Literature Publishing Co., 1885), vol. 3.

———. *Apologeticus,* in *Tertullian,* trans. and ed. Gerald H. Rendall (New York: G.P. Putnam's Sons, 1931).

———. *De Spectaculis,* in ibid.

Thompson, John L. "Patriarchs, Polygamy, and Private Resistance: John Calvin and Others on Breaking God's Rules," *Sixteenth Century Journal* 35/1 (1994):3.

Tierney, Brian. *The Idea of Natural Rights: Natural Rights, Natural Law and Church Law 1150–1625.* Emory University Studies in Law and Religion, no. 5 (Atlanta: Scholars Press, 1997).

Tietz, Gerold. *Verlobung, Trauung, und Hochzeit in den evangelischen Kirchenordnungen des 16. Jahrhunderts* (Phil Fak. Diss., Tübingen, 1969).

Tillyard, E.M.W. *The Elizabethan World Picture* (New York: Vintage Books, n.d.).

Tilney, Edmund. *A Brief and Pleasant Discourse of Duties in Marriage, Called the Flower of Friendshippe* (London, 1571).

Traer, James F. *Marriage and the Family in Eighteenth Century France* (Ithaca, N.Y.: Cornell University Press, 1980).

Treggiari, Susan. *Roman Marriage: Iusti Coniuges from the Time of Cicero to the Time of Ulpian* (Oxford: Clarendon Press, 1991).

Triglott Concordia: The Symbolic Books of the Ev. Lutheran Church German-Latin-English (St. Louis: Concordia Publishing, 1921).

Trusen, Winfried. "Forum internum und gelehrten Rechts im Spätmittelalter Summae confessorum und Traktate also Wegsbereiter der Rezeption," *Zeitschrift der Savigny-Stiftung (Kan. Ab.)* 57 (1971):83.

Tulloch, Gail. *Mill and Sexual Equality* (Hertfordshire and Boulder: Lynne Reinner Publishers, 1989).

Tyndale, William. *An Answer to Sir Thomas More's Dialogue,* ed. H. Walter for the Parker Society (Cambridge: University Press, 1850).

————. *Doctrinal Treatises and Introduction to Different Portions of the Holy Scripture,* ed. H. Walter for the Parker Society (Cambridge: University Press, 1848).

Vajta, Vilmos, ed. *Luther und Melanchthon: Referate und Berichte des Zweiten Internationalen Kongresses für Lutherforschung Münster, 8.–13. August 1960* (Göttingen: Vandenhoeck & Ruprecht, 1960).

van Apeldoorn, L. *Geschiedenis van het nederlandsche huwelijksrecht voor de invoering van de fransche wetsgeving* (Amsterdam: Uitgeversmaatschappij, 1925).

van Bijnkerkshoek, C. *Observationes tumultuariae,* 4 vols., E.M. Meijers et al., eds., (Haarlem, 1926–1962).

van de Kerckhove, M. "La notion de juridiction dans la doctrine des decrètistes et premiers décrétalistes," *Études françiscanes* 49 (1937):420.

van den Brink, Herman. *The Charm of Legal History* (Amsterdam: Adolf M. Hakkert, 1974).

van Overveldt, A.J.M. *De dualiteit van kerkelijk en burgerlijk huwelijk* (Tilburg, 1953).

Vidler, Alec R. *Christ's Strange Work: An Exposition of the Three Uses of God's Law,* rev. ed. (London: SCM Press, 1963).

Vinogradoff, Paul. *The Teaching of Sir Henry Maine* (Oxford: Oxford University Press, 1904).

Walker, Timothy B., and Linda H. Elrod. "Family Law in the Fifty States: An Overview," *Family Law Quarterly* 26 (1993):319.

Walker, Williston. *John Calvin* (New York: Schocken Books, 1960).

Walther, Bernard. *Von den Legitimationen und Bewisung der Siptschafft* (Leipzig, 1558), in Max Rantelen, ed., *Bernard Walters privatrechtliche Traktate aus dem 16. Jahrhunderts* (Leipzig, 1937), 120.

Wardle, Lynn D. "A Critical Analysis of Constitutional Claims for Same-Sex Marriage," *Brigham Young University Law Review* (1996):1.

Watt, Jeffrey R. "The Control of Marriage in Reformed Switzerland, 1550–1800," in W. Fred Graham, ed., *Sixteenth Century Essays and Studies— Later Calvinism: International Perspectives* (Kirksville, Mo.: Sixteenth Century Journal Publishers, 1994).

Weigand, Rudolf. *Die bedingte Eheschliessung im kanonischen Recht* (München: Max Hueber, 1963).

———, ed. *Die Naturrechtslehre der Legisten und Dekretisten von Irnerius bis Accursius und von Gratian bis Johannes Teutonicus* (München: Max Hueber Verlag, 1967).

———. "Ehe-und Familienrecht in der mittelalterlichen Stadt," in Alfred Haverkamp, ed., *Haus und Familie in der spätmittelalterlichen Stadt* (Tübingen: J.C.B. Mohr, 1984), 173.

———. *Liebe und Ehe im Mittelalter* (Goldbach: Keip Verlag, 1993).

———. "Zur mittelalterlichen kirchlichen Ehegerichtsbarkeit: Rechtsvergleichende Untersuchung," *Zeitschrift der Savigny-Stiftung (Kan. Ab.)* 67 (1981):218.

Weitzmann, Lenore J. *The Divorce Revolution: The Unexpected Social and Economic Consequences for Women and Children in America* (New York: Free Press, 1985).

———. *The Marriage Contract: Spouses, Lovers, and the Law* (New York: Free Press, 1991).

Weitzmann, Lenore J., and Ruth B. Dixon. "The Alimony Myth: Does No-Fault Divorce Make a Difference?" *Family Law Quarterly* 14 (1980):141.

Wendel, François. *Le mariage a Strasbourg á l'époque de la réforme 1520–1692* (Strasbourg: Imprimerie Alsacienne, 1928).

Weyrauch, Walter O., and Sanford N. Katz. *American Family Law in Transition* (Washington, D.C.: Bureau of National Affairs, 1983).

Weyrauch, Walter O., Sanford N. Katz, and Frances Olsen. *Cases and Materials on Family Law* (St. Paul: West Publishing Co., 1994).

Whately, William. *A Bride-Bush, or A Wedding Sermon: Compendiously Describing the Duties of Married Persons: By Performing Whereof, Marriage shall be to them a Great Help, which now finde it a little Hell* (London: William Jaagard for Nicholas Bourne, 1617) (STC 25296).

———. *A Care-Cloth: or a Treatise of the Cumbers and Troubles of Marriage* (London: Felix Kyngston for Thomas Man, 1624) (STC 25299).

Wheaton, Robert, and Tamara K. Hareven, eds. *Family and Sexuality in French History* (Philadelphia: University of Pennsylvania Press, 1980).

Whitgift, John. *The Works of John Whitgift*, ed. J. Ayre for the Parker Society, 3 vols. (Cambridge: University Press, 1852).

Williams, George Huntston. *The Radical Reformation*, 3d ed. (Kirksville, Mo.: Sixteenth Century Essays & Studies, 1992).

Wing, John. *The Crovvn Conjugall; or, The Spouse Royall* (London: John Beale for R. Mylbourne, 1632) (STC 25845).

Winnett, A.R. *Divorce and Remarriage in Anglicanism* (New York: St. Martin's Press, 1958).

Winstanley, Gerrard. *The Law of Freedom in a Platform, or True Magistracy Restored,* ed. R.W. Kenny (New York: Schocken Books, 1941).

Witte, John, Jr. "Blest Be the Ties that Bind: Covenant and Community in Puritan Thought," *Emory Law Journal* 36 (1987):579.

———. "The Catholic Origins and Calvinist Orientation of Dutch Reformed Church Law," *Calvin Theological Journal* 28 (1993):328.

———. "The Civic Seminary: The Origins of Public Education in Lutheran Germany," *Journal of Law and Religion* 12 (1996):173.

———. "Moderate Religious Liberty in the Theology of John Calvin," *Calvin Theological Journal* 31 (1996):359.

———. "The Plight of Canon Law in the Early Dutch Republic," in R.H. Helmholz, ed., *Canon Law in Protestant Lands* (Berlin: Duncker & Humblot, 1992), 135.

———. "The Transformation of Marriage Law in the Lutheran Reformation," in John Witte, Jr., and Frank S. Alexander, eds., *The Weightier Matters of the Law: Essays on Law and Religion* (Atlanta: Scholars Press, 1988), 57.

Witte, John, Jr., and Johan van der Vyver, eds. *Religious Human Rights in Global Perspective,* 2 vols. (The Hague and Boston: Martinus Nijhoff, 1996).

Witte, John, Jr., and Thomas C. Arthur. "The Three Uses of the Law: A Protestant Source of the Purposes of Criminal Punishment?" *Journal of Law and Religion* 10 (1994):433.

Witte, John, Jr., and Harold J. Berman. "The Transformation of Western Legal Philosophy in Lutheran Germany," *Southern California Law Review* 62 (1989):1573.

Wolgast, Eike. "Bugenhagen in den politischen Krisen seiner Zeit," in Hans-Gunter Leder, ed., *Johannes Bugenhagen: Gestalt und Wirkung* (Bonn: Evangelische Verlagsanstalt, 1984).

Wollstonecraft, Mary. *A Vindication of the Rights of Women,* ed. Charles W. Hagelman, Jr. (New York: W.W. Norton, 1967).

Wolter, Udo. "Amt und Officium in mittelalterlichen Quellen von 13. bis 15. Jahrhunderts," *Zeitschrift der Savigny-Stiftung (Kan. Ab.)* 105 (1988):246.

Wright, Louis B. *Middle Class Culture in Elizabethan England* (Chapel Hill: University of North Carolina Press, 1953).

Wurtenberger, Thomas, ed. *Existenz und Ordnung: Festschrift für Erik Wolf* (Frankfurt am Main: Klostermann, 1962).

Ziegler, G. *Die Ehelehre der Pönitentialsummen von 1200–1350* (Regensburg: Verlag Friedrich Pustet, 1956).

Zwaan, Ton, ed. *Familie, huwelijk en gezin in West-Europa. Van Middeleeuwen tot moderne tijd* (Amsterdam: Boom/Open Universiteit, 1993).

Zwingli, Uldaricus. *Huldreich Zwinglis Sämtliche Werke,* 18 vols. (Zürich: Theologischer Verlag, 1982).

Index of Biblical References

Index of Subjects and Authors